1 MONTH OF
FREE
READING

at

www.ForgottenBooks.com

By purchasing this book you are eligible for one month membership to ForgottenBooks.com, giving you unlimited access to our entire collection of over 1,000,000 titles via our web site and mobile apps.

To claim your free month visit:

www.forgottenbooks.com/free151532

ISBN 978-1-5280-8583-0
PIBN 10151532

THE LIVES

OF

THE CHIEF JUSTICES

OF

ENGLAND.

FROM THE NORMAN CONQUEST TILL THE DEATH
OF LORD TENTERDEN.

BY

JOHN, LORD CAMPBELL,

Lord Chief Justice and Lord High Chancellor of England.

New and Revised Edition.

WITH ILLUSTRATIONS AND NUMEROUS ANNOTATIONS.

EDITED BY JAMES COCKCROFT.

VOL. V.

NORTHPORT, LONG ISLAND, N. Y.,
EDWARD THOMPSON CO., PUBLISHERS.
1899.

ROBERT DRUMMOND, ELECTROTYPER AND PRINTER, NEW YORK.

CHAPTER XLV.

CHAPTER XLVI.

CHAPTER XLVII.

CHAPTER XLVIII.

CHAPTER XLIX.

CHAPTER L.

CHAPTER LI.

LIST OF ILLUSTRATIONS.

BIOGRAPHICAL NOTES IN VOLUME V.

LIVES

OF THE

CHIEF JUSTICES OF ENGLAND.

CHAPTER XLV.

CONCLUSION OF THE LIFE OF LORD KENYON.

LORD KENYON had been very temperate in his diet, and had enjoyed uninterrupted health till he entered his 70th year. He then began to show symptoms of decay, which some attributed to his defeat in *Haycraft* v. *Creasy*, and some to the dangerous illness of his eldest son. The Chief Justice was exceedingly amiable in all the relations of domestic life, and to this promising young man, who was expected to be the heir of his vast accumulations, he was particularly attached.

In the autumn of 1801, there was imposed upon him the melancholy duty of closing the eyes of him from whom he had expected that the pious office would be performed for himself. When gazing into the open tomb of his first-born, he is said to have exclaimed—" It is large enough for both."

On the first day of next Michaelmas term the Chief Justice returned to his court a sorrow-stricken, heart- broken man. He was hardly able to hold up his head; not even a " *regrating* " case from the Oxford Circuit could exite him ; and as soon as term was over, leaving the Nisi Prius business to be done by Mr. Justice Le Blanc, he went into Wales, in the hope of being recruited by the air of his native mountains. He rallied a little, and came back to London on the approach of Hilary Term; but he was only able to take his seat in court for a single day.

As a last resource he was advised to try the waters of Bath. All would not do. The appointed hour for the termination of his career was at hand. He had now an attack of black jaundice, and it was found that his constitution was entirely exhausted. For several weeks he lay in bed, taking hardly any sleep or nourishment. However, he suffered little pain ; and having retained A.D. 1802.
His death
and burial. his mental faculties to the last, on the 4th of April, 1802, he expired, perfectly resigned to the will of God, and gratefully expressing his sense of the many blessings which he had enjoyed. His remains were conveyed to the family cemetery in the parish of Hanmer, and there deposited in the same grave with those of his His
epitaph. beloved son. A splendid monument has been erected to his memory, containing a minute enumeration of his offices, and of his virtues. But a more simple and touching tribute to him was paid in a letter from his second son,—to whom descended with his title his more amiable qualities :

Touching
praise of
him by his
second son. " He has left a name to which his family will look up with affectionate and honest pride, and which his countrymen will remember with gratitude and veneration as long as they shall continue duly to estimate the great and united principles of religion, law, and social order : no Welshman ever exhibited more eminently two traits of Cambria—warmth of heart and sincerity of character."

Character
of Sir
Leoline
Jenkins
applied to
him. Anxious to suppress nothing that has been said in his praise, I add that the following character of his countryman, the learned civilian Sir Leoline Jenkins, was declared by a respectable writer to be equally applicable to the Cambrian Chief Justice of England :

" Impartial in the administration of justice, without respect of persons or opinions, he was not only just between man and man in all ordinary cases, but also where his intimate friend, his patron, his enemy, or his own interest interfered ; for in a word, he seemed to have loved justice as his life, and the laws as his inheritance, and acted as if he always remembered whose image and commission he bore, and to whom he was accountable for the equity of his decrees. He was a man of excellent piety and unaffected devotion ; he did not use his religion as a cloak to cover or keep him warm, but was early acquainted with religious principles and practices, and through the whole course of his life he was a serious and sincere Christian, of a strong and masculine piety, without any mixture of enthusiasm or superstition."

I must, however, in the discharge of my duty as a biographer, discriminate between his merits and his defects, and having done so, I can by no means consent to his being placed in the first rank of English Judges. That he was a truly religious and strictly moral man, might equally have been said of him had he, according to his original destination, spent his life as an attorney at Nantwich. When placed at the head of the common law as Chief Justice, he did, in the midst of some grumbling and sneering, command a considerable portion of public veneration. He was not only devoted to the discharge of his public duties and zealously desirous to do what was right, but his quickness of apprehension and his professional knowledge generally enabled him to come to a rapid and a sound decision in the various cases which he had to adjudicate. But he was far from being a scientific jurist ; he could very imperfectly explain the rule of law by which he was governed, and when in private he was asked for his reasons, he would answer, " I vow to God that it is so."

Discrimination required in his biographer.

He is said to have been a great favorite with com-

His popu-
larity with
common
juries.

mon juries, and, according to the slang of Westminster Hall, always *to have carried off the verdict.*[1] This was said to be because " he never fired over their heads, and he knew how to hit the bird in the eye." But he never combated the prejudices of the jury. He even

His ill-
usage of
attorneys.

encouraged that universal prejudice of the lower orders against attorneys, by which I have frequently seen the administration of justice perverted. Although bred in an attorney's office and long aspiring no higher than to be an attorney, he seemed to think the whole order pettifoggers, and their occupation almost necessarily disreputable. Instead of restricting his animadversions to peccant individuals, he extended an angry suspicion to a whole class, containing many men as honourable as himself, and much his superiors in education and manners. He talked of striking an attorney off the roll as he might of dismissing a footman who had offended him. A naval officer having been arrested at a ball, Lord Kenyon at once jumped to the conclusion that this must have been by the orders of the plaintiff's attorney, saying that " it must be matter for consideration whether a practitioner who had so misconducted himself ought to remain on the rolls of the court." When a trial, expected to last the whole day, had unaccountably gone off, so that the following causes were struck out, the attorneys not having their witnesses in attendance, he advised that actions should be brought against all the attorneys for negligence.

" His hatred of dishonest practices," says a barrister who attended his Court, " had lit up a flame of indignation in his

1. *i. e.* that juries found upon the facts according to the opinion which he intimated to them. " His very failings won their liking ; his prejudices were theirs ; they with him loved to detect some knavish trick in an attorney ; with him they held in pious horror the fashionable vices of the great, and the faults in his address against taste and correct idiom were beauties in their ears." Townsend, vol. i. p. 65.

WARREN HASTINGS.

breast, but it was an *ignis fatuus* which led him into error.
He gave too easy credit to accusation, and formed an opinion
before he suffered his judgment to cool. He decided while
under the influence of a heated temper, and often punished
with unreflecting severity. The effect of this intemperate
mode of administering justice my memory recalls with painful
recollection in the case of a Mr. Lawless, an attorney and an
honorable member of that profession. He was involved in the
general and groundless proscription of the day. Complaint
was made to the Court against him for some imputed misconduct, grounded on an affidavit which the event proved was a
mass of misrepresentation and falsehood ; but it being on oath
and the charges serious, it was thought sufficient to entitle the
party applying to a rule to show cause why Mr. Lawless should
not answer the matters of the affidavit. Natural justice would
point out, and the practice of the Court was conformable to
it, that he should be heard in answer before he was convicted.
For that purpose a day is given by the rule on which the
party is to show cause, during which time everything is considered as suspended. This indulgence was refused to Mr.
Lawless. Lord Kenyon, in addition to the common form of
the Court's assent to the application 'take a rule to show
cause,' added, 'and let Mr. Lawless be suspended from practising until the rule is disposed of.' He happened to be present
in Court when this unexampled judgment was pronounced, and
heard the sentence which led to his ruin. He rose in a state
of the most bitter agitation : ' My Lord, I entreat you to recall
that judgment ; the charge is wholly unfounded ; suspension
will lead to my ruin ; I have eighty causes in my office.'
What was Lord Kenyon's reply to this supplicatory appeal to
him ? 'So much the worse for your clients, who have employed such a man ! You shall remain suspended until the
Court decides on the rule.' The rule came on to be heard at
a subsequent day after the affidavits on the part of Mr. Lawless
had been filed. The charges against him were found to be
wholly without foundation, and the rule was accordingly discharged. Mr. Lawless was restored to his profession, but not
to his character or peace of mind. He sank under the un-
merited disgrace, and died of a broken heart." [1]

1. Townsend, vol. i. p. 65.

CHAP.
XLV.
Lord
Kenyon
serviceable
in repress-
ing petti-
fogging.
But although individuals might suffer from his precipitancy, Lord Kenyon's strong dislike of chicanery
had a salutary effect upon the practice both of attorneys
and barristers. Sham pleas, which had became much
multiplied, were, by a threat to ask *who had signed them,*
restrained to " judgment recovered," or " a horse given
in satisfaction," and the misrepresentation of authorities
in arguments at the bar was checked by a proposed
rule of Court, requiring that " all cases should be cited
on affidavit."

I ought gratefully to record that he was very kind
to the students who attended the Courts. I cannot say
that I ever heard (with one exception) of his inviting
any of us to dinner, but I have a lively recollection
that our box being near the bench at Guildhall,—while
the counsel were speaking he would bring the record
to us and explain the issues joined upon it which the
jury were to try.[1]

The
student's
ink-bottle
and the
Chief
Justice's
porcelain
vase.
1. The following anecdote I have heard related of Lord Kenyon
by and before very decent people, and it ought not to be lost, as it
illustrates his character and the manners of the age in which he
flourished. In those days retiring-rooms for the use of the Judges
were unknown, and a porcelain vase, with a handle to it, was placed
in a corner of the Court at the extremity of the bench. In the King's
Bench at Guildhall the students' box (in which I myself have often
sat) was very near this corner. One day a student who was taking
notes, finding the ink in his little ink-bottle very thick, used the
freedom secretly to discharge the whole of it into my Lord's porcelain
vase. His Lordship soon after having occasion to come to this corner, he was observed in the course of a few moments to become
much disconcerted and distressed. In truth, discovering the liquid
with which he was filling the vase to be of a jet black color, he
thought the secretion indicated the sudden attack of some mortal
disorder. In great confusion and anguish of mind he returned to
his seat and attempted to resume the trial of the cause, but finding
his hand to shake so much that he could not write, he said that on
account of indisposition he was obliged to adjourn the Court. As he
was led to his carriage by his servants, the luckless student came up
and said to him, " My Lord, I hope your Lordship will excuse me,
as I suspect that I am unfortunately the cause of your Lordship's
apprehensions." He then described what he had done, expressing
deep contrition for his thoughtlessness and impertinence, and saying

TRIAL OF WARREN HASTINGS.

When placed at the head of the common law Lord Kenyon affected to talk rather contumeliously of the *He is rebuked by* Equity Courts. A suitor against whom he had decided, *Thurlow for dis-* threatened to file a bill of discovery. " Go to Chan. *paraging* cery ! " exclaimed the Chief Justice, *"Abi in malam rem."* *the Court of Chan-* Lord Thurlow meeting him soon after, said to him, *cery and solicitors.* " Taffy, when did you first think that the Court of Chancery was such a *mala res?* I remember that you made *a very good thing of it.* And when did solicitors become so very odious as I am told you now represent them ? When they gave you briefs you did not treat them as such atrocious ruffians."

We have nothing to say of Lord Kenyon as an orator or statesman more than as a philosopher. He had no high opinion of Mr. Pitt, to whom he was indebted for his elevation—and he complained that this leader, even after being in office, professed a love for Parliamentary reform, and actually carried through Fox's Libel Bill. He declared that he himself was a loyal *Lord Kenyon's* subject—not a political partisan. He expressed the *eulogy on George III.* most unbounded admiration of the character of George III. This he made the subject of his constant eulogy in his addresses to grand juries on the circuit—and, it being contrary to etiquette for the bar to be present on these occasions, so that the same address may be constantly repeated, he used to sound the royal praises nearly in the same language, and always to conclude with this quotation from Scripture—" Our good King may say with Samuel of old, ' Whose ox have I taken? Whose ass have I taken? Whom have I defrauded?' "

that he considered it his duty to relieve his Lordship's mind by this confession. *Lord Kenyon:* " Sir, you are a man of sense and a gentleman—dine with me on Sunday."

Lord Ellenborough pursued the same practice. I myself have often heard his large seals dangling from his watch-chain rattle against the vase, as he took it in his hand *coram populo*, decorously turning his back upon them.

CHAP
XLV.
His
opinion
given to
George III.
respecting
the Catho-
lic ques-
tion.

In consequence of this warm attachment, George III. had a high opinion of Lord Kenyon, notwithstanding the jokes about his bad Latin and his bad temper, and the subject of Catholic Emancipation arising, addressed to him the following letter:

" Queen's House, March 7, 1795.

" The question that has been so improperly patronized by the Lord Lieutenant of Ireland seems to me to militate against the Coronation Oath and many existing statutes. I have therefore stated the accompanying queries on paper, to which I desire the Lord Kenyon will, after due consideration, state his opinion, and acquire the sentiments of the Attorney General on this most important subject."

The following was the reply:

" Lord Kenyon received your Majesty's commands when he was in the country. He came immediately to town, and encloses what has occurred to him on the question. He has conferred with the Attorney General, and believes there is not any difference in opinion between them. They are neither of them apprized what was the extent of the alteration meditated to be made in Ireland.

" Your Majesty's most obliged and dutiful subject,
" KENYON."

" So long as the King's supremacy and the doctrine, discipline, and government of the Church of England are preserved as the National Church, and the provision for its ministers kept as an appropriated fund, it seems that any ease given to sectarists would not militate against the Coronation Oath or the Act of Union. Though the Test Act appears to be a very wise law, and in point of sound policy not to be departed from, yet it seems that it might be repealed or altered without any breach of the Coronation Oath or Act of Union."

Another interrogatory came from his Majesty to the Chief Justice:

" The King is much pleased with the diligence shown by the Lord Kenyon in answering the question proposed to him, and wishes his further opinion on the state of the question in

Ireland, as drawn up by a Right Reverend Prelate of that kingdom, and on the Petition of the Roman Catholics."

The response was rather oracular :

"The Petition expresses apprehensions of 'proscription, persecution, and oppression.' All grounds of such apprehensions, if such there really are, may be safely removed,—if the late benefits which the Petition admits have not removed them, —without endangering the Established Church or violating the Coronation Oath."

It was greatly to the credit of Lord Kenyon that he went so far in combating the mischievous notions that had been infused into the royal mind, and if the opinion then expressed had been acted upon at the time of the Irish Union, it would have saved a world of woe to the empire.

Lord Kenyon, like all the other judges of his day, highly approved of the severity of the penal code, and would have thought the safety of the state endangered by taking away the capital sentence from forgery,—or from stealing to the amount of five shillings in a shop. Yet he was not such a " hanging judge " as some of his colleagues. A barrister [1] once related the following anecdote in a debate in the House of Commons :

Lord Kenyon for a severe penal code, but not a " hanging judge."

"On the Home Circuit a young woman was tried for stealing to the amount of forty shillings in a dwelling-house. It was her first offence, and was attended with many circumstances of extenuation. The prosecutor came forward, as he said, from a sense of duty ; the witnesses very reluctantly gave their evidence ; and the jury still more reluctantly their verdict of *guilty*. The Judge passed sentence of death. The unhappy prisoner instantly fell lifeless at the bar. Lord Kenyon, whose sensibility was not impaired by the sad duties of his office, cried out in great agitation from the bench, 'I don't mean to hang you ! will nobody tell her I don't mean to hang her ?' I then felt, as I now feel, that this was passing sentence not on the prisoner, but on the law."

1. Edward Morris, Esq., afterwards a Master in Chancery.

CHAP.
XLV.
Specimen
of Lord
Kenyon's
love of
mixed
metaphors.
Lord Kenyon very seldom wrote his judgments. In delivering them his language was sometimes forcible, but arranged without the slightest regard to the rules of composition. In spite of the softening efforts of his reporters in harmonizing his mixed metaphors, we have specimens of his style preserving share a great of its raciness. Thus he fortifies one of his favorite maxims, which Lord Eldon says was constantly in his mouth, *Amo stare supra antiquas vias* [1]—" If an individual can *break down* any of those safeguards which the constitution has so wisely and so cautiously erected, by *poisoning* the minds of the jury at a time when they are called upon to decide, he will *stab* the administration of justice in its most vital parts." But some of the stories circulated respecting his historical allusions and quotations must have been exaggerations or pure inventions. Thus Coleridge in his 'Table Talk' relates that Lord Kenyon in addressing the jury in a blasphemy case, after pointing out several early Christians who had adorned the Gospel, added—"Above all, gentlemen, need I name to you the Emperor Julian, who was so celebrated for the practice of every Christian virtue, that he was called JULIAN THE APOSTLE?" So in the collection of legal anecdotes, entitled 'Westminster Hall,' the noble and learned Lord is represented as concluding an elaborate address, on dismissing a grand jury, with the following valediction: "Having thus discharged your consciences, gentlemen, you may retire to your homes in peace, with the delightful consciousness of having performed your duties well, and may lay your heads upon your pillows, saying to yourselves, 'Aut Cæsar aut nullus.'" In exposing the falsehood of a witness he is supposed to have said, "The allegation is as far from truth 'as old Booterium from the North-

---

1. Twiss's Life of Lord Eldon.

ern Main '—a line I have heard or met with God
knows *wheer* "—{his mode of pronouncing *where*].[1]

Before parting with Lord Kenyon's public character, I ought to mention that although he never returned to poetry after his early flight during his apprenticeship, he left reports of cases begun by him while a
student, and these being edited and published by his
relation, Mr. Job Hammer, inscribe his name in the list
of "noble and royal authors," but I cannot say that
they were of much value to the profession, or that they
confer great glory upon his order.

I have enlivened former Lives of Chancellors and
Chief Justices by their *facetiæ*—but I know nothing
of this sort, either by books or tradition, attributed to
Lord Kenyon, except his address to Mr. Abbot[2] (afterwards Speaker and Lord Colchester). This pompous
little man, while holding under him the office of Clerk
of the Rules, was proceeding, as chairman of a committee of the House of Commons, to examine him very

---

1. Townsend, vol. i. p. 91.

2. Charles Abbot, Lord Colchester, was born at Abingdon, Berkshire, Oct. 14, 1757, and elected from Westminster School to Christ
Church, Oxford. After being called to the bar he practised with
considerable success. In 1795 he entered parliament as member for
Helston, and after having rendered himself particularly conspicuous
by his fervent support of the Seditious Meetings Bill he was appointed chairman of the finance committee. In 1801 he brought in
the Population Bill, and on the formation of the Addington cabinet
was appointed Chief Secretary for Ireland and keeper of the privy
seal. He had already commenced a reform in the Irish government
offices when he was elected Speaker of the House of Commons Feb.,
1802. He gave his casting vote against Lord Melville in 1805, and
during the debate on the Relief Bill in 1815 spoke warmly against
the clause for admitting Catholics to the legislature. Two years
afterwards a severe attack of epilepsy compelled him to resign the
chair, on which occasion he was called to the House of Peers by the
title of Baron Colchester and granted a pension of 4000*l.* a year.
Died May 8, 1829. With him originated the Royal Record Commission, the institution of the Private Bill Office, and an improvement
in the printing of the votes. Some of his speeches have been
printed; also a work by him on "The Practice of the Chester Circuit."—*Cooper's Biog. Dict.*

minutely upon the delicate subject of the perquisites of the Chief Justice. The offended Judge having demurred to answer any further, and being reminded in a solemn manner of the authority of the House of Commons, at last broke out, " Sir, tell the House of Commons that I will not be yelped at by my own turn spit." Of his other recorded sayings I can find nothing more pointed than that in complimenting Serjeant Shepherd,[1] he said, " He has no rubbish in his head "—

1. Sir Samuel Shepherd (1760–1840), lawyer, born on April 6, 1760, was the son of a jeweller in London, a friend of Garrick, and a dabbler in poetry. An epigram by the father is quoted in the *Gentleman's Magazine*, 1805, i. 110. The boy was at the Merchant Taylors' school from 1773 to 1774, and was then at a school at Chiswick, probably that of Dr. William Rose. In July, 1776, he was entered at the Inner Temple, where he became pupil of Serjeant Charles Runnington, who married his sister in 1777. On Nov. 23, 1781, he was called to the bar. Shepherd went the home circuit, and soon acquired a considerable practice both on circuit and in the Court of Common Pleas. Lord Mansfield complimented him, Buller gave him sound advice, and Kenyon remarked " he had no rubbish in his head." With Erskine he spent many long vacations in travel. About 1790 he began to suffer from deafness, and this infirmity increased as years passed away. In 1793 he declined the dignity of King's counsel, but he was created serjeant at law in Easter term, 1796, and in the following Trinity term became King's serjeant. On the death of Serjeant Cockell he rose to be King's ancient serjeant. The Prince of Wales made Shepherd his Solicitor General in June, 1812, and about Christmas, 1813, he was appointed Solicitor General to the Crown. He was knighted on May 11, 1814, and in the spring of 1817 was made Attorney General. From April 11, 1813, to June, 1819, he sat in parliament for Dorchester. In the House of Commons he brought in the Foreign Enlistment Bill and the bill abolishing " the wager of battle and the right of appeal in felony." In the law courts his chief cases were the prosecution in June, 1817, of James Watson for high treason at the Spa Fields meeting in the previous December ("State Trials," xxxii. 26–56), and that of Richard Carlisle for publishing Paine's " Age of Reason." By common consent Shepherd was a sound lawyer, who but for his physical defect could have filled to general satisfaction the highest positions in his profession. He refused the two offices of Chief Justice of the King's Bench and of the Common Pleas, which became vacant in the long vacation of 1818, as he had made up his mind "never to accept a judicial office involving the trial of prisoners." The objection did not apply to the post of Lord Chief Baron of the Court of Exchequer in Scotland, which he held from June, 1819, to February, 1830. He

that a flippant observation being made by a witness respecting a letter supposed to come from a young lady, he said, "Turn the minion out of court,"—and that when he detected the trick of an attorney to delay a trial, he said, "This is the last hair in the tail of procrastination, and it must be plucked out."

When not engaged in his judicial duties, Lord Kenyon led the life of a recluse. He occupied a large, gloomy house in Lincoln's Inn Fields, in which I have seen merry doings when it was afterwards transferred to the Verulam Club. I have often heard this traditional description of the mansion in his time—"All the year through, it is LENT in the kitchen, and PASSION WEEK in the parlor." Some one having mentioned, that although the fire was very dull in the kitchen grate, the *spits* were always bright—"It is quite irrelevant," said Jekyll, "to talk about the *spits*, for *nothing* TURNS *upon them*." Although there was probably a

was raised to the privy council on July 23, 1819. Shepherd became very popular in Edinburgh society, and was on terms of close intimacy with Sir Walter Scott, who praises "the neatness and precision, closeness and truth," of his conversation, the perfect good humor and suavity of his manner, "with a little warmth of temper on suitable occasions." Scott never saw a man so patient under such a distressing malady. Ill health forced Shepherd to resign his post in 1830, when he retired, to the deep regret of Edinburgh society, to a cottage at Streatley in Berkshire, where he owned a small property. For the last three years of his life he was blind. He died on Nov. 3, 1840, and was buried in the churchyard of Streatley, where a monument was erected to his memory. Lord Campbell praises his knowledge of English literature. He and his friend William Adam, Lord Chief Commissioner of the Jury Court, presented in 1834 to the Bannatyne Club, of which they were members, a volume of the "Ragman Rolls" (1291-1296). He was also a member of the Blair-Adam Club, of which William Adam and Sir Walter Scott were leaders, and joined in the club's annual excursions; but his alarm at the Scotch "crags and precipices" once drew from Scott a tirade against cockneyism. A portrait of him was published on April 24, 1812, by J. D. Montague of Southwark. He married, in 1783, a Miss White whom Scott pronounced "fine and fidgety." She died at Hyde Park Terrace, London, on March 24, 1833, aged 74.—*Dict. Nat. Biog.*

good deal of exaggeration in these jests, there can be no doubt that Lord Kenyon deserved censure for the meanness of his mode of living, and his disregard of decent hospitality. The state conferred the liberal emoluments of Chief Justice upon him as a trustee so far as that he should support the dignity of his station— that he should bring together at his board the deserving members of the important profession over which he was appointed to preside—and that he should represent the country to illustrious foreigners who came to study our juridical institutions. Lord Kenyon's dinner-parties consisted of himself, Lady Kenyon, his children, and now and then an old attorney ; and the very moderate weekly bills for such a *ménage* being paid (which they were most punctually), the accumulations were vested in the 3 per cents., till they were sufficient to buy another Welsh farm. Lord Kenyon's hours would not well have suited fashionable company ; for, rising at six in the morning, he and all his household were in bed by ten at night. He is said to have built a comfortable house at Gredington, to which he retired in the long vacation. Under the name of villa, he had a miserable tumble-down farm-house at the Marsh Gate, about half a mile on this side of Richmond, which is still pointed out as a proof of his economy. The walls are mouldering, and by way of an ornamental piece of water may be seen near the door a muddy duck-pond. In Lord Kenyon's time it was guarded by a half-starved Welsh terrier, which was elevated into a higher order of the canine race when the following lines were applied to the establishment :

His villa at Richmond.

> " Benighted wanderers the forest o'er
> Cursed the saved candle and unopened door ;
> While the gaunt mastiff growling at the gate
> Affrights the beggar whom he longs to eat."

To this place the family came regularly on Saturday evenings, after a slight repast in town,—bringing with them a shoulder and sometimes a leg of mutton, which served them for their Sunday dinner. On Monday morning the Chief Justice was up with the lark, and back in Lincoln's Inn Fields before the lazy Londoners were stirring. We have the following amusing account of one of these journeys from a barrister who was patronized by him :

"An old coach came rumbling along and overtook me on the road to London from Richmond. It was one of those vehicles that reminded me of a Duke or Marquis under the old régime of France, rivalling in indigence and want the faded finery of his wardrobe. Its coronet was scarcely discoverable, and its gildings were mouldy ; yet it seemed tenacious of what little remained of its dignity, and unwilling to subside into a mere hackney coach. I believe I might have looked rather wistfully at it (I was then a poor barrister, briefless and speech-less, in the back rows of the court), when I perceived a head with a red nightcap suddenly pop out from the window, and heard myself addressed by name, with the offer of a cast to London. It was Lord Kenyon. He made the journey quite delightful by charming anecdotes of the bar in his own time—of Jack Lee, Wallace, Bower, Mingay, Howorth, the last of whom was drowned, he said, on a Sunday water-excursion in the Thames. The good old man was evidently affected by the regrets which his name awakened, and they seemed the more poignant because his friend was called to his account in an act of profanation. 'But it was the sin of a good man,' he observed, 'and Sunday was the only day a lawyer in full busi-ness could spare for his recreation.' " [1]

The red nightcap had been worn to save his wig. *His dress.* He was curiously economical about the adornment of his head. It was observed for a number of years before he died, that he had two hats and two wigs—of the hats and the wigs one was dreadfully old and shabby, the other comparatively spruce. He always carried into Court with him the very old hat and the comparatively spruce wig, or the very old wig and the comparatively

1. Clubs of London.

spruce hat. On the days of the very old hat and the comparatively spruce wig· he shoved his hat under the bench, and displayed his wig ; but on the days of the very old wig and the comparatively spruce hat, he always continued covered. I have a very lively recol-lection of having often seen him sitting with his hat over his wig ; but I was not then aware of the Rule of Court by which he was governed on this point.[1]

The rest of Lord Kenyon's apparel was in perfect keeping with his *coiffure*. " On entering Guildhall," says Espinasse, " Pope's lines in the Dunciad came across me, and I quoted them involuntarily :

' Known by the band and suit which Settle wore,
His only suit for twice three years and more.'

"Erskine would declare that he remembered the great-coat at least a dozen years, and Erskine did not exaggerate the claims of the coat to antiquity. When I last saw the learned Lord, he had been Chief Justice for nearly fourteen years ; and his coat seemed coeval with his appointment to the office. It must have been originally black, but time had mellowed it down to the appearance of a sober green, which was what Erskine meant by his allusion to its color. I have seen him sit at Guildhall in the month of July in a pair of black leather breeches ; and the exhibition of shoes frequently soled afforded equal proof of the attention which he paid to economy in every article of his dress."

In winter he seems to have indulged in warmer garments; for James Smith,[2] author of the " Rejected

1. Till the middle of the last century the Chancellor is always represented with his hat on. In early times it was round and conical ; and such was Lord Keeper Williams's, although he was a bishop. In Anne's reign three-cornered hats came up. The black cap of the com mon law judges, which has remained unchanged for many ages, is square. With this they used always to be *covered ;* but they wear it now only when passing sentence of death.

2. Horace and James Smith, English humorists and miscella-neous writers, born in London, the former about 1780, the latter in 1775. They first became known by their contributions to *The Pic-Nic,* the *London Review,* and the *Monthly Mirror ;* the poems en-titled " Horace in London," in the last-named periodical, being

Addresses," describing him in Michaelmas term, says— "But we should not have his dress complete were we to omit the black *velvet smalls* worn for many years, and threadbare by constant friction, which he used to rub with most painful assiduity when catechizing the witness. The pocket-handkerchief found in the second-hand silk waistcoat which he bought from Lord Stormont's valet being worn out, he would not go to the expense of another, and, using his fingers instead, he wiped them upon his middle garment, whether of leather or of velvet."

According to other accounts this change in his habits did not begin till the imposition of the Income Tax by Mr. Pitt. Said Rogers the poet, "Lord Ellenborough had infinite wit. When the Income Tax was imposed, he stated that Lord Kenyon (who was not very nice in his habits) intended, in consequence of it, to lay down his pocket-handkerchief." [1]

mostly written by James Smith. In 1812 they brought out their "Rejected Addresses," composed on the occasion of the opening of the new theatre at Drury Lane, the committee of which had requested a number of addresses to be sent in, one of which should obtain the prize. These poems, which are humorous imitations of Coleridge, Wordsworth, Byron, Scott, Crabbe, and other prominent writers of the time, met with brilliant success, and passed rapidly through numerous editions. James Smith wrote for the so-called "entertainments" of Charles Mathews "Trips to Paris," "Country Cousins," and other comic sketches. He died in 1839, and his "Memoirs, Letters," etc., were published by his brother in 1840. Among the other works of Horace Smith we may name the novels of "Brambletye House," "The Moneyed Man," and "Love and Mesmerism." Died in 1849.—*Thomas's Biog. Dict.*

1. Table Talk of Samuel Rogers, p. 196.

Samuel Rogers, F.R.S., F.S.A., a poet, wit, and patron of art, born July 30, 1763, at Stoke Newington, Middlesex. His father was a London banker, and an eminent man among the dissenters. At a very early period of life young Rogers applied himself to the study of art and letters, which he perfected by extensive foreign travels. His first published essay in poetry was an "Ode to Superstition, with some other Poems," 1786. In 1792 appeared "The Pleasures of Memory," a poem in two parts, written in English heroics, with rhyme and with great elegance of language and correctness of thought This work was the means of introducing him to Mr. Fox,

CHAP.
XLV.
His will
directing
his execu-
tors to
avoid the
expense
of a
diphthong.
If we can believe his immediate successor, who had a fair character for veracity, Lord Kenyon studied economy even in the hatchment put up over his house in Lincoln's Inn Fields after his death. The motto was certainly found to be "MORS JANUA VIT*A* "—this being at first supposed to be the mistake of the painter. But when it was mentioned to Lord Ellenborough, "Mis-take!" exclaimed his Lordship, "it is no mistake. The considerate testator left particular directions in his will that the estate should not be burdened with the ex-pense of a *diphthong!* "

Accordingly he had the glory of dying very rich. After the loss of his eldest son, he said with great emotion to Mr. Justice Allan Park, who repeated the words soon after to me—"How delighted George would be to take his poor brother from the earth, and restore him to life, although he receives 250,000*l.* by his decease! "

His de-
scendants.
He was succeeded by this son George, a most warm-hearted, excellent man—to whom it may be easily for-given that he considers the founder of his house a model of perfection, not only in law, religion, and

an introduction that colored the whole career of the poet, for no one could be ten minutes in Rogers's company without hearing some friendly reference to the name of Fox. The death of his father in 1793 left him in the possession of an ample fortune, and shortly afterwards he retired from active participation in business. His third publication, and his masterpiece, in the opinion of many, was his "Epistle to a Friend, and other Poems," 1798. In 1812 he pub-lished another poem, the "Voyage of Columbus," which met with indifferent success. This was followed by "Jacqueline, a Tale," 1814; and "Human Life," 1819. His last and largest publication was his descriptive poem of "Italy," 1822, which passed through several editions. He dedicated the remainder of his literary life to the publication of exquisitely illustrated editions of his "Italy" and his "Poems." For more than half a century he figured in the fore-most rank of London literary society. It may indeed be doubted whether any English poet ever lived so much in the eyes of men and women as the Banker Bard of St. James's Place, where he pitched his tent in 1803. Rogers's "Table Talk" was published shortly after his death, which occurred Dec. 18, 1855.—*Cooper's Biog. Dict.*

morals, but in manners, habits, and accomplishments. To spare the feelings of one so pious, I resolve that this Memoir shall not be published in his lifetime, although I believe that it is chargeable with a desire to *extenuate* rather than to *set down aught in malice.*[1]

I cannot say with a good conscience that the first Lord Kenyon was highly educated and every way well qualified to fill the office of Chief Justice; but he was earnestly desirous to do what was right in it; and he possessed virtues which not only must endear him to his own descendants, but must make his memory be respected by his country.

1. This Memoir was written in the lifetime of George, the second Lord Kenyon, with whom I was in habits of familiar intercourse. He died Feb. 1, 1855, and was succeeded by his eldest son Lloyd, the third Lord, who I have heard does credit to the name he bears, but with whom I have not the honor of any acquaintance.

CHAPTER XLVI.

LIFE OF LORD ELLENBOROUGH FROM HIS BIRTH TILL HIS MARRIAGE.[1]

CHAP.
XLVI.
Feel ngs
of the
biographer
in com-
mencing
the Life of
Lord
Ellen-
borough. I NOW come to a Chief Justice with whom I have had many a personal conflict, and from whom for several years I experienced very rough treatment, but for whose memory I entertain the highest respect. He was a man of gigantic intellect; he had the advantage of the very best education which England could bestow; he was not only a consummate master of his own pro_ fession, but well initiated in mathematical science and one of the best classical scholars of his day; he had great faults, but they were consistent with the qualities essentially required to enable him to fill his high office with applause. ELLENBOROUGH was a *real* CHIEF— such as the rising generation of lawyers may read of and figure to themselves in imagination, but may never behold to dread or to admire.

When I first entered Westminster Hall in my wig and gown, I there found him the "monarch of all he surveyed," and, at this distance of time, I can hardly recollect without awe his appearance and his manner as he ruled over his submissive subjects. But I must now trace his progress till he reached this elevation.

His family. His lot by birth was highly favorable to his gaining distinction in the world—affording him the best facilities and the strongest incentives for exertion. He was

1. When I wrote this Memoir I was still Chancellor of the Duchy of Lancaster, and a member of Lord John Russell's Cabinet.

the younger son of an English prelate of very great learning and very little wealth. His ancestors had long been " statesmen " in the county of Westmoreland —that is, substantial yeomen cultivating a farm which was their own property, and which was transmitted without addition or diminution for many generations. At last one of them was admitted to holy orders without having been at any university, and acted as the curate of the mountainous parish in which his patrimony lay. His son was the famous Dr. Edmund Law,[1] Bishop of Carlisle, who having been sent early to St. John's College, Cambridge, highly distinguished himself there, was elected a fellow of Christ's College, and became one of the shining lights of that society celebrated under the name of the Zodiac. Before being raised to the episcopal bench, he was successively rector of Graystock and of Salkeld, Master of Peterhouse, and a Prebendary of Durham. In politics, like many dignitaries of that day, he was a good Whig, although almost all the inferior clergy were Tories, or rather Jacobites. In religion he strongly inclined to the low Church party, and was suspected of being

1. Edmund Law, a learned bishop, born at Cartmel, Lancashire, 1703. He was educated at Kendal, from whence he removed to St. John's College, Cambridge, where he took his bachelor's degree in 1723, and soon after was elected fellow of Christ's College. In 1727 he proceeded to the degree of master of arts, and in 1732 published a translation of Archbishop King's "Origin of Evil," with notes. He also, while at college, conducted a new edition of Stephens's Latin Thesaurus through the press. In 1737 he was presented to the rectory of Graystock, Cumberland. In 1743 he was promoted to the archdeaconry of Carlisle, which he resigned in 1756, on being chosen master of Peterhouse. About 1760 he was made librarian of the university, and some years afterwards was promoted to the archdeaconry of Stafford and to a prebend in Lincoln Cathedral. In 1768 he was advanced to the bishopric of Carlisle, where he died Aug. 14, 1787. He was the author of "Considerations on the Theory of Religion," "An Inquiry into the Ideas of Space, Time," etc. He also published an edition of Locke's works. Two of his sons came to be bishops, and one a judge.—*Cooper's Biog. Dict.*

somewhat latitudinarian in some of the articles of his faith. He published various theological works, the most famous of which was a treatise "on the Intermediate State "—inculcating the doctrine that the soul cannot be in active existence when separated from the body, and that it is therefore in a continuous sleep between death and the general resurrection.[1] He was married to Mary, daughter of John Christian, Esq., of Unerigg, in Cumberland, and by her had a family of twelve children, among whom were two Bishops and a Chief Justice.

Edward, the subject of this memoir, was one of the youngest of them, and was born in the parsonage of Salkeld on the 16th of November, 1750. Resembling his mother much in features, he is said to have derived from her likewise his manners and the characteristic qualities of his mind. If the following description of the good Bishop be correct, they could not have descended upon the sarcastic Chief Justice *ex parte paternâ*:

" His Lordship was a man of great softness of manners, and of the mildest and most tranquil disposition. His voice was never raised above its ordinary pitch. His countenance seemed never to have been ruffled ; it invariably preserved the same kind and composed aspect, truly indicating the calmness and benignity of his temper. His fault was too great a degree of inaction and facility in his public station. The bashfulness of his nature, *with an exteme unwillingness to give pain*, rendered him sometimes less firm and efficient in the administration of authority than was requisite." [2]

1. It is stated by Townsend (vol. i. 301) and other biographers, that he was likewise author of ' A Serious Call to the Unconverted,' but this very lively work, which should rather be designated ' True Religion made entertaining,' was written by WILLIAM LAW, born in Northamptonshire, and educated at Oxford, who was tutor to the father of Gibbon the historian, and ended his career by becoming a disciple of Jacob Behmen.—*Gibbon's Miscellaneous Works ; Boswell's Life of Johnson.*

2. Archdeacon Paley.

Yet our hero's "Christian" blood will not account for his *irascibility*, as he himself used to declare that in temper his mother was as admirable as the Bishop his father, and when he had reached old age he often expressed a fond respect for his memory.

Little Ned, although often naughty, was the chief favorite of both his parents. He remained at home till he was eight years old, and not only his nurse but the whole family spoke their native dialect in such force, that he retained the Cumbrian pronunciation and accent to his dying hour.[1] Soon after he had been His education. taught to read, he was sent into Norfolk to live with his maternal uncle, the Rev. Humphrey Christian, a clergyman settled at Docking, in that county. Having been At the Charterhouse. a short time at a school of some repute at Bury St. Edmunds, he was removed to the noble foundation of the Charter-house in London.[2] To his solid acquisitions there he ever gratefully ascribed his subsequent eminence in public life, and there, by the special directions of his will, his remains now repose near to those of the founder.

Law continued at the Charterhouse six years, and rose to be Captain of the school. He used to say that while enjoying this dignity he felt himself a much more important character than when he rose to be Chief Justice of England and a Cabinet Minister. At this early period he displayed the same vigor of character and the same mixture of arrogance and *bonhomie* which afterwards distinguished him. He was described by a classfellow who had alternately experienced harshness and kindness from him, as " a bluff, burly boy, at once

1. For example, he called the days of the week " Soonda, Moonda, Toozeda, Wenzeda," &c.

2. He was admitted a Scholar on the 22nd of January, 1761, upon the nomination of the Bishop of London (Dr. Sherlock), and elected an Exhibitioner 2nd May, 1767.

moody and good-natured—ever ready to inflict a blow
or perform an exercise for his schoolfellows." [1]

When he had reached the age of eighteen he was
sent to Cambridge and entered at Peterhouse, of which
his father was still Master. He is said now to have
occasionally indulged pretty freely in the dissipation
which was then considered compatible with a vigorous
application to study, but he never wasted his time in
idle amusements; over his wine he would discuss the
merits of a classical author, or the mode of working a
mathematical problem—and when his head was cleared
by a cup of strong tea, he set doggedly to work that he
might outstrip those who confined themselves to this
thin potation.

He belonged to a club of which William Coxe,[2] then
an undergraduate, afterwards an archdeacon, was the
historiographer. The destined eulogist of Sir Robert
Walpole thus, in flattering terms, described the future
Chief Justice:

" Philotes bears the first rank in this our society. Of
a warm and generous disposition, he breathes all the
animation of youth and the spirit of freedom. His
thoughts and conceptions are uncommonly great and
striking; his language and expressions are strong and
nervous, and partake of the color of his sentiments.

1. Capel Lofft.
2. William Coxe, a successful English historian and writer of
travels, born in London in 1747. He became curate of Denham in
1771, after which he travelled on the continent as tutor of the Marquis of Blandford and other young members of the nobility. He
published "Travels in Russia, Poland, Sweden, and Denmark"
(1784), which are highly prized and interesting, and "Travels in
Switzerland" (1789). He was appointed chaplain to the Tower about
1796, and Archdeacon of Wilts in 1805. Among his most important
works are a "History of the House of Austria" (1792), "Memoirs of
Sir Robert Walpole" (3 vols., 1798), "Memoirs of the Kings of Spain
of the House of Bourbon, 1700-1788" (3 vols., 1813), and "Memoirs
of the Duke of Marlborough" (1817-19). Died in 1828.—*Thomas's
Biog. Dict.*

As all his views are honest and his intentions direct, he
scorns to disguise his feelings or palliate his sentiments.
This disposition has been productive of uneasiness to
himself and to his friends, for his open and unsuspecting
temper leads him to use a warmth of expression which
sometimes assumes the appearance of *fierté*. This has
frequently disgusted his acquaintance ; but his friends
know the goodness of his heart and pardon a foible that
arises from the candor and openness of his temper.
Indeed he never fails, when the heat of conversation is
over and when his mind becomes cool and dispassionate, to acknowledge the error of his nature, and, like a
Roman Catholic, claim an absolution for past as well as
future transgressions. Active and enterprising, he pursues with eagerness whatever strikes him most forcibly.
His studies resemble the warmth of his disposition ;
struck with the great and sublime, his taste, though ele_
gant and refined, prefers the glowing and animated
conceptions of a Tacitus to the softer and more delicate
graces of a Tully." .

I am afraid we must infer that in conversation he
was rather overbearing, and that the love of sarcasm,
which never left him, was then uncontrolled and made
him generally unpopular. However, his straight-
forward manly character, joined to his brilliant talents,
procured him while at the University friends as well as
admirers—among whom are to be reckoned Vicary
Gibbs,[1] Simon Le Blanc and Souldan Lawrence, afterwards his rivals at the bar and associates on the bench.
While an undergraduate, by exercising the invaluable
virtue of self-denial he was upon the whole very industrious,—although he loved society, and said " the great_

1. Sir Vicary Gibbs, an English judge, born at Exeter in 1752. He
distinguished himself in the trials of Hardy, Horne Tooke, and others
for treason in 1794. He became Solicitor General in 1805 and Attorney General in 1807. He was appointed Chief Justice of the Court
of Common Pleas in 1813. Died in 1820.—*Thomas's Biog. Dict.*

est struggle he ever made was in leaving a pleasant party and retiring to his rooms to read."

When the time approached for taking his bachelor's degree, it was confidently expected that he would be senior wrangler and first medallist. His elder brother, afterwards Bishop of Elphin,[1] to whom he was considered much superior, had been second wrangler in a good year. Edward, however, was decidedly surpassed in the mathematical examinations by two men much inferior to him in intellect, but of more steady application. His disappointment was imputed to excess of confidence. He himself took it deeply to heart, and he pretended to be as much ashamed of being third wrangler as if he had got the "wooden spoon." His classical acquirements did carry off the first medal ; but his pride was by no means assuaged, and he continued for the rest of his days to scoff at academical honors. This feeling was embittered by his writing the two following years for bachelors' prizes and gaining nothing beyond fifteen guineas, given by the members for the

1. John Law (1745-1810), Bishop of Elphin, born in 1745, was eldest son of Edmund Law, Bishop of Carlisle, and brother of Edward Law, first Lord Ellenborough, and of George Henry Law, Bishop of Bath and Wells. John was educated at Charterhouse, and proceeding to Christ's College, Cambridge, graduated B.A. 1766, M.A. 1769, and D.D. 1782. He subsequently became a fellow of his college and took holy orders. He was appointed Prebendary of Carlisle in 1773 and archdeacon there in 1777. Five years later, in April, he went to Ireland as chaplain to William Henry Cavendish Bentinck, third Duke of Portland, Lord Lieutenant. Within a few months (August) he was appointed to the see of Clonfert, was translated to that of Killala in 1787, and to that of Elphin in 1795. Dr. William Paley, his successor in the archdeaconry, accompanied him to Ireland and preached his consecration sermon, which has been printed. Law died in Dublin March 18, 1810, and was interred in the vaults of Trinity College Chapel. He married Anne, widow of John Thomlinson of Carlisle and of Blencogo Hall, Cumberland, but had no issue. Law published two sermons : 1. Preached in Christ Church, Dublin, before the Incorporated Society, 1796. 2. Preached in St. Paul's Cathedral, London, at the meeting of the charity school children, 1797. He founded prizes for the study of mathematics in Dublin University.—*Dict. Nat. Biog.*

second best Latin Essay. Although his spoken eloquence was vigorous and impressive, he never could
produce anything very striking when sitting down,
unexcited, at his desk, and his written compositions,
whether in Latin or English, were never remarkable
either for lucid arrangement or purity of style.

He continued to reside at Cambridge two years
after taking his bachelor's degree, with a view to a
fellowship, and these he used to describe as the least
agreeable and least profitable of his life. He still had
fits of application to severe study, but the greatest part
of his time he now devoted to light literature, taking
special pleasure in novels. He said he abominated
such as ended unhappily—but he read all indiscriminately, and while he luxuriated in Fielding[1] and Smol-

1. Henry Fielding, born in 1707, was the third son of General
Fielding, and great grandson of an Earl of Denbigh. His classical
education was received at Eton ; and he afterwards studied law at
Leyden, which, however, he was obliged to leave in his twentieth
year, on failing to receive supplies from home. His father had a
large family, and appears to have been neither rich nor frugal. The
son was fairly left to shift for himself ; and, seeking his fortune in
London, he found, as he says himself, that his choice lay between
being a hackney writer and a hackney coachman. Composition for
the stage was his first pursuit, by which he contrived to lead the life
of a gay young man for about nine years, from 1727 to 1736. During
this time he wrote eighteen plays of one sort or another, which,
though admitted to be dramatic failures, show, in passages innumer-
able, the same vigorous sense and shrewdness, the same keenness of
wit, and the same acuteness of critical discernment which afterwards
characterized his novels. His translated farce of " The Miser " and
his " Mock Doctor " are now oftenest remembered ; but neither these
nor his other comedies and farces possess nearly so much originality
or spirit as his burlesque parodies on the tragic drama, among which
" Tom Thumb " may be noted as being still by far the best thing of
the kind in the English language. The audacity with which in his
farces he satirized public characters is said to have been the main
provocation which led the government to establish a censorship of
acted plays. In 1736 he married an amiable young lady, with whom
he received about 1500l., succeeding about the same time to an
estate of 200l. a year in Derbyshire. He now retired to the country,
where he lived with hospitable and careless extravagance, and found
himself penniless in the course of three years. He returned to
London, resumed his law studies, and was called to the bar. But he

lett, Mrs. Sheridan's ' Sidney Biddulph ' was said to have drawn "iron tears down Pluto's cheek."

His father had much wished to have all his sons in had no success in the practice of his profession, for which, besides other causes, he was now disqualified by frequent attacks of gout. To the anxieties and distresses of a precarious and scanty livelihood was soon added the deep grief caused by the death of his wife, to whom, and to his children, the good-hearted and improvident man of pleasure was warmly attached. For ten years he subsisted by miscellaneous literary drudgery. He made new attempts at dramatic writing ; he published many fugitive essays and tracts, engaged in political controversy as an active Whig partisan, and was the conductor and chief writer of three successive periodical papers aimed at the Jacobites and their principles. About 1742 he wrote " Joseph Andrews," the first of those novels on which his fame depends. Notwithstanding its frequent seriousness, this piece was intended to be, and in many points really is, a parody on the sentimentalism of Richardson's "Pamela." It was followed by "Jonathan Wild," a singular specimen of very vigorous but overdrawn irony. In 1749 he received from the government a small pension, and an appointment as a justice of peace for Middlesex and Westminster. The office, as then regarded and administered, was decidedly one which a gentleman would not have accepted unless through necessity ; and it undoubtedly helped to degrade both Fielding's character and his feelings. Its duties, however, were discharged not only zealously, but with an honorable integrity and disinterestedness altogether new in the occupants of such places. He published an " Inquiry into the Increase of Thieves and Robbers," besides other treatises bearing on law ; he was a remarkably efficient police magistrate ; and one of his last achievements was the extirpating of several gangs of ruffians by whom London was infested. " The History of Tom Jones, a Foundling," was written very soon after Fielding had been forced to embark in these ungenial and harassing employments ; when his health was already quite broken ; and when, by his own public acknowledgment, the honesty with which he filled his office left him so poor that the benevolence of wealthy friends had been required for enabling him to subsist. It is not easy to understand the grounds on which "Tom Jones" has been defended against the charge of immorality ; but in point both of genius and skill in art it is the best novel ever written. It was followed in 1751 by " Amelia," which is very much inferior. The heroine is said to have been designed as a portrait of the author's second wife. In 1752 he attempted a new periodical, which drew him into quarrels with Smollett and other men of letters. His life was fast ebbing away : dropsy had been followed by jaundice and asthma. Ordered by physicians to a southern climate, he sailed for Lisbon and died there in October, 1754, in the forty-eighth year of his age. He left behind him, besides other works, a spiritedly written account of his " Journey to Lisbon."—*Cycl. Univ. Biog.*

the church, but Edward was earnestly bent upon trying his fortune at the bar, and had obtained leave to enter himself of Lincoln's Inn,[1] on the express condition that he was not to begin the study of the law till he had obtained a fellowship, and that, failing this, he should still take holy orders—so that he might have something to depend upon for a subsistence beyond the precarious hope of fees. Meeting with some disappointments in academical promotion, he was strenuously urged to enter the Church, his father having become a bishop, with the power of giving him a living among the fells of Westmoreland ; but at last he was elected a fellow of Trinity College, and the Chief Justiceship was open to him.

A.D. 1773.

It was a fortunate circumstance for him that he embraced the profession of the law *against* the earnest wishes of a father whom he sincerely respected and loved. He thus took a tremendous responsibility upon himself, and had the most powerful motives for exertion, that he might justify his own opinion and soothe the feelings of him whose latter days he hoped to see tranquil and happy. He spurned the idea of retreating upon the Church after a repulse by the Law, and he started with the dogged resolution to overcome every difficulty which he might encounter in his progress. Having obtained a small set of chambers in Lincoln's Inn, he forthwith in good earnest began the study

He studies the law.

---

1. " LINCOLN'S INN.

EDWARD LAW, Gentleman, of St Peter's College, Cambridge, third son of the Right Revd Father in God, Edmond Lord Bishop of Carlisle, is admitted into the Society of this Inn the 10th day of June, in the Ninth year of the Reign of our Sovereign Lord George the Third, by the Grace of God, of Great Britain, France, and Ireland, King. Defender of the Faith, and in the year of our Lord 1769, and hath thereupon paid to the use of this Society the sum o Three pounds three shillings and four pence.

Adm^s B.6
fo 139

Admitted by
R^D SPOONER."

of jurisprudence, not contenting himself with the lucid page of Blackstone and the elegant judgments of Mansfield, but vigorously submitting to whatever was most wearisome and most revolting if considered necessary to qualify him for practice at the English bar. Determined to be a good artificer, he did not dread " the smoke and tarnish of the furnace."

"Moots" and "Readings" having long fallen into disuse, the substituted system of *pupilising* had been firmly established—well adapted to gain a knowledge of practice, but not of principles. A student intended for the common-law courts was expected to work at least two years in the office of a special pleader, copying precedents, drawing declarations and pleas, and having an opportunity of seeing the run of his master's business. The most distinguished instructor in this line at that time was George Wood,[1] on whom Lord Mansfield

1. Mr. Baron Wood was a native of Roystone, near Barnsley, in Yorkshire, his father residing as the clergyman there. He was born in 1740, and being intended for the junior branch of the legal profession was articled to Mr. West, an attorney at Cawthorne. He was so assiduous in his studies and showed so much ability during his articles that at the end of them his master urged him to try his fortune at the bar. This advice he fortunately took, and coming to London he pursued the usual course of preparation at the Middle Temple, and commenced as a special pleader on his own account. He soon got into full practice, and established such a reputation that pupils flocked to him. Among them he gave the initiatory instructions to Mr. Law, afterwards Lord Ellenborough, in 1773: to Mr., afterwards Lord, Erskine, in 1779; and to Mr. Abbott, afterwards Lord Tenterden, in 1787,—besides many others of the most eminent lawyers of the day. So great was his celebrity as a master of the science that when he was called to the bar he was engaged on the part of the Crown in all the state prosecutions commencing in December, 1792. He joined the northern circuit and was as successful in his practice in the country as he was in Westminster Hall. Two stories are told of which he was the hero. On proceeding in a post-chaise to join the circuit with Mr. Holroyd they were addressed by a gentleman of fashionable appearance, who begged to know "what o'clock it was." Mr. Wood politely taking out a handsome gold repeater to answer the question was immediately met by the presentation of a pistol to his breast, and a demand of the watch, which of course he was obliged to resign to the interrogator. The

made the celebrated special-pleading joke about his CHAP.
XLVI. horse *demurring* when he should have *gone to the country*.[1] In his office, Law, by great interest, obtained a desk, and he could soon recite the " money counts " as readily as his favorite poem of ABSALOM AND ACHITOPHEL. We may form a lively notion of his habits and his sentiments at this period from the following letter which, at the conclusion of a sitting of many hours in Mr. Wood's chambers, he wrote to his friend Coxe, then a private tutor to a young nobleman:

His dili-
gence in a
special
pleader's
office.

" June 18th, 1773—Temple, Friday night.

" After holding a pen most of the day in the service of my profession, I will use it a few minutes longer in that of friendship. I thank you, my dearest friend, for

consequence was that he could never appear in court without some learned brother calling out to him, " What's o'clock, Wood ?" . . . . A character so distinguished for legal erudition was not likely to be long neglected by those whose duty it was to supply the vacancies on the bench. Mr. Wood accordingly received his promotion as a baron of the Exchequer in April, 1807, and was knighted soon after. He performed his judicial functions for nearly sixteen years with great advantage to the community and with all the credit to himself which was anticipated from his previous career. In February, 1823, he resigned his seat to Mr. Serjeant Hullock, and lived little more than a year afterwards. His death occurred on July 7, 1824, at his house in Bedford Square ; and he was buried in the Temple Church. He printed for private circulation some valuable "Observations on Tithes and Tithe Laws," discussing the subject with great shrewdness and ability. This treatise was afterwards published, and the principle he recommended for the arrangement of the charge was partially adopted in the bill for the commutation of tithes.—*Foss's Judges of England*.

1. George, though a subtle pleader, was very ignorant of *horse flesh*, and had been cruelly cheated in the purchase of a horse on which he had intended to ride the circuit. He brought an action on the warranty that the horse was " a good roadster, and free from vice." At the trial before Lord Mansfield, it appeared that when the plaintiff mounted at the stables in London, with the intention of proceeding to Barnet, nothing could induce the animal to move forward a single step. On hearing this evidence, the Chief Justice with much gravity exclaimed, " Who would have supposed that Mr. Wood's horse would have *demurred* when he ought to have *gone to the country* ? " Any attempt to explain this excellent joke to *lay gents.* would be vain, and to *lawyers* would be superfluous.

this and every proof of confidence and affection. Let us cheerfully push our way in our different lines: the path of neither of us is strewed with roses, but they will terminate in happiness and honor. I cannot, how. ever, now and then help sighing when I think how inglorious an apprenticeship we both of us serve to ambition—while you teach a child his rudiments and I drudge at the pen for attorneys. But if knowledge and a respectable situation are to be purchased only on these terms, I, for my part, can readily say ' hac mercede placet.' Do not commend my industry too soon; application wears for me at present the charm of novelty ; upon a longer acquaintance I may grow tired of it."

On the contrary, he became fonder and fonder of it. The tautological jargon still used in English law proceedings is disgusting enough, but in the exquisite logic of special pleading rightly understood, there is much to gratify an acute and vigorous understanding. The methods by which it separates the law from the facts, and having ascertained the real question in controversy between the parties, refers the decision of it either to the judges or to the jury, favorably distinguish our procedure from that of any other civilized nation, and have enabled us to boast of a highly satisfactory administration of justice without a scientific legal code.

Law continued working very hard as a special-pleading pupil for two years. During this period he not only grew to be a great favorite with his instructor, but the attorneys who frequented Mr. Wood's chambers became acquainted with his assiduity and skill. The pleadings settled by Mr. Wood and the opinions signed by him were generally written in a very large, bold, pot-hook hand, which they discovered to be Mr. Law's, and although he was much too independent and honorable to resort to any evil arts for the purpose of ingratiating himself, and he was chargeable rather with *hauteur* than with *huggery*, he sometimes got into conversation with the attorneys, and he raised in their minds a very high opinion of his proficiency as well as of his industry.

When he was to cease to be *in statu pupillari* the question arose whether he should immediately be called to the bar, or follow the course recently introduced of practising as a special pleader under the bar—confining himself entirely to chamber practice—drawing law papers and giving opinions to the attorneys in cases of smaller consequence—making his own charges for his work, instead of receiving the spontaneous *quiddam honorarium*, which to a barrister must not be below a well-known *minimum*, but, being above that, he is not at liberty to complain of, however inadequate it may appear. Law was conscious of considerable powers of elocution which he was impatient to display. He not only belonged to a private debating club for students in the Temple, but he had gained applause by an oration at Coachmakers' Hall, then open to spouters in every rank of life. Nevertheless, sacrificing the chance of present *éclat*, he prudently resolved to condemn himself to a period of useful obscurity, and he commenced "special pleader under the bar." He had great success, and business flowed in upon him, particularly from the agents of the Northern attorneys. His charge for answering cases was very small, but he put a modest estimate upon the real value of the commodity which he sold. Many years afterwards, when he was presiding at Nisi Prius, a wrong-headed attorney, pleading his own cause, and being overruled on some untenable points which he took, at last impertinently observed— "My Lord, my Lord, although your Lordship is so great a man now, I remember the time when I could have got your opinion for five shillings." *Ellenborough,*

C.J.: "Sir, I dare say it was not worth the money." This was a far better mode of vindicating the dignity of the Judge and carrying along with him the sympathies of the audience, than fining the delinquent or threatening to commit him for a contempt of court— the course which would probably have been followed by the hasty Kenyon.

His success. Under the bar Law soon made a handsome income; Cambridge men studying for the legal profession were eager to become his pupils at the established fee of one hundred guineas a year or two hundred guineas for three years; and when he made out his bills at Christmas he found that he was doing better than any barrister who could be considered his contemporary— with the single exception of Erskine.

During five long and irksome years did Law continue to devote himself to this drudgery, but his perseverance was amply rewarded, for he not only gained a reputation which was sure to start him with full business at the bar, but he acquired a thorough knowledge of his craft, which few possess who, after a mere course of solitary study, plunge into forensic wrangling.

A.D. 1780.
He is called to the bar. In Hilary Term, 1780, he was called to the bar by the Honorable Society of Lincoln's Inn. Generally speaking, success cannot be anticipated with any confidence for a young barrister, however well qualified to succeed he may appear to be; and our profession well illustrates the Scriptural saying, "The race is not always to the swift, nor the battle to the strong, nor bread to men of understanding, nor honor to men of skill, but time and *chance* happeneth to them all." Nevertheless Law neither felt, nor had reason to feel, the slightest misgivings when he put on his gown, and started for the prize of Chief Justice. Lord Camden and other great lawyers had languished for many years without any opportunity of displaying their acquire-

ments. Law had several retainers given to him by great Northern attorneys on the very day of his call; and not only from family connection, but from his reputation as a special pleader, which had long crossed the Trent, he was sure of finding himself at once in respectable practice. He disdained the notion of attending Quarter Sessions, and he always was inclined to sneer at young gentlemen who tried to force themselves into notice by writing a law book. He calculated that by his knowledge and his eloquence he must speedily be at the head of the Northern Circuit. In general those who practise under the bar as special pleaders do not aspire higher than holding second briefs in a stuff gown, with an *arrière pensée* of being raised to be a puisne judge. The ardor of our *débutant* had not been extinguished or chilled by his long apprenticeship, and he already heard the rustling of his silk gown, and imagined himself wearing the collar of S S, appropriated to the Chief Justice of England.

In the beginning of March, 1780, he joined the circuit at York, causing considerable alarm to those established in business, and curiosity among the disinterested. Without any suspicion of improper arts being used by himself, or of improper influence being exercised in his favor by others, at the opening of the Nisi Prius court a large pile of briefs lay before him. His manner was somewhat rough, and he was apt to get into altercations with his opponents and with the judge; but his strong manly sense, and his familiar knowledge of his profession, inspired confidence into those who employed him; and the mingled powers of humor and of sarcasm which he displayed soon gave him a distinguished position in the Circuit Grand Court held *foribus clausis* among the barristers themselves, in which toasts were given, speeches were made, and verses were recited, not altogether fit for the vulgar ear.

At this period there were never more than two or three King's counsel on any circuit ; and a silk gown was a high distinction to the wearer, not only among his brethren, but in general society,—placing him above the gentry of the country. The Northern leaders then were Wallace and Lee, whom no attorney approached without being uncovered. They were men of great eminence from their personal qualifications, and it was expected that they would speedily fill the highest judicial offices. They were before long taken from the circuit, to the joy of their juniors—Wallace being made Attorney General, and Lee [1] Solicitor Gen-

1. John Lee (1733-1793), lawyer and politician, a member of a family settled in Leeds since the early part of the sixteenth century, was born in 1733. He was the youngest of ten children, and, his father dying in 1736, he was principally brought up under the influence of his mother, a woman of superior talents, who, although a protestant dissenter, was a friend of Archbishop Secker. She designed John for the church, but in spite of his pious disposition and keen interest in theology and in church matters he was more fitted by his blunt and boisterous manner for the law, and he was accordingly called to the bar at Lincoln's Inn and joined the northern circuit. Though his advancement was slow, his learning and dexterity, his ready eloquence and rough humor, eventually gave him an equal share with Wallace of the leadership of the circuit, and he held the office of attorney general for the county palatine of Lancaster till he died. In April, 1769, he appeared before the House of Commons as counsel for the petitioners against the return of Colonel Luttrell for the county of Middlesex. The petition failed, but this debate was long remembered at the bar. The government offered him a seat in the House and a silk gown in 1769, and in 1770 a silk gown, with the appointment of Solicitor General to the Queen, was again offered to him, but he refused both offers on political grounds. On September 18, 1769, he became, however, Recorder of Doncaster. In 1779 he was one of the counsel for Admiral Keppel when he was tried by court-martial for his conduct in the engagement off Ushant on July 12, 1778. Upon his acquittal Keppel sent to Lee a fee of 1000l., and this being refused he presented to each of his counsel, Erskine, Dunning, and Lee, a replica of his portrait by Sir Joshua Reynolds. In 1780 Lee became a King's counsel, and in the second Rockingham administration was appointed Solicitor General, and came into parliament for Clitheroe in Lancashire. Subsequently he was elected for Higham Ferrers, Northamptonshire, and sat for that place till he died. He resigned office on Lord Rockingham's death, but returned to it under the Duke of Portland, and on the death of

eral; but, unluckily for them, they adhered to Mr. Fox and Lord North, and the permanent ascendency of William Pitt after he had crushed the coalition was fatal to their further advancement. Neither of them having reached the Bench, their traditionary fame, transmitted through several generations of lawyers, is now dying away.[1]

Till the beginning of the 19th century the Northern Circuit, in the spring, was confined to Yorkshire and Lancashire. In early times the distance of the four hyperborean counties from the metropolis, and the badness of the roads, rendered it impossible to hold assizes in any of them during the interval between Hilary and Easter Terms—so that a man committed for murder in Durham, Northumberland, Cumberland, or Westmoreland might lie in jail near a twelvemonth before he was brought to trial. At the accession of George III. there were turnpike trusts in the remotest parts of the kingdom, and post-horses were found wherever they

Wallace at the end of 1783 he was promoted to be Attorney General, and held the office until the Duke of Portland was dismissed. In politics he was a thoroughgoing party man. One of his maxims was, "Never speak well of a political enemy." Wilkes spoke of him as having been in the House of Commons "a most impudent dog," and attributed his success there in comparison with other lawyers to this characteristic. Wraxall calls him "a man of strong parts and coarse manners, who never hesitated to express in the coarsest language whatever he thought," and says of him that he "carried his indecorous abuse of the new First Lord of the Treasury to even greater lengths than any other individual of the party dismissed from power." At the bar he was universally known as "honest Jack Lee," was distinguished for his integrity, and amassed a large fortune. Having been injured by a wrench while riding, he was attacked by cancer, and dying on August 5, 1793, he was buried at Staindrop, Durham, a seat which he obtained by his marriage with Miss Hutchinson, by whom he had one daughter. His portrait was painted by Sir Joshua Reynolds in 1786, and was exhibited in that year at the Royal Academy.—*Nat. Biog. Dict.*

1. Wallace's son was made a peer, by the title of Lord Wallace of Knaresdale, in 1828, but died without issue in 1844. Lee, though he filled a great space in the public eye while living, has not in any way added to the permanent "Grandeur of the Law."

were desired ; but the usual superstitious adherence to
ancient customs when the reason for them has ceased,
long obstructed every attempt to improve the administration of justice in England.

The business being finished at York, Mr. Law proceeded with his brethren to Lancaster, where the list of
civil causes was still scanty, although all that arose
within the County Palatine[1] were to be tried here.
Liverpool, compared with what it has since become,
might have been considered a fishing village; Manchester had not reached a fourth of its present population; and the sites of many towns, which now by their
smoke darken the Lancastrian air for miles around,
were then green fields, pastured by cattle, or heathery
moors, valuable only for breeding grouse. Here our

1. Counties palatine are so called from the fact that their lords
had royal rights, equally with the King in his palace (*palatium*). The
earl of a county palatine could pardon treasons, murders, and
felonies ; while all writs were in his name, and offences were said to
be committed against his peace, and not against that of the King.
Palatine counties originated in the time of William I., who practically
created three—Chester, Durham, and Kent—whilst Shropshire had,
until the time of Henry I., palatine rights. These counties were
selected as being especially liable to attack—Chester and Shropshire
from the Welsh Marches, Kent from France, and Durham from
Scotland. The disturbed state of the borders rendered it an easy
task for an earl, who was as powerful as a sovereign in his own
territory, to extend his frontiers at the expense of his enemies.
Kent ceased to be a palatine earldom after the death of Odo of
Bayeux, whilst Pembrokeshire and Hexhamshire, in Northumberland, were made counties palatine. Henry I. granted royal rights
over the Isle of Ely to the Bishop of Ely, and in the year 1351 Lancaster was created a palatine earldom. "The palatine earldom of
Chester," says Bishop Stubbs, "had its own courts, judges, and staff
of officers, constable, steward, and the rest : it had its parliament,
consisting of the barons of the county, and was not until 1541 represented in the parliament of the kingdom." The other counties
palatine, with the exception of Lancaster and Chester, which were
held by the Crown, and of Durham, were assimilated to the rest of
the country during the sixteenth century. The palatine jurisdiction
of Durham remained with the bishop until 1836, whilst the jurisdiction of the palatine courts at Lancaster, with the exception of the
Chancery Court, were transferred to the High Court of Justice by
the Judicature Act of 1873.—*Dict. of Eng. Hist.*

junior **did** not fare so well as at York ; yet he could not
have been indicted at the Grand Court for carrying
. *unam purpuream baggam flaccescentem omnino inanitatis causâ ;*[1] for although Wallace, who was nearly connected with him by marriage, had made him a present
of a bag—an honor of which no junior before could ever
boast on his first circuit—its flaccidity was swelled out
by several briefs, which he received from an attorney of
Ashton-under-Lyne, who used afterwards boastingly to
say, " *I made Law Chief Justice.*"[2]

The assizes being speedily over, Mr. Law returned His slow progress in London.
to London well pleased with his success, and with his
prospects. But in the two following terms he never
opened his mouth in court unless to make a motion
of course,—and he was rather disheartened. It was not
till years afterwards, when the attention of the nation
was fixed upon him as counsel for Mr. Hastings, that his
merits were appreciated by attorneys in London.

When the summer assizes came round he visited all
the six counties which form the Northern Circuit. In
each of them he had a considerable portion of business
—and at Carlisle more than any other junior, his own

---

1. " A purple bag, flaccid because entirely empty."
. These mock indictments were still often in Latin, notwithstanding the statute requiring all proceedings in Courts of Justice to be in
the English tongue, it having been ruled that " no statute is binding
on the Grand Court of the Northern Circuit in which this Court is not
specially mentioned."

2. Now-a-days any young barrister buys a bag, and carries it as
soon after he is called to the bar as he likes ; but when I was called
to the bar, and long after, the privilege of carrying a bag was strictly
confined to those who had received one from a King's counsel. The
King's counsel, then few in number, were considered officers of the
Crown, and they not only had a salary of 40l. a year, but an annual
allowance of paper, pens, and purple bags. These they distributed
among juniors who had made such progress as not to be able to
carry their briefs conveniently in their hands. All these salaries and
perquisites were ruthlessly swept away in 1830 by Lord Grey's reforming Government—and it was full time—as King's counsel had
become a mere grade in the profession, comprehending a very large
number of its members.

qualifications as a lawyer being backed by the respect entertained for the venerable Bishop of the diocese.

His silk gown delayed by his supposed Whiggery.
During seven years he continued to fight his way on the circuit in a stuff gown ; and towards the end of this period he had gained such reputation in addressing juries as nearly to throw out of business several black-letter special pleaders, who were his seniors, and could not be retained along with him when it was intended that he should lead the cause. There was therefore a general wish among his brother circuiteers that he should have silk, and a representation upon the subject was made to Lord Chancellor Thurlow ; but some difficulty arose about conferring this mark of royal favor upon one who was considered a decided Whig. Although measures to encourage free trade, for the improvement of the law, and even for a reform of parliament, were brought forward by the prime minister, the memory of the " Coalition " was green, and the thirst for revenge upon all who had encouraged the attempt to put a force upon the Crown in the choice of ministers was still unsatiated. Thurlow, who soon after, during the King's insanity, intrigued with the Whigs that he himself might retain the Great Seal under them, had down to this time testified peculiar enmity to the whole of them as a party and individually. However, the urgency for Law's promotion increasing, and the Judges who went the Northern Circuit joining in the application, it could no longer be refused.

Law in domestic life.
Before we behold him as a public character, let us take a glance at him in domestic life. It was said that he had rather freely indulged in the gallantries of youth, and that he even for a time followed the example of the then Lord High Chancellor of Great Britain, the great prop of the Church, and chief distributor of ecclesiastical preferment, who openly kept a mistress.[1]

1. Mrs. Harvey, celebrated in the ' Rolliad,' and said to have been much courted by the clergy.

But however this may be, Law was not supposed to
have exceeded what was permitted by the license of
those times, and he was happily forever rescued from
the peril of scandal by being accidentally introduced to
the beautiful Miss Towry, daughter of Mr. Towry, a His court-
commissioner of the navy, and a gentleman of good ship.
family. I myself recollect her become a mature matron,
still a very fine woman, with regular features, and a
roseate complexion; but when she first appeared, she
excited admiration almost unprecedented. Amongst
many others, Law came, saw, and *was* conquered.
Considering his ungainly figure and awkward address,
it seems wonderful that he should have aspired to her
hand among a crowd of competitors—particularly as it
was understood that she had already refused very
tempting proposals. But he ever felt great confidence
in himself, whatever he undertook; he now said, "Faint
heart never won fair lady," and after he had paid her
devoted attention for a few weeks, he asked her father's
leave to address her. The worthy commissioner gave
his consent, having heard that this suitor was considered the most rising lawyer in Westminster Hall.
But the young lady being interrogated, answered by a
decided negative. Still the lover was undismayed—
even (as it is said) after a third rebuff. At last, by the
charms of his conversation, and by the eulogiums of all
her relations, who thought she was repelling a desirable
alliance, her aversion was softened, and she became
tenderly attached to him.

The marriage took place on the 17th day of Octo- His mar-
ber, 1789, and proved most auspicious. Mrs. Law riage.
retained the beauty of Miss Towry; and such admiration did it continue to excite, that she was not only
followed at balls and assemblies, but strangers used to
collect in Bloomsbury Square to gaze at her as she
watered the flowers which stood in her balcony. But

no jealousy was excited in the mind of the husband
even when Princes of the Blood fluttered round her.
For many years the faithful couple lived together in
uninterrupted affection and harmony, blessed with a
numerous progeny, several of whom united their father's
talents with their mother's comeliness.

CHAPTER XLVII.

CONTINUATION OF THE LIFE OF LORD ELLENBOROUGH TILL HE WAS APPOINTED ATTORNEY GENERAL.

LAW had long bitterly complained that his fame was confined to the limits of the Northern Circuit. He had scarcely as yet been employed in a single cause of interest in London, whereas Erskine was already the foremost man in the Court of King's Bench, and had special retainers all over England. Our aspirant believed that if he had a fair opportunity of displaying his powers, he should gain high distinction; but he dreaded that he might never lead in actions of greater interest than *trespass* for an assault, or *assumpsit* on the warranty of a horse, or *covenant* for the mismanagement of a farm, or *case* for the negligent working of a mine.

In the midst of this despondency, he found at his chambers one evening a general retainer for WARREN HASTINGS, ESQ., and instructions to settle the answer to the articles of impeachment,—with a fee of five hundred guineas. This was a much more important occurrence to him than his appointment to be Chief Justice of England, which was the consequence of it, and followed in the natural and expected course of events. He at once perceived that his fortune was made; and in rapid succession he saw with his mind's eye the pleasure to be felt by his family, the mortification of his enemies, the glory that he was to acquire from entering the lists against such antagonists as Burke, Fox, and Sheridan, and the honors of his profession which must in due time be showered upon him. In our juridical history no English advocate has ever had such a field for the display of eloquence as the counsel for the impeached Warren Hastings. Hale could only advise Charles I. to deny the jurisdiction of the High Court of Justice; Lane, in defending the Earl of Strafford, was only permitted to touch upon a technicality; and, till the reign of William III., in cases of high treason, it was only to argue a dry point of law which might incidentally arise that the accused had any assistance from advocacy. Since the Revolution there had been very interesting State Trials, but they only involved the fate of an individual; they exhibited the struggles of retained lawyers against retained lawyers; they turned upon specific acts of criminal conduct imputed to the accused; they were over in a single day, and in nine days more they were forgotten. No one then anticipated that the impending trial of Warren Hastings was to be begun before one generation of Peers and decided by another, but all knew that it involved the mode in which a distant empire had been governed; that it was to unfold the history of some of the most memorable wars and revolutions in Asia; that it was to elucidate the manners and customs of races of men who, though subjected to our dominion, we only imperfectly knew from vague rumor; that in the course of it appalling charges of tyranny and corruption were to be investigated; that the accusers were the Commons of England; that the managers of the impeachment were some of the greatest orators and statesmen England had ever produced, and that upon the result depended not only the existence of Mr. Pitt's administration, but, what was more exciting, the fate of an individual whose actions had divided public opinion

throughout the civilized world—who was considered
by some a monster of oppression, cruelty, and avarice,
and by others a hero, a philanthropist, and a patriot.
The Northern circuiteer, instead of addressing a jury
of illiterate farmers at Appleby, in a small court filled
with rustics, was to plead in Westminster Hall, gor-
geously fitted up for the occasion, before the assembled
Peers in their ermined robes, before the representatives
of the people attending as parties, and before a body
of listeners comprehending all most distinguished for
rank, for talent, and for beauty.

Although Mr. Law had not thought of this retainer
more than of being made Archbishop of Canterbury,
some of his friends had been engaged in a negotiation
for securing it to him. Hastings himself was naturally
desirous that he should be defended by Erskine, who
had acquired so much renown as counsel for Lord
George Gordon, and who had loudly declared his own
personal conviction to be that the ex-Governor General
deserved well of his country. But as the impeachment
had become a party question, and was warmly supported by the leaders of the party to which Erskine
belonged,—although he was not then a member of the
House of Commons, he reluctantly declined an engagement in which his heart would enthusiastically have
prompted the discharge of his professional duties, and
by which he might have acquired even a still greater
name than he has left with posterity. He declared
that he would not have been sorry to measure swords
with Burke, who in the House of Commons had on
several occasions attacked him rather sharply and successfully. "In Westminster Hall," said he, "I could
have smote this antagonist hip and thigh." But Erskine could not for a moment endure the idea of coming
into personal conflict with Fox and Sheridan, whom he
loved as friends, whom he dreaded as rivals, and with

whom, on a change of government, he hoped to be associated in high office.

The bar at this time afforded little other choice. Dunning had become a Peer and sunk into insignifi-·cance; his contemporaries were either connected with Mr. Pitt's Government, or were declining from years and infirmity—and among the rising generation of lawyers, although there was some promise, no one yet had gained a position which seemed to fit him for this "great argument."

The perplexity in which Hastings and his friends found themselves being mentioned in the presence of Sir Thomas Rumbold,[1] who had been in office under him in India, he delicately suggested the name of his brother-in-law,[2] pointing out this kinsman's qualifica-

1. Sir Thomas Rumbold (1736–1791), Indian administrator, third and youngest son of William Rumbold, an officer in the East India Company's naval service, by Dorothy, widow of John Mann, an officer in the same service, and daughter of Thomas Cheney of Hackney, was born at Leytonstone, Essex, on June 15, 1736. . . . Thomas Rumbold was educated for the East India Company's service, which he entered as a writer on Jan. 8, 1752, and sailed for Fort St. George towards the end of the same month. Soon after his arrival in India he exchanged the civil for the military service of the company. He served under Lawrence in the operations about Trichinopoly in 1754, and under Clive at the siege of Calcutta in 1756–7, and for gallantry displayed during the latter operations was rewarded by Clive with a captain's commission. He was Clive's aide-de-camp at Plassey, was severely wounded during the action, and on his recovery resumed his career in the civil service. Part of the years 1762-3 he spent in England on furlough. On his return to India he was appointed chief of Patna, and from 1766 to 1769 sat in the Bengal council. Having made his fortune, Rumbold came home in the latter year, and was returned to parliament for New Shoreham on Nov. 20, 1770. Rumbold returned to India as Governor of Madras in Feb., 1778, and after a distinguished career, in which he coöperated in every way with Warren Hasting, he returned to England in Jan., 1780. He was proceeded against in parliament for corruption and oppression in office. The charges, however, were not established, and at the general election of 1784 he was returned for Weymouth, which he represented until 1790. He died Nov. 11, 1791. (See Dict. Nat. Biog.)

2. Sir Thomas Rumbold had married Joanna, Bishop Law's youngest daughter.

tions in respect of legal acquirements, of eloquence, and, above all, of intrepidity—on which, considering the character of the managers for the Commons, the acquittal of the defendant might chiefly depend. This recommendation was at first supposed to proceed only from the partiality of relationship; but upon inquiry it appeared to be judicious. The resolution was, therefore, taken to employ Law as the leading counsel, associating with him Mr. Plomer,[1] afterwards Vice-Chan-

1. Thomas Plumer, descended from an old and respectable Yorkshire family, was the second son of Thomas Plumer, of Lilling Hall in that county. He was born on October 10, 1753, and at eight years of age he was sent to Eton, where he gained that character for classical ability and suavity of disposition which afterwards distinguished him at University College, Oxford. While William Scott (afterwards Lord Stowell) was regarded as the best tutor in the university, Plumer was considered one of the best scholars. He was elected Vinerian Scholar in 1777, and, taking his degree of B.A. in 1778, became fellow of his college in the next year, and proceeded M A. in 1783. He had become a member of Lincoln's Inn so early as April, 1769, but was not called to the bar till February, 1778. Before that event took place he had the advantage of attending Sir James Eyre on his circuits, and frequently assisted the judge, whose eyes were weak, in taking down the evidence on the trials at which he presided. This employment was of great benefit to him in his future practice, which was principally in the Court of Exchequer. In 1781 he was made a commissioner of bankrupts, and attended the Oxford and also the Welsh circuits, at the end of the latter of which he joined in the revelry of the Horseshoe Club, instituted by the members for their relaxation and indulgence in all sorts of fun and nonsense. (*Notes and Queries*, 2d S. xii. 87, 214.) He soon acquired practice, and stood so high in estimation that he was employed in the defence of Sir Thomas Rumbold at the bar of the House of Commons, and there exhibited such powers that he was selected in 1787 as one of the three counsel to defend Warren Hastings, his coadjutors being Mr. Law and Mr. Dallas, each of whom, as well as he, eventually filled high offices in the law. In 1793 he was made a King's counsel. in which character he was often employed in the public trials that took place during the next ten or twelve years. He successfully defended John Reeves when absurdly prosecuted in 1797 for a libel. In the next year he defended Arthur O'Connor and others on a charge of high treason, one only of the defendants, James O'Coigley, being found guilty. In 1802 he was engaged in the prosecution of Governor Wall for a murder committed twenty years before, in the next year in the prosecution of Colonel Despard for high treason, both of whom were condemned and executed. He

cellor and Master of the Rolls, and Mr. Dallas,[1] afterwards Solicitor General and Chief Justice of the Common Pleas,—in whom Law entirely confided and with whom he ever cordially coöperated. He still

was leading counsel in the defence of Lord Viscount Melville in 1806, on his impeachment by the House of Commons, and contended with so much success against the case of the managers as to procure an acquittal for his noble client on all the ten charges in the articles. Just before this trial, on March 25, 1805, he was appointed a judge on the North Wales Circuit. He had a great reputation as a tithe lawyer, and had much employment before election committees. Of the suppressed volume called "The Book," arising out of the "Delicate Investigation" into the conduct of Caroline, Princess of Wales, in 1806, he was supposed to be, if not the author, at least the corrector, joining with Lord Eldon and Mr. Perceval as her Royal Highness's friends. In April of the next year, on the defeat of the Whig ministry, Mr. Plumer was appointed Solicitor General and was knighted. He then entered parliament for Lord Radnor's borough of Downton, which he continued to represent till he was raised to the bench. He remained Solicitor General for five years, Sir Vicary Gibbs being the Attorney General ; but he does not appear to have taken part in any of the numerous prosecutions instituted by the latter except in the case of the *Independent Whig* when he spoke for two hours in the House of Lords in support of the sentence pronounced against the libellers. On Sir Vicary's elevation to the bench Sir Thomas Plumer succeeded him on June 27, 1812, but filled the post for less than a year, being appointed on April 10, 1813, the first Vice-Chancellor under the statute 53 Geo. III. c. 24. After presiding in the new court for nearly five years, he received another and a last promotion as Master of the Rolls on January 6, 1818. He filled this station till his death, which occurred six years after, on March 24, 1824, when he was buried in the Rolls Chapel.—*Foss's Lives of the Judges.*

1. Robert Dallas was the son of a gentleman of the same name living at Kensington in Middlesex, and his mother was Elizabeth, daughter of the Rev. James Smith, minister of Kilberney in Ayrshire. He became a member of Lincoln's Inn, and trained himself to public speaking at the debating society held at Coachmakers' Hall, according to the common practice of the time. This was of considerable advantage to him when he was called to the bar, and enabled him to produce his arguments with much more ease to himself and with greater effect to the court, in which he soon acquired considerable practice. In January, 1788, he was engaged in the defence of Lord George Gordon. He next appears as one of the counsel for Mr. Hastings, the trial of whose impeachment lasted seven years, from 1788 to 1795, and highly distinguished himself by his exertions, and by his polished addresses to the Lords. Naturally disgusted with the inveteracy of Burke against his client, he gave the relentless prosecutor no credit for patriotic feelings, but, attributing

CHIEF JUSTICE DALLAS.

wore a stuff gown when this retainer was given, but he was clothed in silk before the trial began.

He prepared himself for the task he had undertaken with exemplary diligence and assiduity. Carrying along with him masses of despatches, examinations, and reports, which might have loaded many camels, he retreated to a cottage near the lake of Windermere, and there spent a long vacation more laborious than

his attacks to the innate malignity of his nature, composed this bitter epigram:

> "Oft have we wonder'd that on Irish ground
> No poisonous reptile has e'er yet been found:
> Reveal'd the secret stands of Nature's work—
> She sav'd her venom to produce her Burke."

In 1795 Mr. Dallas received a silk gown: and through all the succeeding years till he was raised to the bench the latter volumes of the State Trials record his efforts either for the defence or the prosecution. Among these his speech on the motion for a new trial in the case of General Picton was separately published. In the meantime he had obtained a seat in the House of Commons, where he represented St. Michael's, Cornwall, in 1802, and afterwards the Scotch boroughs of Kirkaldy, etc. In 1804 he was promoted to the chief justiceship of Chester, and presided there till 1813, when on May 4 he was appointed to the office of Solicitor General and knighted. Six months afterwards he was raised to the bench of the Common Pleas, on November 5, 1813, and on the same day in 1818 he was promoted to the headship of that court. There he presided for five years with acknowledged ability and universal respect. A curious question having been raised in 1823, whether the Lord Lieutenant of Ireland had the same power to confer knighthood after the Union which he undoubtedly possessed before that measure had passed, a meeting of the judges was held in June at Chief Justice Dallas's to consider the point, when they were of opinion unanimously that the Act of Union did not deprive him of his former privilege. It was a matter of some speculation how the right should have remained undisputed for above twenty years, during which it had been frequently exercised, and only now be impugned; and it was suspected that the doubt was invented for the purpose of mortifying Lady Morgan, who had offended the ministers by the freedom of her writings, and whose husband had received an Irish knighthood. ("Lady Morgan's Memoirs," ii. 172.) At this time his health began to break, and he soon found he could no longer undergo the fatigues of his office. He therefore resigned his seat at the end of 1823, and lived little more than one year longer, dying on December 25, 1824. He left several children by his wife, Charlotte, daughter of Lieut. Col. Alexander Jardine.—*Foss's Lives of the Judges.*

the busiest term he had ever known in London. Although possessing copiousness of extempore declamation, he was fond of previously putting down in writing what he proposed to say in public on any important occasion, and there are now lying before me scraps of paper on which he had written during this autumn apostrophes to the Lords respecting the Rohilla war, the cruelties of Debi Sing, and the alleged spoliation of the Begums.

　On the 19th of February, 1788, Mr. Burke having finished a speech of four days, in which he generally opened all the charges, Mr. Fox, his brother manager, proposed that thereafter the charges should be taken separately, and that not only the evidence and arguments should be concluded by both sides, but that the judgment should be given by the Court upon each

before another was taken in hand. Now Mr. Law for the first time opened his mouth as counsel for Mr. Hastings, and strongly resisted this proposal. He distinctly saw that upon the mode of procedure depended the issue of the impeachment, for there not only was a strong prejudice against the accused, which would have rendered perilous a speedy decision upon any part of his case, but the defence really arose from a view of the whole of his conduct while Governor General;—the difficulties in which he was placed palliating, if they did not justify, acts which, taken by themselves, appeared criminal. The managers, feeling the advantage they must derive from having a separate trial, as it were, on each charge, strenuously argued that this was the parliamentary course according to Lord Strafford's case and other precedents,—that the due weight of evidence was most truly appreciated while it was fresh in the memory,—and that facility of conception, notwithstanding the vastness of the subject, might best be attained by subdividing it into parts which the mind might be capable of grasping. Law, in answering them, availed himself of the opportunity to animadvert upon the violent language used by Burke, saying that " the defendant, who was still to be presumed to be innocent till proved to be guilty, had been loaded with terms of invective and calumny in a strain which, never since the days of Sir Walter Raleigh, had been used in an English court of justice." Mr. Fox, interrupting him, said, that " vested with a great trust from the House of Commons, he could not sit and hear such a complaint, which proceeded on the principle that in proportion as the accused was deeply guilty, the accuser, in describing his crimes, was to be considered a calumniator." Law, without any retraction or apology, pursued his argument against the course proposed by the managers, insisting that while it was contrary to the mode of proceeding in the courts of common law, there was no parliamentary precedent to support it. " My Lords," said he, " in answering one charge we may be compelled to disclose to our adversary the defence which we mean to employ upon others. We conceive that the whole case should be before you ere you decide upon any part of it. On the first charge are we, for the purpose of explaining the general policy with which it is connected, to produce all the evidence specifically calculated to repel several others? On the second charge is the whole of the exculpatory evidence to be given over again? Is this just? is it reasonable? is it expedient? Would it be proposed in any other court professing to administer the criminal law of the country?"

The Peers withdrew to their own chamber to deliberate, and on their return to Westminster Hall, the Lord Chancellor Thurlow thus addressed the managers: " Gentlemen, I have it in charge to inform you that you are to produce all your evidence in support of the

CHAP.
XLVII.

His con-
tests with
Burke and
the other
managers
on ques-
tions of
evidence.

prosecution before Mr. Hastings is called upon for his defence."

During the examination of the witnesses there was a constant sparring between the counsel and the managers, and blows were interchanged with all the freedom of *nisi prius*. For example, when Sheridan was examining Mr. Middleton for the prosecution, and finding him rather adverse, addressed some harsh observations to him, Law thus interposed—" I must take the liberty of requesting that the honorable manager will not make comments on the evidence of the witness in the presence of the witness. Such a course will tend to increase the confusion of a witness who is at all confused, and affect the confidence of the most confident. I shall therefore hope that the honorable manager, from humanity and decorum, will be more abstemious."

The managers having entirely failed to prove one particular act of misconduct which they had imputed to Mr. Hastings, Law expressed a wish that in future they would be more cautious in avoiding calumny and slander. Burke answered, with much indignation, that "he was astonished the learned gentleman dared to apply such epithets to charges brought by the Commons of Great Britain, whether they could or could not be proved by legal evidence; it was well known that many facts could be proved to the satisfaction of every conscientious man by evidence which, though in its own nature good and convincing, would not be admitted by the technical canons of lawyers; it would be strange indeed that a well founded accusation should be denominated calumnious and slanderous, because an absurd rule prevented the truth of it from being established."

Law.—" My Lords, I do not mean to apply the terms *calumny* and *slander* to any proceeding of the House of Commons; but I have the authority of that House for declaring that the honorable member has, at your Lordships' bar, used calumnious and slanderous expressions not authorized by them."

Fox.—"My Lords, it is highly irregular and highly indecent in an advocate to allude to what has taken place within the walls of the House of Commons. The learned counsel has done worse, he has misrepresented that to which he presumed to allude. We have offered in evidence the very documents upon the authority of which the Commons preferred the charge now said to be calumnious and slanderous."

Law.—"I cannot justly be accused of improperly referring to proceedings in the House of Commons, as I have only repeated in substance the account given of these proceedings by the honorable manager himself in the hearing of your Lordships—and I have therefore the highest authority for asserting that my client has suffered from calumny and slander."[1]

Fox.—"Here is a new misrepresentation. My honorable friend has not told your Lordships that anything said by the managers at your Lordships' bar was a calumny or a slander, nor said anything which can be tortured into such a meaning. And, my Lords, we will not proceed with the trial till your Lordships have expressed your opinion of the language used by the learned gentleman. We must return to the Commons for fresh instructions."

Thurlow, C.—"The words you complain of must be taken down in writing."

They were taken down accordingly.

Law.—"I acknowledge them and abide by them."

The Peers were about to withdraw for deliberation to their own chamber when it was suggested and agreed that the Chancellor should admonish the learned counsel, "that *it was contrary to order* in the counsel to advert to anything that had happened in the House of Commons; that it was *indecent* to apply the terms *calumny* and *slander* to anything which had been said by their authority, and that such expressions must not be repeated."

1. This refers to a resolution of the House of Commons animadverting on expressions used by Mr. Burke.

The great struggle was, whether the Lords were to be governed by the rules of evidence which prevail in the courts below. These Burke treated with great contempt. On one occasion he said:

> "The accused rests his defence on quibbles, and appears not to look for anything more honorable than an Old Bailey acquittal, where on some flaw in the indictment the prisoner is found *not guilty*, receives a severe reprimand from the Judge, and walks away with the execration of the bystanders. No rule which stands in the way of truth and justice can be binding on this high court."

> *Law.*—"In the name of my client, in the name of the people of England, I protest against such doctrine. The rules of evidence have been established because by experience they have been found calculated for the discovery of truth, and the protection of innocence. If any of them are erroneous, let them be corrected and amended, but let them be equally binding upon your Lordships and the inferior courts. Are you to dismiss every standard of right, and is a party tried at your Lordships' bar—his honor and his life being at stake—to be cast upon the *capricious*, I will not say *corrupt*, opinion entertained or professed by a majority of your Lordships? Why do you summon the Judges of the land to assist you but that you may be informed by them for your guidance what are the rules of law? Unless the rules of law are to prevail, a reference to these reverend sages would be a mockery, and you should order them forever to withdraw."

The Lords very properly held that the rules of law respecting the admissibility of evidence ought to guide them; and during the trial they twenty-three times referred questions of evidence [1] to the Judges, being

---

[1] 1. I have examined the questions and answers as they appear in the Journals of the House of Lords, but they are not instructive, or of much value. With a single exception, they were not so framed as to decide any abstract point, and merely asked whether, under the actual circumstances which occurred, specific evidence was admissible.

One response to a question put was of general application, and

always governed by their advice.[1] But to the very conclusion of the trial Burke bitterly complained, as often as any evidence which the Managers proposed to adduce was excluded in compliance with the opinion of the Judges. On one occasion, when evidence irregularly offered by the Managers in reply had been very properly rejected, a Peer called Burke to order for arguing against a decision of the House. Mr. Hastings's leading counsel contemptuously added, that he would not waste a moment of their Lordships' time in supporting a judgment which, being founded on a rule of law, wanted no other support. *Burke :* "I have become accustomed to such insolent observations from the learned gentlemen retained to obstruct our proceedings, who, to do them justice, are as prodigal of bold assertions as they are sparing of arguments."

might have been advantageously cited in the late case of *Melhuish* v. *Collier*, 15 Q.B. 878.

Question put to the Judges during the Trial of Warren Hastings, Esq.	*Judges' reply to the said question, as entered on the Lords' Journals.*
Feb. 29, 1788.	April 10th.
Whether, when a witness, produced and examined in a criminal proceeding by a prosecutor, disclaims all knowledge of any matter so interrogated, it be competent for such prosecutor to pursue such examination, by proposing a question containing the particulars of an answer supposed to have been made by such witness before a Committee of the House of Commons, or in any other place, and by demanding of him whether the particulars so suggested were not the answers he had so made?	The Lord Chief Baron delivered the unanimous opinion of the Judges, that, when a witness produced and examined in a criminal proceeding by a prosecutor disclaims all knowledge of any matter so interrogated, it is not competent for such prosecutor to pursue such examination, by proposing a question containing the particulars of an answer supposed to have been made before a Committee of the House of Commons, or in any other place, and by demanding of him whether the particulars so suggested were not the answer he had so made.

1. The same course was subsequently followed on the impeachment of Lord Melville, and is now to be considered the established law of parliament.

When the Lords disallowed the evidence of the history of the Mahratta war, Law having merely said, " It would be an insult to their Lordships, and treachery to his client, were he to waste one minute in stating the objections to it," Burke expressed deep regret that so many foreigners were present; but (looking into a box in which sate the Turkish ambassador and his suite, he added) " let us hope that some of them do not understand the English language, as the insolent remarks we are compelled to hear from counsel would be a disgrace to a Turkish court of justice."

Law was more hurt when, at a later period of the trial, having called on Burke to retract an assertion alleged to be unfounded, the Right Honorable Manager, putting on a look of ineffable scorn, merely said in a calm tone, " My Lords, the counsel deserves no answer." Soon after, Law, complaining of the delay caused by the frivolous questions on evidence raised by the Managers, added, " The Right Honorable Manager to whom I chiefly allude, always goes in a circle, never in a straight line. The trial will bring discredit on all connected with it. We owe it to our *common character* to prevent unnecessary delay." " Common character!" angrily interrupted the Manager, "I can never suffer the dignity of the House of Commons to be implicated in the common character of the bar. The learned counsel may take care of his own dignity —ours is in no danger except from his sympathy."

But it was by the rejection of evidence of the alleged cruelties of Raja Debi Sing that Burke was driven almost to madness. His recital of these in his opening speech had produced the most tremendous effect, curdling the blood of the stoutest men, and making ladies shriek aloud and faint away.[1] A witness

---

1. " The treatment of the females cannot be described : dragged from the inmost recesses of their houses, which the religion of the

being called to prove these horrible charges, the counsel for Mr. Hastings objected that the evidence was
inadmissible as there was no mention of such cruelties
in any article of the impeachment, and it was not even
now suggested that Mr. Hastings had directed them,
or in any way sanctioned or approved of them. The
Lords, after consulting the Judges, determined that
the evidence could not be received.

Mr. Burke : " I must submit to your Lordships' decision,
but I must say at the same time that I have heard it with the
deepest concern ; for if ever there was a case in which the
honor, the justice, and the character of a country were concerned, it is that which relates to the disgusting cruelties and
savage barbarities perpetrated by Debi Sing, under an authority
derived from the British Government, upon the poor forlorn
inhabitants of Dinagepore—cruelties and barbarities so fright-
fully and transcendently enormous, that the bare mention of
them has filled with horror every class of the inhabitants of
this country. The impression which even my feeble representation of these cruelties and barbarities in this place produced
upon the hearts and feelings of all who heard me is not to be
removed but by the evidence that shall prove the whole a
fabrication. The most dignified ladies of England swooned at
the bare recital of these atrocities, and is no evidence now to
be received to prove that my forbearing statement fell far
short of the appalling reality ?"
Law : " It is not to be borne that the Right Honorable

country had made so many sanctuaries, they were exposed naked to
public view : the virgins were carried to courts of justice, where
they might naturally have looked for protection, but they looked for
it in vain ; for in the face of the ministers of justice, in the face of
assembled multitudes, in the face of the sun, those tender and
modest virgins were brutally violated. The only difference between
their treatment and that of their mothers, was that the former were
dishonored in open day, the latter in the gloomy recesses of their
dungeon. Other females had the nipples of their breasts put in a
cleft of bamboo and torn off. What modesty in all nations most
carefully conceals, this monster revealed to view, and consumed by
slow fires ; and the tools of this monster, Debi Sing—horrid to tell !
—carried their natural brutality so far as to introduce death into the
source of generation and of life."

Manager shall thus proceed to argue in reprobation of their Lordships' judgments.

Burke : " Nothing can be farther from my intention than to reprobate any decision coming from a Court for which I entertain the highest respect. But I am not a little surprised to find that the learned counsel should stand forth the champion of your Lordships' honor. I should have thought that your Lordships were the best guardians of your own honor· It never could be the intention of the Commons to sully the honor of the House of Peers. As their *coördinate* estate in the legislature the Commons are perhaps not less interested than your Lordships in the preservation of the honor of this noble House ; and therefore we never could think of arguing in *reprobation* of any of its decisions. But I may venture to suggest that the question which you have put to the Judges is not framed in the manner to determine whether what the Commons propose is reasonable or unreasonable. If the Commons had been suffered to draw up their question themselves, they would have worded it in a very different manner, and a very different decision might have been given by your Lordships. It is true that the cruelties of Debi Sing are not expressly charged in the Article to have been committed by the authority of Mr. Hastings ; but the Article charges Mr. Hastings with having established a system which he knew *would* be, and in point of fact *had* actually been attended with cruelty and oppression. The Article does not state by whom the acts of cruelty have been committed, but it states cruelty in general, and of such cruelty so charged the Managers have a right to give evidence. The character of the nation will suffer, the honor of your Lordships will be affected, if when the Commons of England are ready to prove the perpetration of barbarities which have disgraced the British name, and call for vengeance on the guilty heads of those who have been in any degree instrumental in them, the inquiry is to be stopped by a miserable technicality. Suffer me to go into proof of those unparalleled barbarities, and if I do not establish them to the full conviction of this House and of all mankind, if I do not prove their immediate and direct relation to and connection with the system established by Mr. Hastings, then let me be branded as the boldest calumniator that ever dared to fix upon unspotted innocence the imputation of guilt. My

Lords, I have done. My endeavor has been to rescue the
character and justice of my country from obloquy. If those who have formerly provoked inquiry—if those who have said that the horrid barbarities which I detailed had no existence but that which they derived from the malicious fertility of my imagination—if those who have said I was bound to make good what I had charged, and that I should deserve the most opprobrious names if I did not afford Mr. Hastings an opportunity of doing away the impression made by the picture of the savage cruelties of Debi Sing—if these same persons who so loudly called for inquiry now call upon your Lordships to reject the proofs which they before challenged me to bring, the fault is not mine. Upon the heads of others therefore, and not upon those of the Commons of Great Britain, let the charge fall that the justice of the country is not to have its victim. The Commons stand ready to make good their accusation, but the defendant shrinks from the proof of his guilt."

Law [according to the original report of the trial, "with unexampled warmth, whether real or assumed "] : "My Lords, the Right Honorable Manager feels bold only because he knows the proof which he wants to give *cannot* be received. He knows that from the manner in which the charge is worded your Lordships *cannot* if you *would* admit the proof without violating the clearest rules and principles of criminal procedure. But let the Commons put the details of those shocking cruelties into the shape of a charge which my client can meet, and then we will be ready to hear every proof that can be adduced. And if, when they have done that, the much-injured gentleman 1 am now trying to shield from calumny does not falsify every act of cruelty that the Honorable Managers shall attempt to prove upon him, MAY THE HAND OF THIS HOUSE AND THE HAND OF GOD LIGHT UPON HIM." [1]

This imprecation on the head of the client was deemed more cautious than magnanimous, and it was thus criticised by Fox in summing up the evidence on this Article :

1. The reporter, who seems to have had a spite against Mr. Law, adds, " After this ejaculation, delivered in a tone of voice not unlike that of the theatric hero, when he exclaims ' Richard is hoarse with calling thee to battle !' the scene closed."—' History of the trial of Warren Hastings, Esq.,' published by Debrett, Part III. p. 54-56.

"The counsel for the defendant have invoked the judgment of your Lordships and the vengeance of Almighty God,
not on their own heads, but on the head of their client, if the
enormities of Debi Sing, as stated by my Right Honorable
Friend, shall be proved and brought home to him. I know not
how the defendant may relish his part in this imprecation ; but
in answer to it, if the time should come when we are fairly
permitted to enter upon the proof of those enormities, I would
in my turn invoke the most rigorous justice of the Peers and
the full vengeance of Almighty God, not on the head of my
Right Honorable Friend, but on my own, if I do not prove
those enormities and fix them upon the defendant to the full
extent charged by my Right Honorable Friend ; and this I
pledge myself to do under an imprecation upon myself as solemn as the learned gentleman has invoked upon his client."

These imprecations can only be considered rhetori-
cal artifices; both sides were well aware that the con-
tingency on which they were to dare the lightning of
Heaven could never arrive, for the Articles of Impeachment, as framed, clearly did not admit the proof, and a
fresh Article could not then have been introduced. In
truth, the cruelties of Debi Sing had been much ex-
aggerated, and Mr. Hastings, instead of instigating, had
put a stop to them. His counsel must have deliberated
long before they resolved to object to the admissibility
of the evidence, and they were probably actuated by a
dread of the prejudice it might create before it could
be refuted.

Law turned to good account the frivolity and vanity
of Michael Angelo Taylor,[1] a briefless barrister, who,

1. "Michael Angelo Taylor (1757-1834), politician, son and heir
of Sir Robert Taylor, was born in 1757. He matriculated from Corpus
Christi College, Oxford, as gentleman commoner on Oct. 21, 1774,
and graduated B.A. from that body in 1778, but proceeded M.A.
from St John's College in 1781. When only twelve years old he was
admitted to the Inner Temple (Jan. 19, 1769), but changed to Lincoln's Inn on Nov. 30, 1770. He was called to the bar at the latter
inn on Nov. 12, 1774." After several unsuccessful attempts Taylor
was elected to the House of Commons for Poole in 1791, where except
one parliament he sat until his death. Upon first entering politics

although the butt of the Northern Circuit, had con- trived to get himself appointed a Manager. An important point coming on for argument, Law observed— " It is really a pity to waste time in discussing such a point which must be clear to all lawyers; this is no point of political expediency, it is a mere point of law, and my honorable and learned Friend there (pointing to Michael Angelo), from his accurate knowledge of the

he was Tory and supporter of Pitt, but afterwards became a Whig. " Taylor was one of the committee of managers for the impeachment of Warren Hastings, when he assisted Sheridan 'to hold the bag and read the minutes,' and he sat on many important committees of the House of Commons. From 1810 to 1830 he persistently brought before the House the delays which attended the proceedings in Chancery, and for three consecutive years (1814, 1815, and 1816) he drew attention to the defective paving and lighting of the streets of London. His name is still remembered by the measure known as 'Michael Angelo Taylor's Act,' i.e., 'The Metropolitan Paving Act, 1817, 57 Geo. III. cxxix. (Local and Personal),' under which proceedings for the removal of nuisances and other inconveniences from the streets are still taken. It is given *in extenso* in Chitty's 'Statutes' (vol. viii. 1895, title 'Metropolis,' pp. 3-49). Henry Luttrell, in his ' Letters to Julia' (3d edit. 1822, pp. 88-90), describes 'a fog in London —time November,' and appeals to 'Chemistry, attractive aid,' to help us with the assistance of 'the bill of Michael Angelo' (Taylor), who had introduced a bill on 'gas-lighting.' Taylor was a small man, and Gillray in his caricatures always laid stress on his diminutive size. In the 'Great Factotum amusing himself' (1797) he is represented as a monkey ; in 'Pig's Meat, or the Swine flogged out of the Farmyard' (1798), he is a tiny porker ; and in 'Stealing Off—a Prudent Secession ' (November, 1798) he becomes a little pug-dog. In one caricature, that of 'The new Speaker (i.e., the law-chick) between the Hawks and Buzzards,' reference is made to the fact that had the Whigs come into office in 1788 he would have been the Speaker. In February, 1831, his attachment to the Whigs was appropriately rewarded by his elevation to the rank of a privy councillor. He died at his house in Whitehall Garden (long a favorite rendezvous of the Whig party) on July 16, 1834, and was buried on July 23 in the family vault at St. Martin's-in-the-Fields. A half-length portrait of him was painted by James Lonsdale, and an engraving of it was published by S. W. Reynolds on March 7, 1822. A whole-length portrait of his wife (when Frances Vane) as 'Miranda' was painted by John Hoppner. The original belongs to the Marquis of Londonderry, by whom it was exhibited in the 'Fair Women Collection' in the Grafton Gallery in 1894. It has recently been engraved."—*Nat. Biog. Dict.*

law, which he has practised with so much success, can confirm fully what I say." Michael puffed, and swelled, and nodded his head—when Burke ran up to him quite furious, and, shaking him, said, " You little rogue, what do you mean by assenting to this ? "

Law was most afraid of Sheridan, but once ventured to try to ridicule a figurative observation of his that " the treasures in the *Zenana* of the Begum were an offering laid by the hand of piety on the altar of a saint," by asking, " how the lady was to be considered a saint, and how the camels when they bore the treasure were to be laid upon the altar ? " *Sheridan*—" This is the first time in my life that I ever heard of special pleading on a metaphor, or a bill of indictment against a trope ; but such is the turn of the learned gentleman's mind that when he attempts to be humorous no jest can be found, and when serious no fact is visible."

Considering that the Managers were assisted by the legal acumen and experience of Dr. Lawrence, Mr. Mansfield,[1] and Mr. Pigott, it is wonderful to see what

1. James Mansfield. In the year 1729 an act was passed for the regulation of attorneys (St. 2 Geo. II. c. 23), requiring them among other things to be enrolled. Under that statute the father of Sir James Mansfield, who was an attorney practising at Ringwood in Hampshire, is entered on the roll, both of the Common Pleas and Chancery, in November, 1730, as John James Manfield. It has been a question when the' name was altered to Mansfield, and what was the motive. The Ringwood attorney was the son of a gentleman who came to England with one of the Georges and held an appointment in Windsor Castle ; and it was asserted that the attorney thought it more advantageous to him to anglicize his name by calling himself Mansfield. But it is clear that he had not formed this determination in 1730, when he was in practice. Neither had he done so in 1746, when his son, then aged thirteen, was entered at Eton as James Manfield ; nor in 1750, when he appears under the same name on the list for King's College, Cambridge ; nor in 1751, when admitted a scholar, nor in 1754, when nominated a fellow, of that college. But on taking his degree of B.A. in 1755 he signed his name Mansfield. By this date the imputation, which has prevailed, that he made the alteration with the hope of being supposed to be connected with the great Lord Chief Justice entirely falls to the

questions they put and insisted upon.   For example, it
being proved that Mr. Hastings had authorized the

ground, inasmuch as Sir William Murray did not receive the title of
Lord Mansfield till the end of the following year, November, 1756.
He entered the society of the Middle Temple under that name in
February, 1755, and was called to the bar in November, 1758.   He
began to practice in the common law courts, but ultimately removed into Chancery, where he was very successful.   In 1768 he was
one of the counsel for John Wilkes on his application to be admitted
to bail ; and four years afterwards in Michaelmas, 1772, he was made
King's counsel.   On the trial of the Duchess of Kingston for bigamy
in 1776 he appeared for the defendant, when, though he failed in
procuring her acquittal, he succeeded in obtaining her release without any punishment at all.   In the same year he unsuccessfully defended General Smith and Thomas Brand Hollis against a charge of
bribery in the notorious case of the borough of Hindon.   He next
appeared on the part of the Crown on the trials of James Hill for
setting the Rope House at Portsmouth on fire, and of George Strat-
ton and others for deposing Lord Piggott, the Governor of Madras,
and assuming the rule of the settlement.   From his entrance into
parliament in 1774 there is no report of his taking any part in the
debates till just at the close of the session of 1780 ; and his first appearance was somewhat unpropitious, as he excited the risibility of
the whole House by a careless expression about the civil list.   In
September of that year he accepted the solicitor-generalship and
held it during the remainder of Lord North's administration.   While
in office he was engaged in the prosecution of those concerned in the
riots of 1780, and in that of Lord George Gordon he had the disadvantage of replying to the splendid speech of Mr. Erskine for the
prisoner, resulting in an acquittal.   The same duty devolved upon
him on the trial of De La Motte for high treason, whose palpable
guilt insured a conviction.   On the defeat of Lord North's ministry
in March, 1782, Mr. Mansfield was necessarily superseded, and immediately placed himself in the ranks of the opposition.   He was
unfortunate in his first appearance on that side, being called to
order no less than three times for some irrelevant remarks of dangerous tendency, and coming into collision with Kenyon, the new
Attorney General.   Soon after the constitution of the Coalition ministry, which quickly supplanted the administration of Lord Shelburne, Mr. Mansfield was again appointed Solicitor General in
November, 1783, but was fated to be again removed in less than a
month, the Coalition having in its turn succumbed to the ministry
of Mr. Pitt.   In the new parliament called in the following May Mr.
Mansfield had the mortification of surrendering his seat for the
University of Cambridge to the popular minister and never afterwards entered the House.   He remained unemployed for nearly sixteen years, when in 1799 he was constituted Chief Justice of Chester.
Five years afterwards, at the close of Mr. Addington's administration,
he succeeded Lord Alvanly as Chief Justice of the Common Pleas in

letting of certain lands to Kelleram and Cullian Sing,
supposed to be cruel oppressors, they asked the witness—"What impression the letting of the lands to
Kelleram and Cullian Sing made on the minds of the
inhabitants of the country?" Before there was time
to object, the witness blurted out, "They heard it with
terror and dismay." Law insisted that this answer
should be expunged, and that the question should be
overruled, it not being in the competence of the witness
to speak of anybody's feelings but his own. The
Managers standing up strenuously for the regularity
of their question and the fitness of the answer to it, the
Peers adjourned from Westminster Hall to their own
chamber, and, after a reference to the Judges, Lord
Chancellor Thurlow announced to the Managers that
the question objected to could not be regularly put,
and that the answer to it must be expunged. Nearly a
whole day was wasted in this foolish controversy.

A.D. 1792.
Law's
opening of
the defence
On the 14th of February, 1792, and the seventy-
fifth day of the trial, Law thus began to open the defence:

"Your Lordships are now entering on the fifth year of a

April, 1804, and was thereupon knighted. The motto on his rings on
his necessarily taking the degree of a serjeant alludes humorously
to his long exclusion: "Serus in cœlum redeas." On the death
of Mr. Pitt in 1806 and the formation of the Whig ministry he was
pressed to accept the Great Seal, but positively declined the honor;
and his wisdom in the refusal was exemplified by the dismissal of
that party in little more than a year. Though a good average lawyer,
his promotion occurred rather too late in life; and though anxious
to dispense justice in the cases that came before him, he was too apt
to give way to the irritation of the moment. Of this deficiency of
temper the serjeants were not backward in taking advantage; and
towards the end of his career they worried him to such a degree that
he could not always refrain from venting in audible whispers curses
against his tormentors. He was an amiable man, but had not got
rid of the habit of swearing which was too prevalent in his earlier
years. So great was the annoyance that he resigned his post in
Hilary vacation 1814. He lived nearly eight years afterwards, and
died on November 23, 1821, at his house in Russell Square, in the
eigthy-eighth year of his age.—*Foss's Judges of England.*

trial, to which the history of this or any other country furnishes nothing like a parallel; and it at length becomes my
duty to occupy somewhat longer the harassed and nearly exhausted attention of your Lordships, and to exercise reluctantly the expiring patience of my client. Mr. Hastings, by
the bounteous permission of that Providence which disposes
of all things, with a constitution weakened by great and inces-
sant exertions in the service of his country and impaired by
the influence of an unwholesome climate—suffering from year
to year the wounds which most pierce a manly and noble
mind—the passive listener to calumny and insult—thirsting
with an honorable ardor for the public approbation which
illustrious talents and services ever merit—while malignity
and prejudice are combining to degrade him and blacken his
fair reputation in the eyes of his country—subdued by the
painful progress of a trial protracted to a length unexperienced
before by any British subject, and unprecedented in the annals
of any other country—under all these accumulated hardships
Mr. Hastings is alive this day, and kneeling at your Lordships'
bar to implore the protection, as he is sure of the justice, of
this august tribunal.   To a case pampered—I had almost said
corrupted—by luscious delicacies, the advocates of my client
can only bring plain facts and sound arguments ; but we can
show that eloquence has been substituted for proofs, and
acrimony has supplied the place of reasoning.   I could never
be brought to believe that justice was the end looked for,
where vengeance was the moving power."

After an exordium not wanting in dignified solemnity, although creating a wish for more purity and simplicity of diction, he proceeded to take a general view
of the origin of the prosecution, of the charges into
which it was divided, of the feeble manner in which
they had been supported, and of the evidence by which
they were to be repelled.   Upon the whole, he rather
disappointed expectation.   Although he had shown
spirit and energy while wrangling with the managers
about evidence, and although still undaunted by the
matchless power of intellect opposed to him,—now
when he had all Westminster Hall to himself and he

was to proceed for hours and days without interruption or personal contest, he quailed under the quietude, combined with the strangeness and grandeur, of the scene. He by no means satisfied the lively Miss Burney,[1] then attached to the Royal household, who were all, as well as the King and Queen, devoted enemies to the impeachment, and thought no praise sufficiently warm which could be bestowed upon the accused. This is her disparaging language in her Diary :

"To hear the attack the people came in crowds ; to hear the defence they scarcely came in *tête-à-tête*. Mr. Law was terrified exceedingly, and his timidity induced him so frequently to beg quarter from his antagonists, both for any blunders and any deficiencies, that I felt angry even with modest egotism. We (Windham and I) spoke of Mr. Law, and I expressed some dissatisfaction that such attackers should not have had able and more equal opponents. 'But do you not think that Mr. Law spoke well,' cried Windham— 'clear, forcible?' 'Not forcible,' cried I—'I would not say *not clear.*' 'He was frightened,' said Windham ; 'he might not do himself justice. I have heard him elsewhere, and been very well satisfied with him ; but he looked pale and alarmed, and his voice trembled.'"

1. Madame D'Arblay, originally Miss Frances Burney, the second daughter of Dr. Charles Burney, was born at Lynn Regis on June 13, 1752. At an early age she began to exercise herself in works of fiction, tales, and poetry. At fifteen she burned all her early performances, but one of them kept possession of her memory, and gave rise to her first published work, "Evelina ; or the History of a Young Lady's Introduction to the World." It used to be generally understood, and it has been repeatedly stated, that Miss Burney was only about seventeen when this, her first novel, appeared, but in fact it was published in 1778, when she was twenty-six. The work made a very considerable noise in the world. Her second novel, "Cecilia," appeared in 1782. In July, 1786, she was appointed one of the dressers, or keepers of the robes, to Queen Charlotte, and this menial situation she held for five years. In 1793 she married M. Alexandre Piochard D'Arblay, a French emigrant artillery officer, and in 1796 she produced another novel, entitled "Camilla." She survived her husband twenty-two years, dying at Bath on January 6, 1840. Besides the works mentioned above she wrote "The Wanderer," a novel : Memoirs of her father, Dr. Burney ; Diary and Letters, edited by her niece.—*Cooper's Biog. Dict.*

'However, she adds—

" In his second oration Mr. Law was far more animated
and less frightened, and acquitted himself so as almost to
merit as much commendation as, in my opinion, he had merited censure at the opening."

It is a curious fact that the State Trial which, of all
that have taken place in England, excited the most interest is the worst reported. We have no account of
it except from a set of ignorant short-hand writers,
who, although they could take down evidence with
sufficient accuracy, were totally incapable of comprehending the eloquent speeches which were made on
either side. Burke having observed that " virtue does
not depend upon *climates* and *degrees*," he was reported
to have said, " virtue does not depend upon *climaxes*
and *trees*."

The only authentic specimens I can give of Mr.
Law's oratory when he was addressing the Lords on
the merits of the impeachment are the procemium and
the peroration of his speech on the Begum charge,
which are now in my possession, written by his own
hand, and which he had elaborately composed at full
length, and got by heart, although he trusted to short
notes for his comments upon the evidence :

His procemium and peroration on the Begum charge.

" Again, my Lords, after a further period of protracted
solicitude, Mr. Hastings presents himself at your Lordships'
bar, with a temper undisturbed, and a firmness unshaken, by
the lingering torture of a six years' trial.

" God forbid that in the mention of this circumstance I
should be understood to arraign either the justice or mercy of
this tribunal. No, my Lords, all forms of justice have been
well observed. My blame lights on the law, not on your office,
' which you with truth and mercy minister.' As little I advert
to this circumstance as seeking on this account unduly to
interest your Lordships' compassion and tenderness in his
favor. No, my Lords, as he has hitherto disdained to avail
himself of any covert address to these affections, so your Lord-

ships may, I trust, be assured that he does not feel himself
more disposed at this moment than at any former period of
his trial to sully the magnanimity of his past life by the base-
ness of its close.

"He does not even now on his own account merely condescend to lament the unfortunate peculiarity of his destiny
which has marked him out as the only man since man's
creation who has existed the object of a trial of such enduring
continuance ; for, my Lords, he has the virtue, I trust, as far
as human infirmity and frailty will permit, to lose the sense of
his own immediate and peculiar sufferings in the consolatory
reflection which his mind presents to him—that as he is in the
history of mankind the first instance of this extraordinary
species of infliction, so unless he vainly deems of the effect of
this instance upon the human mind, and has formed a rash
and visionary estimate of the generosity and mercy of our
nature, it will be the last.

"He trusts, indeed, that with reference to his own country
at least, he may venture to predict, what the great Roman
historian, Livy, in contrasting a new and barbarous punishment, inflicted in the infancy of the Roman empire, with the
subsequent lenity and humanity of the system of penal laws
which obtained amongst his countrymen, ventured in nearly
the same words to declare—'Primum ultimumque illud supplicium apud Romanos exempli parum memoris legum humana-
rúm fuit.'[1] Dismissing, however, a topic which in the present
advanced stage of this trial has become at least as material for

1. This, it will be recollected, relates to the case of Mettius
Fuffetius, who for his treachery was sentenced to a frightful death
by Tullus Hostilius. The historian in a few lines beautifully narrates
the sentence, the execution, and the behavior of the lookers on :
"Tum Tullus : 'Metti Fuffeti,' inquit, 'si ipse discere posses fidem
ac fœdera servare, vivo tibi ea disciplina a me adhibita esset. Nunc
quoniam tuum insanabile ingenium est, at tu tuo supplicio doce
humanum genus ea sancta credere, quæ a te violata sunt. Ut igitur
paullo ante animum inter Fidenatem Romanamque rem ancipitem
gessisti, ita jam corpus passim distrahendum dabit. EXINDE, DUABIS
ADMOTIS QUADRIGIS, IN CURRUS EARUM DISTENTUM ILLIGAT METTIUM
—DEINDE IN DIVERSUM ITER EQUI CONCITATI, LACERUM IN UTROQUE
CURRU CORPUS, QUA INHÆSERANT VINCULIS MEMBRA, PORTANTES.'
"Avertere omnes a tanta fœditate spectaculi oculos. *Primum
ultimumque illud supplicium apud Romanos exempli parum memoris
legum humanarum fuit*, in aliis gloriari licet, nulli gentium mitiores
placuisse pœnas."—Lib. I. c. 28.

consideration with a view to the happiness and safety of others as his own, the defendant only requests it may for the present so far dwell in your Lordships' memory as to exempt him from the blame of impatience if, thus circumstanced, he has ventured to expect such a degree of accelerated justice as a just attention to other public demands on your Lordships' time may consistently allow.

" He cannot but consider the present moment as on some accounts peculiarly favorable to the consideration and discussion of the many important questions which present themselves for your Lordships' judgment in the course of this trial.

" In a season of recommencing difficulty and alarm we learn better how to estimate the exigence of the moment, and the merit of that moment well employed, than in the calmer season of undisturbed tranquillity.

" We know then best how to value the servant and the service. We hear with awakened attention and conciliated favor the account which vigor, activity, and zeal are required to render of their efforts to save the state—and their success in saving it. In receiving the detail which ardent and energetic service is obliged to lay before us, by a sort of inconsistent gratitude we almost wish to find some opportunities of recompense in the voluntary exercise of our own virtues—some errors which candor may conceal—some excesses which generosity may be required to palliate.

" The same motives which at such a season induce us to appreciate thus favorably the situation, duties, difficulties, and deserts of hazardous and faithful service, induce us also to contemplate with more lively indignation the open attacks of undisguised hostility ; with more poignant aversion and disgust the cold and reluctant requitals of cautious friendship, and with still more animated sentiments of detestation and abhorrence, the treacherous, mischievous attacks of emboldened ingratitude.

" These are sentiments which the present moment will naturally produce and quicken in every mind impregnated with a just sense of civil and political duty. Can I doubt their effect and impression here, where we are taught, and not vainly taught, to believe that elevation of mind and dignity of station are equally hereditary, and that your high court exhibits at once the last and best resort of national justice, and the purest image of national honor?

"To you, my Lords, unadmonished by the ordinary forms and sanctions by which in other tribunals the attention is attracted and the conscience bound to the solemn discharge of judicial duty, the people of England, by a generous confidence equally honorable to themselves and you, have for a long succession of ages entrusted to your own unfettered and unprompted, because unsuspected, honor—have entrusted the supreme and ultimate dispensation of British justice.

"Such then being the tribunal, and such the season at which the defendant is required to account before it for certain acts of high public concernment done in the discharge of one of the greatest public trusts that ever for so long and in so arduous a period fell to the lot of any one man to execute, he cannot but anticipate with the most sanguine satisfaction that fair, full, and liberal consideration of his difficulties and of his duties, of the means by which those difficulties were overcome, and the manner in which those duties were discharged, which he is sure of receiving at your Lordships' hands.

"The great length of your Lordships' time which this trial has already occupied, and the further portion of it which it must yet necessarily consume, renders it unpardonable to waste a moment upon any subject not intimately connected with the very substance of the charges which yet remain to be discussed. I will therefore without delay address myself to the immediate and actual topics which are most intimately connected with the charge now before you, which is contained in the Second Article of Impeachment, and respects principally the supposed injuries of the mother and grandmother of the Nabob of Oude —ladies usually distinguished by the name of the BEGUMS."

A speech of many hours he concluded with this PERORATION:

Peroration.   "I have now at a greater length than I could have wished gone through the vastness of evidence which the managers have thought fit to adduce. and have discussed many of the arguments which they have thought fit to offer in support of this charge, and have brought more immediately before your Lordships' view such parts of that evidence as completely repel the conclusions the managers have attempted to infer from an unfair selection and artificial collation of other parts of that same evidence. I have also generally opened to your Lordships the heads of such further evidence as we shall on our part, in further refutation of the criminal charges contained in this Article, submit to your Lordships' consideration, in order to establish beyond the reach of doubt that Mr. Hastings, in all the transactions now in question, behaved with a strict regard to every obligation of public and private duty, and effectually consulted and promoted the real and substantial interests of the country, and the honor and credit of the British name and character. Stripping this Article therefore of all the extraneous matter with which it has been very artfully and unfairly loaded, and reducing it to the few and simple points of which in a fair legal view of the subject it naturally consists —the questions will be only those which in the introduction to my address to your Lordships on this charge I ventured to state, namely, whether the Begums, by their conduct during the disturbances occasioned by the rebellion, had manifested such a degeee of disaffection and hostility towards the British interests and safety, as warranted the subtraction of the guarantee which had been theretofore voluntarily and gratuitously interposed for their protection ; and next, whether after that guarantee was withdrawn the Nabob was not authorized upon every principle of public and private justice to reclaim his rights, and we to assert our own.

"If there be those who think Mr. Hastings ought to have pursued a formal detailed judicial inquiry on the subject of the notorious misconduct of the Begums, before he adopted any measures of prevention or punishment in respect of them ;— that he should have withheld his belief from the many eye and ear witnesses of the mischief they were hourly producing and contriving against us ;—I say to those who think that the unquestionable and then unquestioned notoriety of a whole country—corroborated by the positive testimony of *all* the officers then in command in that country, speaking to facts within their own observation and knowledge, is not a ground for immediate political conduct—to persons thus thinking I am furnished with little argument to offer. I have no record of the Begums' conviction engrossed on parchment to lay before you—I have only that quantity of evidence which ought to carry conviction home to every human breast accessible to truth and reason.

"God forbid that I should for a moment draw in question the solemn obligation of public treaties. I am contending for their most faithful, honorable, and exact performance. We had pledged our word to grant the most valuable and humane protection—we asked as a recompense only the common offices of friendship and the mere returns of ordinary gratitude. How were they rendered? When the Palace of Shewalla and the streets of Ramnagur were yet reeking with the blood of our slaughtered countrymen;—when that benefactor and friend, to whose protection, as the Begum herself asserts, her dying lord, Sujah Dowla, had bequeathed her, had scarce rescued himself and his attendants from the midnight massacre prepared for him at Benares;—when he was pent up with a petty garrison in the feeble fortress of Chunargur expecting the hourly assault of an elated and numerous enemy;—when his fate hung by a single thread, and the hour of his extinction and that of the British name and nation in India would, according to all probable estimate, have been the same;—in that hour of perilous expectation he cast many an anxious northward look to see his allies of Oude bringing up their powers, and hoped that the long-protected and much-favored house of Sujah Dowla would have now repaid with voluntary gratitude the unclaimed arrears of generous kindness. As far as concerned the son of that Prince, and who by no fault of Mr. Hastings had least benefited by British interposition, he was not disappointed. That Prince who had been in the commencement of his reign robbed of his stipulated rights under the treaties of Allahabad and Benares, and had been unjustly manacled and fettered by that of Fryzabad, which restrained him from his due resort to national treasure for the necessary purposes of national defence and the just discharge of national incumbrances, found an additional motive for his fidelity in the accumulated honorable distresses and dangers of his allies. From the mother and grandmother of that Prince, enriched by his extorted spoils, and bound as they were by every public as well as private tie of gratitude and honor, Mr. Hastings looked, indeed, for a substantial succor; but he looked in vain. It was not, however, as passive and unconcerned spectators that they regarded this anxious and busy scene of gathering troubles. No,

—to the remotest limits of their son's dominions their inveterate hate and detestation of the British race was diplayed in
every shape and form which malice could invent and treachery
assume. In the immediate seats of their own protected wealth
and power, at the reverenced threshold of their own greatness,
in sight of their nearest servant who best knew their genuine
wishes, and was by that knowledge best prepared to execute
them—the British commander of a large force, marching to
sustain the common interests of Great Britain and its allies, is
repelled by the menace of actual hostility from the sanctuary
to which he had fled in assured expectation of safety. At the
same period another British commander, abandoning his camp
to the superior force of a rebellious chief, linked in mischievous confederacy with the Begums, hears amidst the groans of
his own murdered followers the gratulation of his enemies'
success and his own defeat proclaimed in discharges of cannon
from the perfidious walls of Fryzabad. And during all this
dismay and discomfiture of our forces in the neighborhood of
their residence, the eunuchs, the slaves of their palace, under
the very eye of our own insulted officers, array and equip a
numerous and well-appointed force to brave us in the field.

"If these acts do indeed consist with good faith, or are
such light infractions of it as merit no considerable degree of
public animadversion—then I resign Mr. Hastings to the un-
qualified censure of mankind and the overwhelming condemnation of your Lordships. But if to have connived at another's
treachery at such a crisis would have been effectually to prove
and proclaim his own;—if to have continued undiminished to
the Begum the enormous fruits of her own original extortion
and fraud, applied, as they recently had been, to the meditated and half-achieved purpose of our undoing, would have
been an act of political insanity in respect to our own safety,
and of no less injustice to our friend and ally, the proprietor
of these treasures;—then was Mr. Hastings not warranted only,
but required and without alternative or choice compelled, to
apply that degree of lenient, sober, and salutary chastisement,
which was, in fact, administered on this occasion. To have
endured with impunity these public acts of hostile aggression,
would have been to expose our tame irrational forbearance to
the mockery and scorn of all the Asiatic world. Equally removed from the dangerous extremes of unrelenting severity

and unlimited concession, he had the good fortune to preserve in every part of India a dread of our power, a respect for our justice, and an admiration of our mercy. These are the three great links by which the vast chain of civil and political obedience is riveted and held together in every combination of human society. By the due exertion and display of such qualities as these, one faithful servant was enabled to give strength, activity, stability, and permanence, and at last to communicate the blessings of peace and repose to the convulsed members of our Eastern empire. This age has seen one memorable and much-lamented sacrifice to the extreme and excessive indulgence of the amiable virtues of gentleness and mercy.[1] The safety of our country, the order and security of social life, the happiness of the whole human race, require that political authority should be sustained by a firm, regular, and discriminate application of rewards and punishments."

Mr. Law was supposed to do his duty in a manly and effective manner; but Dallas was more polished, and Plomer more impressive. The leading counsel gained renown in his squabbles with Burke about evidence, rather than when he had such an opportunity of making a great oration as Cicero might have envied.

In the early stages of the trial his labor and his anxiety were dreadful, and he often expressed sincere regret that he had been concerned in it; but when he had become familiar with the subject, and public opinion, with which the Peers evidently sympathized, turned in favor of his client, he could enjoy the *éclat* conferred upon him from pleading before such a tribunal, for such a client, against such accusers.

Conclusion of Hasting's trial. At last on the 23d of April, 1795, being the one hundred and forty-fifth day of the trial, and in the tenth year from the commencement of the crimination, he had the satisfaction to hear his client acquitted by a large majority of Peers; and he himself was warmly

1. Alluding, I presume, to the fate of Louis XVI.

congratulated by his friends upon the happy event.
It was expected that Burke would then have shaken
hands with him; but still in Burke's sight Debi Sing
could hardly have been more odious.

Law had long the credit of making the celebrated
epigram upon the leader of the impeachment—

> " Oft have we wonder'd that on Irish ground
> No poisonous reptile has e'er yet been found ;
> Reveal'd the secret stands of Nature's work,—
> She saved her venom to produce her Burke."

But it was composed by Dallas, as I was told, spontaneously, by Dallas himself, when he was Chief Justice
of the Common Pleas. A most rankling hatred continued to subsist between Burke and all Mr. Hastings's
counsel. He regarded them as venal wretches, who
were accomplices in murder after the fact; and they,
in return, believed the accuser to have relentlessly
attempted to bring down punishment upon innocence
that he might gratify his malignity and his vanity.
Yet they had never transgressed the strict line of their
duty as advocates; and he always sincerely believed
that he was vindicating the wrongs of millions of our
fellow-subjects in Asia. The three advocates considered their defence of Mr. Hastings as the most
brilliant and creditable part of their career; and the
accuser, undervaluing his writings against the French
Revolution, which he thought only ephemeral pamphlets, exhorted Dr. Laurence, with his dying breath,
to collect and publish an authentic report of the trial,
saying, " By this you will erect a cenotaph most grateful to my shade, and will clear my memory from that
load which the East India Company, King, Lords, and
Commons, and in a manner the whole British nation
(God forgive them), have been pleased to lay as a
monument on my ashes."

Law's fees, considerably exceeding 3000l., were a

CHAP.
XLVII.
Laws great
advance in
business
from his
fame as
counsel for
Hastings.
poor pecuniary compensation to him for his exertions and his sacrifices in this great cause; but he was amply rewarded by his improved position in his profession. When the trial began he had little more than provincial practice, and when it ended he was next to Erskine—with a small distance between them. Independently of the real talent which he displayed, the very notoriety which he gained as leading counsel for Mr. Hastings was enough to make his fortune. Attorneys and attorneys' clerks were delighted to find themselves conversing at his chambers in the evening with the man upon whom all eyes had been turned in the morning in Westminster Hall—a pleasure which they could secure to themselves by a brief and a consultation. From the oratorical school in which he was exercised while representing Warren Hastings, Law actually improved considerably in his style of doing business; and by the authority he acquired he was better able to cope with Lord Kenyon, who bore a strong dislike to him, and was ever pleased with an opportunity to put him down. This narrow-minded and ill-educated, though learned and conscientious, Chief Justice, had no respect for Law's classical acquirements, and had been deeply offended by the quick-eared Carthusian laughing at his inapt quotations and false quantities. Erskine, who had much more tact and desire to conciliate, was the Chief Justice's special favorite, and was supposed to have his

" ear " or " the length of his foot." Law, having several times, with no effect, hinted at this partiality,—after he had gained much applause by his speech on the Begum charge, openly denounced the injustice by which he suffered. In the course of a trial at Guildhall he had been several times interrupted by the Chief Justice while opening the plaintiff's case, whereas Erskine's address for the defendant was accompanied by smiles and nods from his Lordship, which encouraged the advocate, contrary to his usual habit, to conclude with some expressions of menace and bravado. Law having replied to these with great spirit and effect, thus concluded:

" Perhaps, gentlemen, I may without arrogance assume that I have successfully disposed of the observations of my learned friend, and that the strong case I made for my client remains unimpeached. Still my experience in this Court renders me fearful of the result. I dread a power with which I am not at liberty to combat. When I have finished, the summing up is to follow."

Looking at Erskine he exclaimed,

——" Non me tua fervida terrent
Dicta ferox—"

He then made a bow to the Chief Justice, and as he sat down he added in a low, solemn tone,

——" Di me terrent et JUPITER HOSTIS."

Lord Kenyon, thinking that the quotation must be apologetical and complimentary, bowed again and summed up impartially. When it was explained to him, his resentment was very bitter, and to his dying day he hated Law. But henceforth he stood in awe of him, and treated him more courteously.

At the breaking out of the French Revolution, Law joined the very respectable body of alarmist Whigs who went over to the Government, he being actuated, I believe, like most of them, by a not unreasonable dread of democratical ascendency, rather than by any longing for official advancement. However, he refused offers of a seat in parliament—even after the impeachment was determined. In society he acted the part of a strong Pittite, and he was accused of displaying " renegade rancor " against his former political associates :—but his friends asserted that " he had only been a Whig as Paley,[1] his tutor, had been a Whig, and that he uniformly was attached to the principles of freedom,

1. William Paley, an eminent English writer, born at Peterborough in 1743. He graduated in 1763 at Christ's College, Cambridge, —where he does not appear to have been distinguished for his application,—took holy orders, and was chosen a fellow of his college in 1766. He was subsequently employed as a tutor at Cambridge, and became rector of Musgrove in Westmoreland in 1775, soon after which date he married. In 1782 he was appointed Archdeacon of Carlisle. He published in 1785 "The Principles of Moral and Political Philosophy," regarded by some as the most important of all his works. As a writer he excels in logical power and in clearness of style. He denies the existence of a moral sense, and adopts the maxim that "whatever is expedient is right." He was liberal in theology, was a friend of civil and religious liberty, and earnestly advocated the abolition of the slave-trade. In 1790 he produced an admirable work entitled "Horæ Paulinæ, or the Truth of the Scripture History of Saint Paul evinced." He was appointed a prebendary of St. Paul's in 1794, and was presented to the sub-deanery of Lincoln Cathedral. About 1795 he obtained the rectory of Bishop-Wearmouth. His other principal works are "A View of the Evidences of Christianity" (3 vols., 1794), one of the best works ever written on the subject of which it treats, and "Natural Theology, or Evidences of the Existence and Attributes of the Deity" (1802), which has a very high reputation and has often been reprinted. Paley's utilitarianism and alleged laxity of view respecting certain questions in morals, and in a no less degree his liberalism in politics, were distasteful to George III., who refused positively to appoint him to the episcopate, on his nomination by the Prime Minister. Died May 25, 1805. "This excellent writer," says Mackintosh, "who, after Clarke and Butler, ought to be ranked among the brightest ornaments of the English Church in the eighteenth century, is in the history of philosophy naturally placed after Tucker, to whom, with praiseworthy liberality, he owns his extensive obligations. . . . His style is as near perfection in its kind as any in our language. . . . The most original and ingenious of his writings is the 'Horæ Paulinæ.' 'The Evidences of Christianity' are formed out of an admirable translation of Butler's 'Analogy' and a most skilful abridgment of Lardner's 'Credibility of the Gospel History.' . . . His 'Natural Theology' is the wonderful work of a man who after sixty had studied anatomy in order to write it; and it could only have been surpassed by a man who to great originality of conception and clearness of exposition added the advantage of a high place in the first class of physiologists. . . . It cannot be denied that Paley was sometimes rather a lax moralist,—especially on public duties." (See Mackintosh's "Progress of Ethical Philosophy.") "On one great topic—that of Christian evidence—he has shed new light. By felicity of arrangement and illustration he has given an air of novelty to old arguments, whilst he has strengthened his

although he was always, for the good of the people, a CHAP. XLVII. friend to strong government."

His position on the circuit fully entitled him to the appointment which he now obtained of Attorney General of the County Palatine of Lancaster, and he was fairly destined to higher advancement, when Scott and Mitford, the present law officers of the Crown, should be elevated to the bench.

Meanwhile he conducted some State prosecutions He is opposed to Erskine in Rex v. Walker. in the provinces. Mr. Walker, a respectable merchant at Manchester, and several others being indicted on the false testimony of an informer for a conspiracy to overturn the Constitution, and to assist the French to invade England, Law conducted the case for the Crown, and Erskine came *special* against him. At first the defendants seemed in great jeopardy, and Mr. Attorney of the County Palatine, believing the witness to be sincere, eagerly pressed for a conviction. A point arising about the admissibility of a printed paper, Erskine theatrically exclaimed, " Good God, where am I?"

Law (with affected composure): " In a British Court of justice!"

Erskine (indignantly) : " How are my clients to be exculpated?"

cause by important original proofs. His ' Horæ Paulinæ ' is one of the few books destined to live. Paley saw what he did see through an atmosphere of light. He seized on the strong points of his subject with an intuitive sagacity, and has given his clear bright thoughts in a style which has made them the property of his readers almost as perfectly as they were his own. . . . He was characterized by the distinctness of his vision. He was not, we think, equally remarkable for its extent. He was popular rather than philosophical. He was deficient in that intellectual thirst which is a chief element of the philosophical spirit. He had no irrepressible desire to sound the depths of his own nature, or to ascend to wide and all-reconciling views of the works and ways of God. Moral philosophy he carried backward ; nor had he higher claims in religious than in ethical science. His sermons are worthy of all praise, not, indeed, for their power over the heart, but for their plain and strong expositions of duty and their awakening appeals to the conscience."—*Thomas' Biog. Dict.*

Law (in a still quieter tone) : "By legal evidence."

Erskine (much excited) : "I stand before the people of England for justice."

Law (bursting out furiously) : "I am equally before the people of England for the protection of the people of England ; if you rise in this tone, I can speak as loudly and as emphatically : there is nothing which has betrayed improper passion on my part ; but no tone or manner shall put me down."

In the course of the trial the rivals were reconciled, and tried which could flatter best.

Law : "I know what I have to fear upon this occasion. I know the energy and the eloquence of my learned friend. I have long felt and admired the powerful effect of his various talents. I know the ingenious sophistry by which he can mislead, and the fascination of that look by which he can subdue the minds of those whom he addresses. I know what he can do to-day by remembering what he has done upon many other occasions before."

Erskine : "Since I entered the profession I have met with no antagonist more formidable than my learned friend to whom I am now opposed. While admiring his candor and courtesy I have had reason to know the sharpness of his weapons and the dexterity of his stroke.

> ——' Stetimus tela aspera contra
> Contulimusque manus ; experto credite quantus
> In clypeum assurgat, quo turbine torqueat hastam.' "[1]

An acquittal took place, the guns which were to assist the French being proved to have been brought to fire a *feu-de-joie* on the King's recovery. The informer, being convicted of perjury, was sentenced at the same assizes to stand in the pillory, and to be imprisoned two years in Lancaster Castle.[2]

Law was more successful in prosecuting Mr. Red-

1. This quotation was afterwards applied by Mr. Canning to Lord Brougham.

"We joined our forces and took our stand against his sharp weapons ; experience has taught us how he towers against the (enemy's) shield and with what a whirlwind he hurls the spear."

2. 23 St. Tr. 1055. LIVES OF CHANCELLORS, vi. 465.

head Yorke for sedition, but this prosecution reflects much discredit upon the times in which it took place. The defendant, at a public meeting, had made a speech which he printed and circulated as a pamphlet in favor of a reform in parliament—animadverting with severity upon some of the proceedings of the House of Commons, and accusing that assembly of corruption. He was therefore indicted for a conspiracy " to traduce and vilify the Commons' House of Parliament, to excite disaffection towards the King and his government, and to stir up riots, tumults, and commotions in the realm." Mr. Law, in opening the case to the jury, laid down that " whatever speech or writing had a tendency to lessen the respect of the people for the House of Commons was unlawful." He said, " In no country can a government subsist which is held in contempt. Does not every government under the sun take means, and must it not take means, against such degrading insults? Why in God's name is the united dignity of the empire to be insulted in this way? What is the practical consequence of ridicule thrown on such a body? From the moment that men cease to respect, they cease to obey, and riot and tumult may be expected in every part of the kingdom."

The defendant delivered a very able and temperate address to the jury; but he was repeatedly interrupted by the Judge when making observations which we should think quite unexceptionable. A specimen may be both amusing and instructive:

Defendant.—" You will recollect that the House of Commons in one day, in the midst of a paroxysm of delusion, threw the liberties of the people at the foot of the throne—I mean by the suspension of the Habeas Corpus Act. You will recollect that in consequence of that suspension, every man was unsafe in his person—every man even had reason to tremble for his life."

Rooke, J.[1]—" I must check you, Mr. Yorke, when you talk of the House of Commons throwing the liberties of the people at the foot of the throne."

1. Giles Rooke. This amiable judge bore the same Christian name as his grandfather and father. The former was resident at Rumsey in Hampshire ; and the latter a merchant in London, who became a director of the East India Company. He was the associate of literary men, and indulged himself in some very creditable translations of the classic poets. By his marriage with Frances, daughter of Leonard Cropp of Southampton, he had a numerous family. His third child was the future judge. Giles Rooke was born on June 3, 1743 ; and being sent at an early age to Harrow, then under Dr. Thackery, arrived at the highest class in the school ere he was thirteen. Thence he proceeded to Oxford, where he was matriculated at St. John's College in 1759. There he was an indefatigable student ; and he used to relate his mortification at the only reward he received from the college tutor for the great pains he had bestowed on a copy of Latin verses being the cold remark, " Sir, you have forgotten to put your tittles to your i's." Having taken his degrees of A.B. in 1763 and of A.M. in 1765, he was in 1766 elected to a fellowship of Merton College, which he held till his marriage in 1785 ; and in 1777 he was unsuccessful in a contest for the Vinerian professorship of common law, his opponent, Dr. Woodeson, beating him only by five votes out of 457. Although intended for the legal, it was thought that he preferred the clerical, profession, from his devotion to the study of divinity. But his motive for pursuing the latter was to get rid of early prejudices and a tendency to scepticism and to satisfy himself of the truths of Christianity. The effects of this study and conscientious application were evident in all his future life, producing that character for genuine piety by which he was ever distinguished. The deep impression they made upon him is shown in a small pamphlet containing " Thoughts on the Propriety of Fixing Easter Term." which he published anonymously in 1792. This did not prevent him from preparing for the profession he had chosen ; and having been called to the bar he joined the western circuit, of which he eventually became the leader. His success in business warranted him in accepting the dignity of the coif in 1781 ; and he had the honor of being made King's serjeant in April, 1793. Soon after he succeeded in obtaining verdicts at the Easter assizes against William Winterbotham for preaching two seditious sermons at Plymouth, which, as connected with the French Revolution, were considered especially dangerous, and for which the reverend defendant was sentenced to a large fine and a long imprisonment. At that troubled period it was Sir Giles's lot to be brought very prominently forward. Having been, on November 13 in the same year, appointed a judge of the Common Pleas in the place of Mr. Justice Wilson, and knighted, he delivered in his first circuit a charge to the grand jury at Reading on the excited state of the country ; and in July, 1795, he presided at York on the trial and

Defendant.—" If your Lordship had permitted me, I should
have explained that idea."

Rooke, J.—" I sit here upon my oath, and I cannot suffer any sentiment to pass that is at all disgraceful to that House."

Defendant.—" It was far from my intention. I was only stating that the *Habeas Corpus Act* was suspended, and was about to state the reason why. I consider the *Habeas Corpus Act* and the Trial by Jury as the firmest bulwarks of our liberties ;—certain it is that the legislature thought the country in danger—that it was necessary to strengthen the arm of government, and in some degree to weaken the liberties of the people. May not I, with your Lordship's permission, state what my perception is of the constitution, in order that I may point out where the necessity for reform lies ? "

Rooke, J.—" Annual parliaments and universal suffrage is the general principle upon which the witnesses say you have gone. Now, annual parliaments and universal suffrage are contrary to the established constitution of the country."

Defendant.—" Sir Henry Spelman,[1] treating of the Anglo-

conviction of Henry Redhead Yorke for a conspiracy with others to inflame the people against the government, for which a severe punishment was inflicted. Though not considered a deep lawyer, nor very highly reputed on the bench, he was a mild and merciful judge. A story is told of him that a poor girl, having from the pressure of extreme want committed a theft, was tried before him and reluctantly convicted ; and that, while applauding the jury for giving the inevitable verdict, he declared that he so sympathized with them in their hesitation that he would sentence her to the smallest punishment allowed by the law. He accordingly fined her one shilling, adding, " If she has not one in her possession, I will give her one for the purpose." Towards the end of his life he suffered much from illness, which was greatly aggravated by his grief for the death of his two elder sons. After nearly fifteen years of judicial labors he died suddenly on March 7, 1808, in the sixty-fourth year of his life, during the whole of which he gained the respect of his contemporaries for his strict integrity, his amiable temper, and his love of literature. His wife, Harriet Sophia, daughter of Colonel William Burrard of Walhampton, Hants, and sister of Admiral Sir Harry Burrard-Neale, Bart., survived him till the year 1839. She brought him a large family. One of their sons, the Rev. George Rooke, is Vicar of Embleton in Northumberland, and has kindly furnished many of the foregoing particulars.—*Foss's Judges of England.*

1. Sir Henry Spelman, an antiquary, born at Congham, Norfolk, 1562. He studied at Trinity College, Cambridge, and next in Lincoln's Inn. When very young he wrote a Latin treatise on coats of arms, which procured him admission into the first society of

Saxon government, says that the *Michel-Gemote* met *in annuo parliamento*. Here is the Parliamentary Roll of 5 Ed. II."

Rooke, J.—" The Crown called a parliament annually without an annual election. Septennial parliaments are the law of the land, and I cannot hear you go on in that way."

Defendant.—" Septennial parliaments are unquestionably an actual law of the land ; but what I mean to state is, whether, according to the principles of the Revolution, they ought to be so. May I not state it as my opinion ?"

Rooke, J.—" No."

Defendant.—" Mr. Pitt himself and most of the great men have held the same language."

Rooke, J.—" Not in a court of justice. I am bound by my oath to abide by the law, and I cannot suffer anybody to derogate from it." [1]

antiquaries. In 1604 he served the office of high sheriff of Norfolk ; soon after which he was sent to Ireland as one of the commissioners for settling the titles of lands in that country. He was next appointed a commissioner to inquire into the exaction of fees in the courts and offices of England, for which he received the honor of knighthood. He now fixed his residence in London, where he employed himself in searching records, and studying the Saxon language, the difficulty of acquiring which led him to compile his " Archæologus," as he called it, or, as it was afterwards entitled, the " Glossarium." This great work, however, he did not complete, but published a part of it in 1626 ; and the rest was made up from his papers by Dugdale in 1664. In 1627 Sir Henry compiled a history of the civil affairs of the kingdom, from the Conquest to Magna Charta. His next undertaking was the " Collection of the Councils of the English Church," of which he lived to publish only one volume, in 1639, folio ; and the second was edited, in 1664, by Dugdale. The last labor of Sir Henry was a " History of the Tenures by Knights' Service in England." He died in 1641. Among his other works are " A Treatise concerning Tithes " and " A History of Sacrilege." Sir Henry Spelman, by his will, founded a Saxon lecture at Cambridge, but it was not carried into effect. His son, Sir *John Spelman*, was knighted by Charles I., and made master of Sutton's Hospital. He died at Oxford 1643. He published the Saxon psalter, and wrote "The Life of Alfred the Great," which was published by Hearne 1709. A Latin translation, by Wise, was printed 1678. *Clement Spelman*, the youngest son of Sir Henry, became one of the barons of the Exchequer at the Restoration, and died 1679. *Edward Spelman*, who wrote a treatise on the Greek accents, and translated Xenophon, Cyropædia, and Dionysius Halicarnassensis, was a descendant of the great antiquary. He died 1767.—*Cooper's Biog. Dict.*

1. Rooke was a very meek man ; and at that time, I dare say, most of the other Judges would have held similar language.

After a most intolerant reply from Mr. Law and a summing up, in which the Judge re-stated his doctrines with respect to finding fault with the existing constitution of the House of Commons, the defendant was found guilty and sentenced to two years' imprisonment in Dorchester jail. What must have been the state of public feeling when such proceedings could take place without any censure in parliament, and with very little scandal out of it? The reign of terror having ceased, and Englishmen being again reconciled to liberty, Mr. Redhead Yorke was much honored for his exertions in the cause of parliamentary reform, and he was called to the bar by the Benchers of the Middle Temple.[1]

Law gained very great credit with all sensible men from his conflict with Lord Kenyon about *forestalling* and *regrating*. He had studied successfully the principles of political economy, and he admirably exposed the absurd doctrine that the magistrate can beneficially interfere in the commerce of provisions; but he had the mortification to see his client sentenced to fine and imprisonment for the imaginary crime of buying with a view to raise the price of the commodity.[2]

I now come to what is considered the most brilliant A.D. 1799. passage of the life of the future Lord Ellenborough— Law's triumph his triumph over Sheridan at the trial of Lord Thanet over and Mr. Fergusson for assisting in the attempt to rescue Sheridan. Arthur O'Connor.[3] This trial excited intense interest. The Government was most eager for a conviction,

1. 25 St. Tr. 1003–1154.
2. *R. v. Waddington*, 1 East 166.
3. Arthur O'Connor, an Irish general, born at Bandon, near Cork, in 1767, was a Protestant. He joined the society of United Irishmen, who sent him on a secret mission to France, where he negotiated with General Hoche about the liberation of Ireland. In 1797 or 1798 he was tried on a charge of treason, and acquitted. He entered the French service, and became a general of division in 1804. About 1807 he married Elisa, a daughter of the famous Condorcet. Died in 1852.—*Thomas's Biog. Dict.*

upon my oath ; I know as well as the learned counsel does that I am upon my oath ; and I will say that I saw nothing auxiliary to that escape."

L.—" After what has passed, I am warranted in reminding the honorable gentleman that he is upon his oath. My question is, whether, from the conduct of Lord Thanet and Mr. Fergusson, or either of them, as it fell under your observation, you believe that either of them meant to favor O'Connor's escape ? "

S.—" I desire to know how far I am obliged to answer that question. I certainly will answer it in this way, that from what they did, being a mere observer of what passed, I should not think myself justified in saying that either of them did. Am I to say whether I think they would have been glad if he had escaped ? That is what you are pressing me for."

L.—" No man can misunderstand me ; I ask whether, from the conduct of Lord Thanet and Mr. Fergusson, or either of them, as it fell under your observation, you believe, upon your oath, that they meant to favor the escape of O'Connor ? "

S.—" I repeat it again, that from what either of them did, I should have had no right to conclude that they were persons assisting the escape of O'Connor."

L.—" I ask you again, upon your oath, whether you believe, from the conduct of Lord Thanet or Mr. Fergusson, that they did not mean to favor the escape of O'Connor ? "

S.—" I have answered it already."

Lord Kenyon.—" If you do not answer it, to be sure we must draw the natural inference."

S.—" I have no doubt that they *wished* he might escape ; but from anything I saw them do, I have no right to conclude that they did."

L.—" I will have an answer : I ask you again, whether, from their conduct as it fell under your observation, you do not believe they meant to favor the escape of O'Connor ? "

S.—" If the learned gentleman thinks he can entrap me, he will find himself mistaken."

Erskine.—" It is hardly a legal question."

Lord Kenyon.—" I think it is not an illegal question." [1]

1. I think it is clearly an illegal question. and I am astonished that Erskine so quietly objected to it. I should at once overrule such a question ; for it does not inquire into a fact, or any opinion

L.—" I will repeat the question, whether, from their conduct, as it fell under your observation, you do not believe that
they meant to favor the escape of O'Connor ? "

S.—" My belief is, that they *wished* him to escape ; but
from anything I saw of their conduct on that occasion, I am
not justified in saying so."

Erskine in vain tried to remedy the mischief by re-
examination :

" You were asked by Mr. Law whether you believed that
the defendants wished or meant to favor the escape of Mr.
O'Connor ; I ask you, *after what you have sworn, whether you
believe these gentlemen did any act to rescue Mr. O'Connor ?* "

S.—" Certainly not."

E.—" You have stated that you saw no one act done or
committed by either of the defendants indicative of an intention to aid O'Connor's escape ? "

S.—" Certainly."

E.—" I ask you, then, whether you believe that they did
take any part in rescuing Mr. O'Connor ? "

S.—" Certainly not."

However, the jury could never get over the WISH
that O'Connor should escape;[1] so both defendants
were convicted, and although their right arms were
not cut off—the specific punishment to which it was
said they were liable—they were sentenced to heavy
fines and long imprisonment.[2]

Law recon-
ciled to the
Tories.

There had hitherto been a certain mistrust of Law,
on account of his early Whiggery; but he was now
hailed as a sincere Tory, and his promotion was certain.

upon matter of science, but asks the witness, instead of the jury, the
inference as to the guilt or innocence of the accused to be drawn from
the evidence.

1. Sheridan used afterwards to pretend that he had the best of it,
and that he put Law down effectually. Among other questions and
answers not to be found in the full and accurate report of the short-
hand writer who was present, he used to relate—"When Law said,
'Pray, Mr. Sheridan, do answer my question, without point or epigram,' I retorted, 'You say true, Mr. Law ; your questions are
without point or epigram.'"

2. 27 St. Tr. 821.

LORD ABINGER.

For several more years, however, no vacancy
occurred, and his highest distinction was being leader of the Northern Circuit. There, indeed, he reigned supreme, without any brother being near the throne. He had completely supplanted Serjeant Cockell, who, notwithstanding a most curious nescience of law, had for some time been profanely called " the Almighty of the North." Some juniors had taken the coif without emerging from obscurity, and the only other silk gown on the circuit was worn by " Jemmy Park," whom Law could twist round his finger at any time. Scarlett,[1] in stuff, began to show formidable powers ; but as yet was hardly ever trusted with a lead. Being so decidedly

1. James Scarlett, Lord Abinger, was born 1769 in Jamaica, where his family had long been resident and held considerable property. He was the second son of Robert Scarlett, Esq. At an early age he was sent to England for the purpose of education, and at the age of 17 was entered as a fellow commoner at Trinity College, Cambridge, where he graduated B.A. 1790, M.A. 1794. He was called to the bar in 1791, and rapidly rose to a high position as an advocate. In 1812, and again in 1816, he unsuccessfully contested the borough of Lewes, but in 1818 he entered the House of Commons as member for Peterborough. Mr. Scarlett was not, however, so successful in parliament as he was in the forensic arena. In 1822 he unsuccessfully contested the University of Cambridge, but was at the bottom of the poll. He was, however, re-elected for Peterborough. On the breaking up of the Liverpool administration in 1827 Mr. Canning invoked the assistance of the Whigs, and Mr. Scarlett became Attorney General and received the honor of knighthood. From that period he was a consistent supporter of Conservative principles. He continued to be Attorney General till Jan., 1828, when he was succeeded by Sir Charles Wetherell. In May, 1829, Sir Charles was dismissed from office by the Duke of Wellington on account of his bigoted speech against the Catholic Relief Bill, and the vacant post filled up by the appointment of Sir J. Scarlett, who, without delay, field criminal informations against the principal newspapers which had opposed the policy of the government in regard to Catholic emancipation. He held the Attorney-Generalship until the accession of the Whigs to office in 1830. He subsequently was returned to parliament for Cockermouth and Norwich. Upon the formation of the Peel cabinet in Dec., 1834, he was made Chief Baron of the Exchequer and created Baron Abinger. He died at Bury St. Edmunds, while travelling the Norfolk circuit, April 7, 1844.—*Cooper's Biog. Dict.*

the "Cock of the Circuit," it is not wonderful that Law should crow very fiercely.   According to all accounts, he did become excessively arrogant, and he sometimes treated rudely both his brother barristers and others with whom he came into collision.

His readiness to fight.   He was always ready, however, to give satisfaction for any supposed affront which he offered.   Once he happened, at York, to be counsel for the defendant in an action on a horse-race, the conditions of which required that the riders should be " gentlemen."   The defence was that the plaintiff, who had won the race, was not a " gentleman."   A considerable body of evidence was adduced on both sides, and Mr. Law commented upon it most unmercifully.   The jury found for the defendant that the plaintiff was " not a gentleman." The defeated party blustered much, and threatened to call the audacious advocate to an account.   Law, putting off his journey to Durham for a day, walked about booted and spurred before the coffee-house, the most public place in York, ready to accept an invitation into the field or to repel force by force, because personal chastisement had likewise been threatened.   No message was sent, and no attempt was made to provoke a breach of the peace.

CHAPTER XLVIII.

CONTINUATION OF THE LIFE OF LORD ELLENBOROUGH TILL HE WAS APPOINTED LORD CHIEF JUSTICE.

THE great Northern Leader had reached his fifty- CHAP. first year, and still the political promotion which he so XLVIII. earnestly desired never opened to him. Having till General. then, in his own language, "crawled along the ground without being able to raise himself from it," in the language of his friend Archdeacon Paley, "he suddenly rose like an aeronaut." [1]

Mr. Pitt, in 1801, stepped down from the premiership, and, a new arrangement of legal offices following, Mr. Addington,[2] the new minister, sent for Mr. Law, Feb. 1801.

1. Paley had been chaplain to Law's father, the bishop, who gave him his first preferment, and there was the strictest intimacy between Law and Paley through life. The former, when Chief Justice, has been heard to say, " Although I owed much to Paley as an instructor (for he was practically my tutor at college), I was much more indebted to him for the independent tone of mind which I acquired through his conversation and example : Paley formed my character ; and I consider that I owe my success in life more to my character than to any natural talents I may possess." Law corrected for Paley the proof-sheets of some of his works as they were passing through the press ; and in Law's house in Bloomsbury Square there was an apartment which went by the name of "Paley's room," being reserved for the archdeacon when he paid a visit to the metropolis.

2. Henry Addington, Viscount Sidmouth (*b.* 1755, *d.* 1844), the son of Anthony Addington, Lord Chatham's family physician, was called to the bar about the same time as Pitt, whose intimate friend he was. By Pitt he was persuaded to leave the bar and to turn his attention to political life. He was accordingly returned to parliament as member for Devizes, and soon became conspicuous as a devoted follower of Pitt. In 1789 he was elected Speaker, and pre-

and offering him the Attorney-Generalship, observed,
" That as his ministry might be of short duration, and
the sacrifice to be made considerable, comprising the
lead of the Northern Circuit, to which there was no
return, he would not expect an immediate answer, but
hoped that in two days he might receive one ? " " Sir,"
said Mr. Law, " when such an offer is made to me, and
communicated in such terms, I should think myself
disgraced if I took two days, two hours, or two minutes,
to deliberate upon it; I am yours, and let the storm
blow from what quarter of the hemisphere it may, you
shall always find me at your side."

When he attended in the King's closet to kiss hands
and to be knighted, George III., who had been recently
in a state of derangement and was as yet only partially
recovered, after bidding him " rise Sir Edward," said

sided over the House until, on Pitt's resignation in 1801, he was
invited by the King to form an administration. It was very feeble,
and would scarcely have lived a month if Pitt had not for a time
given it his protection and advice. Addington's ministry was chiefly
signalized by the conclusion of the treaty of Amiens ; but when Pitt
withdrew his support the utter weakness of the cabinet became
very clear, and Addington was forced to make way for his former
leader. There was now a complete breach between the two, and
Addington, who had been created Viscount Sidmouth, attacked Lord
Melville, and through him the Prime Minister, with great vehemence.
After Pitt's death Addington became President of the Council in
the Grenville and Fox administration. In the ministry of Perceval
and the Duke of Portland he had no place ; but when Lord Liverpool came into office in 1812 he was appointed Home Secretary. In
this position his repressive policy, and the hostility he showed to
popular movements, made him remarkably unpopular with the nation at large ; but he maintained his post for several years, until he
resigned it to Sir Robert Peel, 1822, after which he took but little
share in politics. His administration has been described by Macaulay
as one which, in an age pre-eminently fruitful of parliamentary
talents, contained hardly a single man who, in parliamentary talents,
could be considered as even of the second rate. " He was," the same
writer says, " universally admitted to have been the best speaker
that had sate in the Chair since the retirement of Onslow. But
nature had not bestowed on him very vigorous faculties," and his
long occupation of the Chair had unfitted him for the task of heading
an administration.—*Dict. of Eng. Hist.*

to him, " Sir Edward, Sir Edward, have you ever been in parliament ? " and being answered in the negative, added, " Right, Sir Edward ; quite right, Sir Edward ; for now, when you become my Attorney General, Sir Edward, you will not eat your own words, Sir Edward, as so many of your predecessors have been obliged to do, Sir Edward."

In those Ante-Reform-Act days the Government always—easily, and as a matter of course—provided seats in the House of Commons for the law-officers of the Crown, they paying only 500*l.* as a contribution to the Treasury-borough fund. A considerable number of seats were under the absolute control of the minister for the time being, and others, for a consideration in money or money's worth, were placed by borough proprietors at his disposal. The difficulty of getting and keeping a seat in the House of Commons, which now so much influences the appointment to offices, was then never thought of. In consequence, the minister certainly had a more unlimited command of talent and fitness for public service. No one would now think of going back to the "nomination" system, its conveniences being greatly outweighed by its evils ; but the experiment may hereafter be made of allowing certain officers of the Crown, as such, to have voice without vote in the House of Commons.

The new Attorney General, having deposited his 500*l.* with the Secretary to the Treasury, was returned for a close borough, and on the 2nd of March, 1801, he was sworn in at the table.

He seems to have imbibed the doctrine for which I have heard the great Lord Lyndhurst[1] strenuously

1. John Singleton Copley, Lord Lyndhurst, was born at Boston, in New England, May 21, 1772, being the son of John Singleton Copley, the painter, who brought him to England about a year before the outbreak of the American Revolution. He received his education at Trinity College, Cambridge, where he obtained a fellowship ; and

contend, that no allusion ought to be made in parliament to any political opinions entertained or expressed

being appointed a "travelling bachelor," he was enabled, for the
first and only time in his life, to revisit his native country. In 1804
he was called to the bar, and for many years subsequently he went
the Midland Circuit, rising by very slow degrees to professional
eminence. In 1817, having then obtained the leadership of his
circuit, he first brought himself prominently into public notice by the
able manner in which he aided Sir Charles Wetherell in conducting
the prosecution of Watson and Thistlewood, indicted for high treason.
Though previously a Liberal in politics, he so favorably impressed
the Tory leaders by his talents on this occasion that he was soon
employed by them on behalf of the government in several important
state trials ; and in 1818 was appointed chief justice of the county palatine of Chester. Thenceforth he remained for the most part an adherent of the party from which he had received his earliest promotion.
Having entered parliament in 1818, he was appointed Solicitor General
in the Liverpool administration in the following year, and in 1820 he
took a leading part in the proceedings against Queen Caroline, avoiding, by the moderation and skill which he displayed, the censure so
freely bestowed upon most of the parties to the trial. In 1824 he succeeded to the Attorney-Generalship. At the general election of 1826
he was returned by the University of Cambridge, in conjunction with
Lord Palmerston, and a few months later he accepted the mastership
of the rolls. During the early debates on Catholic emancipation in
1827 he strenuously opposed the measure, but, to the surprise of
the public, he entered the Liberal cabinet of Canning as Lord Chancellor, and was raised to the peerage, with the title of Baron Lyndhurst, April 27, 1827. After the death of Canning, in the following
August, he retained the great seal during the short-lived administration of Viscount Goderich, and in that of the Duke of Wellington,
retiring with his colleagues on the triumph of the Whigs in 1830.
Previously to this he had given his full support to Catholic emancipation, declaring that he felt no apprehension for the safety of the
Anglican Establishment. Shortly after retiring from the chancellor-
ship he was appointed Chief Baron of the Exchequer, the duties of
which office he discharged till 1834. Though prevented by official
duties from participating largely in parliamentary proceedings, he
was one of the most strenuous opponents of the Reform Bill, and
upon the resignation of Earl Grey (1832) he endeavored unsuccessfully to form a new Conservative ministry in conjunction with the
Duke of Wellington. He held the great seal again during the brief
administration of Sir Robert Peel (1834), and after retiring from office
devoted himself for several years chiefly to the interests of his party,
becoming one of the most effective leaders of the Tory opposition in
the Upper House. In 1841 Sir Robert Peel formed his second ministry, and Lord Lyndhurst for the third time accepted the great seal,
which he retained till 1846, when he declared himself to be "at the
close of his public, almost of his natural life." He, however, oc-

by any individual before going into parliament. Having
openly and zealously belonged to the Whigs till 1792,—
after changing sides, Law was eager to embrace every
opportunity of attacking or sneering at that party in
their subsequent prostrate condition.

He entered St. Stephen's Chapel [1] too late in life to March 18,
1801.
be a skilful debater; but as often as he spoke he commanded attention by the energy of his manner and the
rotundity of his phrases (reminding the old members
of Thurlow), and he gave entire satisfaction to his
employers. His maiden speech was made in support
of the bill for continuing martial law in Ireland, which
gave courts martial jurisdiction over all offences, with
a power of life and death. He contended that "this
measure had led to the extinction of rebellion in that
country, and that to its operation the House owed their
power of debating at that moment, for without it the
whole empire would have been involved in one common
ruin. The aspect of the late rebellion he conceived to
be unequalled in the history of any country; never
before had rebellion so aimed at the destruction of
all that is venerable in political institutions or sweet
in domestic life—of all the social affections which unite
man to man—of all the sacred sanctions which bind man

casionally took a prominent part in the proceedings of the House of
Lords, supported the Derby ministry of 1852, advocated the war
with Russia, and denounced the policy adopted by Lord Clarendon
in concluding the peace of 1856 as a practical capitulation on the
part of England. Until the infirmities of age overcame him his
speeches, remarkable for their elegant and severely simple style, and
delivered with a voice of singular sweetness and power, were listened
to with unabated interest, and to the day of his death he continued
to exert great influence over the Conservative party. He died in
London Oct. 12, 1863.—*Cooper's Biog. Dict.*

1. St. Stephen's Chapel was a beautiful specimen of rich Decorated Gothic, its inner walls being covered with ancient frescoes
relating to the Old and New Testament history; it was used as the
House of Commons from 1547 till 1834, and its walls resounded to
the eloquence of Chatham, Pitt, Fox, Burke, Grattan, and Canning.
—*Hare's Walks in London*, vol. ii. p. 374.

to his Maker."[1]　Coercive measures for Ireland are always well relished in the House of Commons, and, on a division, eight only mustered in the minority.

Mr. Attorney next argued the necessity for suspend-ing the Habeas Corpus Act in England, asserting that the constitution of the country would not be safe if the bill which was now moved for were not passed.　He said "he would maintain that it was a most lenient measure, and particularly to those against whom it was intended.　To prevent an outbreak of treason, was mercy to the traitors.　Because crimes were not judi-cially proved, their existence must not be denied.　Had it not been for subsequent events, the acquitted and sainted Arthur O'Connor, long the idol of the other side of the House, now confessing his guilt—who had been so lauded as to cause universal nausea—would have gone to his grave loaded with the unmixed praises of his compurgators."[2]　The minority now amounted to forty-two.

Rev. John
Horne
Tooke,
M.P.
When the Rev. John Horne Tooke was nominated as member for the borough of Camelford, the question arose whether a priest in orders was qualified to sit in the House of Commons?　Mr. Attorney learnedly argued for the negative, and zealously supported the bill to prevent such an occurrence in future.　Mr. Horne Tooke had his revenge, and excited a laugh at the dogmatizing method of his opponent, which he pronounced to be "only fit for the pulpit, so that an exchange might advantageously be made between the Law and the Church."[3]

Sir Edward's last speech in the House of Commons was on the claim made by the Prince of Wales against the King for an account of all the revenues of the

---

1. 35 Parl. Hist. 1044.
2. Ib. 1288.
3. 35 Parl. Deb. 1335, 1398.

Duchy of Cornwall during his Royal Highness's minority. The ground taken by him was, that the King had a set off for his Royal Highness's board and education, which overtopped the demand. " Can it be contended," said he, "that the Prince of Wales, after having been maintained one-and-twenty years in all the splendor becoming his elevated rank, may at last call the King to an account for all the money received for that purpose during his minority? The Duchy of Cornwall was granted by Edward III. to his son, that he himself might be relieved from the burthen which had previously been thrown upon him and other Kings of maintaining their heirs at their own expense. It has been clearly shown that the money advanced to this Prince of Wales during his minority exceeds all his revenues, and that the balance is against him. The elegant accomplishments and splendid endowments of this ' *Hope of England* ' prove that he has experienced the highest degree of parental care, tenderness, and liberality."[1] This controversy, though often renewed, was never brought to a final decision ; but the arguments seem conclusively to prove that the revenues of the Duchy of Cornwall belong to the Prince of Wales during his minority, and that he is entitled to an account of them on his coming of age.

The negotiations for a peace with Napoleon as First Consul of the French Republic were now going on, and parliamentary strife was allayed till the results should be known, all parties agreeing that in the mean time no attempt should be made to subvert the government of Mr. Addington. Before this event Sir Edward Law was transferred to another sphere of action.

During the short period of his Attorney-Generalship Governor no prosecution for treason or any political offence arose, Wall's Case. but in his official character he did conduct one of the

1. 36 Parl. Hist. 433.

most memorable prosecutions for murder recorded in our juridical annals. It brought great popularity to him and the Government of which he was the organ, upon the supposition that it presented a striking display of the stern impartiality of British jurisprudence; but after a calm review of the evidence I fear it will rather be considered by posterity as an instance of the triumph of vulgar prejudice over humanity and justice. The alleged crime had been committed twenty years before the trial, and, except in the case of Eugene Aram,[1] there never had been known such an illustration of the

1. Eugene Aram, an English scholar, born at Ramsgill, Yorkshire, in 1704, executed at York for murder Aug. 6, 1759. Aram enjoyed a remarkable reputation for extensive scholarship acquired under the greatest difficulties, his father having been a poor gardener. After his marriage he established himself as a schoolmaster in his native district of Netherdale. In 1734 he removed his school to Knaresborough, where in 1745 he became implicated in a robbery committed by Daniel Clark, a shoemaker of Knaresborough ; and being discharged for want of evidence, he went to London. Clark disappeared mysteriously at the same time. Aram, while employed as school usher in various towns, and in an academy at Lynn in Norfolk, pursued his favorite studies, and was engaged in compiling a comparative lexicon of the English, Latin, Greek, Hebrew, and Celtic languages when he was arrested on the charge of murder. Aram's wife had frequently intimated that he and a man named Houseman were privy to the mystery of Clark's disappearance. Houseman, on being pressed by the coroner, testified that Aram and a man named Ferry were the murderers, and that the body had been buried in a particular part of St. Robert's cave, a well-known spot near Knaresborough. A skeleton was discovered in the exact place indicated, and Houseman's evidence led to Aram's conviction. Aram refused the services of counsel, and conducted his own defence in an elaborate and scholarly manner, making an ingenious plea of the general fallibility of circumstantial evidence, especially that connected with the discovery of human bones. After condemnation he acknowledged his guilt. On the night before the execution he attempted suicide, but was discovered before he had bled to death, and his sentence was carried into effect three days after it was pronounced. Before he attempted suicide he wrote an essay on the subject and also a sketch of his life. Of his "Comparative Lexicon" only passages from the preface are extant. He left a widow and six children. A veil of poetry has been thrown over his fate by Thomas Hood's ballad of "The Dream of Eugene Aram" and Bulwer's romance of "Eugene Aram."—*Appleton's Encyc.*, vol. i. p. 630.

doctrine of our law, that in criminal matters no lapse of
time furnishes any defence, while all civil actions are
barred by short periods of prescription; upon the supposition that the evidence may have perished which
might have proved the charge to be unfounded.
JOSEPH WALL, who had served from early youth as an
officer in the army, and had always been distinguished
for gallantry and good conduct, was, during the American War, appointed Governor of Goree, on the coast
of Africa. With a very insufficient garrison, and with
very slender military supplies, he had to defend this isl-
and from the French, who planned expeditions against
it from their neighboring settlement of Senegal.
Governor Wall performed his duty to his country, in
the midst of formidable difficulties, with firmness and
discretion—and the place intrusted to him was safely
preserved from all perils till peace was re-established.
He was then about to return home, in the expectation
of thanks and promotion, but great discontents existed
among the troops forming the garrison, by reason of
their pay being in arrear. This grievance they imputed
to the Governor, and they resolved that he should not
leave the island till they were righted. Benjamin Armstrong, a sergeant, their ringleader, was brought by him
irregularly before a regimental court martial, and sentenced to receive 800 lashes. Although this whipping
was administered with much severity, he in all proba-
bility would have recovered from it if he had not immediately after drunk a large quantity of ardent spirits:
but his intemperance, together with the wounds inflicted
upon him by the flagellation, and an unhealthy climate,
brought on inflammation and fever, of which he died.
Order was restored, and the Governor returned to
England. However, representations were made to the
authorities at home respecting the irregularity and
alleged cruelty which had been practised, and exag-

gerated accounts of the proceeding were published in
the newspapers, stating among other things that the
Governor had murdered Armstrong and several other
soldiers by firing them from the mouths of cannon. A
warrant was issued against him by the Secretary of
State, he was arrested by a King's messenger, and he
made his escape as they were conveying him from Bath
in a chaise and four. He immediately went abroad, and
he continued to reside on the continent till the peace
of Amiens—when, on the advice of counsel, he came to
England, wrote a letter to the Secretary of State announcing his return, and surrendered himself to take
his trial.

I am old enough to remember the unexampled
excitement which the case produced. The newspapers
were again filled with the atrocities of Governor Wall,
and a universal cry for vengeance upon him was raised.
Among the higher and educated classes a few individuals, who took the trouble to inquire into the facts,
doubted whether he was liable to serious blame, notwithstanding the circumstance against him that he had
fled from justice ; but the mass of the population, and
particularly the lower orders, loudly pronounced
Governor Wall guilty before his trial, and clamored
for his speedy execution.

The trial (if trial it may be called) did come on at
the Old Bailey on the 20th of January, 1802, under a
special commission, issued by the authority of 33 Hen.
VIII., c. 23. The Attorney General, who appeared as
public prosecutor, was conscientiously convinced of
the prisoner's guilt, and, free from every bad motive,
was only desirous to do his duty. He propounded the
law of murder very correctly to the Jury, and I cannot
say that he suppressed any evidence, or put any
improper question to any witness, but he showed a

determined resolution to convict the prisoner. I should not like to be answerable for such a conviction.

Then a very young man, just entered at Lincoln's Inn, I was present at the trial, and, carried away by the prevalent vengeful enthusiasm, I thought that all was right; but after the lapse of half a century, having dispassionately examined the whole proceeding, I come to a very different conclusion.

I have now a lively recollection of the effect produced by the opening speech of the Attorney General, to which, as the law then stood, no answer by counsel was permitted. With professions of candor he narrated the facts in a tone of awful solemnity so as to rouse the indignation of the jury. He particularly dwelt upon the fact, that the men employed to inflict the punishment were not the drummers of the regiment, but African negroes, and he pronounced the punishment wholly illegal, as the sentence could only have been passed by a general court-martial assembled according to the " Articles of War." He allowed, indeed, that if there was a dangerous mutiny all forms might be dispensed with, but insisted that the onus lay on the prisoner to make this clearly out,—and, by anticipation, he sought to discredit the witnesses to be called for the defence. He dwelt with much force upon the circumstance that a despatch written by the prisoner, soon after his return to England, to Lord Sidney, the Secretary of State, was silent as to the supposed mutiny; he palliated the resolution of the soldiers not to permit the Governor to leave the island till their arrears were paid, by observing that, "after his departure, a vast ocean would separate them from their debtor, and considering the precariousness of human life, and particularly in that unhealthy settlement, if they did not press their demand at that period it was possible they might not be in a situation afterwards to urge it with any benefi-

cial effect to themselves." These were the conditions
on which it was said by the Attorney General the
prisoner was entitled to an acquittal : "It will be incumbent on him to show the existence of crime in the
alleged mutineer, the impossibility of regular trial, and
the reasonable fitness of the means substituted and
resorted to in the place of trial. All these things it will
be incumbent on the prisoner to prove. It may likewise be proper for him, in further exculpation of his
conduct, to show how he withdrew himself from justice
at the time when he was first apprehended ; for it
should seem that if he was an innocent man, this was
above all others the convenient time to prove his innocence. It will give me great satisfaction if he is able
to establish that there existed such circumstances as
will make the crime with which he is charged not
entitled to be denominated and considered as murder."

The witnesses for the prosecution represented that
when Armstrong and his associates came up, demand-
ing their arrears, they were unarmed, and that they
returned to their quarters when ordered to do so by the
Governor, so that no extraordinary measures of severity
were necessary—but they admitted that the sentence
had been pronounced by a drumhead court martial,
which the Governor summoned, and they admitted
although where a mutiny is made the subject of
inquiry by a general court martial, it is officially
returned—if a mutiny is repressed at the instant, and a
drumhead court martial is held, it is not returned if the
punishment be short of death. No attempt was made
to show that the prisoner had any spite against Armstrong, or that he was actuated by any improper
motive.

When called upon for his defence Governor Wall
confined himself to a simple narrative, which, if true,
showed that Armstrong had been guilty of most cul-

pable conduct, and that after he had led back the men
to their quarters he still entertained very dangerous designs.

Mrs. Lacy,.the widow of the succeeding Governor who had been second in command when the affair happened, stated on her oath that Armstrong and the seventy soldiers he led on threatened Governor Wall, and swore that if he did not satisfy their demands they would break open the stores and satisfy themselves. She was strongly corroborated by eye-witnesses respecting the dangerous character of the mutiny, and by the opinion of the other officers in the garrison, that extraordinary measures must immediately be taken to repress it. Several general officers who had known the prisoner all his life, and other respectable witnesses, gave him a high character for good temper and humanity. But one of them being cross-examined on the subject by the Attorney General, said that "he had not heard this character of him on the island of Goree," and a witness called in reply to say that a witness examined for the prisoner ought not to be believed on his oath, said that the prisoner's witness was "reckoned a lying, shuffling fellow."

The Jury, after half an hour's deliberation, returned a verdict of *Guilty*, which was received with loud acclamation, and, according to the law as it then stood, the sentence of death, which was immediately passed, was ordered to be carried into execution on the second day after the trial.

Notwithstanding the general satisfaction testified, many were shocked by this proceeding, and petitions for mercy were presented to the King. The case being examined by Lord Eldon, and other members of the Government, there was a sincere desire among them to save the unfortunate gentleman, and a respite for two days was sent to give time for further deliberation—

but there arose such a burst of public resentment as was never known on such an occasion in this country. Still a further respite was granted for three days more, in the hope that reason and humanity might return to the multitude. On the contrary, an open insurrection was threatened, and it was said that the common soldiers and non-commissioned officers of the three regiments of Guards, who would have been called in to quell it, had declared that they would join the rioters, and assist with their own hands in executing the sentence of the law on the murderer of Sergeant Armstrong. The Government had not the courage to grant a farther respite, and Governor Wall was hanged on a gibbet in front of the jail of Newgate, amidst the shouts and execrations of the most numerous mob ever assembled in England to witness a public execution.[1]

Illness of
Lord
Kenyon.

Sir Edward Law was now a good deal disturbed by the near prospect of a vacancy in the office of Chief Justice of the King's Bench. Lord Kenyon, having made a vain effort to discharge his judicial duties in the beginning of Hilary Term, had been ordered by his physician to Bath, and from the accounts of his declining health, it was well understood that he could never sit again. The peace with France being approved of in both Houses, the Catholic question having gone to sleep, the King's health being restored, and Mr. Addington's Government being stronger than any one ever expected to see it, Sir Edward Law would not have been sorry to have continued in the office of Attorney General, but he could not bear the idea of any one being put over his head, and rumors reached

1. 28 St. Tr. 51-178. A writer, who highly approves of the execution of Governor Wall, says, "His inhuman cruelties had so hardened the multitude, that they hailed with exulting shouts his appearance on the scaffold, and triumphed in the knowledge that neither station, nor lapse of time, nor distance, would shield a convicted murderer from his just doom."—*Townsend's Judges*, vol. i. 328.

him that as he could not be considered to have won a right to the office of Chief Justice, from having served only a few months as a law officer of the Crown, it was to be conferred on Erskine, who, since the peace, had been coquetting with the new Prime Minister. I happened to be sitting in the students' box in the Court of King's Bench, on the 5th of April, 1802, when a note announcing Lord Kenyon's death was put into the Attorney General's hand. I am convinced that at this time he had received no intimation respecting the manner in which the vacancy was to be filled up, for he looked troubled and embarrassed, and immediately withdrew.

He did not again appear in Court till the 12th of April, when he was sworn in and took his seat as Chief Justice.[1] Mr. Addington had the highest opinion of him, and never had hesitated about recommending him for promotion. On going home from Court, after hearing of Lord Kenyon's death, Mr. Attorney found a letter from the Prime Minister, announcing that the King would be advised to appoint him, and expressing a confident belief that "when the royal pleasure was taken his Majesty would willingly sanction an appointment likely to be so conducive to the upright and enlightened administration of justice to his subjects." Immediately after Lord Kenyon's funeral, the King's pleasure was formally taken, with the anticipated result, and his Majesty cordially agreed to the proposal that the new Chief Justice should be raised to the peerage.

It was first necessary that he should submit to the degree of the coif, only serjeants-at-law being qualified to preside in the King's Bench, or to be Judges of Assize. In compliment to the peace concluded by his

CHAP. XLVIII.

Law is made Chief Justice of England and a Peer.

---

1. 2 East 253.

patron with the First Consul of the French Republic,
he took for the motto of his rings,

"Positis mitescunt secula bellis." [1]

For his barony he chose from a small fishing village
on the coast of Cumberland a sounding title, to which
there could be no objection, except that having very
often officially to sign it, he was forced afterwards to
write many millions of large characters, beyond what
would have been necessary if he had been contented
with a word of two syllables, without any unphonetic
consonants. [2]

1. "War being ended, the country grows peaceful."
2. At Ellenborough there is a small estate which had been in his
mother's family since the reign of Henry II., and it was supposed
that he was partly induced to take this title as a mark of respect to
her memory.

CHAPTER XLIX.

CONTINUATION OF THE LIFE OF LORD ELLENBOROUGH TILL HE BECAME A CABINET MINISTER.

LORD ELLENBOROUGH'S appointment was generally approved of, and he had the felicity of being promoted without the hostility of an effete predecessor, or the grudge of a disappointed rival, or the envy of contemporaries whom he had surpassed.

His professional qualifications were superior to those of any other man at the bar. Having an excellent head for law, by his practice under the bar he was familiarly versed in all the intricacies of special pleading: although not equally well acquainted with conveyancing, he had mastered its elements, and he could *pro re natâ* adequately understand and safely expatiate upon any point of the law of real property which might arise. He was particularly famous for mercantile law ; and a thorough knowledge of the rules of evidence, and of the principles on which they rested, made his work easy to him at *nisi prius*. Not only had he the incorruptibility now common to all English Judges, but he was inspired by a strong passion for justice, and he could undergo any degree of labor in performing what he considered his duty. He possessed a strong voice, an energetic manner, and all physical requisites for fixing attention and making an impression upon the minds of others. I must likewise state as a great merit that he could cope with and gain an ascendency over all the counsel who addressed him, and that he never had a favorite—dealing out with much impartiality his rebuffs and his sarcasms.   The defects in his judicial aptitude were a bad temper, an arrogance of nature, too great a desire to gain reputation by despatch, and an exces- sive leaning to severity of punishment.

He did not by any means disappoint the favorable anticipations of his friends, although the blemishes were discoverable which those dreaded who had more closely examined his character.   The day when he took his seat in court as Chief Justice, he said privately to an old friend that " his feelings as a barrister had been so often outraged by the insults of Lord Kenyon, he should now take care that no gentleman at the bar should have occasion to complain of any indignity in his court, and that he hoped any one who thought him- self ill-used would resent it."   Yet before the first term was over, he unjustifiably put down a hesitating junior, and ever after he was deeply offended by any show of resistance to his authority.   By good fortune he had very able *puisnes*, so that the decisions of the Court of King's Bench while he was Chief Justice are entitled to the highest respect.   Grose was his coadju- tor of least reputation ; but this supposed weak brother, although much ridiculed,[1] when he differed from his brethren, was voted by the profession to be in the right.   All the others—Lawrence, Le Blanc, Bayley,[2]

His
puisnes.

1. " Qualis sit Grocius Judex uno accipe versu ;
     Exclamat, dubitat, balbutit, stridet et errat."

    " Grocius with his *lantern jaws*
    Throws light upon the English laws."

    2. Sir John Bayley, an English jurist, born in 1763.   He published a " Summary of the Laws of Bills of Exchange " (1789), and became a justice of the King's Bench in 1808.   Died in 1841.—*Thomas's Biog. Dict.*

    " No judge since the act was passed in 1799 granting a pension on retirement after fifteen years' service has declined to avail himself of the privilege for so long a period as Sir John Bayley.   He occu-

SIR JOHN BAYLEY.

Dampier,[1] Abbott, Holroyd [2]—were among the best pied the bench for no less than twenty-six years, with the highest reputation as a lawyer, and undiminished respect and esteem from every one who acted either with or under him. The author of these pages, who is old enough to have advised with him when a serjeant, has been a witness of his whole subsequent career, during which he never heard one word to his disparagement."—*Foss's Judges of England.*

1. Henry Dampier. The Le Dampierres, anciently Counts of Flanders, are the reputed ancestors of this amiable judge, who was not more distinguished for his learning in the law than for his eminence in " *literis humanioribus*" and in general attainments. His father, the Rev. Thomas Dampier, a native of Somersetshire, from being one of the masters at Eton College, was raised to the deanery of Durham, and having married twice was most fortunate in his family. Thomas, the elder of his two sons by his first wife, Anne Hayes, became successively Bishop of Rochester (1802) and Ely (1808); and John, the younger, held a canonry in the latter cathedral. Henry, his only son by his second wife, Frances Walker, by attaining the high rank of a judge in Westminster Hall, claims a notice in these pages. Henry Dampier was born on December 21, 1758, at Eton, and having received his early education there, was elected to King's College, Cambridge, in 1775. He took his degree of B.A. in 1781, and of M. A. in 1784, in the interim proving his assiduity and showing his proficiency by gaining the members' prizes both in 1782 and 1783. Preferring the legal to the clerical profession, for which he was at first intended, he entered the Middle Temple in 1781, and was called to the bar in the customary routine. During the next thirty years he pursued the rugged paths of the law, content with the high character he obtained by his industry and intelligence as an acute counsel, and with the esteem and admiration he acquired by his obliging disposition and his classical as well as legal learning, made more attractive by the brilliancy of his conversation and his wit. Not seeking the addition either of a coif to his wig or a silk gown to his back (honors not then so lavishly bestowed as in the present day), he shone as a junior, whose advice might be surely depended on, and whose advocacy might be safely trusted ; and he was marked out in Westminster Hall as a future judge long before the prophecy could be fulfilled. The high judicial prizes are " few and far between," and the longevity of the then occupants of the bench prevented them from being often drawn. But at last Mr. Justice Grose retired, and Mr. Dampier was appointed his successor in the King's Bench on June 23, 1813, when he was knighted. His career as a judge was doomed to be shorter than any who had lately preceded him ; but it was long enough to cause the sincerest sorrow for its termination, not only to all his ermined brethren, but to the whole bar who practised under him. Ere he

---

2. See note 1, on next page.

lawyers that have appeared in Westminster Hall in my
time.   It was a great happiness to practise before

had graced the bench for two years and a half he died on February
3. 1816. Few have left a name so universally respected. He married in 1790 Martha, daughter of the venerable John Law, archdeacon
of Rochester. She and five of their children survived him ; one of
whom, John Lucius Dampier, was recorder of Portsmouth, and became vice-warden of the Stannaries in Cornwall, the duties of which
he performed most exemplarily till his early death in 1853.—*Foss's
Judges of England.*

1. George Sowley Holroyd.   To the same stirps from which Lord
Sheffield descended, Sir George Sowley Holroyd owed his origin ;
the direct ancestors of both, George and Isaac, being the sons of
Isaac Holroyd of Crawcrofte in Rishworth in the parish of Elland
in the county of York.   The judge was the great-grandson of George ;
and the eldest son of another George, by Eleanor, the daughter of
Henry Sowley of Appleby, Esq., from whom he received one of his
baptismal names.   He was born at York on October 31, 1758, and
was sent in 1770 to Harrow School, then presided over by the Rev.
Dr. Sumner.   From Harrow it was intended that he should proceed
to the university, but in consequence of his father suffering some
severe losses from unfortunate speculations the judge was removed
from Harrow, and in April, 1774, was articled to Mr. Borthwick, an
attorney in London.   At the end of three years he entered Gray's
Inn ; and having, under the pupilage of Mr. (afterwards Sir Alan)
Chambré, acquired by patient assiduity a considerable amount of
legal learning, he commenced business as a special pleader on his
own account in April, 1799.   During the eight years that he pursued this branch of the profession he adopted, with Romilly, Christian, and Baynes, one of the most effective preparations for the con-
tests into which they were about to enter.   Meeting at each other's
chambers, they discussed legal points previously arranged ; one of
them taking the affirmative side, another supporting the contrary
part, and a third summing up the arguments and deciding the question as judge.   On June 26, 1787, he was called to the bar, and about
three months after married Sarah, the daughter of Amos Chaplin,
Esq., who, after bringing him fourteen children, survived him for
seventeen years.   His family connections naturally led him to join
the northern circuit ; and the character he had acquired while under
the bar for solidity of judgment and professional ability secured to
him from the commencement of his forensic career a fair proportion
of business, both in the north and in Westminster Hall.   Ere he had
been called a year his name appears in two cases in the " Term Reports " (ii. 445, 480).   During the twenty-nine years that he remained
at the bar his fee-book shows the rapid increase of his practice,
proving also the advance of his reputation by the number and importance of the cases submitted to his direction.   A story is told
that, when he was forty-eight years of age, Lord Kenyon spoke of
him as " a rising young man " ; but unfortunately for the narrator's

them, and I entertain a most affectionate respect for CHAP. XLIX. their memory.

Lord Ellenborough did not attempt to introduce any His conduct as reform in the practice of his court, or in the prepara- Chief Justice. tion of the preliminary pleadings. The writ of Latitat [1]

credit his lordship's career was finished in 1802, before Mr. Holroyd had attained his forty-fourth year, and when he had as good a practice as any junior member of the bar. Of a retiring disposition, he persisted in declining the offer of a silk gown, and therefore his merits were comparatively unrecognized by the general public ; but among the legal community his superiority was fully acknowledged, and it was said of him that " he was absolutely born with a genius for law." So highly were his instructions esteemed that, while at the bar, no less than forty-seven pupils availed themselves of them, among whom were Mr. Baron Hullock, Mr. Baron Bolland, and Mr. Justice Cresswell. In 1811 he greatly distinguished himself in the celebrated case of privilege, *Burdett* v. *the Speaker of the House of Commons*, by his luminous arguments on behalf of the plaintiff (14 East's Reports 11). In the last years of his practice at the bar he was sent by the government to Guernsey at the head of a commission to inquire into and determine certain " doleances " complained of by persons resident in that island. At length an opportunity occurring, by the death of Sir Henry Dampier, of raising him to a position to which his powers were peculiarly adapted, he was appointed a judge of the King's Bench. In that court he sat for more than twelve years, from February 14, 1816, to November 17, 1828, the date of his resignation, fully sustaining the reputation he had acquired, and largely contributing to the high character of the bench to which he belonged, when associated with such erudite and discriminating judges as Lord Tenterden, Sir John Bayley, and Sir Joseph Littledale. His patience never seemed to be wearied ; his amiable temper was never ruffled ; his decisions were always clear and well founded, for his memory was the storehouse of all the arguments that had ever been advanced for or against the case he was to judge ; and his taste, with no effort at display, was so exquisite that he made the driest subject interesting. The infirmities which obliged him to retire, in three years terminated his life on November 21, 1831, at his residence at Hare Hatch in Berkshire.— *Foss's Judges of England.*

1. Latitat (he lies hid) in English law is the name of a writ calling a defendant to answer to a personal action in the King's Bench. It derives its name from a supposition that the defendant lurks and lies hid, and cannot be found in the county of Middlesex (in which the said court is holden) to be taken there, but is gone into some other county, and therefore requiring the sheriff to apprehend him in such other county.—*Fitz. N. B.* 78. Abolished by stat. 2 Wm. IV. c. 39.

was still as much venerated as the writ of Habeas Corpus, and all the arbitrary and fantastic rules respecting declarations, pleas, replications, rejoinders, surrejoinders, rebutters and surrebutters, which had arisen from accident or had been devised to multiply fees, or had been properly framed for a very different state of society, were still considered to be the result of unerring wisdom, and eternally essential to the due administration of justice. Antiquity was constantly vouched as an unanswerable defence for doctrines and procedure which our ancestors, could they have been summoned from their graves, would have condemned or ridiculed. One obstacle to legal improvement, now removed, then operated most powerfully, though insensibly—that antiquated juridical practice could not be touched without diminishing the profits of offices which were held in trust for the Judges, or which they were permitted to sell.[1] The grand foundation of legal improvement was the bill for putting all the subordinate officers in the courts at Westminster, as well as the Judges, on a fixed salary—allowing fees of reasonable amount to be paid into the public treasury towards the just expenses of our judicial establishment. The Benthamites[2] would go still further and abolish court fees

1. I never saw this feeling at all manifest itself in Lord Ellenborough except once, when a question arose whether money paid into court was liable to poundage. I was counsel in the cause, and threw him into a furious passion by strenuously resisting the demand. The poundage was to go into his own pocket—being payable to the chief clerk—an office held in trust for him. If he was in any degree influenced by this consideration, I make no doubt that he was wholly unconscious of it.

2. Jeremy Bentham (b. 1747, d. 1832), educated at Westminster and Queen's College, Oxford, was originally intended for the bar, but, being possessed of private means, he determined to devote his life to the reformation, rather than the practice, of the law, and wrote numerous works with this object. In spite of their unequal value his books remain a storehouse for the politician and the law-reformer. Indeed, there are few administrative reforms which have not been suggested wholly or in part by Bentham's writings. But his value

JEREMY BENTHAM.

altogether; but there seems no hardship in the general CHAP. XLIX. rule that the expense of litigation shall be thrown upon the parties whose improper conduct must be supposed to have occasioned it. Arbitrators are paid by the party found to be in the wrong, and the burthen of maintaining the Judges appointed by the State ought not to be borne by those who habitually obey the law, and spontaneously render to every man his own.

Upon the accession of Lord Ellenborough, the absurd doctrines about forestalling and regrating were understood, like prosecutions for witchcraft, to be gone for ever on account of the manly stand he had made against them under Lord Kenyon, and there has not since been any attempt to revive them. The internal free trade in corn was thus practically secured, al-

does not only consist in being a suggester of reform on the details of legislation and procedure ; he is also one of the fathers of English jurisprudence. His place in that science is midway between Hobbes and Austin. Hobbes had first discerned the doctrine that whatever be the form of government the sovereign authority is ultimately absolute ; but he had deduced from this the theory of non-resistance. Bentham perceived the fallacy in this deduction, and separated clearly the *legal* necessity for obedience from the *political* duty of resistance. The test of the propriety of political resistance Bentham held to be " Utility," in the sense of the greatest happiness of the greatest number. This maxim, whatever may be its value as the basis of a philosophy, furnishes an excellent rule for practical action. In fact, as Sir Henry Maine has pointed out, by thus making the good of the community take precedence of every other object Bentham offered a clear rule of reform, and gave a distinct object to aim at in the pursuit of improvement. In this respect his influence may be compared with that of the *jus naturæ* in Roman law. Bentham's works, which are very numerous, have been collected by his disciple Bowring (London, 1837), who has prefixed to the collection a sketch of Bentham's method. Those of his writings which will best repay perusal are " The Fragment on Government " (1776), in answer to Blackstone ; " The Book of Fallacies," and " The Tract on Usury." His theory of punishments is contained in " The Principles of Morals and Legislation" (published separately by the Clarendon Press), and in a translation from the French of his disciple Dumont, entitled " The Theory of Legislation " For criticisms of Bentham's philosophy see preface to Green and Grose's edition of " Hume," and W. L. Courtenay, " Criticism on the Philosophy of J. S. Mill."—*Dict. of Eng. Hist.*

though the doctrine that free importation of corn ought to be allowed from foreign countries did not follow for near half a century, and Lord Ellenborough himself would probably have regarded with as much horror such an importation, as did his predecessor a corn-merchant buying wheat at Uxbridge to be resold in Mark Lane.[1]

I do not think that on any other subject the principles were altered by which the Court of King's Bench now professed to be guided. Lord Ellenborough adhered to the rule that in ejectment the legal estate shall always prevail, and that an outstanding term might be set up unless it might be fairly presumed to be extinguished or surrendered, or the defendant was estopped from contesting the title of the claimant. A more liberal and scientific mode, however, was restored of treating commercial questions, the civil law and foreign jurists were quoted with effect, and the authority of Lord Mansfield was again in the ascendent.

Chief Justice Ellenborough's judgments connected with politics and history I propose hereafter to introduce chronologically as I trace his career after he mounted the bench. At present I think it may be convenient to mention some of the more important questions before him, which derive no illustration or interest from the time when they arose, or from any concomitant events.

Lord Ellen-
borough's
decisions. In now looking over the bulky volumes of " **East** " and of " Maule and Selwyn," [2] it is wonderful to ob-

1. Mark Lane is one of the busiest streets in London. It was originally " Mart Lane from the privilege of fair accorded by Edward I. to Sir Thomas Ross of Hamlake, whose manor of Blanch Appleton became corrupted into Blind Chapel Court." In the reign of Edward IV. basket-makers, vine-dressers, and other foreigners were permitted to have shops in the manor of Blanch Appleton and nowhere else in the city.

2. Maule and Selwyn, reporters of the King's Bench from 1813 to 1817. " Without any specific objection to them that I know of,

serve how many of the decisions which they record may already be considered obsolete. A vast majority of them are upon rules of practice and pleading, since remodelled under the authority of the legislature—upon Sessions' law respecting settlements, rating, and bastardy, which has been entirely altered by successive statutes—upon the old Quo warranto law, swept away by the Parliamentary Reform Act and the Municipal Corporations' Amendment Act—upon the law of tithes, abolished by the Tithe Commutation Act—and upon concerted commissions of bankruptcy and the validity of petitioning creditors' debts, which have become immaterial by the new Bankrupt and Insolvent Codes.

I proceed to select a few cases, decided by Lord Ellenborough, which depend upon the common law and the eternal principles of right and wrong, and which must ever be interesting and instructive to those who wish to have a liberal knowledge of our jurisprudence.

In *Rodney* v. *Chambers*[1] the important question Validity of arose upon the legality of a covenant by a husband, who deeds of had been separated from his wife and had been reconciled to her, to pay a certain sum of money annually to trustees for her support in case of a future separation. His counsel contended that such a covenant was contrary to public policy, as tending to encourage the wife to leave her husband, and to disturb the harmony of conjugal life.

Lord Ellenborough.—" I should have thought that it would have fallen in better with the general policy of the law to have prohibited all contracts which tend to facilitate the separation of husband and wife ; but we cannot reject the present on that ground without saying that all contracts which have the same

these Reports are perhaps less cited in daily practice than almost any other Reports of modern times." (*Law Magazine and Law Review*, vol. ix. p. 340.)—*Wallace's Reporters.*
1. 2 East 283.

tendency are vicious—which would extend, for aught I can see, to provisions for pin-money or any other separate provision for the wife, which tends to render her independent of the support and protection of her husband.   Deeds of separation are not illegal, and I cannot see how it is more illegal to provide for future than for present separation." [*Judgment against the husband.*]

Action for Crim.Con., notwithstanding deed of separation.   Whether in consequence of this deed, or from some other cause, the wife soon after separated from her husband and had an affair of gallantry with a military officer. An action for crim. con. being brought, the defence was set up that the plaintiff had voluntarily renounced the society of his wife, and therefore that this action could not be maintained, the *gravamen* of which is the *per quod consortium amisit;* but Lord Ellenborough held that although the husband had made a provision for his wife's separate maintenance, he could not be said to have given up all claim to her society and assistance, and that he sustained an injury from the adultery which brought disgrace upon his name, and might introduce a spurious progeny into his family.[1]

No implied warranty from high price of goods.   In *Parkinson* v. *Lee,*[2] in contradiction to the loose maxim that on the sale of goods a sound price implied a warranty of soundness, Lord Ellenborough, with the rest of the Court, decided that upon a sale of hops, however high the price might be, there was no implied warranty that the commodity should be merchantable, and that in the absence of fraud the governing maxim is *caveat emptor.*[3]

Liability for publication of a libel in England by order of persons living out of England.   Mr. Justice Johnson, an Irish Judge, having been indicted in the Court of King's Bench at Westminster for publishing in the county of Middlesex a libel on Earl Talbot,[4] the Lord Lieutenant of Ireland, and hav-

1. *Chambers* v. *Caulfield*, 6 East 244.
2. 2 East 314.
3. " Let the buyer beware."
4. Sir Charles Chetwynd Talbot, second Earl Talbot of Hensol (1777-1849), born on April 25, 1777, was the elder son of John Chet-

ing pleaded in abatement that as he had been born and
had constantly resided in Ireland, he was only liable to be
tried in the courts of that country, Lord Ellenborough,
in a very elaborate judgment, overruled the plea, thus
concluding :

"If the circumstances of the defendant's birth in Ireland

CHAP.
XLIX.

wynd Talbot, first earl, by his wife Charlotte, daughter of Wills
Hill, first Marquis of Downshire. Charles Talbot, Lord Chancellor,
was his great-grandfather. Charles succeeded to the peerage on the
death of his father on May 19, 1793. He matriculated from Christ
Church, Oxford, on October 11, 1794, and was created M.A. on June
28, 1797. After leaving Oxford he joined Lord Whitworth's embassy
in Russia as a voluntary attaché, and formed a lasting friendship
with his chief. Returning to England about 1800, he devoted himself to the improvement of his estates and to the general promotion
of agriculture in England. In 1803 he took an active part in organ-
izing a volunteer force in Staffordshire to oppose the invasion of
England contemplated by Napoleon. In August, 1812, he was
sworn lord lieutenant of the county, and continued to hold the office
till his death. On October 9, 1817, he was appointed Lord Lieutenant
of Ireland, Sir Robert Peel acting as Irish secretary until 1818. During his term of office he rendered considerable services to the agriculture of the country, in recognition of which he was presented
with the freedom of Drogheda. In 1821, during his viceroyalty,
George IV. visited Ireland, and on that occasion he was created a
Knight of the Order of St. Patrick. Though he steadily opposed
Catholic emancipation, O'Connell gave him credit for impartiality,
and Lord Cloncurry spoke of him as "an honorable, high-minded
gentleman." The discontent in Ireland, however, continued to grow
during his administration, and in December, 1822, he was somewhat
ungraciously superseded by the Marquis Wellesley. In 1839 Talbot
received in recognition of his services as Lord Lieutenant of Staffordshire a testimonial amounting to £1400, which he devoted to
the endowment of a new church at Salt. He was one of the first
peers to support Sir Robert Peel's plan for the extinction of the
duties on foreign corn, and on December 12, 1844, through that minister's influence he was elected a Knight of the Garter. Talbot died
at Ingestre Hall, Staffordshire, on January 10, 1849, and was buried
in Ingestre church on January 20. He married on August 28, 1800,
Frances Thomasine, eldest daughter of Charles Lambert of Beau
Parc in Meath. By her he had ten sons and two daughters. He
was succeeded as third Earl Talbot by his second son, Henry John
Chetwynd, who, on August 10, 1856, succeeded his distant cousin,
Bertram Arthur Talbot, as eighteenth Earl of Shrewsbury. A portrait of the second Earl of Talbot, painted by John Bostock and en-
graved by John Charles Bromley, was published by J. Shepherd at
Newcastle in 1837.—*Nat. Biog. Dict.*

and his residence there at the time of the publication here, have the effect of rendering him not punishable in any court in this country for such publication, this impunity must follow as a consequence from its being no crime in the defendant to publish a libel in Middlesex. Indeed, the argument rests wholly upon this position, that the defendant owed no obedience to the laws of this part of the United Kingdom, so that he has not been guilty of any crime in breaking them. The learned Judge lays down for law that if he remains at Dublin, he may by means of a hired assassin commit a murder in London without being liable to punishment."

The indictment being tried at bar, the libellous letters published in 'Cobbett's Political Register' were proved to be in the handwriting of the defendant, with the Dublin post-mark upon them. They were addressed to the editor of the 'Register' in Middlesex, and they contained a request that he would print and publish them. The defendant's counsel insisted that he was entitled to an acquittal on the ground that the evidence was defective.

Lord Ellenborough.—" There is no question of the fact of publication by Mr. Cobbett, in Middlesex, of that which is admitted to be a libel ; and the only question is, whether the defendant was accessory to that publication ? If he were, the offence is established ; for one who procures another to publish a libel, is no doubt guilty of the publication, in whatever county it is in fact published, in consequence of his procurement."

The other Judges concurred, and the defendant was found GUILTY.[1]

English under-
writers not
liable for
embargo
put on by
the Gov-
ernment of
the as-
sured. The Government of the United States of America having in the year 1808 laid an embargo in American ports on all American ships bound for Great Britain, the owners, who were insured in England, gave notice of abandonment to the underwriters, and claimed a total loss. Lord Ellenborough acquired great glory by

---

1. 6 East 583; 7 East 65.

boldly deciding that, under these circumstances, the English underwriters were not liable. He proceeded on this maxim, that a party insured can never recover for a loss which he himself has occasioned, and he laid down that under every form of government each subject or citizen must be considered as concurring in every act of the supreme power of the country in which he lives:

"The foundation of the abandonment is an act of the American Government. Every American citizen is a party to that act; it has virtually the consent and concurrence of all, and, amongst the rest, the consent and concurrence of the assured. The assured having prevented the vessels from sailing, can they make the detention of the vessels the foundation of an action?"[1]

Where a marriage had been regularly celebrated by *Validity of marriage of illegitimate minor.* a priest in orders, in the face of the church, between a man of full age and a woman under age, who was illegitimate, with the consent of her mother, the father being dead, and they had lived together as man and wife for many years, Lord Ellenborough decided (I think erroneously, although he had the concurrence of two able Judges, Le Blanc and Bayley) that the marriage was void and their children were bastards, because the Court of Chancery had not appointed a guardian to the minor, to consent to the marriage. This most revolting decision might have been avoided by holding on the true principles for construing statutes, that although Lord Hardwicke's Act (26 Geo. II. c. 33) says that all marriages not solemnized in the manner therein mentioned shall be void, this nullification applies only to the marriages of persons in the contemplation of the legislature, and that the marriages of illegitimate minors could not have been in the contemplation of the legislature with respect to this con-

1. 10 East 536. *Conway v. Gray.*

CHAP.
XLIX. sent, as the condition requiring the consent of parents
or guardians could not be fulfilled—so that this being
casus omissus, the marriage in question was valid.   But
Lord Ellenborough's nature was somewhat stern, and
he did not dislike a judgment that others would have
found it painful to pronounce—rather rejoicing in an
opportunity of showing that he was not diverted by
any weak sympathies from the upright discharge of his
duty.[1]

Case of the   However, he was always eager to extend the pro-
HOTTEN-
TOT VENUS tection of British law to all who were supposed to be
oppressed.   Upon an affidavit that an African female,
formed in a remarkable manner, was exhibited in London under the name of the HOTTENTOT VENUS, the
deponents swearing that they believed she had been
brought into this country and was detained here
against her will, he granted a rule to show cause why a
writ of *habeas corpus* should not issue to her keepers to
produce her in court, and that in the mean time the
Master of the Crown-office and persons to be appointed by him should have free access to her :

> At Venus ætherios inter Dea *Candida* nimbos
> Dona ferens aderat.[2]

She appeared before the Master and his associates
magnificently attired, offered them presents, and declared that she came to and remained in this country
with her free will and consent.   A report to this effect
being made to the Court, Lord Ellenborough said,
"We have done our duty in seeing that no human
being, of whatever complexion or shape, is restrained

1. *Priestly* v. *Hughes*, 11 East 1.   Mr. Justice Grose dissented;
the decision was condemned by Westminster Hall, and finally the
law was rectified by the Legislature.   4 Geo. IV. c. 76; 6 and 7 Wm.
IV. c. 85.
2. "But Venus, the fair goddess, appeared between the celestial
clouds, bearing gifts."

of liberty within this realm. Let the rule be discharged."[1]

CHAP.
XLIX.

One of the most important questions which arose in the Court of King's Bench, while Lord Ellenborough was Chief Justice, was, whether the captain of a man-of-war be liable to an action for damage done by her in running down another vessel, without proof of any personal misconduct or default? An award had been made against him by a legal arbitrator, who set out the facts on the face of his award for the opinion of the Court.

Liability of
captain of
a ship of
war for
damage
done by her
negligent
manage-
ment.

Lord Ellenborough.—"Captain Mouncey is said to be liable for the damages awarded in this case, by considering him in the ordinary character of master of the ship by means of which the injury was done. But how was he master? He had no power of appointing the officers or crew on board; he had no power to appoint even himself to the station which he filled on board; he was no volunteer in that particular station, by having entered originally into the naval service; he had no choice whether he would serve or not with the other persons on board, but was obliged to take such as he found there and make the best of them. He was the King's servant stationed on board this ship to do his duty there, together with others stationed there by the same authority to do their several duties. How, then, can he be liable for their misfeasance any more than they for his?" [*Award set aside.*][2]

The only occasion when Lord Ellenborough was ever seriously supposed to be swayed by his own interest, was in deciding whether sailors employed in the lobster-fishery were privileged from being pressed into the Royal Navy. He had an extreme love of turbot, *with lobster-sauce,* and although sailors employed in the deep-sea fishing, where turbots are found, were allowed to be privileged from impressment, the Admiralty had issued orders for impressing all sailors employed in

Lord Ellen-
borough
supposed to
be in-
fluenced by
his love of
lobster
sauce.

1. *Hottentot Venus's Case,* 13 East 384.
2. *Nicholson* v. *Mouncey,* 15 East 384.

collecting lobsters on the rocks and bringing them to Billingsgate. Writs of *habeas corpus* having been granted for the purpose of discharging several who had been so impressed, the counsel for the Crown argued strenuously that upon the just construction of 2 Geo. III. c. 15, and 50 Geo. III. c. 108, they were not entitled to any exemption, not being engaged in the deep-sea fishing.

Lord Ellenborough.—"I think the policy of the legislature seems to have been directed to the better supplying the inhabitants of the metropolis and other parts of the kingdom with fish, and for that purpose to bring sound and well-flavored fish to our markets at a moderate price. It is contended, however, that the protection extends only to those who are engaged in fishing in deep waters, and that lobsters are found in shallow waters. Stat. 50 Geo. III. c. 108, does in its preamble recite that 'various sorts of fish do in the winter retire into the deep water, and that for the supply of the metropolis a larger class of fishing-boats, which cannot be navigated without additional hands, must be employed'; but it enacts, 'that every person employed in *the fisheries of these kingdoms* shall be exempted from being impressed.' Then is not the lobster-fishery a fishery, and a most important fishery, of this kingdom, though carried on in shallow water? The framers of the law well knew that the produce of the deep sea, without the produce of the shallow water, would be of comparatively small value, and intended that the turbot, when placed upon our tables, should be flanked by good lobster-sauce. 'Fisheries of these kingdoms' are words of a large scope, embracing all those fisheries from which fish are supplied in a fresh and wholesome state to the markets of these kingdoms, and all who are engaged in such fisheries are within the equity of the Act. *Let the rule be absolute.*" [1]

May the
executor of
a lady
maintain
an action
for breach
of promise
of mar-
riage? In *Chamberlain* v. *Williamson,* [2] the curious question arose whether the personal representative of a young lady who had died, being forsaken by her lover who had promised to marry her, could maintain an action

1. See *Payne and Thoroughgood's Case.* 1 M. and S. 223.
2. 2 M. and S. 409.

against him for breach of the promise to marry. The plaintiff had recovered a verdict with large damages, but a motion was made in arrest of judgment.

Lord Ellenborough.—" The action is novel in its kind, and not one instance is cited or suggested in the argument of its having been maintained, nor have we been able to discover any by our own researches and inquiries ; and yet frequent occasion must have occurred for bringing such an action. However, that would not be a decisive ground of objection if, on reason and principle, it could strictly be maintained. The general rule of law is *actio personalis moritur cum personâ ;* under which rule are included all actions for injuries merely personal. Executors and administrators are the representatives of the temporal property, that is, the goods and debts of the deceased, but not of their wrongs, except where those wrongs operate to the temporal injury of their personal estate. If this action be maintainable, then every action founded on an implied promise to a testator, where the damage subsists in the previous personal suffering of the testator, would also be maintainable by the executor or administrator. All actions affecting the life or health of the deceased ; all such as arise out of the unskilfulness of medical practitioners ; the imprisonment of the party brought on by the negligence of his attorney ; all these would be breaches of the implied promise by the persons employed to exhibit a proper portion of skill and attention. Although marriage may be considered as a temporal advantage to the party, as far as respects personal comfort, still it cannot be considered in this case as an increase of the individual transmissible personal estate, but would operate rather as an extinction of it. We are of opinion that this judgment must be arrested."

An action being brought by the Earl of Essex against the Honorable and Reverend Mr. Capel, which charged that the defendant had committed a trespass in breaking and entering his grounds, called Cashiobury Park, and with horses and hounds destroying the grass and herbage, and breaking down his fences, the defendant justified, that the fox being a noxious animal and liable to do mischief, he, for the purpose of killing and destroying him, and as the most effectual means of doing so, broke and entered the park with hounds and horses, and hunted the fox. Replication, that his object was —not to destroy the fox but, the amusement and diversion afforded by the chase. After two witnesses had been examined, Lord Ellenborough interrupted the further progress of the cause:

"This is a contending against all nature and conviction. Can it be supposed that these gentlemen hunted for the purpose of killing vermin, and not for their own diversion? Can the jury be desired to say, upon their oaths, that the defendant was actuated by any other motive than a desire to enjoy the pleasures of the chase? The defendant says that he has not committed the trespass for the sake of the diversion of the chase, but as the only effectual way of killing and destroying the fox. Now, can any man of common sense hesitate in saying that the principal motive was not the killing vermin, but the sport? It is a sport the law of the land will not justify, without the consent of the owner of the land, and I cannot make a new law accommodated to the pleasures and amusements of these gentlemen. They may destroy such noxious animals as are injurious to the commonwealth, but the good of the public must be the governing motive."

Illegality of cock-fighting. Nor was more countenance shown by the Chief Justice to a barbarous sport formerly in great favor with country squires, but which the increased refinement of modern manners has tended to discourage. He refused to try an action for money had and received for a wager on a cock-fight:

"This must be considered a barbarous diversion, which ought not to be encouraged or sanctioned in a court of justice. I believe that cruelty to these animals in throwing at them forms part of the dehortatory charge of judges to grand juries, and it makes little difference whether they are lacerated by sticks and stones, or by the bills and spurs of each other. There is likewise another principle on which I think an action on such wagers cannot be maintained. They tend to the degradation of courts of justice. It is impossible to be engaged

in ludicrous inquiries of this sort consistently with that dignity
which it is essential to the public welfare that a court of
justice should always preserve. I will not try the plaintiff's
right to recover the four guineas, which might involve questions on the weight of the cocks and the construction of their
steel spurs."[1]

It had long been a disputed question whether the Consuls not privileged as public ministers. consul of a foreign Prince residing in this country, and acknowledged as such by our Government, be privi-leged from arrest for debt. A motion was at last made to discharge out of custody the consul of the Duke of Sleswick Holstein Oldenburg, who had been arrested for a debt contracted by him as a merchant in this country:

Lord Ellenborough.—"Every person who is conversant with
the history of this country is not ignorant of the occasion
which led to the passing of the statute 7 Anne, c. 12. An
ambassador of the Czar Peter had been arrested, and had
put in bail; and this matter was taken up with considerable
inflammation and anger by several of the European Courts,
and particularly by that potentate. In order to soothe the
feelings of these powers the act of parliament was passed, in
which it was thought fit to declare the immunities and privileges of ambassadors and public ministers from process, and
it was enacted 'that in case any person should presume to
sue forth or prosecute any such writ or process, such persons
being thereof convicted, should be deemed violators of the
law of nations and disturbers of the public repose, and should
suffer such penalties and corporal punishment as the Lord
Chancellor or the Chief Justice of the Queen's Bench or
Common Pleas, or any two of them, should adjudge to be inflicted.' Thus was conferred a great and extraordinary power,
which I am glad to think belongs in no other instance to those
functionaries. The act goes on to declare that 'all writs and
processes that shall in future be sued forth, whereby the person of any ambassador or other public minister of any foreign
Prince or State may be arrested or imprisoned, shall be deemed
to be utterly null and void.' Here the question is, if this defendant be an ambassador or other public minister of a foreign

---

1. *Squires* v. *Whisken*, 3 Camp. 140.

Prince or State?   He certainly is a person invested with some authority by a foreign Prince ; but is he a public minister? There, is I believe, not a single writer on the law of nations, nor even of those who have written looser tracts on the same subject, who has pronounced that a consul is *eo nomine* a public minister."

Having minutely examined the authorities, and pointed out that there was no usage to show that by the law of nations a consul is entitled to any exemption from being sued in courts of justice as any ordinary person, a rule was pronounced for continuing the defendant in custody.[1]

Privilege of
House of
Com'mon⁵
to imprison
for con-
tempt. Lord Ellenborough, in the great case of *Burdett* v. *Abbott*,[2] stoutly maintained the doctrine denied by the plaintiff, that the House of Commons has power to imprison for a contempt.   Having examined all the authorities cited, he observed,

" Thus the matter stands on parliamentary precedent, upon the recognition by statute, upon the continued recognition of all the Judges, and particularly of Lord Holt, who was one of the greatest favorers of the liberties of the people, and as strict an advocate for the authority of the common law against the privileges of parliament as ever existed.   I should have thought that this was a quantity of authority enough to have put this question to rest.   Why should the House of Commons not possess this power?   What is there against it?   A priori, if there were no precedents upon the subject, no legislative recognition, no opinions of Judges in favor of it, it is essentially necessary to the House of Commons, and they must possess it ; indeed they would sink into utter insignificance and contempt without it.   Could they stand high in the estimation and reverence of the people, if, whenever they were insulted, they were obliged to wait the comparatively slow proceedings of the ordinary Courts of law for their redress?—that the Speaker with his mace, should be under the necessity of going before a Grand Jury to prefer a bill of indictment for an insult offered to the House? "

1. *Viveash* v. *Becker*, 3 M. and S. 284.
2. 14 East 1.

He then repelled with indignation the quibbling ob-jections made to the form of the warrant, and vindicated the right of the officers to break open the outer door of the plaintiff's house for the purpose of apprehending him.

But I think he did not lay down with sufficient discrimination and accuracy the limits within which parliamentary proceedings may be published without danger of an indictment. Mr. Creevey, M.P. for Liverpool, in a debate in the House of Commons respecting the collection of the public revenue, had made a speech in which he pointed out some alleged misconduct of an Inspector General of Taxes. An inaccurate account of this speech having been published, he printed and circulated a full and correct one. For this he was indicted, on the ground that it reflected on the Receiver General, and therefore was a libel. His counsel contended that he was absolutely entitled to an acquittal on the admission made by the prosecution, that the supposed libel was a true report of a speech made in the House of Commons. This was very properly overruled by Le Blanc, J., the presiding Judge, on the authority of the conviction and punishment of the Earl of Abingdon, who, having quarrelled with his steward, made a scurrilous speech against him in the House of Lords, which he maliciously published with intent to defame him—but the learned Judge erroneously (I think) told the Jury that "if there was anything in Mr. Creevey's published speech which reflected on the prosecutor, the publication of it was a misdemeanor." The defendant being found *Guilty*, a motion was made for a new trial on the ground of misdirection:

Lord Ellenborough.—" The only question is, whether the occasion of the publication rebuts the inference of malice arising from the matter of it ? We cannot scan what the defendant said within the walls of the House of Commons ; but has he a

CHAP. XLIX.

Doubtful doctrine in Rex v. Creevey.

right to reiterate these reflections to the public ?—to address them as an *oratio ad populum*, in order to explain his conduct to his constituents ? The Jury have found that the publication was libellous, and I can see no ground for drawing the subject again into discussion."

The rule was refused, and the defendant was sentenced to pay a fine of 100*l.*—but if his object *bonâ fide* was to explain his conduct to his constituents, I think he was entitled to a new trial and to an acquittal.

Freedom of literary criticism. Lord Ellenborough nobly maintained the freedom of literary criticism.—Sir John Carr,[1] Knight, a silly author, brought an action against respectable booksellers for a burlesque upon certain foolish Travels which he had given to the world, relying upon a recent decision of Lord Ellenborough in *Tabbart* v. *Tipper*.

Lord Ellenborough.—" In that case the defendant had falsely accused the plaintiff of publishing what he had never published. Here the supposed libel only attacks those works of which Sir John Carr is the avowed author ; and one writer, in exposing the absurdities and errors of another, may make use of ridicule, however poignant. Ridicule is often the fittest instrument which can be employed for such a purpose. If the reputation or pecuniary interests of the party ridiculed suffer, it is *damnum absque injuria*. Perhaps the plaintiff's Tour in Scotland is now unsalable ; but is he to be indemnified by receiving a compensation in damages from the person who may have opened the eyes of the public to the bad taste and inanity of his composition ? Who prized the works of Sir Robert Fil-

1. Sir John Carr, a writer of travels, was born in Devonshire 1772, and practised as an attorney in the Middle Temple, London. He received the honor of knighthood from the Lord Lieutenant of Ireland about 1805, and died July 17, 1832. He published " Fury of Discord," a poem ; " The Stranger in France," " Tour from Devonshire to Paris," " The Sea-side Hero," a drama ; " A Northern Summer, or Travels round the Baltic, through Denmark, Sweden, Russia, part of Poland, and Prussia," " The Stranger in Ireland," which gave rise to an excellent *jeu d'esprit*, entitled " My Pocket Book," by Edward Dubois ; " Caledonian Sketches," " Descriptive Travels in the Southern and Eastern Parts of Spain and the Balearic Isles," and a volume of poems.—*Cooper's Biog. Dict.*

mer after he had been refuted by Mr. Locke,[1] but shall it be CHAP.
said that he might have maintained an action for defamation XLIX.

[1]. John Locke, born at Wrington, near Bristol, on August 29th, 1632; died at Oates, in Essex, on October 28th, 1704. A name than which there is none higher in English philosophical literature; the name of a Man surpassed by no one in that worth which constitutes the dignity of an independent English gentleman.—It is not our intention to offer in this place an analysis of the celebrated "Essay Concerning the Human Understanding"; suffice it to touch rapidly on those main points which constitute it a landmark—on the circumstances in which it arose, and the peculiarities that gave it historic significance. Falling, like Kant after him, on a period of one-sidedness or dogmatism—when statements accurate in the main had, through their imperfection as representatives of the whole truth, been twisted into assertions of error -Locke found the freedom of the Human Understanding attacked by the Cartesians with the weapon named by them "Innate Ideas." Inquiry he found—fearless and rational—stopped at both its termini : truths clearly within its reach were repudiated because in pretended conflict with so-called Innate Ideas ; and regions apparently beyond the sphere of our faculties were on the same authority sketched out and described with the pedantry of a mechanical Surveyor. To determine the length of our line was therefore Locke's first resolve ; nor can it be asserted that his preliminary war with Innate Ideas is—in the sense in which he looked at the subject—wholly unsuccessful. Rightly interpreted, his theory is this—no authoritative belief can be found in the Mind which has not an origin in Experience ; and the most extensive or nearly universal Beliefs existing are shaped and colored by the varying experience of the men and nations entertaining them. The thesis, so stated, cannot be impugned ; neither the value of its assertion at the epoch of Locke : but our philosopher fails in establishing the proposition which he supposed to be his thesis, viz., that there are no Beliefs in the mind of man which, although suggested by, and in their forms dependent on, Experience, cannot yet be explained unless we attribute to the Thinking Faculty a proper and independent Modifying Force. Des Cartes himself did not think as Locke imagined he thought : and to that illustrious Man the first three chapters of the Essay have therefore no true reference. Following out his partial, because controversial, first view, Locke proceeds to unfold in what manner every recognized or defensible notion belonging to the Human Understanding may grow up in it. An imperfect first view, we have said—for while looking at the error he misses the truth of the Cartesians : he never even proposed to establish by a preliminary and rigorous analysis what those characteristics of our various classes of Ideas are of which every just philosophy must give an account. Missing therefore, not unnaturally, some of their main characteristics, confounding necessity and infinity with the simple attributes of generality and immensity, he proceeds to deduce all the forms and results of the Understanding

against that great philosopher, who was laboring to enlighten
and to ameliorate mankind? We really must not cramp

from our pure Sensations, and the operation on these of what he
terms Reflection. Closely scrutinized, Locke's Reflection amounts to
nothing more than the exercise of Memory, Comparison, and the processes known as Association. The exercise of the Mind as a voluntary Agency indeed seems to remain; but, as Leibnitz soon pointed
out, and as subsequent History showed, the descent from this
Scheme was easy towards the undisguised Sensationalism of Con-
dillac and the French School of the close of last century. To charge
John Locke—as sound and practical a thinker as ever lived—with the
extravagances of these hypothetic schemes were the worst injustice;
nevertheless there is no precaution against the largest excesses of
sensational philosophy in his mode of presenting the genesis of
human thought; and it cannot be gainsayed that the "Essay" in
several important directions has been the parent among ourselves
of as much mischief as could well find place amidst the realities of
the English mind. Utterly antagonistic to absolutism in thought or
life, not less repellent of the doctrines of Sir Robert Filmer than of
all theocratic dogmatism, this remarkable work seemed, however, to
harmonize with our notions of rational liberty; and it became the
favorite text-book of our best men during the difficult periods when
Locke wrote. Himself practically imbued with the sense of person-
ality and independence in all things, our Philosopher stood by
constitutional Liberty, suffered with it, and shared its triumphs.
Menaced by the Court party—as corrupt a court as the sun ever shone
on then reigned in England—he withdrew to Holland, and for a time
found shelter. During this voluntary exile his name was erased
from the roll of the Students of Christ Church, Oxford, in consequence
of a Royal Mandate; and the spirit of persecution went so far as to
demand the rendition of our philosopher from the States General.
Better times, however, were dawning on England. At the Revolution in 1688 Locke returned in the fleet that brought home our future
queen, the Princess of Orange; and henceforward his career was
prosperous. His residence in Holland, however, was not without
avail to him. Associating chiefly with dissentient Protestants, he
acquired a truer notion of that cardinal principle on the strength of
which alone Protestantism can live; and he showed this in his Letters on Toleration, as well as in the just freedom of his Exegesis.—
It is seldom that a personal History so much delights one as that of
John Locke. Not only can no one discern a stain on the nature and
career of the great Englishman, but his practical career is everywhere in strictest accordance with the principles he labored to
establish. Firmly attached to the cause of Toleration, civil or religious, he scrupled not to suffer for either; nor did his opposition to
any faction ever drive him from moderation and justice, disincline
him to appreciate his opponents aright or to conceal the excesses of
the party whose fortunes he mainly espoused. He accepted Human
Liberty as a basis of his philosophy, and practically stood by that.

observations upon authors and their works. Every man who publishes a book commits himself to the judgment of the public, and any one may comment upon his performance. He may not only be refuted, but turned into ridicule if his blunders are ridiculous. Reflection on personal character is another thing. Show me any attack on the plaintiff's character unconnected with his authorship, and I shall be as ready to protect him; but I cannot hear of malice from merely laughing at his works. The works may be very valuable for anything I know to the contrary, but others have a right to pass judgment upon them. The critic does a great service to society who exposes vapid as well as mischievous publications. He checks the dissemination of bad taste, and saves his fellow subjects from wasting their time and their money upon trash. If a loss arises to the author, it is a loss without injury; it is a loss which the party ought to sustain; it is the loss of fame and profit to which he never was entitled. Nothing can be conceived more threatening to the liberty of the press than the species of action before the Court. We ought to resist an attempt against fair and free criticism at the threshold." [1] [*Verdict for the Defendants.*]

A good specimen of Lord Ellenborough's *nisi prius* Trespass manner in his opinion upon the question, whether a by balloons considered. man by nailing to his own wall a board which overhangs his neighbor's field is liable to an action of trespass:

" I do not think it is a trespass to interfere with the column of air superincumbent on the close of another. I once had occasion to rule on the circuit that a man who from the outside ·of a field discharged a gun into it, so that the shot must have struck the soil, was guilty of breaking and entering it. A very learned Judge who went the circuit with me, having at first doubted the decision, afterwards approved of it, and I believe that it met with the general concurrence of those to whom it was mentioned. But I am by no means prepared to say that firing across a field *in vacuo*, no part of the contents

Few writers, before or since, in England have had a finer sense of the respect owing to the determinations of the personal Conscience.— The student is specially recommended to the admirable life of John Locke by Lord King.—*Dict. of Univ. Biog.*

1. *Carr* v. *Hood* and another, 1 Campb. 355.

touching it, amounts to a *clausum fregit.* Nay, if this board commits a trespass by overhanging the plaintiff's field, the consequence is that an aeronaut is liable to an action of trespass at the suit of the occupier of every house and inch of ground over which his balloon passes in the course of his voyage. Whether the action lies or not, cannot depend upon the length of time for which the superincumbent air is invaded. If any damage arises from the overhanging substance, the remedy is by an action on the case."[1]

Privilege of counsel to criminate an attorney   Peter Hodgson, an attorney, having sued Mr. Scarlett, the celebrated counsel (afterwards Lord Abinger and Chief Baron of the Exchequer), for speaking these words, " Mr. Hodgson is a fraudulent and wicked attorney," it appears that the words were spoken in an address to the jury in a trial involving the good faith of a transaction which Mr. Hodgson had conducted:

Lord Ellenborough.—" The law privileges many communications which otherwise might be considered calumnious, and become the subject of an action. In the case of master and servant the convenience of mankind requires that what is said in fair communication between man and man, upon the subject of character, should be privileged if made *bonâ fide* and without malice. So a counsel intrusted with the interests of others, and speaking from their information, for the sake of public convenience, is privileged in commenting fairly on the circumstances of the case, and in making observations on the parties concerned and their agents in bringing the cause into court. Now the plaintiff in this case was not only the attorney, but was mixed up in the concoction of the antecedent facts, out of which the original cause arose. It was in commenting on this conduct that the words were used by the defendant. Perhaps they were too strong, but the counsel might *bonâ fide* think them justifiable and appropriate. They were relevant and pertinent to the original cause in which they were spoken, and consequently this action is not maintainable."[2]

Richard Thornton having been tried at Warwick

1. *Pickering* v. *Rudd,* 4 Campb. 220.
2. *Hodgson* v. *Scarlett,* 1 Barn. and Ald. 232.

upon an indictment, in the King's name, for the murder
of Mary Ashford, and found *Not Guilty* by the jury,
William Ashford, her brother and heir-at-law, sued out
an appeal of murder against him. The appellee being
brought by writ of *habeas corpus* into the Court of
King's Bench to plead, he pleaded *vivâ voce* as follows :
" Not Guilty, and I am ready to defend the same by
my body," and thereupon taking off a gauntlet which
he wore from his right hand, he threw it on the floor
of the court. The appellor having obtained time for
that purpose, with a view to deprive the appellee of the
privilege of trial by battle, put in a counter-plea, setting
forth evidence of circumstances tending strongly to
prove his guilt. To this the appellee put in a replication, setting forth facts in his favor, and his former
acquittal. The appellor demurred. The question was
then very learnedly argued, whether upon this record
the appellee was entitled to insist upon trial by battle ?

Lord Ellenborough.—" The cases which have been cited in
this argument, and the others to which we ourselves have referred, show very distinctly that the general mode of trial by
law in a case of appeal is by *battle*, at the election of the appellee, unless the case be brought within certain exceptions—
as for instance, where the appellee is an infant, or a woman, or
above sixty years of age—or where the appellee is taken with
the manor, or has broken prison. In addition to all these,—
where, from evidence which may be adduced, there is a violent
presumption of guilt against the appellee, which cannot be re-
butted. Without going at length into the discussion of the
circumstances disclosed by the counter-plea and replication, it
is quite sufficient to say that this case is not like those in
Bracton,[1] it is not one with conclusive evidence of guilt. Con-

1. Henry de Bracton, an English lawyer, was a native of Devonshire, and bred at Oxford, where he was created doctor of civil law.
Applying himself afterwards to the study of the laws of England, he
rose to great eminence at the bar, and in 1244 was by King Henry
III. made one of the judges itinerant. At present he is chiefly
known by his learned work "De legibus et consuetudinibus Angliæ,"
first printed 1569, and reprinted 1640. It is a finished and systematic

trary evidence must be admitted if there were a trial by jury. The consequence is, that trial by battle having been duly demanded, this is the legal and constitutional mode of trial, and it must be awarded. The law of the land is in favor of the trial by battle, and it is our duty to pronounce the law as it is, and not as we may wish it to be. Whatever prejudices therefore may justly exist against this mode of trial, still as it is the law of the land the Court must pronounce judgment for it."

The public now expected to see the lists prepared in Tothill Fields, and the *battle* fought out before the Judges, for whom a special tribunal was to have been erected; but the appellor, who was much inferior in strength to the appellee, cried *craven*, and declining to proceed, the appellee was discharged.[1]

LordEllen-
borough in
the House
of Lords.

Bidding adieu to pure law, which I am afraid may be thought by many " rough and crabbed," I must now present Lord Ellenborough to my readers as a Peer of Parliament, and give some account of trials before him of a political and historical aspect. Some expected that he would have great success in the Upper House, —and, as often as he spoke there, he made a considerable sensation by his loud tones and strong expressions; but he was not listened to with much favor, for their lordships thought that he was not sufficiently refined and polished for their delicate ears, and they complained that he betrayed a most unjudicial violence.

His maiden
speech.

May 13,
1802.

His maiden speech, which gave an alarming earnest of these faults, was in the debate on the definitive treaty of peace with France. Having apologized to another

performance, giving a complete view of the law as it stood at the time the work was composed. Bracton was deservedly looked up to as the first source of legal knowledge, even as late as the days of Sir Edward Coke, who took this author as his guide in all his inquiries into the foundation of our law.—*Cooper's Biog. Dict.*

1. *Ashford* v. *Thornton*, 1 Barn. and Ald. 405. In consequence of the scandal occasioned by this case, stat. 59 Geo. III. c. 46 was passed, abolishing criminal appeals, and trial by battle in writs of right which till then might have been demanded.

Peer, who had risen and begun to speak at the same CHAP.
time with him, and expressed his extreme reluctance to XLXI.
obtrude himself upon their Lordships so very soon
after taking his seat among them,—he addressed himself to Lord Grenville's objection, that, contrary to
usage, and sound diplomacy, this treaty did not renew
or recognize former treaties:

"With regard to the noble Lord's argument, that by the
omission the public law of Europe has become a dead letter, I
am astonished to observe a man of talents fall into such a mistake. To what use would the revival of all the solemn nonsense and important absurdity contained in those treaties have
contributed? Are they not replete with articles totally inap-
plicable to the present situation of Europe, and are they not
for this reason become unintelligible trash and absolute waste
paper? With respect to the Cape of Good Hope, the cession
of which is so much deplored, I say, my Lords, that we are well
rid of it. There is no advantage in that post, and the expense
of it would have been so great that the country would soon
have complained of its retention."

So he went over all the articles of the treaty, and
concluded with expressing his warm thanks to the ministers—

"who had taken the helm of State when others had abandoned
it, and who had restored the blessings of peace to their exhausted country." [1]

This bullying style of oratory was not favorably received, but, luckily for the orator, on this occasion he
could do no harm, Whigs as well as Ministerialists being determined to vote for the treaty,—and the minority of violent anti-Gallicans who censured it amounted
only to sixteen. [2]

Lord Ellenborough was quite insensible of the impression made by his violence, and soon after, there
being an attack on ministers, he began his defence of

1. 36 Parl. Hist. 718.
2. *Ibid.*, 738.

them by saying that "he could not sit silent when he heard the capacity of able men arraigned by those who were themselves most incapable, and when he saw ignorance itself pretending to decide on exuberant knowledge possessed and displayed by others."[1] The Chief Justice of England being a peer may, with propriety and effect, take part in the debates of the House of Lords on important questions of statesmanship, such as the causes of war and the conditions of peace, but he should comport himself rather as a judge calmly summing up evidence and balancing arguments, than as the retained advocate of the Government or of the Opposition.

His ex-
posure of
the Athol
job.
Lord Ellenborough, till he himself became a cabinet minister, did not again break out with violence, save in opposing a job so gross that he was rather applauded for boldly pronouncing its true character. The Athol family, for certain rights in the Isle of Man, of which they were deprived, had been superabundantly compensated ; but many years after the bargain into which they had voluntarily and gratefully entered, they made a claim for further compensation,—which the Government, at a time when prodigality of expenditure ranked among ministerial virtues, was disposed to grant. A bill was introduced into parliament for the purpose, and this bill, without Lord Ellenborough's determined opposition to it, would have been quietly smuggled through. He began by moving that certain additional papers upon the subject should be printed, and that the second reading of the bill should be postponed till there might be an opportunity of perusing and considering them. This was resisted by the Earl of Westmoreland :

Lord Ellenborough.—" My Lords, when I look at the papers just now printed, and still reeking from the press, so that I can-

1. 36 Parl. Hist. 1572.

not open them without endangering my health—when I look at a folio volume of 140 uncut pages, presented this day by the noble Earl, I cannot but enter my solemn protest against pretending to debate the merits of this bill under such circumstances—against a proceeding which could only be sanctioned by parliament in the worst and most corrupt times. I do not ask for a long delay, but I hope that noble Lords will consult their own dignity, and show some deference to public opinion, by granting a short time for gaining necessary information, that we may see whether we are not robbing the Exchequer to put the plunder into the pocket of an accomplice. I pause for a reply. [Having sat down for a few moments he thus resumed.] Then I am to understand, my Lords, that it is your intention to proceed with this bill to-night. With the imperfect lights I have, I shall try and expose to you some of the deformities of the bill. In the first three lines of the preamble, it tells three lies. The Isle of Man was never granted in sovereignty by the King of England, but to be held in petty sergeanty by the presentation of two falcons to the King at his coronation. This must have been known to the author of the bill—yet 'like a tall bully'—I will not finish the line. When the noble Earl talks of acts of parliament not binding the Isle of Man, I am astonished at the puerility of the argument ; if Acts of Parliament cannot bind the Isle of Man, the Act passed in 1765 for the purchase of the Isle is a nullity. Then we have the assertion that the compensation given to the late Duke of Athol was inadequate. The late Duke named his own sum,[1] and in the course of forty years his family have re-

1. John Murray, third Duke of Athol (1729-1774), eldest son of Lord George Murray, by his wife Amelia only surviving child and heiress of James Murray of Glencarse and Strowan, was born May 6, 1729. For some time he was captain in a company of Lord Loudoun's regiment of foot, afterwards the 54th. At the general election in 1761 he was chosen member of parliament for Perth. On the death of his uncle James, second Duke of Athol, Jan. 8, 1764, Murray, who besides being nearest male heir, had married Lady Charlotte Murray, the Duke's only surviving child, laid claim to the dukedom of Athol. As, however, his father, Lord George Murray, had been forfeited, he deemed it advisable to petition the King that his claim to the dukedom might be allowed. The petition was referred by the King to the House of Lords, who on Feb. 7, 1764, resolved that he had a right to the title. His wife, on the death of her father, the second duke, succeeded to the sovereignty of the Isle of

ceived 177,000*l.* more than they were entitled to. You propose to open on its hinges a door to fraud, which, like a door
described in 'Paradise Lost,' if once opened will never be shut
again. Never did I witness a gross job present itself in parliament in such a bodily form as this. In a few days parliament will be dispersed, and let us not return to our respective
homes with the stigma of having passed such a bill. Let us
not at a moment like this, when all classes are ground down
with taxes, add to their burdens by voting a boon to mendi-
cant importunity. If indeed our supplies were unlimited, if
we could draw upon them without any fear of exhaustion, if
the resources of the stage grew like the fabled Promethean
liver under the beaks and talons of the vultures by whom they
are lacerated and devoured, then indeed we might yield to this
demand. The times are critical ; our dangers are great—the
state of our finances is hopeless ; let us not, my Lords, imitate
the conduct of reckless sailors in a storm, who, when they see
the vessel driving on the rocks, instead of trying to save her,
throw up the helm, abandon the sails, and fall to breaking
open the lockers. If we would avoid the thunderbolts of
divine vengeance which seem ready to burst upon us, let us
rather deck ourselves in the robes of virtue, and with the love
of God let us try to recover the love of the people, of whom

Man, and to the ancient English barony of Strange, of Knockyn,
Wotton, Mohun, Burnel, Basset, and Lacy. For some time negotiations had been in progress with the English government for the
union of the sovereignty to the English crown ; and in 1765 an act
of parliament was passed to give effect to a contract between the
lords of the treasury and the Duke and Duchess of Athol for the
purchase of the sovereignty of Man and its dependencies for
70,000*l.*, the Duke and Duchess retaining their manorial rights, the
patronage of the bishopric and other ecclesiastical benefices, the
fisheries, minerals, etc. The arrangement rendered them very unpopular in Man, and the 42d, or Black Watch under Lord John
Murray, had to be stationed in the island to maintain order. The
money received by the Duke and Duchess was directed to be laid
out and invested in the purchase of lands of inheritance in Scotland,
to be inalienably entailed on a certain series of heirs. The Duke
and Duchess had also a grant of an annuity of 2000*l.* for their lives.
Athol was chosen a representative peer in succession to the Earl of
Sutherland, who died Aug. 21, 1764, and he was rechosen in 1768.
In 1767 he was invested with the Order of the Thistle. He died at
Dunkeld on Nov. 5, 1774, and was succeeded by his son John, fourth
Duke of Athol.—*Nat. Biog. Dict.*

we ought to be the protectors, not the spoliators. Be the
event what it may, *liberavi animam meam.*"[1]

Several "silken barons" having complained of this
language as too strong and unparliamentary, Lord
Ellenborough said, " The attack made upon me would
have been just had I said anything wantonly to give
pain to any noble Lord ; but my observations were applied to the measure, not to any individual whatever;
and by no milder words than those I used could the
measure be truly characterized."[2]

When the war was renewed after the truce follow- Right of
the Crown
ing the supposed treaty of peace signed at Amiens,[3] to the
military
services of
all subjects.

1. " I have freed my mind."

2. 5 Parl. Deb. 773-792. After all, to the great discredit of Mr.
Pitt's second administration, the bill passed.

3. Treaty of Amiens (March 25, 1802), between England and
France, put an end for the time to the great war which had lasted since
1793. The mutual losses during the preceding years, the complete
supremacy of the English fleet, and the blow given to the northern
alliance by the battle of Copenhagen, and, on the other hand, the de-
feats inflicted on England's Continental ally, Austria, in 1800, and the
Treaty of Luneville, which she concluded with France, Feb. 9, 1801,
led both governments to desire a cessation of hostilities. The treaty
was the work of the Addington ministry. In the previous October
the preliminaries had been agreed to and signed, but some troublesome negotiations had to be gone through, before it was finally rati-
fied at Amiens, by Lord Cornwallis on the part of England, and by
Joseph Bonaparte, assisted by Talleyrand, for France. According
to it, England gave up all its conquests but Trinidad and Ceylon.
The Cape of Good Hope was restored to the Dutch, but was
to be a free port. Malta was to go back to the Knights of St.
John, under the guarantee of one of the great powers. "Cet
article est le plus important de tout le traité, mais aucune des
conditions qu'il renferme n'a été exécutée; et il est devenu le
pretexte d'une guerre qui s'est renouvelée en 1803, et a duré sans
interruption jusqu'en 1814." (*Histoire des Traités*, vi. 149). Porto
Ferrajo was to be evacuated. On the other hand, the Republic
of the Ionian Islands was acknowledged: the French were to withdraw from Naples and the Roman States ; the integrity of Portugal
was to be guaranteed; Egypt was to be restored to the Porte; and,
finally, the Newfoundland fisheries were to be placed on the same
footing as they held before the war began. These terms, as noticed
above, were not considered sufficiently satisfactory by the English;
consequently the peace was of very short duration, war being
declared against Bonaparte in 1803.—*Dict. of Eng. Hist.*

Lord Ellenborough, in supporting the Volunteer Con-
solidation Bill, very stoutly defended the prerogative
of the Crown to call out the whole population for the
defence of the realm :

"In an age of adventurous propositions," said he, " I did
not expect that any noble Lord would have ventured to question this radical, essential, unquestionable, and hitherto-never-
questioned prerogative.   My Lords, from the earliest period of
our history we have been a military people ; and this right,
inherent in the Crown from the Norman Conquest, cannot be
abandoned without an act of political suicide.   I hold in my
hand a copy of the Commission of array passed in the fifth year
of Henry IV., referred to By Lord Coke in his Fourth Institute, written in the reign of James I., acknowledged by him to
be law, and never since repealed or modified.   Here, my
Lords, we have a solemn recognition of the power of the
Sovereign to require in case of insurrection, or the apprehension of invasion, the services of all his subjects capable
of bearing arms—in the words of the Commission, *potentes et
habiles in corpore.*   This power, my Lords, is inherent in the
supreme executive government in every state.   Vattel[1] and
the other writers on the Law of Nations are unanimous in
saying that the power exists in all countries, royal or repub-
lican, which have anything like civilized rule.   As to the noble
Lord's supposition that this prerogative enables the King to
throw all classes indiscriminately into the ranks, I say such an
abuse of it is not necessary, and would not be tolerated ; men
upon the contemplated emergency are to be employed accord-

1. Emrich von Vattel, a celebrated Swiss jurist and writer, born in
the principality of Neufchâtel in 1817.   He studied at the Universi-
ties of Bâle and Geneva, and in 1741 visited Berlin, where he
published his "Defence of the System of Leibnitz," (in French,
1742), dedicated to Frederick the Great.   In 1746 he was sent as
Polish minister to Berne by Augustus, Elector of Saxony and King
of Poland.   He published in 1758 his principal work, entitled "The
Right of Nations, or the Principles of Natural Law applied to the
Conduct and Affairs of Nations and Sovereigns," which has passed
through numerous editions and been translated into the principal
European languages.   He was the author of other works on various
subjects, the most important of which is entitled "Questions of
Natural Law, and Observations on Wolff's Treatise on the Law of
Nature" (1762).   Died in 1767.—*Thomas' Biog. Dict.*

ing to their habits of life, and to the modes in which they would be most useful. But I trust that in case of extreme necessity no individual who bears the semblance of a man, who values his country and his domestic ties, and who knows his duty to fight body to body, *pro aris et focis*,[1] will stickle about the mode in which his energies can be most advantageously brought into action. My Lords, unfitted even as I am by education and habit for a campaign, yet in such a case of extreme necessity I should not think I did my duty to my country or to my children, if I did not cast this gown from my back, and employ every faculty of my mind and of my body to grapple with the enemy."

His martial ardor was much applauded, and appeared the more wonderful from his speaking on this and all other occasions in the House of Lords attired in his black silk robes and with a judicial wig.[2] His hearers likewise recollected the well-known fact that when Attorney-General he had enlisted in a volunteer corps, and had never been promoted to the ranks out of the awkward squad, the drill-serjeant having in vain tried by chalk and other appliances to make him understand the difference between his right foot and his left, or with which of them he was to step forward on hearing the word " MARCH!"

The only other considerable speech which he made before Mr. Pitt's death was against Lord Grenville's motion for a committee on the Catholic Petition, when he so violently opposed any further concession to the Roman Catholics, that the public were much surprised to find him sitting, soon after, in the same Cabinet with Lord Grenville and Charles Fox. We cannot be surprised that this Cabinet was so short-lived, although it contained "all the talents" of the country. Lord Ellenborough very sensibly and forcibly pointed out on

His hostility to the Roman Catholics.

1. "For altars and homes," *i. e.*, for God and his country.
2. Lord Denman was the first Chief Justice who appeared in the House of Lord *en bourgeois*.

CHAP.
XLIX.

this occasion the inconvenience arising from giving power to religionists owning the supremacy of a foreign pontiff; but he caused a smile when, in describing the danger of the Pope again subjecting Great Britian to his sway, he quoted the lines—

> " Jam tenet Italiam, tamen ultra pergere tendit
> Actum inquit nihil est, nisi Pœno milite portas
> Frangimus et mediâ vexillum pono suburrâ." [1]

Trial of
Colonel
Despard for
treason.

Although Lord Ellenborough's success as a debater in the House of Lords was doubtful, he was securing to himself a great reputation as a Criminal Judge. He presided with applause at the trial of Colonel Despard for high treason in plotting the insane scheme to establish a republic after massacring the King, the royal family, and the greatest number of the members of both Houses of Parliament. I was present at

Feb. 7,
1803.

this trial, and well remember the Chief Justice's very dignified, impressive, and awe-inspiring deportment. He caused some dissatisfaction by thus abruptly and sarcastically snubbing the great Nelson,[2] who, when

1. This appears much less absurd now, after Pio Nono's creation of the archbishopric of Westminster, and his partition of all England into Roman Catholic sees —*September*, 1855.
"Now he holds Italy, yet he aims to pursue his conquests further; he says nothing has been accomplished, unless we break through the gates with the Phœnician soldiery, and place the standard in the middle of the Subura."

2. Horatio, Viscount Nelson, (*b*. 1758, *d*. 1805) was the son of the Rector of Burnham Thorpe in Norfolk. He went to school first at Norwich, and afterwards at North Walsham. In 1771 he went to sea with his uncle in the *Raisonnable*, but soon returned, and was commissioned to the *Triumph* at Chatham. In 1773 his uncle's influence obtained a place for him in an expedition to the Arctic Seas. The expedition was at one time in great danger, but eventually returned in safety. He was then ordered to the East Indies, where, after serving eighteen months, he was invalided home. In 1777 he received his commission as second lieutenant of the *Lowestoffe*, ordered to Jamaica. In the West Indies he soon became noticeable for his bravery and application, and in December, 1778, he was appointed to command the *Badger*, from which he was transferred in the following June as post-captain to the *Hinchinbrook*. In the spring of 1780 he was appointed to command an expedition against San Juan

NELSON BRONTE.

called to give the prisoner a character, was proceeding to describe his gallant conduct in several actions: " I

in the Isthmus of Panama. The expedition ended in failure, not through any fault of Nelson's, but on account of the deadly nature of the climate, against which only 380 out of 1800 men were proof. Nelson himself was so shattered by the exertions he had gone through that he had to go to England to recruit his health. In 1783 he was appointed to the *Boreas* bound for the West Indies, where he found himself senior captain. In this position he became involved in some troublesome disputes, and finally in a lawsuit, owing to his determination to enforce the Navigation Act. On the breaking out of the French War in 1793 he was appointed to the *Agamemnon*, of sixty-four guns, to proceed to the Mediterranean. In 1796 Sir John Jervis took the command in the Mediterranean, and Nelson became at the same time commodore. After various encounters with Span-ish and French ships, he joined the main fleet off Cape St. Vincent, where, on February 14, 1797, he took a conspicuous part in the great battle, and contributed much to the victory. Nelson was now ad-vanced to the rank of rear-admiral, and commanded the inner squad-ron at the blockade of Cadiz. In July he conducted a night attack on Santa Cruz, which failed through the darkness ; Nelson himself lost his right arm. Early in the following year he rejoined Lord St. Vincent in the *Vanguard*, and was immediately despatched in com-mand of a small squadron to watch the movements of the French fleet in the Mediterranean. On August 1 he came in sight of them anchored in Aboukir Bay, near Alexandria. He at once attacked with such fury and skill that, after the battle had raged all night, the whole French fleet, with the exception of four ships, was either taken or destroyed. The victory was hailed with delight in Eng-land, where honors were showered upon Nelson from all sides, and he was created Baron Nelson. There was work for him next to do at Naples in trying to strengthen that kingdom to resist France. At Naples Nelson's infatuation for Lady Hamilton led him to bolster up the decaying monarchy of the Bourbons, and to commit the only act of injustice recorded of him—the execution of Caraccioli. In the spring of the year 1800 Nelson returned to England, and in the fol-lowing year he was sent as second in command under Sir Hyde Parker to the Baltic, and on April 2 bore the chief part in the bom-bardment of Copenhagen. Nelson was made a viscount, and on the recall of Sir Hyde Parker was left in sole command. On his return to England he was at once appointed to a command extending from Orford Ness to Beachy Head. He organized an attack on the flotilla lying at Boulogne, but the expedition failed in its immediate object, though it had the effect of terrifying the French. On the war breaking out afresh in 1803 he was appointed to the command of the Mediterranean fleet, and took his station off Toulon. From May, 1803, to August, 1805, Nelson left his ship only three times, so con-stant was his watch for an opportunity of engaging the enemy. But when the alliance of Spain and France was concluded, Napoleon deam sorry to be obliged to interrupt your Lordship, but we cannot hear what I dare say your Lordship would give with great effect, the history of this gentleman's military life."

At two in the morning I saw the Chief Justice put on the black cap to pronounce the awful sentence of the law on Colonel Despard[1] and his associates, and I heard him utter these thrilling sentences:

" After a long and I trust a patient and impartial trial, you have been severally convicted of the high treasons charged

termined to carry out his long-intended invasion of England. The combined fleets put out of port. Nelson went in search of them. From January to April, 1805, he beat about the Mediterranean ; then pursued them to the West Indies. Here they were in advance of him, and he was baffled by conflicting accounts of their movements. At length he followed them northwards, and on July 19 anchored off Gibraltar, but could hear no tidings of them. Unrelentingly he resumed his search round the Bay of Biscay and the coast of Ireland, and returning, joined Admiral Cornwallis off Ushant on August 15, where he received orders to proceed to Portsmouth. There he learnt that Admiral Calder had fallen in with them off Cape Finisterre on July 22, and that they had put into Vigo to refit. He again offered his services, which were eagerly accepted, and on September 29 he was off Cadiz. Villeneuve hesitated to obey peremptory orders to put to sea, but at length he ventured out, and on October 21 gave Nelson his long-wished-for opportunity. The fleets met off Trafalgar, and in the battle which ensued the French and Spanish fleets were utterly destroyed. The victory was, however, only obtained at the cost of Nelson's life. He died at the early age of forty-seven. " Yet," as Southey says, " he cannot be said to have fallen prematurely, whose work was done."—*Dict. of Eng. Hist.*

1. Edward Marcus Despard, an Irishman, who early entered upon a military life, and became an able engineer. At the close of the American war he served in the West Indies, where he distinguished himself by an expedition on the Spanish main, in which he had for a coadjutor Captain, afterwards Lord, Nelson. For his services there he was made lieutenant-colonel. In 1784 he was appointed English superintendent at Honduras ; but his conduct causing him to be suspended, he demanded an investigation. This, however, was refused him, when he became violent against the government and was sent to Coldbath Fields prison, whence he was removed to the House of Industry at Shrewsbury, and next to Tothill Fields, Bridewell. On his liberation he attempted to seduce the soldiery, and having collected some followers, held meetings at alehouses, to which no persons were admitted without taking a treasonable oath. At these assemblies it is said that various plans were devised for

upon you by the indictment. In the course of the evidence
which has been laid before the Court, a treasonable conspiracy has been disclosed of enormous extent and most alarming magnitude. The object of that conspiracy, in which you have borne your several very active and criminal parts, has been to overthrow and demolish the fundamental laws and established government of your country; to seize upon and destroy the sacred person of our revered and justly-beloved Sovereign; to murder the various members of his royal house; to extinguish the other branches of the legislature of this realm, and, instead of the ancient limited monarchy, its free and wholesome laws, its approved usages, its useful gradations of rank, its natural and inevitable as well as desirable inequalities of property, to substitute a wild scheme of impracticable equality, holding out, for the purpose of carrying this scheme into effect, a vain and delusive promise of provision for the families of the *heroes* (falsely so called) *who should fall in the contest*—a scheme equally destructive of the interests and happiness of those who should mischievously struggle for its adoption as of those who should be the victims of its intended execution. This plan has been sought to be carried into effect in the first place by the detestable seduction of unwary soldiers from their sworn duty and allegiance to his Majesty and by the wicked ensnaring of their consciences by the supposed obligation of an impious and unauthorized oath, and next by the industrious association to this purpose of the most needy or the most unprincipled persons in the lowest ranks of society. It is, however, wisely ordained by Divine Providence, for the security and happiness of mankind, that the rashness of such counsels does for the most part counteract and defeat the effects of their malignity, and that the wickedness of the contrivers falls ultimately upon their own heads, affording at the same time the means of escape and security to the intended victims of their abominable contrivances. The leagues of such associates are at all times false and hollow. They begin in treachery to their king and country, and they end in schemes of treachery towards each other. In the present instance your crimes have

the murder of the King; and, at last, it was determined to make the attack when his majesty went to the Parliament House. The plot being discovered, he and several other persons were arrested, and being found guilty, suffered on the scaffold in 1803.—*Beeton's Biog. Dict.*

been disclosed and frustrated through the operation of the same passions, motives, and instruments by which they were conceived, prepared, forwarded, and nearly matured for their ultimate and most destructive accomplishment. Upon the convicted contrivers and instruments of this dangerous but abortive treason it remains for me to perform the last painful part of my official duty. As to you, Colonel Edward Marcus Despard, born as you were to better hopes, intended and formed, as it should seem, by Providence for better ends ; accustomed as you have hitherto been to better habits of life and manners, pursuing as you once did, together with the honorable companions of your former life and services (who have appeared as witnesses to your character during that period), the virtuous objects of loyal and laudable ambition ; I will not at this moment point out to you how much all these considerations and the degraded and ignominious fellowship in which you now stand enhance the particular guilt of your crime, sharpening and embittering, as I know they must, in the same proportion the acuteness and pungency of your present sufferings. I entreat you, however, by the memory of what you once were, to excite and revive in your mind an ardent and unceasing endeavor and purpose during the short period of your remaining life to subdue that callous insensibility of heart of which, in an ill-fated hour, you have boasted, and to regain that salutary and more softened disposition of the heart and affections which I trust you once had, and which may enable you to work out that salvation which, from the infinite mercy of God, may even yet be attainable by effectual penitence and prevailing prayers. As to you, John Wood (naming eight others), the sad victims of his seduction and example, or of your own wicked, discontented, and disloyal purposes, you afford a melancholy but I hope an instructive example to all persons in the same class and condition with yourselves—an example to deter them by the calamitous consequences which presently await your crimes from engaging in the same mischievous and destructive counsels and designs which have brought you to this untimely and ignominious end. May they learn properly to value the humble but secure blessings of an industrious and quiet life, and of an honest and loyal course of conduct—all which blessings you have in an evil hour wilfully cast from you. The same recommendation which

I have already offered to the leader in your crimes and the companion in your present sufferings as to the employment of the short remainder of your present existence I again repeat, and earnestly recommend to every one of you ; and may your sincere and deep penitence obtain for you all hereafter that mercy which a due and necessary regard to the interest and security of your fellow-creatures will not allow of your receiving here. It only remains for me to pronounce the sentence of the law upon the crime of which you are convicted. That sentence is, and this Court doth adjudge that, &c."

Then came the dreadful enumeration of the barbarities which the law at that time adjudged to be inflicted on traitors—now commuted for hanging and beheading.[1]

Colonel Despard and six of his associates actually were executed ;—and, the revolting parts of the sentence being remitted, the public did not complain of undue severity. The temptation to engage in such conspiracies, which promise suddenly to elevate those who engage in them to power, wealth, and fame, cannot be counteracted by the dread, on failure, as a term of imprisonment, or even of transportation with the hope of a speedy recall. An attempt for selfish purposes to overturn the monarchy and to inundate the country with blood cannot be leniently treated as a mere " political offence."

Lord Ellenborough was soon after placed in a most difficult situation on a trial for libel, the prosecutor being no other than Napoleon Buonaparte. This autocrat having extinguished liberty in France and conquered the continent of Europe, was resolved to put down free discussion in England, as a preliminary to the extension of his empire over the British Isles. He was galled by the severe strictures on his conduct which appeared in the London journals, and he remonstrated upon the subject to our ministers, but received for answer that

Trial of Peltier for a libel on Napoleon Buonaparte.

1. 28 St. Tr. 315–528.

the law, which in England is supreme, gave them no power to interfere. At last there came out in the AMBIGU, a periodical in the French language, published in London by M. Peltier, a French emigrant, a poem and other articles, which in one sense might be construed into an exhortation to assassinate the First Consul. A new representation was made by the French ambassador, and the Attorney-General was directed to file a criminal information against the Editor. The most objectionable passage contained the following allusion to the fabled death and apotheosis of Romulus:

" Il est proclamé Chef et Consul pour la vie . . . . . .
Pour moi, loin qu'à son sort je porte quelque envie,
Qu'il nomme, j'y consens, son digne successeur ;
Sur le pavois porté qu'on l'église EMPREUR ;
Enfin, et Romulus nous rappelle la chose,
Je fais vœu . . . dès demain qu'il ait *l'apothéose.*"

At the trial before Lord Ellenborough and a special jury, Mr. Perceval,[1] then Attorney General, soon after

1. Spencer Perceval (*b.* 1762, *d.* 1812), was the second son of John, Earl of Egmont, and was educated at Harrow and Trinity College, Cambridge. In 1786 he was called to the bar, and ten years later took silk. At the same time he entered parliament as M. P. for Northampton, and was soon noticed by Pitt as a promising member. In supporting the Treason and Sedition Bills he rendered good service to the government. Addington appointed Perceval his Solicitor-General, and in 1802 Attorney-General, in which capacity he had to conduct the prosecution of Peltier for a libel on Bonaparte, and in spite of the briliant defence of Sir James Mackintosh, he secured a verdict of guilty. He held that office until Pitt's death in 1806. In March, 1807, he became Chancellor of the Exchequer, and on the death of the Duke of Portland in 1809 he was named First Lord of the Treasury. At that time the war in the Peninsula was being carried on : Napoleon had as yet received no check on the Continent ; England was spending millions in encouraging the nations of Europe to offer an effectual resistance to him. Foreign politics were thus all engrossing, and scarcely any attention was paid to the reforms at home, which were so badly needed. For three years his ministry lasted, and then on May 11. 1812, he was shot by one Bellingham, in the lobby of the House of Commons. Nothing could have happened so opportunely for Perceval's reputation as his murder, which raised him to the position of a martyr. From having been really a minister of moderate abilities, by his death he suddenly became, in public estimation a political genius, a first-rate financier, and a powerful

prime minister, evidently ashamed of the task imposèd
upon him, tried to make out that the defendant really
wished to instigate assassination ; and Mackintosh,[1] in
one of the finest essays ever composed, argued that the
publications complained of were mere pieces of jocularity, and that it was the duty of the jury to resist this

orator. We can now look back more calmly and see in him a man
of shrewd sense, imperturbable temper, narrow views, and restless
ambition, which, to his credit, never led him astray from the path
of integrity.—*Dict. of Eng. Hist.*

1. Sir James Mackintosh, a distinguished author and statesman,
born at Aldowrie, near Inverness, Oct. 24, 1765. After having
studied at Aberdeen and Edinburgh he graduated in medicine 1787,
but subsequently chose the law as his profession. Previous to his
call to the bar he visited the Continent, and on his return published
his "Vindiciæ Gallicæ," 1791, in defence of the French Revolution
and its English admirers against the accusations of Mr. Burke. This
work produced a great sensation, and had the effect of materially
checking the tide of popular opinion, which then ran in favor of Mr.
Burke's sentiments. In 1799 Mackintosh delivered, in the hall of
Lincoln's Inn, a course of lectures on the Law of Nature and Nations.
in allusion to which Pitt said that " he had never met with anything
so able or so elegant on the subject in any language." In 1803 Mackintosh appeared as advocate on behalf of M. Peltier, who had been
indicted for a libel on the First Consul of France, and defended his
client in a speech which was pronounced by Lord Ellenborough to be
" the most eloquent oration he had ever heard in Westminster Hall."
On Dec. 21, 1803, he received the honor of knighthood, and was appointed recorder, or criminal judge, of Bombay, where he resided for
several years, distinguished by his temperate and impartial administration of justice, and his active zeal in behalf of literature and
science. In 1813 he was elected M. P. for Nairn, in Scotland, and he
continued to sit in the House of Commons till his death. Whilst in
parliament he supported all liberal measures ; but his efforts were
chiefly directed towards the amelioration of the criminal code, the
rigor of which he was one of the most active in opposing. In 1822
he was elected lord-rector of the university of Glasgow, and in the
following year was re-elected to the same dignity. In Dec., 1830, on
the formation of Earl Grey's administration, he was appointed one
of the commissioners for the affairs of India. Died May 30, 1832.
His principal works are "Vindiciæ Gallicæ," already noticed ; "Dis-
course on the Study of the Law of Nature and Nations ;" "Dissertation on Ethical Philosophy ;" "History of England, B.C. 55 to A.D.
1572," 3 vols. in Lardner's Cabinet Cyclopædia ; "Life of Sir Thomas
More ;" "History of the Revolution in England in 1688." His
Miscellaneous Works were published in 3 vols. 8vo., 1846.—*Cooper's
Biog. Dict.*

effort to enslave the press in the only country in which it could proclaim truth to the world.

Lord Ellenborough.—" Gentlemen, it is my duty to state to you that every publication which has a tendency to promote public mischief, whether by causing irritation in the minds of the subjects of this realm that may induce them to commit a breach of the public peace or may be injurious to the morals and religion of the country, is to be considered a libel. So, if it defames the characters of magistrates and others in high and eminent situations of power and dignity in other countries, expressed in such terms or in such a manner as to interrupt the friendly relations subsisting with foreign states in amity with us, every such publication is what the law calls a libel. Cases of this sort have occurred within all our memories. Lord George Gordon published a libel on the person and character of the Queen of France, and another person grossly vituperated Paul, the late Emperor of all the Russias. In both these cases there were prosecutions, convictions, and judgments, and I am not aware that the law on which these proceedings were founded was ever questioned. If the publication contains a plain and manifest incitement to assassinate magistrates, as the tendency of such a publication is to interrupt the harmony subsisting between the two nations, the libel assumes a more criminal complexion. What interpretation do you put on these words ?—' As for me, far from envying his lot, let him name, I consent to it, his worthy successor ; carried on the shield, let him be elected Emperor. Finally (Romulus recalls the thing to mind) I wish that on the morrow he may have his apotheosis.' This is a direct wish by the author, that if Buonaparte should be elected Emperor of that country, of which he then held the government, his death might be instantaneous—or that his destruction might follow on the next day. Everybody knows the supposed story of Romulus. He disappeared ; and his death was supposed to be the effect of assassination. If the words were equivocal and could bear two constructions, I should advise you to adopt the mildest ; but if these words can bear this sense and this only, we cannot trifle with our duty; we cannot invent or feign a signification or import which the fair sense of the words does not suggest."

He then proceeded to comment on other passages,
and according to the fashion which still prevailed under a supposed injunction of Mr. Fox's Libel Bill not to be found there, he declared that in his opinion the publication was libellous.   Thus he concluded :

"Gentlemen, I trust that your verdict will strengthen the relations by which the interests of this country are connected with those of France, and that it will illustrate and justify in every part of the world the unsullied purity of British Courts of Justice, and of the impartiality by which their decisions are uniformly governed."

In spite of a verdict of *Guilty*, which the jury under this direction immediately returned, hostilities were very soon renewed with France. Owing to this rupture the defendant was not called up to receive judgment—a very undignified course on the part of the Government ; for the prosecution, if justifiable, must be considered as having been commenced to vindicate the majesty of English law—not to humor the First Consul of the French republic.'

While Mr. Addington remained prime minister, Lord Ellenborough warmly supported him as a partisan ; but when Mr. Pitt resumed the helm, the Chief Justice confined himself almost entirely to the discharge of his official duties, and seemed to have renounced politics for ever.

1. 28 St. Tr. 529–620.

CHAPTER L.

CONTINUATION OF THE LIFE OF LORD ELLENBOROUGH
TILL THE TRIAL OF LORD COCHRANE.

CHAP.
L.
A.D. 1806.
The Chief
Justice a
member of
the Cabi-
net.

ON the death of Mr. Pitt, after the signal failure of his last confederacy for the humiliation of France, a new ministry was to be formed, and so deplorable was the state of public affairs, that the King's antipathy to Mr. Fox could no longer exclude him from office. Lord Ellenborough little thought that he himself could in any way be comprehended in the new arrangement. However, instead of forming a Cabinet of Lord Howick,[1] Lord Grenville, and those in whose principles

1. Charles Grey, second Earl, an eminent English statesman and champion of parliamentary reform, was the eldest son of the first Earl Grey. He was born at Fallowden, near Alnwick, in March, 1764, and educated at Cambridge. Entering parliament in 1786, as member for Northumberland, he became a constant supporter of the Whig party and a warm personal friend of Fox. He had won a prominent position by his splendid talents and eloquence, when he was appointed by the House a member of the committee to manage the impeachment of Warren Hastings, in 1788. "At twenty-three," says Macaulay, "he had been thought worthy to be ranked with the veteran statesmen who appeared as the delegates of the British Commons at the bar of the British nobility."

When the Whig party was disorganized by hostility to the French Revolution, Fox and Grey remained constant to their principles, and were the leaders of the opposition. Mr. Grey was one of the founders of the "Society of the Friends of the People," a political association formed in 1792 to promote reform in parliament. In the stormy and critical times which followed, when the more timid Whigs deserted to the dominant party, when liberal principles were stigmatized as Jacobinical, when the coercive policy of Pitt was supported by large majorities, Mr. Grey did not falter in his devotion to the popular cause. In 1793 he presented a petition for a change in the system of representation, and advocated it in an impressive speech. In

Mr. Fox agreed and with whom he had been lately
acting in opposition, it was arranged that there should

1797 he again made an unsuccessful effort for reform in the House of Commons. On the formation of the Whig ministry of Fox and Grenville, in 1806, Mr. Grey, who had recently received the title of Lord Howick, was appointed first lord of the admiralty. At the death of Fox, September, 1806, Lord Howick succeeded him as secretary of foreign affairs and leader in the House of Commons. The most memorable act of this brief ministry was the abolition of the slave-trade, which he cordially supported. The Whig cabinet was dissolved in March, 1807. In the same year, Lord Howick, at the death of his father, became Earl Grey, and a member of the House of Lords. In 1812 the prince-regent solicited Lords Grey and Grenville to accept places in his Tory cabinet; but they declined thus to sacrifice their consistency and principles, and continued to be the opposition leaders in the House of Lords. In 1829 Lord Grey concurred in the passage of the Catholic Emancipation Bill, which had long been a fundamental point in his political creed.

The cause of Reform in 1830 received a new impulse by the accession of William IV., and the second French revolution. Wellington was compelled to resign, and Earl Grey became premier, adopting for his policy peace, retrenchment, and reform. The first Reform bill having been defeated in 1831, the ministers dissolved parliament and appealed to the people, who returned to the new House a large majority of Liberals. A second bill passed the House of Commons, but was lost in the Upper House. The measure finally triumphed in June, 1832. The Reformed Parliament, which met in 1833, abolished colonial slavery and the monopoly of the East India Company. In consequence of dissensions in the cabinet, Lord Grey resigned in July, 1833. He died in 1845. He had married in 1784 Mary E. Ponsonby, and left eight sons, the eldest of whom is the third Earl Grey. —*Thomas's Biog. Dict.*

Macaulay, in his Essay on Warren Hastings, says : " Nor, though surrounded by such men, did the youngest manager pass unnoticed. At an age when most of those who distinguish themselves in life are still contending for prizes and fellowships at college, he had won for himself a conspicuous place in parliament. No advantage of fortune or connection was wanting that could set off to the height his splendid talents and his unblemished honor. At twenty-three he had been thought worthy to be ranked with the veteran statesmen who appeared as the delegates of the British Commons, at the bar of the British nobility. All who stood at that bar, save him alone, are gone, culprit, advocates, accusers. To the generation which is now in the vigor of life, he is the sole representative of a great age which has passed away. But those who, within the last ten years, have listened with delight, till the morning sun shone on the tapestries of the House of Lords, to the lofty and animated eloquence of Charles Earl Grey, are able to form some estimate of the powers of a race of men among whom he was not the foremost."

be a *broad bottom* administration, and that, to please the
King, Mr. Addington, now become Lord Sidmouth,
should be asked to join it. He refused to go in alone,
thinking that in that case he might be a cipher, and it
was conceded to him that he should bring in a friend
with him. He named Lord Ellenborough, to whom
personally no objection could be made. The Great Seal
was offered to the Chief Justice, and pressed upon him;
but he positively refused it, partly from a misgiving as
to his competency to preside in Equity, and still more
from a foreboding that the new ministry, although it
was to include "all the talents" of the country, might
be short lived. One great object which the Whigs had
in view was to make Erskine Chief Justice of the
King's Bench, an office for which he was allowed to be
eminently competent; whereas his qualifications for
the woolsack were deemed very doubtful. Lord Ellenborough advised that an attempt should be made to
induce Sir James Mansfield, the Chief Justice of the
Common Pleas, to take the Great Seal, that Erskine
might succeed him; but the offer being made, he at
once said " No!"—manfully giving as his reason to the
King and to his friends who pressed him to accept, that
all his children were illegitimate, although he had married their mother after their birth, and he would not
have their illegitimacy constantly proclaimed by accepting a peerage. Lord Ellenborough said "Nothing now
remains but for Erskine to become Chancellor himself"
—and he swore a great oath that he would make a very
fair one. With this assurance Fox and Grenville
assented to the appointment, and Erskine, considering
Equity mere play compared to the common law, very
readily acceded to it.

Lord Ellenborough announced his own determination in the following letter to his brother, the Bishop of
Elphin :

" MY DEAR BROTHER,

" I have not yet the means of communicating any
certain intelligence on the subject of Irish arrange-
ments, or should have written to you many days ago.
I presume that Lerd Redesdale will not retain the
Great Seal of Ireland. Public report gives it to Mr.
Ponsonby.[1]

" That of Great Britain was offered me last week
by Lord Grenville and Mr. Fox, but which for several
reasons both of duty, propriety, and prudence I declined. I have had the honor of being placed in the
cabinet without any wish on my part, and indeed
against my wishes—but a sense both of public and private duty has obliged me to accept a situation for the
present, which I could not have refused without materially disturbing an arrangement which is, I think,
necessary for the public interests at the present moment. I assure you that I have no motive of ambition
or interest inducing me to mix in politics, and will not
suffer myself to bear any part in them which can trench

1. George Ponsonby, Lord Chancellor of Ireland, the third son
of John Ponsonby, was born, March 5, 1755. His brother William
Brabazon Ponsonby was the first baron Ponsonby. After an education received partly at home and partly at Trinity College Cambridge,
George was called to the Irish bar, in 1780. Through family influence his success was assured and he entered parliament and held
office several times. His reputation as a lawyer grew steadily, and in
1790, as counsel with Curran, he supported the claims of the common
council of Dublin against the court of aldermen in their contest over
the election of lord mayor and received their thanks for his conduct
of their case. He advocated the cause of catholic emancipation in
company with Grattan and Curran. After the union on March 2,
1801, he took his seat in the imperial parliament. There he opposed
a motion for funeral honors to Pitt, on the ground that to do otherwise " would be virtually a contradiction of the votes I have given
for a series of years against all the leading measures of that minister." On the formation of the Fox, Grenville ministry, he received
the seals as Lord Chancellor of Ireland. Though holding the office
for barely a year, he retired with the usual pension of 4000l. a year.
He afterwards took an active part in politics, especially in matters
relating to Ireland, until his death upon July 8, 1817. See *Dict. of
Nat. Biog.*

upon the immediate duties of my judicial situation. I am aware that I shall incur much obloquy in the hopes of doing some good, and remain,

"My dear Brother,

"Ever most sincerely and affectionately yours,

"ELLENBOROUGH.

"Bloomsbury Square, Thursday,
February 13, 1806."[1]

It seems strange to us that the incongruity of the positions of Cabinet Minister and Chief Justice should not have struck "All the Talents," but in the hurry of the moment no attention was paid to it by any member of the new Government. The members of the new Opposition had more leisure and were more acute. As soon as the list of the Cabinet was published, violent paragraphs appeared in the newspapers against the unconstitutional conduct of the Whigs, and notices of motion upon the subject were given in both Houses of Parliament.

Lord Ellenborough was taken by surprise when this storm arose, and he was much annoyed by it. Although his seat in the Cabinet was not to be accompanied with any profit, the new dignity had considerably tickled his vanity, and he was really in hopes that he might be of service to the country—particularly in watching over the Church establishment, and checking any concession to the Roman Catholics. He was fully convinced that the objection now started was unfounded, but he made up his mind that he would not condescend to discuss the question in parliament, and thus he addressed the Bishop of Elphin:

"Bloomsbury Square, March 1, 1806.

"MY DEAR BROTHER,

"My entire occupations for some time past at

1. Earl of Ellenborough's MSS.

Westminster and Guildhall have excluded me from the means of learning any news worth sending you.

"A question comes on on Monday in both Houses, which is brought forward under so much misconception of its true merits, and so much party heat and violence, that I shall not wonder if it is carried. The object of those by whom it is brought forward is to obtain a vote of censure upon my appointment to a situation in the Cabinet, on the ground of a supposed incompatibility in that situation in his Majesty's councils with my judicial situation and duties. I think it the more dignified and becoming course not to attend the House upon the occasion. If any vote of the kind intended should be carried, it is my determination to resign my situation as a Privy Councillor; with the duties of which I shall consider the vote (if it has any meaning at all) as pronouncing my judicial function as incompatible. The vote, if it comes at all, must be under an entire ignorance or misunderstanding of the history of the country and the precedents respecting the situation I fill, its proper and usual duties, and the political duties which the Legislature and the Sovereign have from time to time in the most anxious and important periods connected therewith. You will find this displayed in the debate by Lord Grenville and Mr. Fox, who are fully masters of the subject. I have thought it proper to give you this hint that you may be prepared to expect and to understand the conduct I am determined to adopt.

"Yours, my dear Brother,
"Ever most affectionately,
"ELLENBOROUGH."

When the motions came on, it appeared that there was no ground for apprehension as to the immediate result, for in the House of Commons the proposed cen-

as the names of the Lord Chancellor, or the First
Lord of the Treasury, or the Secretaries of State, for
the time being. Without this body the monarchy
could not now subsist, and any writer describing our
polity would point it out as one of the most important
institutions in the state. To say therefore that whoever may without impropriety be sworn of the Privy
Council, may without impropriety be introduced into
the Cabinet, is a mere quibble wholly unworthy of
Mr. Fox and Lord Grenville. Their concession that
the Chief Justice should absent himself from the Cabinet when the expediency of commencing prosecutions
for treason or sedition was to be discussed, is decisive
against them, and they did not attempt to answer the
observation that the circumstance of the Chief Justice
being a member of the Cabinet, however pure his conduct might be, was sure to bring suspicion upon the
administration of justice before him in all cases connected with politics. The mischief is not confined to
the period when he actually continues a Cabinet minister; for when his party is driven from power, although all his colleagues are deprived of their offices,
he still presides in the Court of King's Bench, and
there is much danger that in Government prosecutions
he will be charged with being actuated by spite to his
political opponents. As to the fact of the Chief
Justice having been a member of a council of regency,
the precedents might as well have been cited of Chief
Justices in the King's absence governing the realm,
and deciding causes in the AULA REGIS. The only real
precedent was that of Lord Mansfield from 1757 to
1765, and that was strongly condemned at the time by
Lord Shelburne and other great statesmen. The resolution to keep Lord Chief Justice Ellenborough in the
Cabinet gave a dangerous shake to the new Government; and public opinion being so strong against it,

the advantage expected from it was not enjoyed, for, from a dread of injuring his judicial reputation, he took little part in debate, and remained silent on occasions when, professing to be an independent peer, he might legitimately have rendered powerful help to the Government. It is said that Lord Ellenborough himself ere long changed his opinion, and to his intimate friends expressed deep regret that he had ever been prevailed upon to enter the Cabinet.[1]

1. The following letters, which passed at the time between Lord Ellenborough and Mr. Perceval, then beginning to take the lead of the Tory party, have been communicated to me. Considering the eminence of the writers and the permanent interest of the subject, I think it right that they should be preserved :

MR. PERCEVAL TO LORD ELLENBOROUGH.

" MY DEAR LORD,

" I believe Mr. Spencer Stanhope will certainly give notice to-morrow in the House of Commons of his intention to submit some motion to the House on the subject of your Lordship's situation in the Cabinet. Feeling as I do upon the subject, and convinced as I am after a great deal of reflection upon it, that the propriety of the appointment cannot be maintained in argument, I should think that I acted unkindly, if not treacherously, by you (especially as with these feelings I shall be obliged to take a part myself in the debate upon this motion), if I did not once more, with great earnestness, recommend to you the expediency of reconsidering the subject, and of retiring willingly in deference to the public sentiment from the situation in question. I advise it the more readily because I am sure you do not covet the situation yourself, and that you are risking your own character, which is too important a public possession to be risked lightly, out of deference to the opinions and feelings and wishes of others, rather than your own. And however unpleasant it may be either to you or your friends to take a step which apparently acknowledges that you have fallen into an error ; yet, as you may depend upon it, it will come to this at last, or else raise a ferment of which at present you have no conception, and in which your new friends will leave you to yourself ; it must be clearly less unpleasant to you, when the implied acknowledgment will amount to no more than that you have committed an error, into which under the circumstances any person might very naturally have fallen, than to wait till the time when this implied acknowledgment will not only be that you have committed an error, but that you have tried to persevere in it after it was pointed out to you, and against, if not the force of argument, at least the weight of public opinion. Your friends who advise you against the step which I now recom-

While the "Talents" remained in office the only
Government measure on which the Lord Chief Justice

mend, cannot, I am certain, see this subject in all its bearings or
they could not, as your friends, so advise you. You and they both,
living perhaps encircled a good deal by your own friends (who bor-
row their impressions upon such subjects in great measure from
yourselves, and do little more than reflect back upon your own
opinions), do not come in contact with the opinion of the public. It
requires some effort, as I feel at this moment, to communicate an
unwelcome truth, and therefore few people will have the hardihood
to tell you how apparently unanimous the public opinion is against
the Government on this point. The confidence and kindness with
which you have uniformly favored me, have drawn from me this
frank exposure of my sentiments. I trust you are not offended at it.
As far as party feeling against the Government could go, I assure
you I should covet the discussion. And I cannot trace in my own
mind any improper bias which actuates me, unless indeed the disinclination which I feel to be forced into a situation where my duty
will oblige me to take a part in a debate, possibly unpleasant to your
feelings, may be deemed an improper bias.

" I am, my dear Lord,

" Yours most truly and faithfully,

" SP. PERCEVAL.

" Lincoln's Inn Fields, Feb. 23, 1806."

LORD ELLENBOROUGH TO MR. PERCEVAL.

" MY DEAR SIR,

" I should not truly state my own feelings upon the occasion,
if I did not say that I received on many accounts very great pain
from the perusal of your letter.

" You will no doubt conscientiously pursue your own line of conduct. I have only to request that you will have the charity to suppose that I am equally guided by principles of duty, when I declare
my intention of abiding and conforming to the sense which parliament may think fit to express on my subject. I would, as you advise me to do, retire in deference to the public sentiment, if I was
perfectly satisfied that the sentiment of the unprejudiced part of the
public did not accord with my own—but I am yet to learn that the
judgment of those who consider the question without party bias is
against me, and am wholly at a loss to discover what duties, in
respect of advice to the Crown, are cast upon me in the character of
what is called a Cabinet Councillor which do not already attach upon
me as a Member of the Privy Council, under the oath I have taken
in case his Majesty should think fit to require my advice as a Privy
Councillor (as he has often done that of others) upon subjects relative to the executive Government of the country. However, as you
tell me you are 'convinced that the propriety of the appointment
cannot be maintained in argument,' I will forbear to waste your
time or my own in unavailing discussions, and remain, with thanks

spoke in the House of Lords was the Bill for abolish- CHAP.
ing the Slave Trade; and of his speech on this occasion; L.

for the frankness and explicitness of your communication, and a
strong sense of former kindness, very sincerely yours,

" ELLENBOROUGH."

MR. PERCEVAL TO LORD ELLENBOROUGH.

" Lincoln's Inn Fields,
Monday evening, Feb. 24.

" MY DEAR LORD,

" I cannot possibly permit the letter which I received from
you this morning, to be the last which should pass between us upon
the subject to which it relates. I cannot fail to perceive that you
are much offended by my former letter; and I must endeavor to remove, as far as I can, the grounds for that offence, which any objectionable expressions in it may have afforded. If there is any one
word in it which intimates or insinuates the slightest or most distant
suspicion that you will not act, or have not acted, upon this occasion,
as upon all others, upon what you conceive to be the true principles
of duty, or which conveys the least ground for your thinking it
necessary to request that I would have *the charity to suppose* that you
would act upon such principles, I can only say that I have been most
unfortunate in the language which I have used, and have conveyed
a sentiment directly the reverse of what I felt, as well as of what I
intended to convey. From some expressions of my letter, which you
repeat, underlined, I fear that in expressing strongly what I strongly
felt, I have used language which you have thought disrespectful; if
I have done so, I am extremely sorry for it, and ask your pardon
most readily for the *manner* in which I have executed my purpose.
But for the *matter* of it, I am so conscious that I never acted by you
or anybody under a more sincere impression of personal regard, than
in writing that letter, that though I must be sorry for my failure, I
should even now reproach myself if I had not sent it.

" When I referred to the sentiments of the public being against
the Government upon this question, I ought certainly to have been
aware that nothing is more difficult than to collect with any accuracy
the public opinion. But I did so refer to them because I had conversed with, and collected the sentiments of, many persons wholly
unconnected with party, of different descriptions, some of them members of our own profession (whose judgments form no unimportant
criterion), and also of several persons *friendly to the present Government*, and I have not met with a single one who has doubted of the
impropriety of the appointment. You say ' that you are yet to learn
that the judgment of persons who consider the question without
party bias is against you.' I fully believe that you are so, and it
was my belief of this which is my only justification for troubling you
with my letter. Your situation is so elevated that you have no
chance of obtaining information upon such a subject, unless some
real friend will, as I have done, risk, with the hope of serving you,

which seems to have been elaborate and eloquent, the following is the only record extant:

"Lord Ellenborough supported the bill in a variety

the chance of offending. I have exposed myself to that chance and I fear have been unfortunate. Even now I doubt whether you distinguish between the *illegality*, which you certainly may strongly contest, and the *impropriety* of this appointment, its inexpediency, its tendency to diminish (not the true upright and independent administration of justice, for in your instance I am sure that will never be), but the satisfactory administration of it in the opinion, or, if you please, the prejudices of the people. It was this impropriety that I stated (in terms which I wish I had not used because they offended you) could not be maintained in argument. I will, however, trouble you no further, and should be ashamed of having troubled you so long, but for the concluding sentence of your note, in which, in expressing a strong sense of my *former* kindness, you too plainly imply that in this instance you suppose me to have departed from it. And I thought it but due to that kindness and friendship which I wished still to retain, or recover, not to spare myself any trouble in endeavoring to remove as far as I can the unfavorable impression you have received. I hardly know how to hope that, under the immediate effect of present impressions, your opinion of my former letter can be changed. I hope, however, you will do me the favor to keep what I have written, and if when temporary feelings may have passed by, you will fairly ask yourself what possible motive I could have had to have written an unpleasant letter to you on this or on any other subject, except that which I profess, I think you will be convinced that you can find no trace of any intentional departure from the most friendly kindness and good will in anything I have done. I am, my dear Lord, very sincerely yours,

"SP. PERCEVAL."

"Tuesday morning."

LORD ELLENBOROUGH TO MR. PERCEVAL.

" MY DEAR SIR,

I received your letter this morning as I was setting out for Guildhall, or would have immediately thanked you for the kind terms in which it is written and the friendly spirit it breathes. Nothing will give me, I assure you, more pain than that events should occasion an interruption of that confidence and regard between us from which I had long derived so much satisfaction, and which I had once hoped would endure as long as we both live. I cannot but acknowledge that the admonitions to retire and some other expressions in your letter appeared to me of an harsher tone and temper than you would, I thought, on consideration have been pleased with yourself or have adopted in any communication with me, but they excited more of sorrow than of anger in my mind. Upon the principal question between us I forbear to say one word—

of arguments, and, adverting to the speech of a noble CHAP.
and learned Lord (Eldon), expressed his astonishment L.
that any noble Lord who had supported and approved
of the same measure, in the shape of an order of council, should oppose this bill, unless it was that they proceeded from different men. The ex-Chancellor and the
Chief Justice thereupon got into a sharp altercation,
which was put an end to by Lord Lauderdale [1] requiring the clerk at the table to read the Standing Order
against *taxing speeches.*" [2]

Lord Ellenborough regularly attended the trial of Impeach-
Lord Melville,[3] and as to the 2d, 3d, 5th, 6th, 7th, and ment of
Lord Mel-
ville.

in the position in which it at present stands it cannot be further
touched by either of us with any degree of delicacy.

"I remain, with a sincere regard for your character and conduct
which I feel neither time nor events ever can efface,

"Most faithfully yours,

ELLENBOROUGH."

1. James Maitland, Earl of Lauderdale. an able Scottish Whig
statesman, born in 1759, was the son of the seventh Earl of Lauderdale, and was first styled Lord Maitland. About 1781 he was elected
to the House of Commons, where he acted as the political friend of
Fox, and in 1787 was chosen one of the managers of the impeachment of Hastings. He inherited the title of Earl in 1789, and was
chosen one of the Scottish representative peers in 1790. He favored
the French republic, and opposed the war against the French which
began in 1793. In 1806 he became a peer of the United Kingdom
and keeper of the seal of Scotland, and was sent by Mr. Fox to Paris
with full powers to negotiate a peace, but without success. On the
fall of the Whig ministry in 1807 he gave up the seal of Scotland.
He died in 1839, leaving his title to his son James. He wrote several
treatises on finance and political economy.—*Thomas's Biog. Dict.*

2. Parl. Deb., vol. vii., p. 234.

3. Henry Dundas, Viscount Melville (born 1740, died 1811), was
the son of Robert Dundas, who was for many years President of the
Court of Session. Having adopted the bar as his profession, he
made his way with wonderful rapidity to the top of the ladder, being
Solicitor-General in 1773 and Lord Advocate two years later. In
this position he threw himself eagerly into politics, abandoning the
law. Attached to a ministry which, after a long period of office, was
at last falling beneath a weight of obloquy, Dundas exhibited so
much spirit and ability that he was at once recognized as promising
to rise to the highest power. Not the smallest source of his rising
reputation was the minute knowledge he displayed with regard to

CHAP.
L. 8th Articles, laying his hand on his breast, said with great emphasis and solemnity, " GUILTY, UPON MY HONOR." The acquittal of the noble viscount upon the 2d Article, charging him with having connived at the improper drawing of money by Mr. Trotter, without alleging that he himself derived any profit from the money so drawn, showed that impeachment can no longer be relied upon for the conviction of state offences, and can only be considered a test of party strength. Almost all good Tories said NOT GUILTY, and the independent course taken by Lord Ellenborough very much raised him in public estimation.[1]

The following letter shows that he acted cordially with Mr. Fox, and was confidentially consulted by that great statesman in the attempt then made to bring

Indian affairs. On the fall of North's ministry, Lord Rockingham was not slow to avail himself of Dundas's services, which were employed in the treasury of the navy, an office which he held also under Lord Shelburne. He retired, however, on the formation of the Coalition (1783), but did not have long to wait before he resumed his old post under Pitt. In June, 1788, he resigned that place to become President of the Board of Control with a seat in the Cabinet. With Pitt he resigned in 1801, and was raised to the peerage. In 1804 he again followed Pitt into office, and was appointed First Lord of the Admiralty, where he remained until 1806, when he was impeached for misappropriation of public money during his former period of control over the Navy Treasury. Pitt defended his faithful follower and colleague with his utmost ability, but a strong case was brought against him, and when the numbers on division were equal, the Speaker gave his casting vote against Lord Melville. Pitt was quite broken down by the blow, and did not live long enough to see the censure reversed by the Lords in 1807, after which the name of Lord Melville. which had been erased, was restored to the Privy Council list. He had retired, however, to Scotland, and never again took any part in public affairs ; and in retirement he died in May, 1811. That Dundas had been " guilty of highly culpable laxity in transactions relating to public money," no one can doubt ; but no loss had accrued to the state in consequence, and it was undeniable that he had exhibited a most praiseworthy energy in taking some steps to remedy the hopeless confusion and mismanagement which had for many years prevailed at the Admiralty.—*Dict. of Eng. Hist.*

1. 29 St. Tr. 549–1482.

about a pacification with Napoleon contrary to tne CHAP.
L. wishes of the King:

" Secret and Confidential.

" Many thanks to you, my dear Lord, for your note. The argument is quite satisfactory, and I should hope Holland would not be a point on which there would be much difficulty. I have heard something to-day which makes me apprehend that internal difficulties, and those from the highest quarter, will be the greatest. I hope nothing will prevent your attending, Monday, at eleven, for a consultation of greater importance in all its consequences never did nor never can occur. Shall we shut the door for ever to peace with France? Shall we admit that a council and ministers are nothing? that the opinion of the K. is everything, from what suggestions soever he may have formed that opinion? These are questions of some moment. Let us act honorably and fairly (in as conciliating a *manner* as possible, I agree). We may be foiled, the country may be ruined, but we cannot be dishonored. I am, with great regard, my dear Lord,

" Yours ever,

"St. Anne's Hill, Saturday evening." " C. J. Fox.

On the death of Mr. Fox Lord Ellenborough con- Dismissal of "All the Talents." tinued a cabinet minister, under Lord Grenville, till the entire dissolution of the government of All the Talents. March, 1807. Notwithstanding his objection to Roman Catholics sitting in parliament, he had given his consent in the Cabinet to the little bill (which produced such great effects) for permitting Roman Catholics to hold the rank of field officers in the army; but when the rupture actually took place his sympathies were with the King, and he declared it to be not unreasonable or unconstitutional that the King's ministers should be required to pledge themselves to propose no farther concessions to the Roman Catholics.[1] However, the

1. Lord Ellenborough had once looked favorably on the claims of the Irish Roman Catholics, but had become much afraid of them by the representations of his brother, the Bishop of Elphin, who had been exposed to serious perils in the Irish Rebellion of 1798, in which

CHAP.
L.

Chief Justice parted on good terms with Lord Gren-ville, who gave him the following testimony to his honorable conduct while they had acted together in the Cabinet:

"Downing Street, March 13, 1807.

"MY DEAR LORD,

"The matter which has of late occupied our attention is now brought to a state which appears to leave no possibility of the further continuance of the Government. Although I have the misfortune of differing from your Lordship on the expediency of the measures which have been in question, yet the frank and honorable conduct which has at all times marked every part of the share which you have taken in the delibera-tions and measures of the Government while it subsisted, makes me extremely anxious to have, if possible, the satisfaction of conversing with you to-morrow morning, previous to my going to the Queen's house, in order that I may have the opportu-nity of stating to you the course which we have taken during the last two days, and the grounds on which we have acted.

"Whatever be the course of the events to which these trans-actions may lead, I shall ever retain a strong sense of the con-duct which you have held on all occasions during the time that we have acted together, and a sincere respect for your character.

"I have the honor to be, my dear Lord,

"Most truly and faithfully,

"Your most obedient humble servant,

"GRENVILLE."

he displayed great gallantry. When Lord Cornwallis during the insurrection was riding with his staff at the head of a column in march, the first object he saw through the haze one morning was the Bishop on horseback coming to join him with a sword by his side, and pistols in his holsters. This same Bishop carried off in his carriage from his own door a country neighbor, whom he heard was to join the rebels the next day—and drove him 20 miles into Dublin. He had induced him to enter by courteously offering *a lift*, but the moment the door of the carriage was closed upon his friend, he collared him and told him he was his prisoner, and the coachman, having his orders, whipped his horses into a gallop.—The Bishop had all the qualities of a Christian pastor, but it was thought that, if in the law, he would have made a still better Chief Justice than his brother Edward, although it is rather doubtful whether Edward in the church would have displayed the mild virtues expected in a Bishop.

Henceforth, Lord Ellenborough, estranging himself entirely from the Whigs, entered into a still closer alliance with Lord Sidmouth, and, till his friend and patron again returned to office under Lord Liverpool, joined the small Addingtonian opposition in the House of Lords.

Accordingly, on the motion for the restoration of Feb. 18, 1808. the Danish Fleet, he declared "that in his opinion Lord Ellen- there was no act that had ever been committed by the borough's speech on Government of this country which so much disgraced the restora- tion of the its character and stained its honor as the expedition to Danish Copenhagen; as an Englishman he felt dishonored fleet. whenever the national honor was tarnished; the expedition reminded him of

'—— the ill-omen'd bark
Built in th' eclipse, and rigg'd with curses dark.'

He thought the object it had in view was most unjustifiable, and that even the success of that object would bring great calamity upon the country. When necessity was pleaded, noble Lords should recollect that this plea rested on an overwhelming inevitable urgency to do a particular act—not *on mere predominating convenience*. Many persons considered it justification enough that it might be very convenient for the country in this instance to apply to its own use what belonged in full property to another. This doctrine he was so much in the habit of reprobating at the *Old Bailey* that he could not help expressing himself with some warmth when he found it set up and acted upon by their Lordships."[1]

Having defended the Bill by which the Attorney His alterca- tion with General was empowered to hold to bail in cases prose- Lord Stan- cuted by him, and Earl Stanhope having said that such hope. language might have been expected from Jeffreys or Scroggs, Lord Ellenborough thus retorted:

1. 10 Parl. Deb. 655.

" My Lords, from my station as Chief Justice of
England I am entitled to some degree of respect; but I
have been grossly calumniated by a member of this
House, who has compared me to monsters who in
former reigns disgraced the seat of justice—such as
Scroggs and Jeffreys. I shall treat the calumny and
calumniator with contempt."

Earl Stanhope.—" I meant no such comparison, and
if the noble and learned Lord from intimate acquaintance has found a resemblance, this must be one of his
singularities; but his rash precipitancy in misapplying
what fell from me, convinces me that it might be dangerous to delegate the power created by the Bill even
to the noble and learned Lord."[1]

The Bill passed, but, being most unnecessary and
most odious, it was not acted upon by any Attorney
General, not even by Sir Vicary Gibbs, its author, who,
by his oppressive multiplication of ex-officio informa-
mations, brought himself and his office into sad dis-
repute.

Feb. 1810.   One of these informations which excited much
interest was filed against Mr. Perry, the proprietor of
the ' Morning Chronicle.' He was a gentleman of
considerable talents and high honor, who did much to
raise to respectability and distinction the profession
of a journalist in this country. He abstained from all
attacks on private character; he was never influenced
by any mercenary motive; and his paper, although
strongly opposed to the Tory Government, steadily
adhered to true constitutional principles. An article
in the ' Morning Chronicle,' after calmly discussing the
Catholic question, thus concluded: " What a crowd of
blessings rush upon one's mind that might be bestowed
upon the country in the event of a total change of system! Of all monarchs indeed since the Revolution,

1. 11 Parl. Deb. 710.

the successor of George III. will have the finest opportunity of becoming nobly popular."

Sir Vicary's information alleged that the defendant "being a malicious, seditious, and evil-disposed person, and being greatly disaffected to our Sovereign Lord the King and to his administration of the government of this kingdom, and most unlawfully, wickedly, and maliciously designing, as much as in him lay, to bring our said Lord the King, and his administration of the government of this kingdom, and the persons employed by him in the administration of the government of this kingdom into great and public hatred and contempt among all his liege subjects, and to alienate and withdraw from our said Lord the King the cordial love and affection, true and due obedience, fidelity and allegiance of the subjects of our said Lord the King, did print and publish a certain scandalous, malicious, and seditious libel" [setting out the words which I have copied].

Mr. Perry appeared as his own counsel, and defended himself with singular modesty, tact, and eloquence.

At his request the following paragraph was allowed to be read from the same newspaper:

" The Prince has thought it his duty to express to his Majesty his firm and unalterable determination to preserve the same course of neutrality which he has maintained, and which, from every feeling of dutiful attachment to his Majesty's person, from his reverence of the virtues and from his confidence in the wisdom and solicitude of his Royal Father for the happiness of his people, he is sensible ought to be the course that he should pursue."

Lord Ellenborough, in summing up to the Jury, after commenting upon the weight to be given to this paragraph, thus proceeded:

" The next and most important question is, what is
the fair, honest candid construction to be put upon the
words standing by themselves. Is the passage set out
in the information *per se* libellous? The first sentence
easily admits of an innocent interpretation. 'What a
crowd of blessings rush upon one's mind that might be
bestowed upon the country in the event of a total
change of system!' The fair meaning of the expression, 'change of system,' I think is a change of political
system—not a change in the frame of the established
government—but in the measures of policy which have
been for some time pursued. By 'total change of system' is certainly not meant subversion or *demolition*,
for the descent of the crown to the successor of his
Majesty is mentioned immediately after. The writer
goes on to speak of the blessings that may be enjoyed
upon the accession of the Prince of Wales; and therefore cannot be understood to allude to a change inconsistent with the full vigor of the monarchical part of
the constitution. Now I do not know that merely
saying there would be blessings from a change of
system, without reference to the period at which they
may be expected, is expressing a wish or a sentiment
that may not be innocently expressed in reviewing the
political condition of the country. The information
treats this as a libel on the person of his Majesty, and
his personal administration of the government of the
country. But there may be error in the present system, without any vicious motives, and with the greatest virtues, on the part of the reigning Sovereign. He
may be misled by the ministers he employs, and a
change of system may be desirable from their faults.
He may himself, notwithstanding the utmost solicitude
for the happiness of his people, take an erroneous view
of some great question of policy, either foreign or
domestic. I know but of ONE BEING to whom error

may not be imputed.   If a person who admits the wisdom and the virtues of his Majesty, laments that in the
exercise of these he has taken an unfortunate and
erroneous view of the interests of his dominions, I am
not prepared to say that this tends to degrade his
Majesty, or to alienate the affections of his subjects.   I
am not prepared to say that this is libellous.   But it
must be with perfect decency and respect, and without
any imputation of bad motives.   Go one step farther,
and say, or insinuate, that his Majesty acts from any
partial or corrupt view, or with an intention to favor
or oppress any individual or class of men, and it would
become most libellous.   However, merely to represent
that an erroneous system of government obtains under
his Majesty's reign, I am not prepared to say exceeds
the freedom of discussion on political subjects which
the law permits.   Then comes the next sentence : 'Of
all monarchs, indeed, since the Revolution, the successor of George the Third will have the finest opportunity of becoming nobly popular.'   This is more
equivocal ; and it will be for you, gentlemen of the
Jury, to determine what is the fair import of the words
employed.   Formerly it was the practice to say, that
words were to be taken in the more lenient sense : but
that doctrine is now exploded ; they are not to be
taken in the more lenient or more severe sense ; but in
the sense which fairly belongs to them, and which they
were intended to convey.   Now, do these words mean
that his Majesty is actuated by improper motives, or
that his successor may render himself nobly popular by
taking a more lively interest in the welfare of his subjects?   Such sentiments, as it would be most mischievous, so it would be most criminal to propagate.
But if the passage only means that his Majesty during
his reign, or any length of time, may have taken an
imperfect view of the interests of the country, either

respecting our foreign relations, or the system of our internal policy, if it imputes nothing but honest error, without moral blame, I am not prepared to say that it is a libel. The extract, read at the request of the defendants, does seem to me too remote in point of situation in the newspaper to have any material bearing on the paragraph in question. If it had formed a part of the same discussion, it must certainly have tended strongly to show the innocence of the whole. It speaks of that which everybody in his Majesty's dominions knows, his Majesty's solicitude for the happiness of his people; and it expresses a respectful regard for his paternal virtues. What connection it has with the passage set out in the information, it is for you to determine. Taking that passage substantively and by itself, it is a matter, I think, somewhat doubtful, whether the writer meant to calumniate the person and character of our august Sovereign. If you are satisfied that this was his intention by the application of your understandings honestly and fairly to the words complained of, and you think they cannot properly be interpreted by the extract which has been read from the same paper, you will find the defendants *guilty*. But if, looking at the obnoxious paragraph by itself, you are persuaded that it betrays no such intention; or if, feeling yourselves warranted to import into your consideration of it a passage connected with the subject, though considerably distant in place and disjoined by other matter, you infer from that connection that this was written without any purpose to calumniate the personal government of his Majesty, and render it odious to his people, you will find the defendants *not guilty*. The question of intention is for your consideration. You will not distort the words, but give them their application and meaning as they impress your minds. What appears to me most material, is the substantive paragraph itself ; and if you consider it as meant to represent that the reign of his Majesty is the only thing interposed between the subjects of this country and the possession of great blessings, which are likely to be enjoyed in the reign of his successor, and thus to render his Majesty's administration of his government odious, it is a calumnious paragraph, and to be dealt with as a libel. If, on the contrary, you do not see that it means distinctly, according to your reasoning, to impute any purposed maladministration to his Majesty, or those acting under him, but may be fairly construed as an expression of regret that an erroneous view has been taken of public affairs, I am not prepared to say that it is a libel. There have been errors in the administration of the most enlightened men. I will take the instance of a man who for a time administered the concerns of this country with great ability, although he gained his elevation with great crime—I mean *Oliver Cromwell.* We are at this moment suffering from a most erroneous principle of his government in turning the balance of power against the *Spanish* monarchy in favor of the House of *Bourbon.* He thereby laid the foundation of that ascendency which, unfortunately for all mankind, *France* has since obtained in the affairs of *Europe.* The greatest monarchs who have ever reigned—monarchs who have felt the most anxious solicitude for the welfare of their country, and who have in some respects been the authors of the highest blessings to their subjects, have erred. But could a simple expression of regret for any error they had committed, or an earnest wish to see that error corrected, be considered as disparaging them, or tending to endanger their government? Gentlemen, with these directions the whole subject is for your consideration. Apply your minds candidly and uprightly to the meaning of the passage in question;

distort no part of it for one purpose or another; and let your verdict be the result of your fair and deliberate judgment."

The defendant was acquitted.[1] As soon as the foreman of the jury had pronounced the verdict, Sir Vicary Gibbs, the Attorney General, turning round to me, said, "We shall never get another verdict for the Crown while the Chief Justice is in opposition." His Lordship certainly since the dissolution of the Talents Administration had kept up an intimacy with Addington and the Grenvilles, but it was a mere piece of Mr. Attorney's spleen to suppose that the Judge was actuated by any desire to mortify the existing Government, although the possibility of such a suspicion is argument enough against a Chief Justice of the King's Bench ever being a member of any Cabinet.

Lord Ellenborough had a violent hatred of libellers, and generally animadverted upon them with much severity. He soon after did his best to convict Leigh

Hunt,[2] then the editor of the EXAMINER, upon an

---

1. 31 St. Tr. 335 ; 2 Campb. 398.

2. James Henry Leigh Hunt, an English author, born in Southgate, Middlesex, Oct. 19, 1784, died at Putney, Aug. 28, 1859. His father, a West Indian, married an American lady, and practised law in Philadelphia till the Revolution broke out, when he warmly espoused the cause of the Crown and had to leave the country. He went to England, took orders, and became tutor to Mr. Leigh, nephew of the Duke of Chandos, after whom he named his son. Leigh Hunt was educated at Christ's Hospital, which he left in his fifteenth year, spent some time in the office of his brother, an attorney, and then obtained a place in the war office. In 1808 he left the war office, and with his brother established the "Examiner," a liberal journal, which he edited for many years and rendered exceedingly popular ; it was noted for the fearlessness of its criticism and the freedom of its political discussions. Three times the Hunts were prosecuted by the Government ; first, for the words, "Of all monarchs, indeed, since the Revolution, the successor of George III. will have the finest opportunity of becoming nobly popular " ; second, for denouncing flogging in the army ; third, when a fashionable newspaper had called the Prince Regent an Adonis, for adding "a fat Adonis of fifty." On the first the prosecution was abandoned,

ex-officio information for publishing an article against CHAP. L. the excess to which the punishment of flagellation had been carried in the army:

"Gentlemen," said he to the jury, "we are placed in a most anxious and awful situation. The liberty of the country—everything that we enjoy—not only the independence of the nation, but whatever each individual among us prizes in private life, depends upon our fortunate resistance to the arms of Buonaparte and the force of France, which I may say is the force of all Europe combined under that formidable foe. It becomes us, therefore, to see that there is not in addition to the prostrate thrones of Europe an auxiliary within this country, and that he has not the aid for the furtherance of his object of a British press. It is for you, between the public on the one hand, and the

on the second the verdict was for acquittal, but on the third the brothers were sentenced to a fine of £500 each, and two years' imprisonment. They rejected offers to remit the penalties on condition that the paper should change its tone, and underwent the full sentence; but so much popular sympathy was excited in their behalf that the cells were transformed into comfortable apartments, constantly supplied with books and flowers. Here Leigh was visited by Byron, Moore, Lamb, Shelley, and Keats, and here he wrote "The Feast of the Poets" (1814), "The Descent of Liberty, a Mask" (1815), and "The Story of Rimini" (1816), which immediately gave him a place among the poets. He also continued to edit the "Examiner" while in prison. His pecuniary affairs having become badly involved, in June 1822, on the invitation of Byron and Shelley, he went to Pisa, Italy, to assist them in editing the "Liberal," a journal intended to be ultra-liberal in both literature and politics. Shelley's death occurred in July, and Hunt resided with Byron for several months; but the journal proving a failure and the association uncongenial, the poets separated with decidedly unpleasant impressions of each other. Hunt remained in Italy for some years, and after his return to England published "Recollections of Lord Byron and some of his Contemporaries." In this book the character of Byron was set forth in so unfavorable a light that his friends, especially Moore, retorted upon its author in the severest manner. Years afterward Hunt confessed that he was ashamed of it. From this time his life was constantly devoted to the production of books. Shortly before his death he collected and arranged a complete final edition of his poems.—*Appleton's Encyc.*, vol. ix., p. 68.

subject on the other, to see that such a calamity does
not overwhelm us. Is this the way of temperate discussion? The first thing that strikes us is this ONE
THOUSAND LASHES in large letters. What is this but
to portray the punishment as a circumstance of horror,
and excite feelings of detestation against those who
had inflicted and compassion for those who had suffered
it? Then he goes into an irritating enumeration of
the miseries which do arise from the punishment, and
which do harrow up the feelings of men who consider
them in detail. This punishment is an evil which has
subsisted in the eyes of the legislature and of that
honorable body who constitute the officers of the army,
and it has not been remedied. If there are persons
who really feel for the private soldier, why not remedy
the evil by private representation?[1] But when, as at
this moment, everything depends on the zeal and
fidelity of the soldier, can you conceive that the ex-
clamation ONE THOUSAND LASHES, with strokes underneath to attract attention, could be for any other purpose than to excite disaffection? Can it have any
other tendency than that of preventing men from
entering into the army? Can you doubt that it is a
means intended to promote the end it is calculated to
produce? If its object be to discourage the soldiery, I
hope it will be unavailing. These men who are represented as being treated ignominiously have presented a
front—and successfully—to every enemy against which
they have been opposed. On what occasion do you
find the soldiery of Great Britain unmanned by the
effect of our military code? This publication is not to
draw the attention of the legislature or of persons in

1. This reminds one of the Emperor Alexander's observation
when he visited England in 1815, that "he thought the English
'Opposition' a very useful institution, but he rather wondered why
they did not convey their remonstrances to the King's Ministers in
private."

authority with a view to a remedy, but seems intended to induce the military to consider themselves as more degraded than any other soldiers in the world—and to make them less ready at this awful crisis to render the country that assistance without which we are collectively and individually undone. I have no doubt that this libel has been published with the intention imputed to it, and that it is entitled to the character given to it by the information." [1]

Nevertheless, to the unspeakable mortification of the noble Judge, the jury found a verdict of *Not Guilty*. [2]

Such scandal was excited by the mode in which Government prosecutions for libel were now instituted and conducted, that Lord Holland brought the subject before the House of Lords, and, after a long speech, in which he complained of the power of the Attorney General to file criminal informations, and the manner in which it had recently been abused, moved for a return of all informations *ex-officio* for libel from 1st January, 1801, to 31st December, 1810.

Lord Ellenborough : "The motion of the noble Baron includes the period during which so humble an individual as myself had the honor of filling the office of Attorney General. Whether he means to refer to my conduct I know not—but as he made no allusion to it, I do not think myself bound to defend what has not been attacked; but I must say with reference to the learned gentlemen who succeeded me, that their dis-

---

1. This was manifestly usurping the functions of the jury as to matter of fact; but it was then erroneously supposed to be in conformity to the power given by Fox's Libel Act, which is merely for the Judge to deliver his opinion on matter of law as in other cases.

2. 31 St. Tr. 367. This acquittal was mainly produced by the eloquence of Mr. Brougham; but in spite of all his efforts another client was convicted at Lincoln before Baron Wood, for publishing the same libel in a country newspaper. *Rex* v. *Drakard*, 31 St. Tr. 495.

CHAP. charge of their public duty ought not lightly or
L. captiously to be censured nor made the subject of
invidious investigation on grounds of hazardous conjecture. The law of informations *ex-officio* is the law of
the land, resting on the same authority with the rights
and privileges which we most dearly prize. It is as
much law as that which gives the noble Lord the right
of speaking in this House; it is as much law as the
law which puts the crown of this realm on the brow of
the Sovereign. If the noble Lord questions the expediency of the law of informations, why not propose
that it be repealed? This would be the direct and
manly course. I deprecate in this House violent and
vague declamations. [*Hear! hear!* from Lord Holland.] I am aware to what I subject myself. The
noble Lord may call all that I have said a mere *tirade*.
[*Hear! hear!* from Lord Holland.] I am used to
tumults and alarms—they never yet could put me
down. Were I to die next moment, I will not yield
to violence. My abhorrence of the licentiousness of
the press is founded on my love of civil liberty. The
most certain mode of upsetting our free constitution is
by generating a groundless distrust of the great officers
of justice, and teaching the people to despise the law
along with those who administer it. I repeat that I
know nothing more mischievous in its tendency than
inoculating the public mind with groundless apprehensions of imaginary evils."

The violence of this language called forth considerable animadversion from several noble Lords. Lord
Stanhope declared that he was afraid of entering into
any controversy with the " vituperative Chief Justice "
—justifying himself by the example of a peer celebrated for his politeness, of whom he told this anecdote:
Lord Chesterfield, when walking in the street, being
pushed off the flags by an impudent fellow, who said

to him, " I never give the wall to a scoundrel," the
great master of courtesy immediately took off his hat,
and, making him a low bow, replied, " Sir, I always
do." [1]

Lord Holland: " The noble and learned Chief Justice has complained of the vehemence and passion with
which I have delivered myself; but he should have had
the charity to recollect that I have not the advantage
of those judicial habits from which he has profited so
much. The practice of the duties of the highest
criminal judge and the exercise of temper which those
duties require can alone bring the feelings of men to a
perfect state of discipline, and produce even in the
delivery of the strongest opinions the dignified and
dispassionate tone which ever adds grace to the noble
and learned Lord's oratorical efforts, and has so signally
marked his demeanor in this night's debate."

Sir James Mackintosh, who was present at this
debate, in giving an account of it, says :—" I was much
delighted with the ingenious, temperate, and elegant
speech of Lord Holland on the abominable multiplication of criminal informations for libels, and much disgusted with the dogmatism of Lord Ellenborough's
answer. Lord Holland spoke with the calm dignity of
a magistrate, and Lord Ellenborough with the coarse
violence of a demagogue." [2]

The Chief Justice's next remarkable appearance in March 22, 1813.
the House of Lords was in a discussion respecting the Lord Ellen-
" Delicate Investigation." While he was in the Cabi- borough and the
net in 1806 a commission had been addressed to him " DELI- CATE IN-
and several others by George III. to inquire into certain VESTIGA- TION."
charges brought forward against the Princess of Wales.
After examining many witnesses, they presented a
report acquitting her of conjugal infidelity, but stating

1. 19 Parl. Deb. 129-174.
2. Life of Mackintosh.

that she had been guilty of great levity of conduct, and recommending that she should be admonished to conduct herself more circumspectly in future.[1]   These animadversions excited the deep resentment of her Royal Highness and her friends, and were complained of in various publications and speeches, which asserted that the secret inquiry before the Commissioners had been carried on unfairly, that improper questions had been put, and that the evidence had not been correctly taken down.   Without making any motion, or giving any notice, the noble and learned Lord rose in his place, and thus addressed his brother Peers:

"My Lords, various considerations have at different moments operated upon my mind to induce me to forbear the execution of a task which now, after the most mature and deliberate consideration, I am compelled to perform as a duty that I owe to my own character and honor, as well as to the character and honor of those who were joined with me in a most important investigation.   The first of these considerations was a consciousness of rectitude, I hope not presumptuously indulged, which made me backward in noticing the slanderous productions recently circulated against the conduct of individuals employed in situations of the highest trust.   To have betrayed an anxious irritability of feeling would have appeared to imply an acknowledgment of imperfection among those who have faithfully discharged an arduous and painful duty.   There are

1. I have seen the original draught of the Report in Lord Ellenborough's handwriting, and the draught of a second very elaborate Report by him upon a communication to the Commissioners from the King. After a very long commentary on the evidence of the witnesses, the Commissioners say that "there are no sufficient grounds for bringing Her Royal Highness to trial for adultery; but that she had comported herself in a manner highly unbecoming her rank and her character." Lord Ellenborough appears throughout the whole affair to have taken infinite pains to get at the truth, and to have been actuated by a most earnest desire to do impartial justice to all parties. _

cases where a sufficient vindication may be found in the candid judgment of mankind, where opportunities of forming an opinion not very erroneous are afforded to the public. Such, however, is not the situation of the individual who now addresses your Lordships. When the exculpation rests solely in the hands of the person accused, it becomes him, on the credit of the esteem and respect with which his assertion has been hitherto received, to employ that assertion, given in a manner the most solemn and impressive, for his own vindication."

After adverting to his reluctance to run any risk of making disclosures contrary to his oath as a Privy Concillor, and stating the issuing of the Commission, he thus proceeded :

" In that Commission I found my name included; but the subject of inquiry, the intention to issue the Commission, and the Commission itself, were all profound secrets to me, until I was called upon to discharge the high and sacred duty that upon me was thus imposed. I felt that much was due to this command, and it was accompanied with some inward satisfaction that the integrity and zeal with which I had endeavored to discharge my public functions, had made a favorable impression upon the mind of my Sovereign; notwithstanding which, the mode in which this command was obeyed has been made the subject of the most unprincipled and abandoned slanders. It has been said, that after the testimony had been taken in a case where the most important interests were involved, the persons intrusted had thought fit to fabricate an unauthorized document, purporting to relate what was not given, and to suppress what was given in evidence. My Lords, I assert that the accusation is as false as hell in every part ! What is there, let me ask, in the transactions of my past life—what is there in the gen-

eral complexion of my conduct, since the commencement of my public career, that should induce any man
to venture on an assertion so audacious? That it is
destitute of all foundation would, I trust, be believed
even without my contradiction; but where it originated
or how it was circulated I know not. I will not trench
on the decorum that ought to be observed in the
proceedings of this House further than in such a case
is necessary; but I will give the lie to such infamous
falsehood, and I will, to the last hour of my existence,
maintain the truth of that which I know to be founded
on fact. It occurred to me, my Lords, that in order to
facilitate the proceedings, and at the same time to
conduct them with the secrecy that was so important,
it would be fit to select a person, in whom especial
confidence might be reposed, for the purpose of recording the examinations, by taking down the evidence from
the mouth of the witness in the most correct form.
I thought that both the secrecy and accuracy required
would be best consulted and secured by appointing
an honorable and learned gentleman, who then held
the office of Solicitor General, Sir Samuel Romilly.[1]
On every occasion when testimony was given, with

1. Sir Samuel Romilly was the son of a jeweller in Frith Street,
Westminster, and born there March 1, 1757. His education was
private and contracted; after which he became a clerk in an attorney's office, but left that situation to study in one of the inns of court.
In 1783 he was called to the bar; and for several years confined his
practice to draughts in equity. At length he rose to distinction in
the court of chancery; and in the last administration of Mr. Fox was
made solicitor-general, when he received the honor of knighthood.
When the party to whom he was attached went out of office, he also
retired; but still continued in parliament, where he displayed great
powers in debate. He exerted himself in endeavoring to effect a
revision of the criminal code, with a view to the limitation of capital
punishments to a few heinous offences; on which subject he published an able pamphlet; as he also did another against the erection
of the office of vice-chancellor. The death of this eminent man was
melancholy. Shocked at the loss of his wife, who died of a dropsy,
in the Isle of Wight, he became delirious, and destroyed himself,
Nov. 2, 1818.—*Cooper's Biog. Dict.*

only one exception, we had the benefit of his presence ;
but on that single occasion, whether it was that the
commissioners found themselves at leisure to proceed, or
whether they were unwilling that the witnesses should
be called upon unnecessarily to attend again, I do not
exactly remember ; but it so happened that we determined to pursue our inquiries without his aid, for a
messenger who had been despatched for Sir Samuel
Romilly returned with information that he could not
be found. It then occurred to my noble colleagues and
to myself that we could take down the evidence ourselves, and as I was in the particular habit of recording
testimony (discharging, I believe, twice as much of that
duty as any other individual in the kingdom) it was
resolved that on that evening I should hold the pen. I
complied; and I declare and make the most solemn
asseveration (which I should be happy, were it possible,
to confirm and verify under the sacred sanction of an
oath), that the examination that evening taken down by
me proceeded, in every part, from the mouth of the
witness—that the testimony, at its termination, was read
over to the witness—that the witness herself read and
subscribed her name to the concluding sheet, as she
had previously affixed her initials to that on which the
evidence was commenced. Were I to advert to the
terms in which that evidence was couched, I fear that I
should be trenching upon the terms of the oath by
which my duty is bound; but thus much I may say,
upon the character of the paper (which I wish could be
laid before the House without provoking a discussion
or leading to improper disclosures, that I would not for
a thousand reasons have promulgated), that if it could
be inspected, the strongest internal evidence would be
found upon its face to show that it was a genuine
production as taken from the mouth of the witness: if
it could be consulted, many interlineations would be

noticed, qualifying and altering the text according to the wish of the witness, and every individual reading it with the application of common sense, would find that these alterations could only have been made at the time the person was under examination. I do not think that I bestow upon myself too great a share of praise, when I say that I may take credit to myself at least for accuracy in details of this kind, and I will venture to maintain that there is not in the original document one word which was not uttered, approved and signed, after the most deliberate consideration by the witness.

"My Lords, if I could be guilty of the negligence, or rather the wickedness imputed, are my noble colleagues and friends so negligent or so wicked as to connive at a crime of such unparalleled enormity? I am not aware that a syllable the witness wished to add was omitted, and I speak from the most perfect recollection and the most decided conviction when I say, that the minutes made by me contained the whole of the evidence, and nothing but the evidence, of the person then under examination. I am not in the habit of making complaints against publications; but if in any case it were necessary, it would be more peculiarly so in the present, where I am charged with a crime not only inconsistent with the functions of the high office I hold, but inconsistent with the integrity that, as a man, I should possess. Surely, for myself and my noble friends, I may be allowed to insist that we anxiously and faithfully discharged a public duty, and I hope, in the face of the House and of the country, we shall stand clear of this most base and miscreant imputation.

"I have heard it said, but the charge can only originate in the grossest stupidity, that we, as Commissioners, misbehaved ourselves in various respects. Folly, my Lords, has said, that in examining the witnesses we put leading questions. The accusation is ridiculous—it is almost too absurd to deserve notice. In the first place, admitting the fact, can it be objected to a Judge that he puts leading questions? Can it be objected to persons in the situation of the Commissioners that they put leading questions? I have always understood, after some little experience, that the meaning of a leading question was this, and this only, that the Judge restrains an advocate who produces a witness on one particular side of a question, and who may be supposed to have a leaning to that side of the question, from putting such interrogatories as may operate as an instruction to that witness how he is to reply to favor the party for whom he is adduced. The counsel on the other side, however, may put what questions he pleases, and frame them as best suits his purpose, because then the rule is changed, for there is no danger that the witness will be too complying. But even in a case where evidence is brought forward to support a particular fact, if the witness is obviously adverse to the party calling him, then again the rule does not prevail, and the most leading interrogatories are allowed. But to say that the Judge on the bench may not put what questions, and in what form he pleases, can only originate in that dulness and stupidity which is the curse of the age. Folly says again, that the testimony of the witness should have been recorded in question and answer. When, I ask, was it ever done? is there a single instance of the kind? will the most gray-headed judicial character in the country show a solitary example of the kind? It is impossible; and undoubtedly the most convenient mode was for the witness to see his evidence in one unbroken narrative, without the interruption of questions composed of words which he never employed—it is the language of the witness and not of the interrogator that is required. Such accusations are the offspring of a happy union of dulness and

stupidity, aided by the most consummate impudence
that was ever displayed.

" It would, I confess, be a great satisfaction to my
mind and to those of my noble colleagues, if we had
any means, without violating sacred and indispensable
obligations, of attesting the truth of these facts; but
the nature of the inquiry forbids it. We cannot produce the evidence itself; I dare not give the explanation that would set the matter for ever at rest; and in
the situation I hold, and under all the circumstances,
it is impossible that the Prince Regent should be
addressed that the original document might be laid
before the House.

" My Lords, this malignant and unfounded charge—
this base and nefarious calumny—is one of the worst
symptoms of the times in which we live. It shows an
indifference in the public mind as to truth and falsehood; it originates in malice and is supported by ignorance; it is tossing firebrands in all directions, leaving
those who are in danger from the flames to escape as
well as they can, sometimes almost by a miracle. This,
my Lords, is one of the most hazardous attempts; it is a
cruel attack upon those who are unable to defend themselves. We have struggled, but I hope not in vain, to
defeat the nefarious and horrible design. I feel that it is
impossible to give the accusation a more positive denial.
I have declared that it is false from the commencement
to the conclusion, and I shall sit down ashamed that it
has been necessary for me to say anything: I feel
almost ashamed that any vindication was required. I
do not say that I am personally indifferent on a question of such undoubted magnitude; but if it regarded
myself only, I could be well content to leave such degraded calumnies to their own refutation. I was called
upon to discharge a public duty; that duty I assert I
discharged faithfully; and that I took down the depo-

sitions fairly, fully, and honestly, I protest on my most CHAP.
L.
solemn word and asseveration. I have spoken merely
to vindicate myself and my colleagues. That vindication I trust is complete. We only wish to stand well in
the opinion of our country as honest men who have
faithfully discharged a great and painful duty; and let
it be recollected, that having no means of resorting to
proof, we are compelled to rest our exculpation on a
flat, positive, and complete denial." [1]

All candid men believed that the investigation had
been carried on with perfect fairness,—but the violence
of the noble and learned Lord's vindication was re-
gretted, and many questioned the soundness of his positions as to the unlimited right of a Judge to put leading questions, and still more denied that in such an inquiry it was proper to give only the substance of the
evidence of the witnesses, compounding questions and
answers,—instead of writing down the questions and the
answers at full length, so as to obviate the possibility of
misrepresentation or mistake.

For several Sessions following, Lord Ellenborough
took no part in debate upon any political subject, and
confined his efforts in the House of Lords to a strenuous opposition to Bills for amending either the civil or
criminal law, all which he denounced as Jacobinical
and Revolutionary.

In 1816 he zealously supported the severe Alien 11th June,
Bill which ministers still considered necessary after the 1816.
return of peace; and, to show that at common law the
King has a right by the royal prerogative to send all
aliens out of the kingdom, he cited a petition of the
merchants of London in the reign of Edward I., praying that monarch to do so. On a subsequent evening
Earl Grey ventured to question the bearing of this

1. 25 Parl. Deb. 207.

precedent, which, he said, had been brought forward in " the proud display of a noble and learned Lord."

Lord Ellenborough.—" I rise, my Lords, to repel with indignation the base and calumnious imputation against me by the noble Earl, of having falsified a document, namely, the Petition of the City of London to Edward I. I hold in my hand a copy of that document, and its contents will show how unjustly I have been attacked."

Having read it in a loud and angry voice, he added in a very softened tone as he was about to resume his seat :

" I thought it due, my Lords, to my own character to make this explanation, *and I trust that I have done it without any asperity of language.* [A loud laugh from both sides of the House.] That laugh awakens a sentiment in my mind which I will not express. All I shall say is, that a man who is capable of patiently enduring the imputation of having falsified a document is capable of that atrocity." [1]

Lord Ellenborough's last speech in the House of Lords was on the 12th of May, 1817, in opposition to Lord Grey's motion for a censure on Lord Sidmouth's circular letter, inviting all the magistrates of England to interfere for the purpose of putting down seditious publications, and telling them that it was their duty to imprison all the authors and vendors who could not give bail for their appearance at Quarter Sessions to answer indictments against them. Recollecting that he owed his promotion as Attorney General and as Chief Justice to the Home Secretary, who was now accused, and who was generally supposed to have been guilty of a great indiscretion, if not of an illegal stretch of authority, he redeemed the pledge he had given in these words, " I am yours, and let the storm

1. 34 Parl. Deb. 1069–1143.

blow from what quarter of the hemisphere it may, you shall always find me at your side." The noble and learned Lord now delivered a very long and elaborate argument to prove that, by the common law of England, Justices of the Peace have power to hold to bail in cases of libel. This was answered by Lord Erskine, who insisted that the assumed power was an entire novelty and a dangerous usurpation. The Lords, persuaded by the learning and eloquence of the Chief Justice, or blindly determined to support the Government, rejected the motion by a majority of 75 to 19.[1]

After the permanent insanity of George III. and the establishment of the Regency, Lord Ellenborough was a member of the Queen's Council, to assist her in the custody and care of the King's person. In this capacity he had a daily report sent to him in a red box, which was handed up to him on the bench, and he frequently attended meetings of the Council at Windsor. Having been absent from one of these, he received the following letter from Lord Eldon, which gives an interesting account of the afflicted monarch and his family during this calamity:

LordEllenborough a member of the Queen's Council, as Custodian of the King's person during the Regency.

A.D. 1811.

"(*Confidential.*)

" MY DEAR LORD,

" The Archbishop being from town, I trouble you with a sketch of yesterday's proceedings at Windsor, your absence from which I greatly lamented, especially as the King wished to see you, and you would have been glad to see him.

" We had good and bad. Upon our arrival we received the daily account signed by all the doctors and Dundas. You must *see that*, it being by far the best account we have ever had. They state, I think, that no delusions had been betrayed for three days,—Bott,

1. 36 Parl. Deb. 445-516.

CHAP.
L.
the page, said none since Tuesday. They stated that, if the schemes and plans remained, they remained in a less degree than they had been before observed to exist; and they unanimously recommended that the King should have greater freedom and liberties, and more of communication with others than had been allowed him—that this would try the solidity, and enable them to judge of the permanence of his improved state.

"I then desired them, by a written question, to *specify* in writing *what* they recommended, and not to leave us to judge of what was to be done under their *general* recommendation.

"They recommended — then in writing — unanimously:

"1. That Colonel Taylor [1] should be with the King, his intercourse limited in degree, that is, as I understand it, by their prudence.

"2. That the King's chaplain should read the daily prayers in *his room*, not his chapel.

"3. That Lord Arden, Lord St. Helens, and others of that description, should visit and walk with him.

"4. That he should have his keys restored to him.

"Whilst they were consulting on these measures, the Dukes of York [2] and Kent [3] came to the Council, *as*

1. Sir Herbert Taylor, an English general, born in 1775. He was private secretary to the Duke of York, and to George III. Died in 1839.—*Thomas' Biog. Dict.*

2. Frederick Augustus, Duke of York (*b.* 1763, *d.* 1827), was the second son of George III., and, as early as his elder brother, broke away from the rigid discipline by which their parents fondly hoped to preserve them from the evils of the world. At the age of twenty-one he was created Duke of York and Albany, and Earl of Ulster. But already in his third year he had been elevated by his father to the half-secularized bishopric of Osnabrück. In 1791 he married Charlotte, eldest daughter of Frederick William, King of Prussia, when his income was increased by a vote of £30,000 per annum. In

3. See note 1, on next page.

we believed, by the Queen's desire, to represent that
their walk had been very uncomfortable; that the King betrayed no delusion, but that he was very, very full of plans and schemes, much more so than he had lately been to the Duke of York, and that they were particularly alarmed at his conversation about having his keys. I should here tell you that the Queen sent for me immediately upon my arrival at Windsor, and, in a conversation I had with her Majesty and the Princess Augusta, expressed great apprehensions about the keys, both representing great improvement in the King. I found that this subject had been mentioned on *Wednesday* to the Council then at Windsor, and that the King had learnt that it was under their consideration. The Dukes also stated that the King's conversation was hurried, and did not admit of their saying

1793 he was placed in command of an expedition to the Netherlands, to act with the Prince of Saxe-Coburg against France. Though giving some proof of personal gallantry, he soon made it clear that his royal birth was his only qualification for command. Fortunately for England the duke became disgusted at his want of success, and retreated, leaving Abercromby in command. As a reward for the military ability displayed in this campaign, he was in 1795 appointed Commander-in-chief of the Forces, and in 1799 was again entrusted with the command of an expedition to the Low Countries, in which, however, the only successes gained were due to Abercromby. The campaign finally ended in a disgraceful convention with the French. The duke was compelled to resign his office because of the shameful disclosures as to the way in which he allowed his mistress, Mrs. Clarke, to influence the military appointments, but was later restored to his old office under his brother's regency. His last act in public life was a most violent speech in the House of Lords against Catholic Emancipation in 1826. In the following January he died.—*Dict. of Eng. Hist.*

1. Edward, Duke of Kent, father of Victoria, Queen of Great Britain, and the fourth son of George III., was born in 1767. He studied at Göttingen and Geneva. In 1790 he entered the army, and three years later assisted in the capture of Saint Lucia. In 1796 he was appointed lieutenant-general, and in 1799 was created Duke of Kent and Strathern and Earl of Dublin. In 1802 he became Governor of Gibraltar; but, his rigid discipline producing a mutiny, he was soon after recalled. In 1818 he married a daughter of the Duke of Saxe-Coburg. The Duke of Kent was a liberal patron of benevolent enterprises. He died in 1820.—*Thomas' Biog. Dict.*

CHAP.
L.
one word.   This was all delivered by the Dukes themselves to Dr. Halford,[1] and afterwards to us, and by

1. Sir Henry Halford (1766–1844) physician, was second son of
Dr. James Vaughan, a successful physician of Leicester, who devoted
his whole income to educating his seven sons, of whom John became
judge of the court of common pleas, Peter, Dean of Chester, and
Charles Richard, envoy extraordinary to the United States.   The
sixth son, Edward Thomas, was father of Dean Vaughan, master of
the Temple.   Henry, born at Leicester on Oct. 2d, 1766, entered at
Christ Church, Oxford, and graduated B.A. in 1788 and M.D. in
1791.   After studying some time at Edinburgh he settled in
London, having borrowed 1000*l.* on his own security.   His good
manners and learning soon made him friends, and he was elected
physician to the Middlesex Hospital in 1793, and Fellow of the Royal
College of Physicians in 1794, having been appointed physician
extraordinary to the King in the previous year.   In March, 1795, he
married Elizabeth Barbara, the third daughter of Lord St. John, and
by 1800 his practice had so greatly increased that he gave up his
hospital appointment.   He inherited a large property on the death
of Lady Denbigh, widow of his mother's cousin, Sir Charles Halford,
seventh baronet, and subsequently changed his name from Vaughan
to Halford by act of parliament in 1809.   George III., who had a
strong liking for him, created him a baronet in the same year, and
he subsequently attended George IV., William IV., and Queen
Victoria.   For many years after Dr. Matthew Baillie's death he was
indisputably at the head of London practice.   He was president of
the College of Physicians from 1820 till his death, an unbroken tenure
which was by no means favorable to reform and progress ; but he
was largely instrumental in securing the removal of the college in
1825 from Warwick Lane to Pall Mall East.   He was made K.C.H
on this occasion and G.C H. by William IV.   He died on March 9,
1844, and was buried in the parish church of Wistow, Leicestershire.
His bust by Chantrey was presented to the College of Physicians by
a number of the fellows.   His portrait by Sir Thomas Lawrence is
at Wistow.   He left one son, Henry, who succeeded to the title,
and one daughter.   Halford was a good practical physician with
quick perception and sound judgment, but he depreciated physical
examination of patients, knew little of pathology and disliked innovation.   His courtly, formal manners and his aristocratic connection
served him well.   His chief publications were first given as addresses
to the College of Physicians, his subjects being such as "The
Climacteric Disease." "Tic Douloureux," "Shakspeare's Test of
Insanity" ("Hamlet," Act III., Scene 4), "The Influence of some of
the Diseases of the Body on the Mind," "Gout," "The Deaths of
some Illustrious Persons of Antiquity," etc.   Halford is described by
J. F. Clarke (Autobiographical Recollections) as vain, cringing to
superiors, and haughty to inferiors.   James Wardrop, surgeon to
George IV., termed him "the eel-backed baronet."   Some charges
of unprofessional conduct are made against him by Clarke, who

the Council it was all delivered in charge to all the physicians for their serious consideration.

"In the meantime, the Master of the Rolls and I went to the King, he having himself desired to see you and us. His manner to me was much kinder, and he had in the course of a week observed to Willis[1] that he thought me entitled to a belief on his part that I was right in what I had done, though he could not make it out how I could be so, and why I had not resigned the Seal. Willis had told him that I could not resign the Seal, that his Majesty was not well enough to accept it on resignation, and that the Prince, till he was Regent, could not have it offered to him, and that therefore it could not be resigned till the act his Majesty blamed on my part was done. He expressed surprise he had not adverted to this himself. The Queen or Princess Augusta[2] had told me that he

further states that when Charles I.'s coffin was opened in 1813 he obtained possession of a portion of the fourth cervical vertebra, which had been cut through by the axe, and used to show it at his dinner-table as a curiosity. This may be held to be confirmed by Halford's minute description of this bone in his "Account." Halford published : 1. "An account of what appeared on opening the Coffin of King Charles I." 4to, 1813. 2. "Essays and Orations delivered at the Royal College of Physicians," 1831 ; 3d edition, 1842. 3. "Nugæ Metricæ," English and Latin, 1842, besides several separate addresses and orations.—*Nat. Biog. Dict.*

1. Francis Willis, an eminent English physician, born in Lincolnshire about 1720. He studied at Brazennose College, Oxford, and in 1740 entered holy orders ; but he subsequently devoted himself to the study of medicine—particularly mental diseases. He attended King George III. during his attack of insanity, and his successful treatment of his case procured for him a high reputation. He founded an establishment for the insane at Greatford, in Lincolnshire, where his labors were attended with extraordinary success. His personal influence over his patients is said to have been wonderful. Died in 1807.

2. Augusta Sophia (1768-1840), princess, daughter of George III. and his sixth child, was born at Buckingham House, London, Nov. 8th, 1768. The public reception on her birth took place on Sunday, Nov. 13, when two young girls, discovered carrying away the cups in which their caudle had been served, and secreting cake, were reprimanded on their knees ("George III., his Court and Family,"

studiously called me Lord Eldon, and not Chancellor,
or to that effect, and that he had told his family that
when you and Grant and I were with him, he had been
as reserved as he could towards me, and had avoided
calling me Chancellor, but that he was in good humor
again. Both Grant and I thought him so: his conversation was calm, quiet, connected, admitting of free
conversation on our part, all the subjects good, the
whole manner right. I think Grant will tell you we
left the room sunk with grief that there could be anything wrong where all appeared so right. He said not
a syllable, however, of himself, his situation, or his
plans, and we understood it to be his determination not
to make any request of any kind, of anybody, respecting himself. Upon our return at the end of three-
quarters of an hour's visit, which concluded in a
dignified bow upon Willis's coming in, and a kind

vol. I., p. 317). Princess Augusta is several times mentioned in
Mme. d'Arblay's diary ; she was sprightly enough in her manner to
endure considerable banter from " Mr. Turbulent " March 1st, 1787,
and to be called " la Coquette corrigée " by him, on her supposed
attachment to the Prince Royal of Denmark, then visiting at the
castle (ibid., pp. 281, *et seq.*); She was partner to her brother, the
Duke of York, in the historical country dance on the evening of the
day, June 1, 1789, when the duke had fought the duel with Colonel
Lennox, and the Prince of Wales had resented the colonel's presence
amongst his sisters by breaking up the ball ("Annual Register,"
1827, p. 438). She accompanied the king and queen later in the
month to Weymouth, joining in the chorus of "God save the King"
at Lyndhurst ("Diary of Royal Tour," 1789). In 1810 she was in
attendance on her father, helping him to take exercise at Windsor.
In 1816, May 2, she was at Carlton House at the marriage of her
niece, the Princess Charlotte. In May, 1818, she gave 50l. to the
National Society for the Education of the Poor. On July 15, 1819,
she played and sang some of her own musical compositions to Mme.
d'Arblay (Diary, vol. VII., p. 270). In 1820 she was again at Windsor
attending to her father, whose death in that year was the occasion
of her being supplied with residences of her own at Frogmore, and
at Clarence House, St. James's. In this position of head of an
establishment the princess showed the same pleasantness and
patience she had shown in her parents' homes ; and died at Clarence
House, Sept. 22, 1840, in her 72d year ("Annual Register," 1840,
p. 176). She was buried at Windsor Oct. 2.—*Nat. Biog. Dict.*

speech towards me as Chancellor, we found that the doctors were ready with their written paper (which you must see), stating that, *upon full consideration of all circumstances*, they still recommended the measures before mentioned, *including the restoration of the keys.*

" We were much puzzled, but we all agreed that we could not venture to control the doctors' unanimous and deliberate advice.

" We, therefore, in a written paper, advised the Queen to restore the keys ;—in that paper stating (for her sake) that she had hitherto retained them under our advice ; and in another paper we directed the physicians, if any improper use of the keys was at- tempted, to interpose to prevent it, and inform the Council of the occurrence. This was necessary, as the keys open presses in which there are papers of con- sequence, and, it is understood, jewels of value. Tay- lor's attendance is to see that nobody sees any papers but the King, T. being acquainted with them all ; and he has orders not to obey any orders either about pa- pers, jewels, or other things. Willis and Bott expressed the utmost confidence that the King would do nothing wrong with his keys. Bott stated that he could not have answered for that a week ago, but all thought the recovery going on very rapidly.

" The prayers were to be said in the private room, because the physicians wished that the King should not yet go to the chapel, which is up stairs, as that step would lead him to think that he was to be up stairs as much as he wished. We desired that a particular account might be sent us to-day of the effect of all this, which you will receive in the course of circulation. I have detailed this as accurately as I can remember it, because it's natural *you* should know it, and because it tends to show, I think, that attendance at meetings becomes now of much importance. One of the doctors observed to

CHAP.
L.
the D. of M. that, in all this illness, much of improper communication as the King had made, he had never said a syllable upon state matters.   This, I believe, was Baillie.[1]

"In our papers of yesterday, which upon the Archbishop's return you should see, we noticed your absence, as we did the Duke of Montrose's[2] formerly, that, if we

1. Matthew Baillie, a celebrated physician and anatomist, born in Lanarkshire, Scotland, in 1761, was a brother of Joanna Baillie.   He studied at the University of Glasgow, where his father, the Rev. James Baillie, was professor of divinity.   Through the influence of his maternal uncle, the eminent anatomist William Hunter, he applied himself to the study of medicine at Oxford, where he graduated in 1789, and soon after was made a member of the College of Physicians.   In 1783 he succeeded Hunter as lecturer on anatomy.   He became physician to George III. and the royal family about 1810, and acquired a very extensive practice in London.   He was distinguished for his skill in diagnosis.   His "Morbid Anatomy of some of the most Important Parts of the Human Body" (1795) is esteemed a standard work, and has been translated into German, French, and Italian.   He also wrote "Lectures and Observations on Medicine," (1825.)   He died in 1823, bequeathing to the College of Physicians his medical library and anatomical collection.—*Thomas' Biog. Dict.*

2. "James Graham, third Duke of Montrose (1755-1836), born Sept. 8, 1755, was eldest son of William, second Duke of Montrose. Educated at Trinity College, Cambridge, he proceeded M.A. jure natalium in 1775.   On Sept. 11, 1780, he was elected M.P. for Richmond in Yorkshire, and sat for Great Bedwin in Wiltshire in the parliaments of 1784 and 1790.   He joined Pitt's administration in December, 1783, as a lord of the treasury, and held the post until April 8, 1789.   He opposed Fox's East India Bill in 1783, proposed Addington (afterwards Viscount Sidmouth) as speaker on May 8, 1789, and at the end of the same year moved the address on the Spanish convention.   From Aug. 6, 1789, until February, 1791, he was paymaster general of the forces, jointly with Lord Mulgrave.   On Aug. 8, 1789, he became vice-president of the board of trade and a member of the privy council.   On his father's death (Sept. 23, 1790) he succeeded to the dukedom.   From Dec. 7, 1790, till 1795 he was master of the horse ; served as commissioner for the affairs of India May 16, 1791, until Oct. 22, 1803, and was lord justice general of Scotland from Jan. 14, 1795, until his death, when the office was amalgamated with that of lord president of the court of session.   In 1803 he moved the address of the House of Lords to the King on his escape from the conspiracy of Colonel E. M. Despard.   He was president of the board of trade, under Pitt, from June 7, 1804, until the change of administration on Pitt's death in February, 1806, and for the most of that time was also joint postmaster general.   In 1805 he voted for

are blamable, it may be recorded that you are not so.
I have communicated these matters to the Prince last night, who was very good-humored and reasonable upon them.

" Yours, my dear Lord,
"ELDON."

When this letter was written Lord Eldon had not really been taken into favor by the Regent, and, on the contrary, he expected to be speedily turned out of office. He therefore still clung with tenacity to the forlorn hope of the King's recovery, and he was exceedingly anxious to have Lord Ellenborough's co-operation in case there should appear to be any ground for restoring his Majesty to the throne. But the Regent soon after having for ever renounced " his early friends," Lord Eldon changed his tactics, and encouraged the belief that the King was incurably mad. Lord Ellenborough appears to have refused always to join in any of these intrigues, and to have been only solicitous that the truth should be disclosed, and that justice should be done to the King, to the Prince, and to the Nation.[1]

Lord Melville's acquittal. Under the Duke of Portland he again became (April 4, 1807) master of the horse, and held the office until his resignation in 1830; was lord chamberlain, in succession to the Marquis of Hertford, from December, 1821, to May, 1827, and from Feb. 18, 1828, to July 15, 1830. Montrose was chancellor of the university of Glasgow from December, 1780, until his death; was lord lieutenant of the counties of Stirling and Dumbarton; and was knight of the order of the Thistle from June 14, 1793, until March 26, 1812, when he was made a knight of the Garter. A disparaging estimate of his character and abilities is to be found in the ' Greville Memoirs.' He obtained for the highlanders permission to resume the national dress, which had long been prohibited by law. He married, on Feb. 22, 1785, Jemima Elizabeth, daughter of John, second Earl of Ashburnham, and had by her an only son, who died in infancy. He married again, on July 24, 1790, Caroline Maria, daughter of George, fourth Duke of Manchester, by whom he had two sons and five daughters. He died at his mansion in Grosvenor Square on Dec. 30, 1836, and was buried in the mausoleum of the Earls of Montrose at Aberuthven in Perthshire."—*Nat. Biog. Dict.*

1. See Lives of Chancellors, ch. 201.

CHAPTER LI.

CONCLUSION OF THE LIFE OF LORD ELLENBOROUGH.

CHAP.
LI.
A.D. 1814-
1817.
Trial of
. Lord
Cochrane.

I HAVE now only to mention some criminal cases which arose before Lord Ellenborough in his later years. Of these the most remarkable was Lord Cochrane's, as this drew upon the Chief Justice a considerable degree of public obloquy, and causing very uneasy reflections in his own mind, was supposed to have hastened his end. In the whole of the proceedings connected with it he was no doubt actuated by an ardent desire to do what was right, but, in some stages of it, his zeal to punish one whom he regarded as a splendid delinquent, carried him beyond the limits of mercy and of justice.

Lord Cochrane [1] (since Earl of Dundonald) was one

1. Thomas Cochrane, tenth Earl of Dundonald, son of Archibald, was born at Annsfield, Lanarkshire, Dec. 14, 1775. In consequence of his father having impoverished himself through his devotion to scientific pursuits, the son, although heir to a peerage, had to start in life with no other expectations than those arising from his own exertions. When in his eighteenth year he entered the navy, and displayed such valor that in course of time he was placed in command of a vessel, and decorated with the order of the Bath. In the intervals which he passed on shore he became M. P., first for Honiton and afterwards for Westminster; but by persistently calling attention to the abuses which then disgraced the navy, he rendered himself highly obnoxious to the government, which seized the earliest opportunity of putting him to silence. In 1814 a rumor was spread that Napoleon had fallen, in consequence of which the Funds suddenly rose, and Lord Cochrane and some friends of his sold out to a large amount. The news, however, proved false; and as the chief actor in the fraud was known to have changed his dress at Lord Cochrane's, suspicion naturally fell upon his lordship, who, being brought to trial, and found guilty, was sentenced to pay a fine of 1000*l*, to undergo a year's imprisonment, and to stand in the

of the most gallant officers in the English navy, and
had gained the most brilliant reputation in a succession of naval engagements against the French. Unfortunately for him, he likewise wished to distinguish himself in politics, and, taking the Radical line, he was returned to parliament for the city of Westminster. He was a determined opponent of Lord Liverpool's[1] ad-

pillory. He was also deprived of the order of the Bath and his rank in the navy, and expelled from the House of Commons. One part of the sentence, however—that relating to the pillory—was remitted. The electors of Westminster again chose him as their representative, and, breaking out of prison, he took his seat in the House, but was recaptured, and his constituents were consequently deprived of his services until the expiration of his sentence. In 1818 he went abroad, and served with distinction in various foreign navies. When the Whigs came into power in 1830 his rank in the British navy was restored to him, and in the following year he succeeded his father as Earl of Dundonald. He now continued to obtain promotion in his profession, until, in 1854, he attained the rank of rear-admiral. Died Oct. 30, 1860. He enjoyed a high reputation for his scientific acquirements, and was the author of a pamphlet entitled, "Observations on Naval Affairs" and on some collateral subjects; as well as of two interesting volumes of Autobiography.—*Cooper's Biog. Dict.*

1. Robert Banks Jenkinson, second Earl of Liverpool (born 1770, died 1828), son of the first earl, was educated at the Charterhouse and Christ Church, Oxford, where he was the contemporary and friend of Canning. He entered political life under Pitt's auspices, and was returned for Rye before he had attained his majority. On his father being created Earl of Liverpool, he became, in 1796, Lord Hawkesbury. In the Addington ministry he was Foreign Secretary, and had charge of the negotiations which ended in the Treaty of Amiens; but when Pitt returned to office, in 1804, Lord Hawkesbury went to the Home Office. On Pitt's death, the king earnestly wished him to become Premier, but he very wisely declined the troublesome office, as he did also on the fall of Lord Grenville's ministry, in 1807, contenting himself with being Home Secretary. On Perceval's assassination, he imprudently yielded to the urgency of the Prince Regent and became Premier. He at once became the object of popular hatred by his opposition to reform, especially in the shape of Catholic Emancipation, and the adoption of arbitrary coercion to suppress the violent discontent, which gathered head during the period of his ministry. His unpopularity was still further increased by his introduction of a bill of pains and penalties against Queen Caroline, which he afterwards withdrew. He was struck down by paralysis in 1827, and died after lingering in a state of imbecility for nearly two years. It has been said of him that "his talents were far

ministration, and at popular meetings was in the habit of delivering harangues of rather a seditious aspect, which induced Lord Ellenborough to believe that he seriously meant to abet rebellion, and that he was a dangerous character. But the gallant officer really was a loyal subject, as well as enthusiastically zealous for the glory of his country. He had an uncle named Cochrane, a merchant, and a very unprincipled man, who, towards the end of the war, in concert with De Berenger,[1] a foreigner, wickedly devised a scheme by

inferior to his virtues ; and he is entitled to respect, but not to admiration. In honesty, as a minister, he has never been surpassed; in prejudices, he has rarely been equalled."—*Dict. of Eng. Hist.*

1. "Toward the end of 1813 Cochrane's uncle, Sir Alexander Forrester Inglis Cochrane, was appointed to the command-in-chief on the North American station, and went out in a frigate, leaving his flagship, the Tonnant, to be equipped and brought out by his nephew, who was nominated his flag captain. While engaged in fitting out the Tonnant, Cochrane became acquainted with a Captain de Berenger, a French refugee and officer in one of the foreign regiments, who was recommended to him as a skilled rifle instructor and pyrotechnist, in which capacities he was anxious to secure his services for the Tonnant. There is no reason to doubt that de Berenger was fully qualified for this post ; but he was also gifted with an unscrupulous impudence. On Feb. 20, 1814, while at Dover, he sent word to the admiral at Deal (whence the news was brought to London) that he was Lord Cathcart's aide-de-camp, and was the bearer of intelligence from Paris to the effect that Bonaparte had been killed, that the allies were in full march on Paris, and that immediate peace was certain. The Funds rose suddenly, and then fell heavily; out of the fluctuation one of Cochrane's uncles, who had taken the name of Johnstone, netted, it was said, a very large sum. De Berenger meanwhile posted up to London, took a hackney coach and drove to Cochrane's house in Green Street, changing his dress on the way from the scarlet coat of a staff officer to his own green coat of a rifleman, and in Green Street again changing into plain clothes which he borrowed from Cochrane. He was traced to Green Street, and Cochrane thus learning that he was the perpetrator of the swindle, gave information that led to his arrest. De Berenger, Johnstone, and with them Cochrane were thus all apprehended and brought to trial. The case of Cochrane, who knew absolutely nothing of the affair, was mixed up with that of the others, who were undoubtedly guilty; all were convicted, and Cochrane was sentenced to pay a fine of £1,000, to stand in the pillory for an hour, and to be imprisoned in the King's Bench Prison for a year. The standing in the pillory was remitted, probably because Sir Francis Bur-

which they were to make an immense fortune by a specu-lation on the Stock Exchange. For this purpose they were to cause a sudden rise in the Funds, by spreading false intelligence that a preliminary treaty of peace had actually been signed between England and France. Everything succeeded to their wishes; the intelligence was believed, the Funds rose, and they sold on time bargains many hundred thousands of 3 per cents. before the truth was discovered. It so happened that Lord Cochrane was then in London, was living in his uncle's house, and was much in his company, but there is now good reason to believe that he was not at all implicated in the nefarious scheme. However, when the fraud was detected—partly from a belief of his complicity, and partly from political spite, he was included in the indictment preferred for the conspiracy to defraud the Stock Exchange.

The trial coming on before Lord Ellenborough, the noble and learned Judge, being himself persuaded of the guilt of all the defendants, used his best endeavors that they should all be convicted. He refused to ad-journ the trial at the close of the prosecutors' case about nine in the evening, when the trial had lasted twelve hours, and the Jury as well as the defendants' counsel were all completely exhausted, and all prayed for an adjournment. The following day, in summing up, prompted no doubt by the conclusion of his own mind, he laid special emphasis on every circumstance which might raise a suspicion against Lord Cochrane, and elaborately explained away whatever at first sight appeared favorable to the gallant officer. In conse-

dett, his fellow-member for Westminster, avowed his intention of standing with him, and the government feared a riot ; but his name was struck off the list of the navy (June 25) ; he was expelled from the House of Commons (July 5) ; and, with every possible indignity, from the number of knights of the Bath."—*Nat. Biog. Dict.* s. n. Cochrane.

quence the Jury found a verdict of GUILTY against all
the defendants.

Next term Lord Cochrane presented himself in
Court to move for a new trial, but the other defendants
convicted along with him did not attend. He said
truly that he had no power or influence to obtain
their attendance, and urged that his application was
founded on circumstances peculiar to his own case.
But Lord Ellenborough would not hear him, because
the other defendants were not present.[1] Such a rule
had before been laid down, but it is palpably contrary
to the first principles of justice, and it ought immediately to have been reversed.

Lord Cochrane was thus deprived of all opportunity
of showing that the verdict against him was wrong, and
in addition to fine and imprisonment, he was sentenced
to stand in the pillory. Although as yet he was generally believed to be guilty, the award of this degrading
and infamous punishment upon a young nobleman, a
member of the House of Commons, and a distinguished
naval officer, raised universal sympathy in his favor.
The Judge was proportionably blamed, not only by the
vulgar, but by men of education on both sides in politics and he found upon entering society and appearing
in the House of Lords that he was looked upon coldly.
Having now some misgivings himself as to the propriety of his conduct in this affair, he became very
wretched. Nor was the agitation allowed to drop
during the remainder of Lord Ellenborough's life, for
Lord Cochrane, being expelled the House of Commons,
was immediately re-elected for Westminster; having
escaped from the prison in which he was confined
under his sentence, he appeared in the House of Commons ; in obedience to the public voice, the part of his
sentence by which he was to stand in the pillory was

1. 3 Maule and Selwyn, 10, 67.

remitted by the Crown; and a Bill was introduced into CHAP.
parliament altogether to abolish the pillory as a pun- LI.
ishment, on account of the manner in which the power
of inflicting it had been recently abused. It was said
that these matters preyed deeply on Lord Ellenborough's mind and affected his health. Thenceforth
he certainly seemed to have lost the gaiety of heart
for which he had formerly been remarkable.[1]

In Trinity Term, 1817, there came on at the King's Trial of
Bench bar the memorable trial of Dr. James Watson for high
for high treason, when the Chief Justice exerted him- treason.
self greatly beyond his strength, having to contend
with the eccentric exuberance of Sir Charles Wetherell,[2] greatly piqued against the Government because,
though a steady Tory, he had been passed over when
he expected to have been appointed Solicitor General,
—and with the luminous energy of Sergeant Copley,
who on this occasion gained the reputation which in
rapid succession made him, with universal applause,
Chief Justice of Chester, Solicitor and Attorney General, Master of the Rolls, Lord Chancellor, and Baron
Lyndhurst.[3] These two distinguished advocates, cor-

1. Many years afterwards, Lord Cochrane's case being reconsid-
ered, he was restored to his rank in the navy, he was entrusted with
an important naval command, and eulogies upon his services and
upon his character were pronounced by Lord Brougham and other
Peers.

2. Sir Charles Wetherell, an English lawyer, born in 1770, was a
son of the Dean of Hereford. He was called to the bar in 1794, and
acquired extensive practice in the court of chancery. Though he
was an ultra Tory and was king's counsel, he defended the Spafield
rioters, who were tried for treason in 1817. In 1820 he was returned
to parliament for Oxford. He became solicitor general in 1824, and
attorney general in 1826. Having resigned in 1727, he was reap-
pointed in 1828, but retired from office in 1829, because he was opposed to the Roman Catholic emancipation. By his hostility to the
Reform bill he rendered himself so unpopular that he was attacked
by a mob at Bristol in 1831, and narrowly escaped death. Died in
1846.—*Thomas' Biog. Dict.*

3. Lord Castlereagh was sitting on the Bench during the trial,
and expressing great admiration of his Whig-Radical eloquence, is

dially concurring in the tender of their services, were
assigned as counsel for the prisoner, and struggled
with unsurpassed zeal in his defence. Conscientiously
believing that the insurrection in which Watson had
been engaged was planned by him for the purpose
of overturning the Monarchy, the venerable Judge was
honestly desirous of obtaining a conviction. But,
quantum mutatus ab illo—he presented only a ghost-like
resemblance of his former mighty self. When Sir
Charles Wetherell described Castle, the accomplice, the
principal witness for the Crown, as "an indescribable
villain" and "a bawdy-house bully," the enfeebled Chief
Justice exclaimed that "terms so peculiarly coarse
might have been spared out of regard to the decorum
of the Court," and he animadverted severely upon some
of the gesticulations of the same irrepressible counsel,
threatening to proceed to a painful act of authority if
the offence were repeated; but the deep, impressive
tones and the heart-stirring thoughts with which from
the bench he used to create awe and to carry along with
him the sympathies of the audience were gone; and,
notwithstanding formidable proofs to make out a case
of treason, an acquittal was early anticipated.

The trial having lasted seven long days, the Chief
Justice was much exhausted, and in summing up he
was obliged to ask Mr. Justice Bayley to read a considerable part of the evidence. His strength being
recruited, he thus very unexceptionably concluded his
charge:

"You must now proceed to give that verdict which
I trust you will give from the unbiassed impulse of
honest and pure minds acting upon the subject before
you, and which will have the effect of affording protection and immunity to the prisoner at the bar if he shall

said to have added, "I will set my *rat-trap* for him—baited with
Cheshire cheese."

be found entitled to protection and immunity from the charges made against him; but, in another point of view, affording also that security to the laws and people of this land, and to its government as it subsists under those laws and is administered by the King and the two Houses of Parliament; thus satisfying your own conscience and the expectation of your country, unbiased by any consideration which might affect the impartiality of that justice which you are under so many solemn sanctions this day required to administer. Gentlemen, you will consider of your verdict."

He then asked them whether they would take some refreshment before they left the bar,—when the foreman, in a tone which made the Chief Justice's countenance visibly collapse, said, " My Lord, we shall not be long." Accordingly after going through the form of withdrawing and consulting together, they returned and pronounced their verdict, to which they had long made up their minds. NOT GUILTY,—and thereupon all the other prisoners who were to have been tried on the same evidence were at once acquitted and liberated.[1]

In the following autumn Lord Ellenborough made a short tour on the Continent in the hope of re-establishing his health. He at first rallied from change of scene, but ere long unfavorable symptoms returned, and he seems to have had a serious foreboding that his earthly career was drawing to its close. A deep sense of religion had been instilled into his infant mind by his pious parents: this had never been obliterated; and now it proved his consolation and his support. While at Paris he composed the following beautiful prayer, which may be used by all who wish like him with a grateful heart to return thanks for the past bounties of

---

1. 32 St. Tr. 1-1074.

Providence, and, looking forward, to express humble resignation to the Divine will:

His prayer
when his
health and
strength
were
declining.
"Oh God, heavenly Father, by whose providence and goodness all things were made and have their being, and from whom all the blessings and comforts of this life, and all the hopes and expectations of happiness hereafter, are, through the merits of our blessed Saviour, derived to us, Thy sinful creatures, I humbly offer up my most grateful thanks and acknowledgments for Thy Divine goodness and protection, constantly vouchsafed to me through the whole course of my life, particularly in indulging to me such faculties of mind and body, and such means of health and strength, as have hitherto enabled me to obtain and to enjoy many great worldly comforts and advantages.

"Grant me, oh Lord, I humbly beseech Thee, a due sense of these Thy manifold blessings, together with a steadfast disposition and purpose to use them for the benefit of my fellow-creatures, and Thy honor and glory. And grant, oh Lord, that no decay or diminution of these faculties and means of happiness may excite in my mind any dissatisfied or desponding thoughts or feelings, but that I may always place my firm trust and confidence in Thy Divine goodness; and whether the blessings heretofore indulged to me shall be continued or cease, and whether Thou shalt give them or take them away, I may still, in humble obedience to Thy Divine will, submit myself in all things with patience and resignation to the dispensations of Thy Divine providence, humbly and gratefully blessing, praising, and magnifying Thy holy name for ever and ever. Amen.

"Paris, 1817."

When Michaelmas Term returned he was able to take his seat in the Court of King's Bench, but he was frequently obliged to call in the assistance of the puisne CHAP. LI. judges to sit for him at nisi prius.

The trial of William Hone[1] coming on at Guild- Trial of William Hone. hall, although there was a strong desire to convict him, for he had published very offensive pasquinades on George IV., the task of presiding was intrusted to Mr. Justice Abbott. The defendant was charged by three different informations with publishing three parodies, entitled "The late John Wilkes's Cate- chism," "The Political Litany," and "The Sinecurist's Creed." He was not at all supposed to be formidable, not being hitherto known as a demagogue; but in truth he defended himself with extraordinary skill and

1. William Hone, a political pamphleteer and compiler of popular antiquities, began life in an attorney's office, at first in London, and subsequently at Chatham. In 1800 he established himself as a book- seller in Lambeth Walk, from which he removed to St. Martin's Churchyard, close to the present Charing Cross. In 1806 he com- menced his singular literary career by issuing an edition of Shaw's "Gardener." An attempt at establishing a savings' bank, as well as a new publishing speculation, followed, both being failures. In 1811 he was appointed by the booksellers their "trade auctioneer," and, a short time before, had been engaged in the compilation of the index to Froissart. But he was quite unfitted for business, and while engaged in the above post he was occupied in investigating the abuses in lunatic asylums : he was soon a bankrupt for the sec- ond time. His family now consisted of seven children, and he gained a livelihood by writing for the "Critical Review" and the "British Lady's Magazine." He next opened a bookseller's shop in Fleet Street, but his ill-fortune still continued ; it was twice plun- dered. In 1815 he was the publisher of the "Traveller" news- paper, and soon after began to publish those bold political pam- phlets and satires which made him universally known, and led to his being tried for three days in the Court of King's Bench. He was acquitted, however, and a large sum of money was collected by sub- scription for him, with which he established himself once more in business, and once more failed. From this time he was occupied in the compilation and publication of those well-known books which will continue to preserve his name. The chief of these were "Ancient Mysteries Described," "The Every-day Book," "The Table Book," and "The Year Book," his last work being an edition of "Strutt's Sports and Pastimes of the English." *B.* at Bath, 1779; *d.* at Tottenham, 1842.—*Beeton's Biog. Dict.*

tact, and at the end of the first day's trial he obtained a verdict of acquittal amidst the shouts of the mob.

This being related to the enfeebled Chief Justice—his energy was revived, and he swore that at whatever cost he would preside in Court next day himself, so that conviction might be certain, and the insulted law might be vindicated. Accordingly he appeared in Court pale and hollow-visaged, but with a spirit un-broken, and more stern than when his strength was unimpaired. As he took his place on the bench, " I am glad to see you, my Lord Ellenborough," shouted Hone; " I know what you are come here for; I know what you want." " I am come to do justice," retorted the noble and learned Lord ; " my only wish is to see justice done." " Is it not rather, my Lord," said Hone, " to send a poor bookseller to rot in a dungeon ? "

The subject of this day's prosecution was " The Political Litany," and the course taken by the defend-ant, with great effect, was to read a vast collection of similar parodies composed by writers of high celebrity from Swift to Canning. Some of these exciting loud laughter in the crowd, the indignant Judge sent for the Sheriffs to preserve order, and fined them for their negligence. In summing up to the Jury he reminded them that they were sworn on the Holy Evangelists and were bound to protect the ritual of our Church from profanation :

" There are many things," said he, " in the parodies you have heard read which must be considered pro-fane and impious, although divines and statesmen may be the authors of them ; but this parody of the defend-ant transcends them all in profanity and impiety. I will deliver to you my solemn opinion, as *I am required by Act of Parliament to do ;* under the authority of that Act, and still more in obedience to my conscience and my God, I pronounce it to be a MOST IMPIOUS AND

PROFANE LIBEL. Hoping and believing that you are Christians, I doubt not that your opinion is the same."

The usual question being put when the jury after a short deliberation returned into Court,—the Chief Justice had the mortification to hear the words NOT GUILTY pronounced, followed by a tremendous burst of applause, which he could not even attempt to quell.

But he was still undismayed, and declared that he would proceed next day with the indictment on "The Sinecurist's Creed." This was a most indiscreet resolution.

The whole of Hone's third trial was a triumph, the jury plainly intimating their determination to find a verdict in his favor. He read parallel parodies as on the preceding days, and at last came to one said to be written by Dr. Law, the late Bishop of Carlisle, the Judge's own father. *Lord Ellenborough* (in a broken voice): " Sir, for decency's sake forbear." Hone withdrew it, and gained more advantage by this tasteful courtesy than the parody could have brought him, had it been ever so apposite. After a similar summing up as on the preceding day, there was the like verdict, accompanied with still louder shouts of applause.

Bishop Turner, who was present at the trial, and accompanied the Chief Justice home in his carriage, related that all the way he laughed at the tumultuous mob who followed him, remarking that " he was afraid of their *saliva*, not of their *bite :*" and that passing Charing Cross he pulled the checkstring, and said, " It just occurs to me that they sell the best red herrings at this shop of any in London; buy six." The popular opinion, however, was that Lord Ellenborough was killed by Hone's trial, and he certainly never held up his head in public after.

When the day again came round for the Judges to choose their Summer Circuits, he chose the Home, and

CHAP.
LI.

He is un-
able to go
the
Summer
Circuit.

appointed the days for holding the assizes at each place upon it; but as the time for his departure approached, his strength was unequal to the task, and he accepted the offer of LENS,[1] a King's Sergeant, an excellent lawyer and an accomplished scholar (whom he greatly wished to have for his successor as Chief Justice), to go in his stead. On this occasion he wrote the following

1. " John Lens (1756–1825), serjeant at law, son of John Lens, a well-known land agent in Norwich, was born there on Jan. 2, 1756. He was educated first at a school in Norwich, and then by the Rev. John Peele. In 1775 he matriculated at St. John's College, Cambridge. He graduated B.A. in 1779, when he was fourth wrangler and chancellor's medallist, and M.A. in 1782. After leaving Cambridge he entered at Lincoln's Inn, whence he was called to the bar in 1781. He at first joined the Norfolk circuit, but soon transferred himself to the western circuit, which he led for many years. On June 12, 1799, he became a serjeant at law, and in 1806 King's serjeant. His practice was extensive, and his position at the bar eminent. He was named a lay fellow of Downing College in its charter in 1800, was treasurer of Serjeant's Inn in 1806, succeeded Spencer Perceval in 1807, as counsel to the university of Cambridge, and was engaged in numerous celebrated cases, of which the chief were the action of Charles Perkin Wyatt, surveyor general of crown lands in Canada, against General Gore, governor of Upper Canada, for libel, in 1816, and the Cranborne Chase boundaries case in the same year. He sat as commissioner of assize at Guildford and Maidstone in 1818. He had been a friend and adherent of Fox, was a Whig by conviction, and might, had he chosen, have represented the university of Cambridge in parliament. But he was as indifferent to honors as he was completely disinterested. In December 1813, on the appointment of Sir Robert Dallas to the bench of the common pleas, he declined the solicitor generalship, although it was pressed upon him by the prime minister at the request of the prince regent, his personal friend. His independence at length became proverbial, and the toast ' Serjeant Lens and the independence of the bar ' was given at public dinners. In 1817 he retired from his circuit, at the height of his powers, in order to make way for younger men, but continued to practice in London, acting also as commissioner of assize on the home circuit in 1818. He refused the chief justiceship of Chester, and Lord Ellenborough strongly recommended him as his own successor in the office of lord chief justice. He died at Ryde in the Isle of Wight on Aug. 6, 1825. He had married in 1818 Mrs. Nares, widow of John Nares, Esq., son of Sir George Nares, a judge of the common pleas. His wife predeceased him on June 15, 1820. A portrait of Lens was at Serjeants' Inn."—*Nat. Biog. Dict.*

letter to his trusty clerk, who had served him faithfully CHAP.
many years: LI.

"St. James's Square, July 1, 1818.

"DEAR SMITH,

"Mr. Sergeant Lens seems to prefer taking his own carriage and a pair of horses, with a pair to be put before them from his jobman, to having the use of my chariot, drivers, and horses which I offered him. John will attend him as circuit butler on a horse, with which I will provide him. You will attend to all things material to the Sergeant's convenient accommodation, and see that they be fully supplied in all respects. The Sergeant as going in my place will, I presume, sit at each place on the circuit on the Civil side or the Crown side, as I should have done myself, viz., on the Civil side at Hertford, and on the Crown side at Chelmsford. You can apply to me if any matter of doubt should occur—which, however, I do not expect. I am going out of town to Roehampton.

"Yours, &c.,
"ELLENBOROUGH."

He afterwards took up his quarters at Worthing on the coast of Sussex, in hopes of benefit from the sea air. While there he wrote the following letters to his anxious clerk, who had a sincere regard for his kind master, besides holding an office worth 2000l. a year on his master's life:

"September 17th, 1818.

"DEAR SMITH,

"I think I am better, though but little, on my legs; and this fine weather gives me opportunity for beneficial exercise and exposure to the fresh air. Charles, who is with his family at Bognor, has been over to me here—as has Lushington from the same place. I shall be glad to see you when we are within distance of each other. Keep me properly apprised of your change of place from time to time, and believe me,

" Ever most sincerely,
" ELLENBOROUGH."

" October 1st, 1818.

" DEAR SMITH,

" I leave this place for Brighton for a month, on Saturday morning next. I have not gained much ground since I left town, and unless I make a progress which I do not expect, I shall not be able to look business in the face very soon. I am very lame in one of my legs from an erysipelas affection, which has settled there. I have likewise a troublesome cough, proceeding from the same cause. The Chief Justice of the Common Pleas [1] is here, and better, upon the whole, than I expected to find him. He is, however, very weak in body, and can hardly sustain himself against any fatigue. I shall be glad to see you.

" Yours very sincerely,
" ELLENBOROUGH."

Before this he had found that all hope of returning to the discharge of his public duties must be renounced, and he had with firmness made up his mind to seek repose, that he might prepare for the awful day when he himself was to stand before the tribunal of an almighty, an omniscient, but merciful Judge.

The last stage of his judicial career has been thus graphically described :

" Nature had exhibited evident symptoms of decay before his strenuous and ill-judged efforts on the trial of Hone ; his frame had been shaken by violent attacks of gout, and during the Hilary and Easter terms of 1818 his absence from Court became more frequent, and his calls on the Puisne Judges for assistance in the sittings

---

1. Sir Vicary Gibbs, who was then dying.

after term were often, though reluctantly, renewed. The fretfulness of his manner, and his irritable temperament, proved clearly the workings of disease when he occasionally re-appeared in the submissive and silent hall, and the frequent interruptions of " I will not recast the practice of the Court ; I do not sit here as pedagogue to hear first principles argued. What are the issues ? What can you mean by wandering thus wildly from the record ? I will not tolerate such aberration ; I cannot engender or inoculate my mind with a doubt ; I will not endure this industry of coughing ; " attested his impatient anxiety, and fast growing inability to sustain the toils of office. To the last he clung to his situation with adhesive grasp, and girded himself with a sort of desperate fidelity to perform its duties, at a time when, as he wrote to a friend, ' he could scarcely totter to his seat, and could only take notes *manu lassissimâ et corpore imbecillo.*' [1] During the calm of the recess he deluded his spirits with the hope that he might resume his duties once more. The physicians recommended Bath, but his failing health rendered the journey hazardous; and, just before Michaelmas term commenced, tardily and with repining, he was compelled to announce to the Chancellor his inability to remain." [2]

The following is his melancholy missive on this occasion :

"Worthing, September 21, 1818.

" My Dear Lord,

" The decay of many of my faculties, particularly of my eyesight, which I have painfully experienced since the beginning of the present year, strongly admonishes me of the duty which I owe to the public and myself on that account ; and as I have now held the office of Chief Justice of the Court of King's Bench for more

1. " With a heavy hand and a weak body."
2. Townsend, vol. i. 389.

than sixteen years, viz. from the 12th day of April, 1802, I am entitled, under the Acts of Parliament, to request, which I most humbly do, the permission of His Royal Highness the Prince Regent for leave to retire on the first day of next term, upon that amount of pension which by those Acts of Parliament His Royal Highness the Prince Regent is authorized to grant to a Chief Justice of the King's Bench retiring after a period of fifteen years' service. If I had been able to depend upon my strength for the due and satisfactory execution of my most important office for a longer period, I should not now have tendered my resignation to His Royal Highness."

The Chief Justice without any servility, had always been a special favorite at Carlton House, and his proffered resignation drew forth the following graceful letter of condolence from the PRINCE REGENT :

Compli-
mentary
letter to
him from
the Prince
Regent. " MY DEAR LORD,

"I have only this moment been informed of your arrival in town, and I cannot suffer it to pass without conveying to you the heart-felt grief with which I received from the Chancellor a few days ago, his report of the melancholy necessity under which you have found yourself of tendering your resignation, and of your retiring from public life. As to my own private feelings upon this most sad occasion, I will not attempt their expression ; indeed, that would be quite impossible—but as a public man I do not hesitate most distinctly to state, that it is the heaviest calamity, above all in our present circumstances, that could have befallen the country. My Lord, your career, since the moment you took your seat, and presided in the high court committed to your charge, can admit of but one sentiment, and but of one opinion ; it has been glorious to yourself, and most beneficial to the nation. You have afforded an example combining wisdom with every other talent and virtue which exalt your character, and place it beyond all praise. With these sentiments, and such a picture before me, where can I hope to find, or where can I look for that individual who shall not leave a blank still in that great machine, of which you were the mainspring and brightest ornament? If, however, my dear friend, there can be consolation for us under such afflicting circumstances, that consolation is, that you carry with you into your retirement the veneration, gratitude, and admiration of the good, and the unbounded love and affection of those who have had the happiness of associating more intimately with you in private life. I confess that the magnitude of the loss we are about to sustain presses so heavily upon me, that I have not the power of adding more than that my constant and most fervent wishes for your health, comfort, and happiness will ever attend you, and that I remain always,

"My dear Lord,

"Your most sincere and affectionate friend,

"GEORGE, P. R.[1]

"Carlton House, October 18th, 1818."

1. George (Augustus Frederick) IV., King of Great Britain, the eldest son of George III. and Queen Charlotte, was born on the 12th of August, 1762. His education was confided in 1771 to Lord Holderness as governor, and Markham, Bishop of Chester, as preceptor, who both resigned in 1776. Their places were supplied by the Duke of Montague and Dr. Hurd. His natural abilities were above mediocrity, but were not diligently or wisely improved. In his youth he became an object of his father's invincible aversion, and by a natural consequence attached himself to the Whig party, who were also treated as enemies by the King. He exhausted prematurely the resources of sensual indulgence, and was deeply involved in debt by gaming and extravagance. About 1786 he married privately Mrs. Fitzherbert, a Roman Catholic lady, who was the object of his most lasting attachment. This marriage was illegal, and, when the subject was broached in parliament, was publicly disowned by the Prince of Wales. The pressure of pecuniary difficulties rendered a regular marriage necessary, as the King refused to supply his extravagant wants except on the condition that he should marry. In

On the 6th day of November the Chief Justice went through the trying ceremony of executing his deed of

1795 he married his cousin, Caroline Amelia Elizabeth, a daughter of the Duke of Brunswick, who became the mother of the Princess Charlotte in 1796, and whom he treated with studied neglect, if not contempt. A final separation took place in 1796, and scandalous reports against her honor were circulated. The King having become, through insanity, incompetent for the duties of royalty, the Prince of Wales was appointed regent in February, 1811. He retained in office the Tory ministry of Mr. Percival, abandoning his former political friends, who accused him of ingratitude. The foreign policy of the prince regent was the same as that of George III. The war against the French was prosecuted with vigor and success in the Peninsula. In June, 1812, war was declared against the United States, with which a treaty of peace was concluded in December, 1814. Lord Liverpool succeeded Percival as prime minister in 1812. The only child of the Prince Regent, the Princess Charlotte, died in 1817. On the death of his father, George IV. ascended the throne, on the 29th of January, 1820. Great excitement was produced by the process instituted by the ministry in 1820 against Queen Caroline, for alleged infidelity to her husband. The majority for the ministers on this question in the House was so small that they abandoned the case. The prime minister, Lord Liverpool, having been prostrated by apoplexy, was succeeded by Mr. Canning in April, 1827. On the death of Canning, in August of the same year, Viscount Goderich became premier. In January, 1828, a new ministry was formed under the Duke of Wellington. A bill for the relief of Roman Catholics from political disabilities was passed after a long contest, in April, 1829. George IV. died in June, 1830, and was succeeded by his brother, the Duke of Clarence, as William IV. George IV. had no public virtues, and took little interest in the affairs of government.— *Thomas' Biog. Dict.*

Thackeray's summary of this Prince's character, although so well known, is yet worthy of repetition. " To make a portrait of him at first seemed a matter of small difficulty. There is his coat, his star, his wig, his countenance simpering under it: with a slate and a piece of chalk, I could at this very desk perform a recognizable likeness of him. And yet after reading of him in scores of volumes, hunting him through old magazines and newspapers, having him here at a ball, there at a public dinner, there at races and so forth, you find you have nothing—nothing but a coat and a wig and a mask smiling below it—nothing but a great simulacrum. His sire and grandsires were men. One knows what they were like ; what they would do in given circumstances ; that on occasion they fought and demeaned themselves like tough good soldiers. They had friends whom they liked according to their natures ; enemies whom they hated fiercely ; passions, and actions, and individualities of their own. The sailor King who came after George was a man ; the Duke

resignation, which cost him a deeper pang than draw-ing his last breath. This world had now closed upon him, and before another opened there was a dreary interval, in which, reduced to insignificance, he had the dread of suffering severe pain as well as cold neglect.

His family had flattered themselves that when re-lieved from the anxiety of business, to which he was inadequate, he would rally, and that he might long be spared to enliven and to comfort them ; but the excite-ment of office being removed, he only sunk more rapidly.

Having ever been a firm believer in Christianity, he was now supported by a Christian's hope. In a short month after his resignation it was evident that his end His death. was approaching, and having piously received the last consolations of religion, he calmly expired at his house in St. James's Square in the evening of Sunday, the

of York was a man, big, burly, loud, jolly, cursing, courageous. But this George, what was he? I look through all his life, and recognize but a bow and a grin. I try and take him to pieces, and find silk stockings, padding, stays, a coat with frogs and a fur collar, a star and blue ribbon, a pocket-handkerchief prodigiously scented, one of Truefitt's best nutty brown wigs reeking with oil, a set of teeth and a huge black stock, underwaistcoats, more under-waistcoats, and then nothing. I know of no sentiment that he ever distinctly uttered. Documents are published under his name, but people wrote them—private letters, but people spelt them. He put a great George P. or George R. at the bottom of the page and fancied he had written the paper ; some bookseller's clerk, some poor author, some *man* did the work ; saw to the spelling, cleaned up the slovenly sentences, and gave the lax, maudlin slipslop a sort of consistency. He must have had an individuality ; the dancing-master whom he emulated, nay, surpassed—the wig-maker who curled his toupee for him—the tailor who cut his coats, had that. But, about George, one can get at nothing actual. That outside, I am certain, is pad and tailor's work ; there may be something behind, but what? We cannot get at the character ; no doubt never shall. Will men of the future have nothing better to do than to unswathe and interpret that royal old mummy ? I own I once used to think it would be good sport to pursue him, fasten on him, and pull him down. But now I am ashamed to mount and lay good dogs on, to summon a full field and then to hunt the poor game."—*Thackeray's Four Georges.*

13th of December, 1818. On the 22d of the same
month his remains were interred in the cemetery of
the Charter-House,[1] by the side of those of Mr. Sutton,[2] its honored founder. The funeral was attended

[1]. The buildings of the Charter-House were presented to several
of the king's favorites in turn, and in 1565 were sold by the Norths
to the Duke of Norfolk, who pulled down many of the monastic
buildings, and added rooms more fitted to a palatial residence.
Thomas Howard, Earl of Suffolk, second son of the Duke of Norfolk,
beheaded for Mary Queen of Scots, sold the Charter-House for
13,000*l.* to Thomas Sutton, of Camps Castle, in Cambridgeshire, who
had made an enormous fortune in Northumbrian coal-mines. He
used it to found (1611) a hospital for aged men and a school for
children of poor parents—the "triple good" of Bacon, the "masterpiece of English charity" of Fuller. In 1872 the school was removed
to Godalming, supposed to be a more healthy situation, and the
land which was occupied by its buildings and playground was sold
to the Merchant Tailors for their school. But the rest of the foundation of Sutton still exists where he left it.

The *Charter-House* (shown by the Porter) is entered from the
Square by a perpendicular arch, with a projecting shelf above it,
supported by lions. Immediately opposite is a brick gateway belonging to the monastic buildings, which is that where the "arm of
Houghton was hung up as a bloody sign to awe the remaining
brothers to obedience," when his head was exposed on London
Bridge. The second court contains the Master's house, and is faced
by the great hall of the Dukes of Norfolk. By a door in the right
wall we pass to a *Cloister*, containing monuments to Thackeray, John
Leech, Sir Henry Havelock, old Carthusians, and Archdeacon Hale,
long a master of the Charter-House. Hence we enter *Brook Hall*, to
which Brook, a master of the Charter-House, whose picture hangs
here, was confined by Cromwell : another door leads to the *Chapel*,
of which the groined entrance dates from monastic times, but the
rest is Jacobian. On the left of the altar is the magnificent alabaster
tomb of Sutton, who died Dec. 12, 1611, a few months after his
foundation of the Charter-House. The upper part of the tomb repre-
sents his funeral sermon, with the poor brethren seated round. On
the cornice are figures of Faith and Hope, Labor and Rest, Plenty
and Want. The whole is the work of *Nicholas Stone* and *Jansen of
Southwark*. Opposite is an interesting tomb of Francis Beaumont,
an early master. The monument of Edward Law, Lord Ellenborough, is by *Chantrey*. There are tablets to Dr. Raine and other
eminent masters.—*Hare's Walks in London*.

2. Thomas Sutton, founder of the Charter-House, was born at
Knaith, Lincolnshire, about 1532. He was educated at Eton, and
next at Cambridge, after which he studied law at Lincoln's Inn. On
becoming secretary to the Earl of Warwick he was made master of
the ordnance at Berwick, where he signalized himself during the

by all the dignitaries of the law and many distinguished men from other ranks of life, and its pomp was rendered more solemn by a dense fog, which only permitted to the eye a dim glimpse of the procession.[1]

rebellion raised by the earls of Northumberland and Westmoreland. On account of his services at that period he obtained a patent for the office of master-general of the ordnance in the North for life. In 1573 he commanded one of the batteries which compelled the castle of Edinburgh to surrender to the English. While thus employed he made an accession to his fortune by the purchase of lands and mines in the bishopric of Durham. He afterwards increased his property by marriage, and, on turning merchant, prospered in all his undertakings. In 1611 he purchased the dissolved Charter-House for 13000*l.*, and began the hospital as it now stands, with an intention of being the first master, but died before its completion, Dec. 12, the same year. At his death he was the richest commoner in the kingdom.—*Athen. Cantab.* iii. 49–53.

1. From the family of his clerk, Mr. Smith, I have in my possession the originals of the two following letters, which I cannot refrain from copying, as they seem to me very creditable to all who are mentioned in them. They particularly show the subject of this memoir in a most amiable point of view, and prove that if at times he was regardless of giving pain to his equals, he must have been uniformly kind to dependants:

"Lofty and sour to them who loved him not ;
But to those men who sought him, sweet as summer."

The first, announcing Lord Ellenborough's death to Mr. Smith, is from the Honorable Charles Law, his second son, and the other, inviting Mr. Smith to the funeral, is from the present Earl of Ellenborough :

"Southampton Row, 8 o'clock.
"MY DEAR FRIEND,
"It has become my melancholy duty to announce to you the death of my beloved parent. He breathed his last about six o'clock, without a sigh and without a struggle. If you could call on me this evening, it would much oblige me.
"Yours, very sincerely and faithfully
CHAS. E. LAW.

"St. James Square, Dec. 18, 1818.
"MY DEAR SIR,
"I am sure the long and intimate connection you had with my father, and the regard you naturally entertained for him, would make you desirous of joining his family in the performance of the last duties to his memory ; and I am equally sure, from my knowledge of the gratitude my father felt for your very useful and faithful services, and of the esteem in which he held your character, that it would have been gratifying to him to think that his remains would

On a tablet near the spot where his dust reposes, there is the following simple inscription to his memory :

His
Epitaph.

In the Founder's vault are deposited the remains of
EDWARD LAW, LORD ELLENBOROUGH,
son of EDMUND LAW, LORD BISHOP of CARLISLE,
Chief Justice of the Court of King's bench from April
1802 to November 1818,
And a Governor of the Charter-House.
He died December 13, 1818, in the 69th year of his age ;
and in grateful remembrance of
the advantages he had derived through life from his
Education
upon the Foundation of the Charter-House,
desired to be buried in this Church.

His character.

His character has been thus drawn by one who knew him well :

He was not a man of ambition; he had still less of vanity. He received with satisfaction certainly, but without the smallest excitement, the appointment of Attorney General, the Chief Justiceship, and the Peerage. I never knew any man, except the Duke of Wellington,[1] who was so innately just. He thoroughly

be attended to the grave by you. Allow me, therefore, to request that you will proceed with us from this house on Tuesday morning before half-past seven.
                    "Very truly and faithfully yours,
                                        "E.

· "I have great pleasure in communicating to you that my late respected father has, in testimony of your long and faithful services, bequeathed to you the watch and gold chain he usually wore, and a small sum for the purchase of some memorial of him."

1. Arthur Wellesley, Duke of Wellington (b. 1769, d. 1852), was the fourth son of the first Earl of Mornington. He was educated at Eton, and afterwards at the military college at Angers, where he studied under the celebrated Pignerol. He entered the army in Mar., 1787. His career in the field commenced in Holland (1794), under the Duke of York. He shared the hardships of this campaign, occupying the post of honor, the rear guard. He received a colonelcy in 1796. His next service was in India, where he passed through the whole of the Mysore War, and the Siege of Seringapatam, being attached to the Nizam's contingent of horse. In July, 1799, he was nominated Governor of Seringapatam and Mysore, and the command in chief of the army of occupation was entrusted to him. He exercised the great powers conferred upon him in such a

WELLINGTON STATUE.

loved justice—strict justice, perhaps, but still justice.
He was also thoroughly devoted to the performance

way as to deserve and obtain the gratitude and respect of the natives, and to display his own extraordinary talents for organization and command. While thus employed he found it necessary to take the field against the marauder Dhoondiah Waugh, whom he routed and slew. In 1803 he was raised to the rank of major-general, and shortly afterwards the Mahratta War broke out. Major-General Wellesley was appointed to the command of the force destined to restore the Peishwa to his throne after the conclusion of the Treaty of Bassein, as well as to act against the Mahratta chiefs. Operations in the Deccan were quickly opened, and concluded by Wellesley's brilliant victory at Assye (Sept. 23, 1803), and Argaum (Nov. 19), which effectually subdued the opposition of Scindiah and the Rajah of Berar. Shortly after the close of the Mahratta War, General Wellesley quitted India, and after an absence of five years landed once more in England. In 1807 he was appointed Chief Secretary to the Lord-Lieutenant of Ireland. In the following August he was nominated to a command in the expedition to Copenhagen, and rendered important services, for which he received the special thanks of parliament. On July 12 the same year he started with a command of 10,000 men for Portugal, the Portland ministry having sent these troops at the request of the Portuguese government, who feared the ambitious designs of Napoleon. He landed successfully at Mondego, marched on Lisbon, and defeated the French at Rolica. Sir Harry Burrard, who had been appointed over Wellesley's head, now arrived and took the command, and countermanded all Wellesley's dispositions for the attack on Junot at Torres Vedras. The French therefore assailed the English at Vimiera, and again Sir Harry Burrard prevented the English success being decisive by forbidding Wellesley to pursue and cut off the French retreat to Torres Vedras. The Convention of Cintra roused the general indignation of England against the expedition and its commanders, and especially and most unwarrantably against Wellesley. He returned to England and resumed his Irish duties and his seat in parliament. In 1809, when the French had entirely occupied the Peninsula, Wellesley was sent out again with 24,000 men. He landed at Lisbon (April 22), marched against Soult, who was strongly posted at Oporto, and drove him into Galicia. The state of his commissariat rendered it impossible to pursue and march on Madrid as he had intended ; while the obstinacy and imbecility of the Spanish generals rendered co-operation impossible. In spite, therefore, of the crushing victory of Talavera he was obliged to retreat. The next year was occupied with the inroad of Napoleon, the victory of Busaco, and the successful defence of the lines of Torres Vedras. At last in 1812, after the capture af Badajos and Ciudad Rodrigo, Wellington began his march across Spain by defeating the French at Salamanca ; opened the road to Madrid ; and marched from thence to Burgos. He was, however, compelled to retire once more

ot his duty.   I have heard him say that no private consideration could absolve a man from the execution of

to the Portuguese frontier.   In 1813 he marched straight to Vittoria,
and from victory to victory till Soult was finally routed at Orthez,
and the abdication of Napoleon ended the great Peninsular War
At the close of the campaign he was for his services created Marquis
of Douro and Duke of Wellington; the House of Commons voted
him an annuity of 10,000*l.*, which was afterwards commuted for
the sum of 400,000*l.*, and on July 1 the thanks of the House were
conveyed to him by the Speaker.   The highest honors were conferred on him by the allies, and he was made a field-marshal in each
of the principal armies of Europe.   In August he proceeded to
Paris to represent the British government at the court of the Tuil-
eries.   He remained five months, and bore a principal share in the
negotiations of this year.   In Jan., 1815, the Duke was accredited
to Vienna as one of the representatives of Britain at the Congress
of the European Powers, and united with Austria and France in resisting the demands of Russia and Prussia.   In February Napoleon
broke loose from Elba, and Wellington was appointed commander-
in-chief against him.   The Hundred Days ended at Waterloo and
the allied armies marched on Paris, where Wellington had the
greatest difficulty in restraining the Prussian desire for vengeance :
and it was in consequence of his advice that the army of occupation, which was to have remained for five years, evacuated France
at the end of three.   The military career of the duke thus came to
an end.   In Oct., 1818, while attending the Congress of Aix-la-
Chapelle, he was offered and accepted the office of Master-General
of the Ordnance, with a seat in the Cabinet.   He took no prominent part, however, in the administration of home affairs, though
he shared the odium which accrued to the government from its
coersive policy.   He represented Great Britain at the Congress of
Verona in 1822, and protested against the armed intervention of the
French court in the affairs of Spain.   In 1826, he was sent on a
special mission to St. Petersburg for the purpose of promoting a
peaceable settlement of the Greek question.   In the following year
he refused to serve under Mr. Canning, and resigned the post of
Commander-in-Chief which had naturally come to him on the death
of the Duke of York.   In 1828, he himself became Prime Minister of
England.   The Canningites were allowed to retain their seats for a
short time, but very soon dissensions arose, and they were either
driven out or resigned spontaneously.   The great question of
Roman Catholic Emancipation had now for a quarter of a century
occupied the attention of the legislature, and had become not so
much a question of abstract principle and policy as of national peace
and security.   The continued anarchy of Ireland, the interminable
division of cabinets, the distraction of imperial councils, and the
utter impossibility of maintaining such a state of things, at last
satisfied the duke and Sir Robert Peel that the time had come when
the clamorous demand of the Roman Catholics should be conceded.

public duty—that should the person dearest to him in CHAP.
the world die, he would go into court next day if LI.

The premier had a clear perception of the difficulties to be encoun-
tered, and the sacrifices which must be made in thus surrendering
the citidel of Protestant ascendency, but having made up his mind
that this measure was necessary, he carried it through resolutely
and characteristically.   His policy was announced in the speech
from the throne (Feb. 5, 1829), and so vigorously was the measure
pressed, that in spite of the most determined opposition, the Relief
Bill passed both Houses by a large majority, and in little more
than a month became law.   The ministry of the duke was greatly
weakened by his victory over the principles and prejudices of his
party.   His opponents were not conciliated, while many of his old
supporters had become furious in their indignation.   The duke
failed to read the signs of the times, and his obstinate opposition to
Parliamentary Reform caused the downfall of his ministry, the accession of Earl Grey (1831), and the passing of the Reform Bill
At the final passage of the Bill, Wellington, at the request of the
king, left the House of Lords, followed by about a hundred peers,
to allow the Bill to pass.   All through this period the tide of
popular feeling ran strongly against the duke, who found it necessary to protect his windows from the mob by casings of iron.
When the excitement of the Reform agitation had subsided, popular
feeling towards him gradually changed ; and during the rest of his
life he retained a firm hold on the affections of the English people.
In 1834 the king announced his intention to recall the duke to his
councils, but the latter insisted that Sir Robert Peel was the proper
person to be placed at the head of the government, and himself accepted the post of Foreign Secretary.   In 1835 he retired with his
leader and never again took charge of any of the great civil depart-
ments of state.   In 1841, on the return of his party to power, he
accepted a seat in the Cabinet, but without office ; though he took
an active part in the business of the country.   In 1842, he again
became Commander-in-Chief, and was confirmed in the office for life
by patent under the Great Seal.   When the Irish famine brought the
Anti-Corn-law agitation to a crisis, he changed with Peel, and gave
that minister the warmest and most consistent support in his new
commercial policy.   It was in fact mainly through the duke's influence that the opposition of the great territorial magnates was withdrawn.   On the complete breakup of the Conservative party in
1846, the duke formally intimated his final retirement from political
life, and never again took any part in the debates in the House of
Lords except on military matters.   But he continued to take the
warmest interest in the welfare of the army, the country, and the
sovereign, and was regarded by the queen as a friendly and intimate adviser.   With the nation the popularity of "the duke" during
his later years was extraordinary and almost unique.   Wherever he
appeared he was received with enthusiasm and affection.   On
Sept. 14, 1852, he died at Walmer Castle, where he resided as

physically capable of doing so. When he took as his motto *compositum jus fasque animi,*[1] he stamped his own character upon his shield."

Of Lord Ellenborough as a Judge little remains to be said. Notwithstanding his defects, which were not small, it must be admitted that he filled his high office most creditably. He had an ascendency with his brethren, with the bar, and with the public, which none of his successors have obtained, and since his death his reputation has in no degree declined.[2] His bad temper and inclination to arrogance are forgotten, while men bear in willing recollection his unspotted integrity, his sound learning, his vigorous intellect, and his manly intrepidity in the discharge of his duty.

As a legislator his fame depends upon the Act (Lord Ellenborough's Act, 43 Geo. III. c. 58) which goes by his name, the only one he ever introduced into parliament,—by which ten new capital felonies were created, and the revolting severity of our criminal code was scandalously aggravated. Some of these, which before were only misdemeanors, might without impropriety have been made clergyable felonies, punishable with

Warden of the Cinque Ports. Of Wellington's eminence as a general there is no question. In an age of great commanders he was one of the greatest ; inferior to few of his contemporaries, save the great opponent whose designs he so often defeated. The integrity, honesty, and disinterested simplicity of his private character are equally little open to doubt. His position as a statesman admits of no dispute. That he did not altogether comprehend the spirit of the age in which he lived, and that he offered an unbending front to reform which in the end he was obliged to accept, can scarcely be denied.—*Dict. of Eng. Hist.*

1. " Law and justice."

2. The unenviable awe which he inspired into his brother Judges may be imagined from the following statement of Lord Brougham : " I remember being told by a learned Serjeant, that at the table of Serjeants' Inn, where the Judges met their brethren of the coif to dine, the etiquette was in those days never to say a word after the Chief Justice, nor ever to begin any topic of conversation. He was treated with more than the obsequious deference shown at Court to the Sovereign himself."

long imprisonment or transportation; but punishing them with death raised a cry against capital punishment, even in cases of murder, where it is prompted by nature, sanctioned by religion, and necessary for the security of mankind. However, Lord Ellenborough, with many of his contemporaries, thought that the criminal code could not be too severe. He strenuously opposed all the efforts of Sir Samuel Romilly in the cause of humanity, and was as much shocked by a proposal to repeal the punishment of death for stealing to the value of five shillings in a shop, as if it had been to abrogate the Ten Commandments:

" I trust," said he, " your Lordships will pause be- His approval of a fore you assent to a measure pregnant with danger to severe the security of property, and before you repeal a statute penal code. which has been so long held neccssary for public security, and which I am not conscious has produced the smallest injury to the merciful administration of justice. After all that has been stated in favor of this speculative humanity, it must be admitted that the law as it stands is but seldom carried into execution, and yet it ceases not to hold out that terror, which alone will be sufficient to prevent the frequent commission of the offence. It has been urged by persons speculating in modern legislation, that a certainty of punishment is preferable to severity—that it should invariably be proportioned to the magnitude of the crime, thereby forming a known scale of punishments commensurate with the degree of offence. Whatever may be my opinion of the theory of this doctrine, I am convinced of its absurdity in practice. . . . Retaining the terror, and leaving the execution uncertain and dependent on circumstances which may aggravate or mitigate the enormity of the crime, does not prove the severity of any criminal law ; whereas to remove that salutary dread of punishment would produce injury to the criminal, and break down the barrier which prevents the frequent commission of crime. The learned Judges are *unanimously agreed* that the expediency of justice and the public security require there should not be a remission of capital punishment in this part of the criminal law. My Lords, if we suffer this bill to pass, we shall not know where to stand—we shall not know whether we are on our heads or on our feet. If you repeal the Act which inflicts the penalty of death for stealing to the value of five shillings in a shop, you will be called upon next year to repeal a law which prescribes the penalty of death for stealing five shillings in a dwelling house, there being no person therein—a law, your Lordships must know, on the severity of which, and the application of it, stands the security of every poor cottager who goes out to his daily labor. He, my Lords, can leave no one behind to watch his little dwelling and preserve it from the attacks of lawless plunderers; confident in the protection of the laws of the land, he cheerfully pursues his daily labors, trusting that on his return he shall find all his property safe and unmolested. Repeal this law, and see the contrast: no man can trust himself for an hour out of doors without the most alarming apprehensions that on his return every vestige of his property will be swept away by the hardened robber. My Lords, painful as is the duty—anxious as the feelings of a Judge are—unwilling as he is to inflict the tremendous penalties of the law—there are cases where mercy and humanity to the few would be injustice and cruelty to the many. There are cases where the law must be applied in all its terrors. *My Lords, I think this, above all others, is a law on which so much of the security of mankind depends in its execution, that I should deem myself neglectful of my duty to the public if I failed to let the law take its course.*"

The Chief Justice scoffed "at that speculative and

modern philosophy which would overturn the laws that a century had proved to be necessary—on the illusory opinions of speculatists.

" I implore you, " he said, in one of his latest addresses to the Lords, " not to take away the only security the honest and industrious have against the outrages of vice and the licentiousness of dishonesty. There is a dangerous spirit of innovation abroad on this subject, but against which I ever have been, and always shall be, a steady opposer. I seek no praise—I want no popular applause ; all I wish is, that the world may esteem me as a man who will not sacrifice one iota of his duty for the sake of public opinion. My Lords, 1 shall never shrink from the fulfilment of the most arduous task from fear of popular prejudice."

The degree to which Lord Ellenborough's powerful mind was perverted by early prejudice, may be seen from the following entry in the Diary of Sir Samuel Romilly.

" Lord Lauderdale told me that soon after my pamphlet appeared, in 1810, he had some conversation about it with Ellenborough, who told him, that though the instances were very rare, yet it sometimes became necessary to execute the law against privately stealing in shops, and that he had himself left a man for execution at Worcester for that offence. The man had, he said, when he came to the bar, lolled out his tongue and acted the part of an idiot ; that he saw the prisoner was counterfeiting idiocy, and bade him be on his guard ; that the man, however, still went on in the same way ; whereupon Lord Ellenborough, having put it to the jury to say whether the prisoner was really of weak mind, and they having found that he was not, and having convicted him, left him for execution. Upon which Lord Lauderdale asked the Chief Justice what law there was which punished with death the counter-

feiting idiocy in a court of justice ; and told him that
he thought his story was a stronger illustration of my
doctrines than any of the instances which I had mentioned."

Lord Ellenborough was equally opposed to every
improvement in the law of Debtor and Creditor, and
prophesied the utter ruin of commercial credit and the
subversion of the empire if the invaluable right of ar-
resting on mesne process should ever be taken away,
or the fatal principle of *cessio bonorum* [1] should ever be
recognized in this country, so as that an honest insolvent might be entitled to be discharged out of prison
on yielding up the whole of his property to his creditors. [2]

I may perhaps feel some little pride in beholding
England, after the passing of bills, which I had the
honor to introduce into parliament, to take away " the
invaluable right," and to establish " the fatal principle,"
—more wealthy and more prosperous than she ever
was before.

His dislike
of foreign
laws.   Lord Ellenborough had seen very little of foreign
countries, and was rather intolerant of what he considered unEnglish. While in Paris, he went to attend
a criminal trial at the Cour d'Assises, but when the
interrogatory of the prisoner began, he made off, saying
that it was contrary to the first principles of justice to
call upon the accused to criminate himself. He saw
still stronger reason to be disgusted with their civil
procedure. He had hired a carriage by the day, with
a coachman, from the *remise*. On one of the *quais* the
coachman, by furious driving, wilfully damaged some
crockery-ware exposed to sale by an old woman. She
screamed ; a *sergent de ville* came up, the carriage was
stopped, and Milord Anglais was called upon to pay a

1. Surrender of goods.
2. 19 Parl. Deb 1169-1172 ; 20 Parl. Deb. 229, 606-7.

large sum of money by way of *amende*. He denied his liability, and insisted that, according to the doctrine of *Macmanus* v. *Cricket*, 1 East, 106, the only remedy was against the coachman himself, or against the keeper of the *remise ;* but he was cast, and had to pay damages and costs.

The Chief Justice deserves great credit for the exercise of his influence in the appointment of puisne Judges. Lord Chancellor Eldon was in the habit of consulting him on this subject, and of being guided by his advice. Free from all petty jealousy, he chose for his colleagues Bayley, Dampierre, Holroyd, and Abbott.[1]

He never appeared before the world as an author, and, from the want of attention to English composition which prevails at English seminaries, he was signally unskilful in it. In his written judgments, as they appear in the law reports, he betrays an utter disregard of *rhythm*, and his hereditary love of *parenthesis* is constantly breaking out.[2]

It was in sarcastic effusions from the bench, and in jocular quips when mixing in society on equal terms with his companions, that he acquired his most brilliant renown. Westminster Hall used to abound with his *facetiæ*, and some of them (perhaps not the best) are still *cited*.

A young counsel who had the reputation of being a His facetiæ.

1. I have had the opportunity of reading the letters between Lord Eldon and Lord Ellenborough about the appointment of Judges; but such correspondence ought to remain for ever "secret and confidential."

2. It is related of his father, the Bishop of Carlisle, that in passing a work through the press, the proof-sheets, which were promised to be sent regularly, soon stopped, and that going to the printing office to remonstrate, the *Devil* said to him, "Please you, my Lord, your Lordship's MS. has already used up all our parentheses, but we have sent to the letter founder's for a ton extra, which we expect to be sent in next week."

very impudent fellow, but whose memory failed him
when beginning to recite a long speech which he had
prepared, having uttered these words—" The *unfortunate client* who appears by me—the *unfortunate client*
who appears by me—My Lord, my *unfortunate client* "
—the Chief Justice interposed, and almost whispered in
a soft and encouraging tone—" You may go on, Sir—so
far the Court is quite with you."

Mr. Preston,[1] the famous conveyancer, who boasted
that he had answered 50,000 cases, and drawn deeds
which would go round the globe, if not sufficient to
cover the whole of its surface, having come special
from the Court of Chancery to the King's Bench to
argue a case on the construction of a will, assumed that
the Judges whom he addressed were ignorant of the

1. Richard Preston (1768–1850), legal author, only son of Rev.
John Preston, of Okehampton, Devonshire, was born at Ashbur-
ton in the same county in 1768. He began life as an attorney, but
attracted the notice of Sir Francis Buller, by his first work, " An
Elementary Treatise by Way of Essay on the Quantity of Estates,"
Exeter 1791, 8vo. By Buller's advice he entered in 1793 at the Inner
Temple, where, after practising for some years as a certificated conveyancer, he was called to the bar on May 20, 1807, was elected a
bencher in 1834, in which year he took silk, and was reader in 1844.
Preston represented Ashburton in the Parliament of 1812-18, and
was one of the earliest and most robust advocates of the imposition of
the corn duties. He had invested a large fortune, derived from his
conveyancing practice, in land in Devonshire. In law, as in politics,
he was intensely conservative, and thought the Fines and Recoveries
Act a dangerous innovation ; but his knowledge of the technique of
real property law was profound, and his works on conveyancing are
masterpieces of patient research and lucid exposition. He was for
some time professor of law at King's College, London. He died on
June 20, 1820, at his seat, Lee House, Chulmleigh, near Exeter.
Besides the work mentioned in the text Preston was author of : 1.
" A Succinct View of the Rule in Shelley's Case," Exeter, 1794, 8vo.
2. A volume of "Tracts " (on cross-remainders, fines and recoveries,
and similar subjects), London, 1797, 8vo. 3. " A Treatise on Conveyancing," London, 1806–9, 2 vols., 8vo.; 2d edit., 1813 ; 3d edit ,
1819–29 8vo. 4. "An Essay in a Course of Lectures on Abstracts of
Title," London, 1818, 8vo.; 2d edit., 1823-4, 8vo. He also, edited in
1828, Sheppard's "Touchstone of Common Assurances," London,
8vo.—*Nat. Biog. Dict.*

first principles of real property, and thus began his erudite harangue—"An estate in *fee simple*, my Lords, is the highest estate known to the law of England." "Stay, stay," said the Chief Justice, with consummate gravity, "let me take that down." He wrote and read slowly and emphatically, "An estate—in fee simple—is —the highest estate—known to—the law of England;" adding, "Sir, the Court is much indebted to you for the information."[1] There was only one person present who did not perceive the irony. That person having not yet exhausted the Year Books, when the shades of evening were closing upon him, applied to know when it would *be their Lordships' pleasure* to hear the remainder of his argument? *Lord Ellenborough.*—"Mr. Preston, we are bound to hear you out, and I hope we shall do so on Friday—but alas! pleasure has been long out of the question."

Another tiresome conveyancer having, towards the end of Easter Term, occupied the Court a whole day about the *merger of a term*, the Chief Justice said to him, "I am afraid, Sir, the TERM, although a long one, will *merge* in your argument."

1. Chief Justice Gibbs once told me this anecdote of Serjeant Vaughan, who, although a popular advocate and afterwards made a Judge, was utterly ignorant of the rudiments of the law of real property, and terribly alarmed lest he should commit some absurd blunder. "He was arguing a real property case before me, of which he knew no more than the usher, and he laid down Preston's proposition that 'an estate in fee simple is the highest estate known to the law of England.' I, wishing to frighten him, pretended to start, and said, 'What is your proposition, brother Vaughan?' when, thinking he was quite wrong and wishing to get out of the scrape, he observed, 'My Lord, I mean to contend that an estate in fee simple is *one of* the highest estates known to the law of England—that is, my Lord, that it may be under certain circumstances—and sometimes is so." But the learned Serjeant had good qualities, which rendered him very popular—although when he was promoted to the Bench by the interest of his brother, Sir Henry Halford, physician to George IV., it was said by the wags that he had a better title than any of his brethren, being a Judge *by prescription.*

James Allan Park, who had the character of being very sanctimonious, having in a trumpery cause affected great solemnity, and said several times in addressing the Jury, " I call Heaven to witness—as God is my Judge," &c.—at last Lord Ellenborough burst out—" Sir, I cannot allow the law to be thus violated in open Court. I must proceed to fine you for profane swearing—five shillings an oath." The learned counsel, whose risibility was always excited by the jokes of a Chief Justice, is said to have joined in the laugh created by this pleasantry.

Mr. Caldecot,[1] a great Sessions lawyer, but known

1. " Thomas Caldecott, (1743-1833) lawyer, book collector, and Shakespearean student, was educated at New College, Oxford, where he obtained a fellowship and proceeded B.C.L. on Oct. 24 1770. He was called to the bar at the Middle Temple; afterwards became a bencher, and was for many years a prominent member of the Oxford circuit. He published, in continuation of Sir James Burrow's ' Reports,' two volumes of ' Reports of Cases relative to the duty and office of a Justice of the Peace from 1776 to 1785' (2 vols. 1786, 1789). Caldecott died at the age of ninety, at Dartford, at the end of May, 1833. He best deserves to be remembered as a book collector and Shakespearean student. He laid the foundation of his library at an early age, and at his death it was singularly rich in sixteenth-century literature. He was a regular attendant at the great book sales, and many of Farmer's, Stevens's, West's, and Pearson's books passed to him. He bequeathed to the Bodleian an invaluable collection of Shakespearean quartos, some of which cost him the merest trifle, but the bulk of his library was sold by auction by Messrs. Sotheby between Dec. 2 and 7, 1833. Dr. Dibdin, the bibliographer, described the rarest books in three papers contributed to the Gentleman's Magazine for 1834 (pt. 1. pp. 59, 195, 284). Caldecott had views of his own on Shakespearean editing. Dibdin describes him as ' the last of the old breed of Shakespearean commentators of the school of Johnson and Stevens,' and he certainly had characteristic contempt for Malone, Stevens, and the Shakespearean scholars of his own day. After many years' labor he published privately in 1832 a volume containing ' Hamlet' and ' As You Like It,' with elaborate notes. This was intended to be the first instalment of a final edition of Shakespeare. But the compilation proved singularly feeble and was not continued. Caldecott was well acquainted with ' honest Tom Warton' and Bishop Percy, and entered heartily into the former's quarrels with Ribson, whom he styles in a letter to Percy, ' that scurrilous miscreant.'—*Nat. Biog. Dict.*

as a dreadful *bore*, was arguing a question upon the rate-
ability of certain lime quarries to the relief of the poor,
and contended at enormous length that, " like lead and
copper mines, they were not rateable, because the lime-
stone in them could only be reached by deep *boring*,
which was matter of science." *Lord Ellenborough, C.
J.*—" You will hardly succeed in convincing us, Sir,
that every species of *boring* is ' *matter of science.*' "

A declamatory speaker (Randle Jackson,[1] counsel
for the E. I. Company), who despised all technicalities,
and tried to storm the Court by the force of eloquence,
was once, when uttering these words, " In the book of
nature, my Lords, it is written "—stopped by this question from the Chief Justice, " Will you have the goodness to mention the *page*, Sir, if you please? "

A question arose, whether, upon the true construction of certain tax acts, *mourning coaches* attending a
funeral were subject to the post-horse duty? Mr.
Gaselee,[2] the counsel for the defendant, generally con-

1. " Randle Jackson (1757–1837), parliamentary counsel, son of
Samuel Jackson of Westminster, was matriculated at Oxford July 17,
1789, at the age of thirty-two (Foster, *Alumni Oxonienses*). A member
first of Magdalen Hall, afterwards of Exeter College, he was created
M.A. May 2, 1793. In the same year, on Feb. 9, he was called to the
bar by the Middle Temple (Foster; the Georgian Era 11, 548, says
by Lincoln's Inn). He was admitted *ad eundem* at the Inner Temple
in 1805, and became a bencher of the Middle Temple in 1828. Jackson won a considerable reputation at the bar, and acted as parliamentary counsel of the East India Company and of the corporation
of London. Five or six of his speeches delivered before parliamentary committees or the proprietors of East India stock on the griev-
ances of cloth-workers, the prolongation of the East India Company's charter, etc., were printed. Jackson died at North Brixton
March 15, 1837. Besides his speeches, Jackson published: 1. ' Considerations on the Increase of Crime,' London, 1828, 8vo. 2. ' A
Letter to Lord Henley, in answer to one from his Lordship requesting a vote for Middlesex, and with observations on his Lordship's
plan for a reform in our church Establishment,' London, 1832, 8vo."
—*Nat. Biog. Dict.*

2. " Sir Stephen Gaselee (1762–1839), justice of the court of common
pleas, was the son of Stephen Gaselee, an eminent surgeon at Portsmouth, where he was born in 1762. He was admitted a student at

sidered a dry special pleader, aiming for once at eloquence and pathos, observed—"My Lords, it never
could have been the intention of a Christian legislature
to aggravate the grief felt by us in following to the
grave the remains of our dearest relatives, by likewise
imposing upon us the payment of the post-horse duty."
Lord Ellenborough, C. J.—"Mr. Gaselee, may there not
be some danger in sailing up into these high sentimental latitudes?"

A very doubtful *nisi prius* decision being cited
before him, he asked, "Who ruled that?" Being
answered "The Chief Justice of the Isle of Ely "—he
replied—"Cite to me the decisions of the 'Judges of the
land — not of the Chief Justice of the Isle of Ely "—
adding in a stage whisper, " who is only fit to *rule*—a
copybook."[1]

A Quaker coming into the witness box at Guildhall
without a broad brim or dittoes, and rather smartly
dressed, the crier put the book into his hand and was

Gray's Inn on Jan. 29, 1781, but he was not called to the bar until
Nov. 20, 1793. He had the advantage of being a pupil of Sir Vicary
Gibbs, under whose instruction he became a skilful special pleader.
He joined the western circuit, and was so much respected as a careful and well-informed junior, that when, after twenty-six years'
practice, he was made a king's counsel in Hilary term, 1819, his professional income was probably diminished. Though he was not orator enough to commence practice as a leader, his deserved reputation
for legal knowledge soon recommended him for a judge's place. On
the resignation of Sir John Richardson, he was selected on July 1,
1824, to supply the vacant justiceship in the common pleas, became
a serjeant-at-law July 5, 1824, and was knighted at Carlton House
on April 27 in the following year. In that court he sat for nearly
thirteen years, with the character of a painstaking and upright judge.
He was a vice-president and an active member of the Royal Humane
Society, and is said to have been the original of the irascible judge
represented by Dickens in the trial of *Bardell* v. *Pickwick*, under the
name of Justice Starleigh. He resigned his judgeship at the end of
Hilary term, 1837, and after two years' retirement died at 13 Montague Place, Russell Square, London, on March 26, 1839. His wife
was Henrietta, daughter of James Harris, of the East India Company's service."—*Nat. Biog. Dict.*

1. This was Christian, a far-away cousin of Lord Ellenborough.

about to administer the oath, when he required to be
examined on his *affirmation.* Lord Ellenborough asking if he was really a Quaker, and being answered in the
affirmative, exclaimed, " Do you really mean to impose
upon the Court by appearing here in the disguise of a
reasonable being?"

A witness dressed in a fantastical manner having
given very rambling and discreditable evidence, was
asked in cross-examination, "What he was?" *Witness—*
"I employ myself as a surgeon." *Lord Ellenborough,
C. J.*—" But does any one else *employ you as a surgeon?*"

A volunteer corps of Wesminster shopkeepers, while
exercising in Tothill Fields, being overtaken by a violent
storm of wind and rain, took shelter in Westminster Hall,
while he was presiding in the adjoining Court of King's
Bench. *Lord Ellenborough, C. J.*—" Usher, what is the
meaning of that disturbance?" *Usher.*—"My Lord, it
is a volunteer regiment *exercising*, your Lordship."
Lord Ellenborough, C. J.—" *Exercising!* We will see
who is best at that. Go, Sir, to the Regiment, and inform it, that if it depart not instantly I will commit
it the custody of a tipstaff." The noble and learned
Lord seems to have forgotten his own military enthusiasm when he exercised in the awkward squad of the
" DEVIL'S OWN."

At a Cabinet dinner of " All the Talents" Lord ——
being absent, and some one observing that he was
seriously ill, and like to die: " Die!" said Lord Ellenborough—" why should he die? What would he *get*
by that?"

Henry Hunt,[1] the famous demagogue, having been

1. Henry Hunt, a political agitator and mob orator, born in Wiltshire Nov. 6, 1773. The quiet pursuit of farming he quitted in order
to embark on the troubled sea of politics; and his hearty advocacy
of extreme Radical doctrines soon rendered him the darling of the
mob. A meeting over which he presided at Manchester (1819) was
dispersed by the authorities; and Mr. Hunt, being prosecuted, was

brought up to receive sentence upon a conviction for holding a seditious meeting, began his address in mitigation of punishment, by complaining of certain persons who had accused him of "stirring up the people by *dangerous eloquence." Lord Ellenborough, C. J.* (in a very mild tone).—"My impartiality as a Judge calls upon me to say, Sir, that in accusing you of that they do you great injustice."

The following dialogue between the same Chief Justice and the same demagogue we have on the authority of Mr. Justice Talfourd,[1] who was present at it:

sentenced to two years and a half imprisonment, to pay a fine of 1000*l.*, and to give surety for his future good conduct. On his liberation, he made a kind of triumphal entry into London. After several unsuccessful attempts to enter parliament, he was at last elected for Preston; but, to the astonishment of his admirers, his eloquence, so effective out of doors, produced little or no effect in the House of Commons. Died Feb. 13, 1835.—*Cooper's Biog. Dict.*

1. "That a devotion to literature and the possession of a poetic genius are not necessarily incompatible with abstruser studies, nor absolute impediments to professional success, is exemplified in the career of Sir Thomas Noon Talfourd, who from the beginning to the end of his life united to the labors of the law the more agreeable avocations of an essayist, a poet, and a dramatist. The union of these apparently opposite studies did not prevent him from obtaining a considerable mastery of both: nor did the general reputation of this double occupation induce the legal world to suppose that he would neglect or fail in his exertions for them, because he employed himself occasionally in lighter pursuits. It is not, perhaps, too much to say that he owed his success and his promotion as much to his literary as to his legal character; and it is not improbable that in the future he will be remembered more as the author of ' Ion' and as the friend and biographer of Charles Lamb than as one of the judges of Westminster Hall. This divided empire, however, of literature and law is not one to be recommended, and the success in this instance must be taken more as the exception than as the rule. Thomas Noon Talfourd was the son of Edward Talfourd, a brewer at Reading, not in very prosperous circumstances, and of a daughter of the Rev. Thomas Noon, an independent minister there. He was born at Reading on January 26, 1795. His education commenced at the dissenters' school at Mill Hill, and proceeded at the grammar school at Reading. then holding a high character under the guidance of the celebrated Dr. Valpy. At the latter were strengthened and confirmed those poetic and dramatic inclinations which he had shown

"Lord Ellenborough had come down after an interval, CHAP. during which his substitutes had made slow progress, and was LI.

from his earliest youth, and the indulgence of which had hitherto been confined to the sacred dramas of Hannah More, and works of that class. He displayed his talent in some juvenile pieces, long since suppressed; but he always attributed his future more matured efforts to the classical taste which he imbibed from his accomplished preceptor. After gaining many of the prizes and other distinctions of the school, stern necessity obliged him to quit the flowery paths of elegant literature, and to seek the means of subsistence in London. There, to support himself, he obtained employment as a newspaper reporter, and as a regular contributor to periodical publications. At the same time he sought instruction in the intricacies of law from the eminent special pleader, Mr. Joseph Chitty; and to qualify himself for the grade of a barrister he partook of all the initiatory dinners at the Middle Temple, no further preparation being at that time required. His novitiate being completed he was called to the bar on February 9, 1821, and attended the Oxford circuit, where for some time he was engaged in reporting the assize business for the "Times," and obtained great credit for the impartial manner in which he detailed the exertions of his colleagues, and for the modest avoidance of his own name when he happened to be engaged. Thus gaining the respect of his associates, his genial qualities soon made him a general favorite; and the observance of his industry in reporting, and the competent knowledge which it indicated, brought him a gradual increase of business from those who distribute professional favors. To these recommendations was added a powerful and attractive style of oratory, which greatly availed him when taking a leading part, and at the end of twelve years the position he had secured justified him in applying for the distinction of a silk gown. He took the degree of a serjeant in 1833; and when the court of Common Pleas was soon after opened to all barristers he received a patent of precedence which gave him rank in all the courts. He had two years before been selected as deputy recorder of the town of Banbury. From this time he proceeded with distinguished success, and eventually became the acknowledged head of his circuit. In the metropolis also he shared with the eminent counsel who then graced the courts the conduct of the more important conflicts that engaged them; never sacrificing the interests of his clients to a love of display, and being as successful in their management and gaining as many verdicts as the most popular of his competitors. Two events occurring in the year 1835 tended greatly to extend his fame,—his entrance into parliament as the representative of his native town, and the appearance of his tragedy of 'Ion' on the stage. In the former he soon became conspicuous, not only for his oratorical powers, by which lawyers do not generally make themselves acceptable to the House, but for two great measures which he advocated with extraordinary zeal and effect; one securing to the mother the right to have access to her children

rushing through the list like a rhinoceros through a sugar plantation, or a Common Serjeant in the evening through a paper of small larcenies ; but just as he had non-suited the plaintiff in the twenty-second cause, which the plaintiff's attorney had thought safe till the end of a week, and was about to retire to his turtle, with the conviction of having done a very good morning's work, an undeniable voice exclaimed, 'My Lord!' and Mr. Hunt was seen on the floor with his peculiar air—perplexed between that of a bully and a martyr. The Bar stood aghast at his presumption ; the ushers' wands trembled in their hands ; and the reporters, who were retiring after a very long day, during which, though some few City firms had been crushed into bankruptcy, and some few hearts broken by the results of the causes, they could honestly de-

as long as her character is unstained; and the other securing to the author an extended period during which he or his family may enjoy the fruits of his labors. To the next parliament of 1841 Mr. Serjeant Talfourd was not returned, but in that of 1847 he resumed his seat for Reading till his elevation to the bench. His dramatic efforts during this interval did not meet with the brilliant success that attended the production of 'Ion.' They consisted of 'The Athenian Captive,' and the 'Massacre of Glencoe,' which were both acted, and 'The Castilian,' which was privately circulated. His other publications were numerous, among the most important of which were 'Vacation Rambles,' a 'Life of Charles Lamb,' and an 'Essay on the Greek Drama,' contributed to a cyclopædia. It was not till eight-and-twenty years after his call to the bar, and sixteen years after he took the degree of serjeant, that he was admitted into the judicial college. Upon the lamented death of Mr. Justice Coltman, Serjeant Talfourd was called upon, in July 1849, to take his place as a judge of the Common Pleas: where he received the accustomed honor of knighthood. The periodical press was loud in the expression of the universal feeling of pleasure which the appointment occasioned; and during the five years that he administered justice on the bench he did not disappoint the general expectation. Though not what is called a black-letter lawyer, his great good sense and extreme desire to do justice, his vigorous intellect and his practical experience, his personal amiability and urbanity towards all, made him a most satisfactory judge. His career was closed by an awful termination. While delivering his charge to the grand jury at Stafford on March 13, 1854, and recommending in emphatic terms a closer connection between the rich and the poor, he was, in the middle of an effective passage, suddenly struck with apoplexy, and ere a few moments had elapsed had gone to his great account. He married in 1821 the daughter of Mr. John Towell Rutt, a merchant of London and one of his earliest friends. She survived him, having brought him a numerous family."—*Foss's Judges of England.*

scribe as ' affording nothing of the slightest interest except to
the parties,' rushed back and seized their note-books to catch
any word of that variety of rubbish which is of ' public interest.' My Lord paused and looked thunders, but spoke none.
'I am here, my Lord, on the part of the boy Dogood,' proceeded the undaunted Quixote. His Lordship cast a moment's
glance on the printed list, and quietly said, ' Mr. Hunt, I see
no name of any boy Dogood in the paper of causes,' and
turned towards the door of his room. ' My Lord!' vociferated
the orator, ' am I to have no redress for an unfortunate youth ?
I thought your Lordship was sitting for the redress of injuries
in a court of justice.' ' O no, Mr. Hunt,' still calmly re-
sponded the Judge—' I am sitting at Nisi Prius ; and I have
no right to redress any injuries, except those which may be
brought before the jury and me, in the causes appointed for
trial.' ' My Lord,' then said Mr. Hunt, somewhat subdued
by the unexpected amenity of the Judge, ' I only desire to
protest.' ' Oh, is that all ?' said Lord Ellenborough : ' by all
means protest, and go about your business !' So Mr. Hunt
protested and went about his business ; and my Lord went
unruffled to his dinner, and both parties were content."[1]

While the old Lord Darnley, against whom Lord
Ellenborough had a special spite, was making a tiresome
speech in the House of Lords, he rose up and said,
with that quaint and dry humor which rarely suffered
his own muscles to relax, but loud enough to be heard
by three-fourths of the Peers present, " I am answerable to God for my time, and what account can I give
at the day of judgment if I stay here any longer ?"

A very tedious Bishop having yawned during his
own speech, Lord Ellenborough exclaimed, " Come,
come, the fellow shows some symptoms of taste, but
this is encroaching on our province."

Of Michael Angelo Taylor, who, though very short
of stature, was well knit, and thought himself *a very
great man*—Lord Ellenborough said, " his father, the
sculptor, had fashioned him for *a pocket Hercules.*"

1. Talfourd's " Vacation Rambles."

CHAP. LI.

At the coming in of the "TALENTS" in 1806, Erskine himself pressed the Great Seal upon Ellenborough, saying that " he would add to the splendor of his reputation as Lord Chancellor." Ellenborough knowing that on his own refusal, Erskine was to be the man, exclaimed, "How can you ask me to accept the office of Lord Chancellor when I know as little of its duties as you do?"[1]

Being told that the undertaker had made a foolish mistake in the hatchment put up on Lord Kenyon's house after the death of that frugal Chief Justice, MORS JANUA VITA, his successor exclaimed, " No mistake at all, Sir—there is no mistake—it was by particular directions of the deceased in his will—it saved the expense of a diphthong!"

From these sayings it might be thought that he was uniformly cynical and even acrimonious, but he spoke rather from a love of fun than from any malignity, and he had in him a large stock of good humor and *bonhomie*, which, producing little epigrammatic point, is in danger of being forgotten. He was an extremely agreeable companion. "The pungency of his wit," said an old class-fellow, "his broad, odd, sometimes grotesque jokes, his hearty merriment, which he seemed to enjoy, rather by a quaint look and indescribable manner than by any audible laughing, altogether formed a most lively and delightful person, whether to hear or see."

LordEllenborough in domestic life.

In domestic life Lord Ellenborough was exceedingly amiable, though on rare occasions a little hasty. It was reported that Lady Ellenborough, by doing what all ladies then considered very innocent, trying to smuggle some lace, caused the family coach to be seized as forfeited, and that he calmly said, " We have only to pay the penalty." But if Rogers is to be believed, he

1. *Ex relatione* the present Earl of Ellenborough.

did not show such equanimity when he thought that a bandbox had been improperly put into the carriage by her Ladyship. The author of the 'Pleasures of Memory' used often to relate the following anecdote:

"Lord Ellenborough was once about to go on the circuit, when Lady Ellenborough said that she should like to accompany him. He replied that he had no objection, provided she did not encumber the carriage with bandboxes, which were his utter abhorrence. During the first day's journey, Lord Ellenborough, happening to stretch his legs, struck his foot against something below the seat. He discovered that it was a bandbox. Up went the window and out went the bandbox. The coachman stopped, and the footmen, thinking that the bandbox had tumbled out of the window by some extraordinary chance, were going to pick it up, when Lord Ellenborough furiously called out, 'Drive on!' The bandbox accordingly was left by the ditch-side. Having reached the county-town where he was to officiate as Judge, Lord Ellenborough proceeded to array himself for his appearance in the Court-house. 'Now,' said he, 'where's my wig—where is my wig?' 'My Lord,' replied his attendant, 'it was thrown out of the carriage window.'"[1]

Lord Ellenborough was above the middle size, and sinewy, but his figure was ungainly, and his walk singularly awkward. He moved with a sort of semirotary step, and his path to the place to which he wished to go was the section of a parabola. When he entered the court he was in the habit of swelling out his cheeks by blowing and compressing his lips, and you would have supposed that he was going to snort like a war horse preparing for battle. His spoken diction, although always scholarlike, rather inclined to the sesquipedalian; his intonation was deep and solemn,

His figure and manner.

1. Table Talk of Samuel Rogers, p. 197.

CHAP.
LI.

Imitation
of the Chief
Justice by
Charles
Mathews
the come-
dian.

—and certain words he continued through life to pronounce in the fashion he had learned from his Cumbrian nurse. These peculiarities, which were of course
well known to the public, made him a favorite subject
for mimicry. Charles Mathews,[1] the celebrated come·
dian, who had unrivalled felicity of execution in this
line,—to the infinite delight of a crowded theatre,
brought the Lord Chief Justice on the stage in the
farce of LOVE, LAW, AND PHYSIC. His Lordship did
not appear as one of the *Dramatis Personæ*, but *Flexible*,
the Barrister (personated by Mathews), in giving an
account of a trial in which he had been counsel, having
very successfully taken off Erskine and Garrow,—when
he came to the summing up, in look, gesture, language,
tone, and accent, so admirably represented the Lord
Chief Justice of the King's Bench, that the audience,
really believing they were in the presence of the ven-

1. CHARLES MATHEWS, a celebrated comedian, was born in London June 28, 1776, and after receiving a sound education at Merchant
Taylor's School, was apprenticed to his father, who kept a bookseller's shop in the Strand. To the horror of his family, who were rigid
Methodists, he showed a decided inclination for the stage, and after
appearing as an amateur at several provincial theatres obtained an
engagement at the Theatre Royal, Dublin. His histrionic reputation, however, was built up some years later on the York circuit, he
having joined the company of the well-known Tate Wilkinson. On
May 16, 1803, he made his first appearance on the London boards at
the Haymarket Theatre, as ' Jubal' in ' The Jew,' and he continued
to act there during several seasons with considerable success. In
1804 he was engaged at Drury Lane, and in 1812 at Covent Garden,
having risen to the highest rank among the professors of the mimic
art. Among the characters in which he mostly excelled were ' Maw-
worm,' ' Sir Fretful Plagiary,' ' Morbleu,' ' Monsieur Mallet,' ' Dick
Cypher,' and ' Multiple,' in the ' Actor of All Work.' In 1818 he
abandoned the regular drama and commenced a species of entertainment in the form of a monologue, which, under the name of ' Mathews at Home.' proved highly successful, and drew large audiences
not only in the metropolis, but in almost every theatre in the kingdom, and also in the United States, which he twice visited. The
result of his first voyage across the Atlantic suggested the materials
for a new entertainment called ' A Trip to America.' Mr. Mathews
died at Plymouth, June 28, 1835.—*Cooper's Biog. Dict.*

erable Judge, remained in deep and reverential silence till he had concluded, and then after many rounds of applause made him give the charge three times over. Mrs. Mathews, in her entertaining 'Memoirs of her husband,' says " When he came to the Judge's summing up, the effect was quite astounding to him, for he had no idea of its being so received. The shout of recognition and enjoyment indeed was so alarming to his nerves, so unlike all former receptions of such efforts, that he repented the attempt in proportion as it was well taken, and a call for it a second time fairly upset him, albeit not unused to loud applause and approbation." The Lord Chief Justice was exceedingly shocked to find all the papers next morning filled with comments on his charge in the famous case of *Litigant* v. *Camphor*, and in a fury he wrote to the Lord Chamberlain, requiring his interposition, and observing, that since the 'Clouds of Aristophanes,' in which Socrates was ridiculed, there had not been such an outrage on public decency. The Lord Chamberlain appears immediately to have effected his object, in a private audience with Mathews, by a courteous representation, without even a hint of authoritative proceedings. According to Mrs. Mathews, "his Lordship was soon satisfied that he had no occasion to use any argument to influence the performer, for Mr. Mathews proved to him at once that he had fully resolved, from the moment he found his imitation received with such extraordinary vehemence, not to repeat it." Notwithstanding urgent and vociferous requests and complaints of the audience at subsequent representations of LOVE, LAW, AND PHYSIC, the Judge's charge was heard no more in public. But soon afterwards Mathews received an invitation from the Prince Regent to Carlton House, and in the course of the evening H.R.H. began to speak of the extraordinary sensation caused by *Flexible's* recent

imitation, adding that he would have given tne world
to have been present. Mathews well understood the
royal hint, but was much embarrassed, for, glancing
his eye round, it fell upon the Lord Chamberlain, who
was looking particularly grave. The Prince observing
Mathews's hesitation, said, "Oh don't be afraid; we're
all *tiled* here. Come, pray oblige me. I'm something
of a mimic myself. My brother here (turning to the
Duke of York) can tell you that my Chancellor Thurlow is very tolerable, only that I do not like to swear
up to the mark. It was not so well that you should
produce Chief Justice Ellenborough on the public
stage, but here you need have no scruples." "The
Prince was in raptures," says Mrs. Mathews, "and declared himself astonished at the closeness of the imitation, shutting his eyes while he listened to it with excessive enjoyment, and many exclamations of wonder
and delight, such as *Excellent! Perfect! It is he himself!* The Duke of York manifested his approval by
peals of laughter, and the Princes afterwards conversed
most kindly and agreeably on the subject with my husband and the high personages present."

His por-
trait by
Lawrence.   Posterity may have a favorable and correct
notion of Lord Chief Justice Ellenborough, from a
portrait of him by Sir Thomas Lawrence,[1] in his judi-

1. Sir Thomas Lawrence, a celebrated English portrait-painter,
born at Bristol in 1769. His artistic talents were marvellously developed in early childhood, when he was also remarkable for his
memory, musical voice, and personal beauty. It is stated that he
drew with a crayon accurate likenesses of eminent persons about
the age of six years. In 1782 he became a pupil of Prince Hoare at
Bath, and soon acquired the grace, inspiration, and delicacy of manner which rendered him unrivalled among contemporary English
artists in the expression of female beauty. He removed to London .
in 1787, and was admitted as an associate of the Royal Academy in
1791. In 1792 he succeeded Sir Joshua Reynolds as first painter to
the king. From that time he was abundantly patronized at the rate
of one hundred guineas for a full-length portrait. In 1797 he
painted a portrait of Mrs. Siddons, which is one of his master-
pieces. Between 1814 and 1820 he painted, by order of the prince-

cial robes, which, covering his awkward limbs, repre-
sents a striking likeness of him, and yet makes him
appear dignified by portraying his broad and commanding forehead, his projecting eyebrows, dark and
shaggy, his stern black eye, and the deep lines of
thought which marked his countenance.

He lived in a handsome style suitable to his station His style of
and the splendid emoluments which then belonged to living.
the Chief Justiceship of the King's Bench. At first
these did not exceed 8000*l.* a year, but on the death of
Mr. Way, appointed by Lord Mansfield, the great
office of Chief Clerk of the Court of King's Bench fell
in, which formed a noble provision for him and his
family.[1] Soon after he was made Chief Justice he left
Bloomsbury Square for a magnificent house in St.
James's Square.[2] To give an idea of its size to an old

regent, the King of Prussia, the Emperor of Austria, Pope Pius VII.,
Wellington, and many famous generals and statesmen. He received the honor of knighthood in 1815, and visited Vienna and
Rome in 1819. On the death of Benjamin West, in 1820, Sir Thomas
was elected president of the Royal Academy. Died in 1830. He
excelled in the art of imparting ideal beauty to his subjects without
departing from the reality. Among his master-pieces are portraits of Benjamin West, John Kemble, Curran, Lord Erskine, Lady
Cowper, and the Duchess of Sutherland.—*Thomas' Biog. Dict.*

1. It is said that he heard of Way's death while he was riding in
Hyde Park, and that he immediately dismounted at a house in
Knightsbridge and executed a deed filling up the office, lest he
should die before appointing to it.

2. The two short streets on the right of Pall Mall lead into St.
James's Square, which dates from the time of Charles II., when the
adjoining King Street and Charles Street were named in honor of
the King, and York Street and Duke Street in honor of the Duke of
York. In the centre was a Gothic conduit, which is seen in old
prints and maps of London, with a steep gable and walls of colored
bricks in diamond patterns. Its site is now occupied by a statue of
William III. by the younger Bacon, 1808. The great Duke of Ormond lived here in Ormond House, and his duchess died there. No.
3 was the house of the Duke of Leeds.

" When the Duke of Leeds shall married be
To a fair young lady of high quality,
How happy will that gentlewoman be
In his grace of Leeds' good company !

lawyer who lived in Chancery Lane, and to whom he was describing it, he said, " Sir, if you let off a piece of ordnance in the hall, the report is not heard in the bed rooms." [1] He likewise bought a beautiful villa at Roehampton, which might almost rival Lord Mans-field's at Caen Wood. Nevertheless from fees and offices the profits of which he was entitled to turn to his own use, he left above 240,000*l.* to his family, be-sides the office of Chief Clerk of the King's Bench, commuted to his son for 7000*l.* a year during life.

His
children. Five sons and five daughters survived him. He bequeathed 2000*l.* a-year to his widow, and 15000*l.* to each of his younger children. The eldest, to whom the residue and the great office fell, is the present Earl of Ellenborough,[2] one of the most distinguished states-

> She shall have all that's fine and fair,
> And the best of silk and satin shall wear ;
> And ride in a coach to take the air,
> And have a house in St. James's Square."

No. 15, which belonged to Sir Philip Francis, was lent to Queen Caroline (1820), and was inhabited by her during the earlier part of her trial. No. 16 was the house of Lord Castlereagh, who lay in state there in 1822. No. 17, the Duke of Cleveland's, is an interest-ing old house, and contains a fine picture of Barbara, Duchess of Cleveland, by Sir Peter Lely. No. 21, in the south-east corner, is Norfolk House, and has been inhabited by the Dukes of Norfolk since 1684. Hither Frederick Prince of Wales, when turned out of St. James's by George II., took refuge with his family till the pur-chase of Leicester House; and here George III. was born, June 4, 1738, being a seven-months' child, and was privately baptized the same day by Seeker, Bishop of Oxford."—*Hare's Walks in London.*

1. This was the first instance of a common law judge moving to the "West End." Hitherto all the common law judges had lived within a radius of half a mile from Lincoln's Inn; but now they are spread over the Regent's Park, Hyde Park Gardens, and Kensington Gore.

2. Edward Law, first Earl of Ellenborough, a Tory statesman, and a son of Lord Ellenborough, was born in 1790. He inherited the title of baron in 1818, and was appointed lord privy seal in 1828. During the brief ministry of Sir Robert Peel in 1835 he was presi-dent of the Board of Control. He was appointed Governor-General of India in 1842, and, having annexed Scinde and Gwalior by con quest, was recalled in 1844 and raised to the rank of earl. He was

LORD ELLENBOROUGH.

men of the nineteenth century,—who, by his eloquence and his administrative powers, has added fresh splendor to the name which he bears.

Charles,[1] the second son, having risen by his own merit to be Recorder of London, and Member of Parliament for the University of Cambridge, died at an early age.

I have great pleasure in concluding this Memoir of Lord Chief Justice Ellenborough with a few artless but sweet and affecting lines from a Monody on his death, written by his favorite daughter ELIZABETH,— then a little girl in the school-room,—now the LADY COLCHESTER:

first lord of the admiralty in 1845 and 1846. On the accession of the Derby-Disraeli ministry, in February, 1858, he became president of the Board of Control. The publication of a despatch in which he condemned Lord Canning's conduct in India, gave so much offence that Ellenborough resigned a few months after his appointment. The House of Lords, by a majority of nine, rejected a motion to censure him for his conduct in this affair. Died 1871.—*Thomas' Biog. Dict.*

1. "Charles Ewan Law (1792–1850), recorder of London, second son of Edward Law, first baron Ellenborough, by his wife, Anne, daughter of George Phillips Towry of the victualling office, was born on June 14, 1792. He was educated at St. John's College, Cambridge, where he graduated M.A. 1812 and LL.D. 1847. Having been admitted a member of the Inner Temple in 1813, Law was called to the bar on Feb. 7, 1817, and subsequently became a member of the home circuit. At a by-election in March, 1835, occasioned by the elevation of Charles Manners-Sutton to the House of Lords as Viscount Canterbury, Law was returned unopposed to the House of Commons for the University of Cambridge as the colleague of Henry Goulburn, with whom he continued to represent the constituency until his death. The only occasion on which his seat was contested was at the general election of 1847, when he was returned at the head of the poll as a protectionist, while Goulburn only narrowly escaped being defeated by Viscount Fielding. Law was a staunch tory, but did not take any prominent part in the debates of the House of Commons. He was a man of moderate abilities (*Law Magazine*, XLIV. 291). He died at No. 72 Eaton Place, Belgrave Square, London, on Aug. 13, 1850, aged 58, and was buried on the 20th of the same month at St. John's Church, Paddington, whence his remains were subsequently removed to Wargrave, Berkshire."—*Nat. Biog. Dict.*

" Ye who have mourn'd o'er life's departing breath,
 And view'd the sad and solemn scene of death,
 Whilst hanging still o'er him whose soul is fled,
 Have ye not felt the awful, silent dread,
 Which strikes the soul as we in vain deplore
 His loss, whose presence ne'er can cheer us more !
 Those eyes are closed, whose fond approving glance
 Could once the bliss of each gay joy enhance ;
 Those lips are seal'd—where truth for ever reign'd,
 Where wisdom dwelt, and piety unfeign'd !
            *   *   *   *   *

 Such was the father whom we now bewail,
 But what can tears or poignant grief avail?
 Can they recall him to this earth again ?
 False, flatt'ring hope ! ah ! wherefore art thou vain ?
            *   *   *   *   *

 Rais'd above earth and ev'ry earth-born care,
 For Heav'n's eternal joys our souls prepare,
 Till ev'ry feeling, taught on high to soar,
 Our hearts shall taste of bliss unknown before.

" *St. James's Square, Dec.* 1818."

LORD TENTERDEN.

LIFE OF LORD TENTERDEN, FROM HIS BIRTH TILL HIS ELEVATION TO THE BENCH.

The subject of this memoir seems to offer an un- promising task to the biographer. Lord Tenterden was of very obscure origin; scarcely an anecdote remains of his schoolboy days; his university career, though highly creditable, was not marked by any extraordinary incidents; while at the bar he was more distinguished by labor than brilliancy; he did not even attain the easy honor of a silk gown; till raised to the Bench he never held any office more distinguished than that of " Devil to the Attorney General;" he neither was, nor wished to be, a member of the House of Commons; when made a puisne Judge he was believed to have reached the summit of his ambition; afterwards unexpectedly placed in the House of Lords, his few speeches there were distinguished for flatness or absurdity; he was dull in private life as well as in public; and neither crimes nor follies could ever be imputed to him. Yet is his career most instructive, and by a writer who does not depend upon wonder-stirring vicissitudes, it might be made most interesting. The scrubby little boy who ran after his father, carrying for him a pewter basin, a case of razors and a hair-powder bag, through the streets of Canterbury, became Chief Justice of England, was installed among the Peers of the United Kingdom, attended by the whole profession of the law, proud of him as their leader; and when the names of orators and statesmen illustrious in their day have perished with their frothy declamations, Lord Tenterden will be respected as a great magistrate, and his judgments will be studied and admired.

Although there be something exciting to ridicule in the manipulations of barbers,—according both to works of fiction and to the experience of life, there is no trade which furnishes such striking examples of ready wit, of entertaining information, and of agreeable manners.[1] This superiority of barbers may have at first arisen from their combination of bleeding and bone-setting with shaving and haircutting—but since they ceased to act as surgeons it can only by accounted for by their being admitted to familiar intercourse with their customers in higher station, whom they daily visit,—and by the barber's shop being the grand emporium for the circulation of news and scandal.

Lord Tenterden's father and mother.
At the corner of a narrow street, opposite to the stately western portal of the Cathedral of Canterbury, stood a small house, presenting in front of it a long pole, painted of several colors,—with blocks in the window, some covered with wigs and some naked,—a sign over the door, bearing the words " ABBOTT, HAIRDRESSER,"

1. One of the most intimate friends I ever had in the world was Dick Danby, who kept a hairdresser's shop under the Cloisters in the Inner Temple. I first made his acquaintance from his assisting me, when a student at law, to engage a set of chambers ; he afterwards cut my hair, made my bar wigs, and assisted me at all times with his valuable advice. He was on the same good terms with most of my forensic contemporaries. Thus he became master of all the news of the profession ; and he could tell who were getting on and who were without a brief,—who succeeded by their talents and who hugged the attorneys,—who were desirous of becoming puisne judges and who meant to try their fortune in parliament,—which of the Chiefs was in a failing state of health, and who was next to be promoted to the collar of SS. Poor fellow ! he died suddenly, and his death threw a universal gloom over Westminster Hall,—unrelieved by the thought that the survivors who mourned him might pick up some of his business,—a consolation which wonderfully softens the grief felt for the loss of a Nisi prius leader.

—and on the sides of the door "Shave for a penny— hair cut for twopence, and fashionably dressed on reasonable terms." This shop was kept by a very decent, well-behaved man, much respected in his neighborhood, —who had the honor to trim the whole Chapter and to cauliflower their wigs as they were successively in residence,—and who boasted that he had thrice prepared his Grace the Archbishop for his triennial charge to the clergy of the diocese. But he was not the pert, garrulous, bustling character which novelists who introduce heroes of the razor and scissors love to portray. He was depicted by one who had known him well for many years as "a tall, erect, primitive-looking man, with a large pig-tail, which latterly assumed the aspect of a heavy brass knocker of a door.[1] From his clerical connection he had a profound veneration for the Church, which we shall see was inherited by his offspring. His wife, in her humble sphere, was equally to be praised, and without neglecting her household affairs, she was seldom absent from the early service of the Cathedral.

Struggling with poverty, their virtues were rewarded with a son, who thus modestly recorded their merits on his tomb,

"Patre vero prudenti, matre piâ ortus."[2]

This was Charles, their youngest child, the future Chief Justice of England, who was born on 7th of October, 1762.

A.D. 1762.
Birth of
Lord Tenterden.

His infancy offered no omens or indications of his future eminence. Though always steady and well behaved, he was long considered a very dull lad, and it is said that his father, who intended that he should succeed him as a barber, used to express apprehensions lest he should be obliged to put the boy to another

1. Gentleman's Magazine.
2. "Born of a wise father and a pious mother."

trade requiring less genius.   Having learned to read at a dame's school, little Charley used to be employed in carrying home the wigs that had been properly frizzed and pomatumed, and he would accompany his father on the morning rounds to be made in the Cathedral close and in other parts of the city.   We have transmitted to us a graphic description of the old gentleman "going about with the instruments of his business under his arms, and attended frequently by his son Charles, a youth as decent, grave, and primitive-looking as himself.[1]

But the youth's obscure destiny, which seemed inevitable, was suddenly changed to one highly intellectual, and he became nearly the finest classical scholar and the very best lawyer of his generation in England.

This he owed to his admission on the foundation of the King's School, connected with Canterbury Cathedral, which had been founded by Henry VIII. and was then taught by Dr. Osmund Beauvoir, who was not only a very learned man but an admirable teacher, and eager to discover and to encourage talent in the boys under his care, whether of high or of humble degree.   Young Abbott, notwithstanding his demureness, was soon found out by this discriminating master, and as great pains were bestowed upon him as if he had been the son of a Duke or an Archbishop.   We have interesting portraits of him in his boyhood by two of his schoolfellows.   Says Sir Egerton Brydges,[2] who pretended to

1. Gentleman's Magazine.

2. Sir Samuel Egerton Brydges, a genealogist and miscellaneous writer, second son of Edward Brydges, Esq., of Wooton Court, Kent, where he was born Nov. 30, 1762.   He received his academical education at Queen's College, Cambridge, though he quitted the university without graduating.   Afterwards he was called to the bar. In 1790, after the death of the last duke of Chandos, Mr. Brydges incited his elder brother to prefer a claim to the barony of Chandos, alleging his descent from a younger son of the first Brydges who bore that title.   The consideration of this claim was long procras-

be a descendant of the Plantagenets, of the Tudors, and of Charlemagne :

"From his earliest years he was industrious, apprehensive, regular and correct in all his conduct—even in his temper, and prudent in everything. I became acquainted with him in July, 1775, when I was removed from Maidstone to Canterbury school. I was about six or seven weeks his junior in age, and was placed in the same class with him, in which, after a short struggle, I won the next place to him, and kept it until I quitted school for Cambridge in autumn, 1780, in my eighteenth year. Though we were in some degree competitors, our friendship was never broken or cooled. He always exceeded me in accuracy, steadiness, and equality of

tinated, but in 1803 the House of Peers pronounced its decision 'that the petitioner had not made out his claim to the title and dignity of Baron Chandos." Mr. Brydges never lost an opportunity to protest in the press against this decision, and he even stooped to the drudgery of editing a Peerage of 9 volumes, in order that a few of its pages might transmit to posterity an account of his wrongs. That the claim was actually groundless was proved beyond dispute in a volume published in 1834 by George Frederick Beltz, Lancaster herald. Latterly, it may be remarked, Mr. Brydges used to add to his signature the words "per legem terræ, B. C. of S.," meaning Baron Chandos of Sudeley. He was for some years M.P. for Maidstone, and in 1814 was created a baronet. In 1818 he quitted England, and died near Geneva Sept. 8, 1837. Mr. Brydges was among the first of the modern school of sonnetteers, and commenced his literary career by publishing a volume of Sonnets and other Poems, 1785. This was followed by a host of other works, chief among which were "Mary de Clifford," a novel; "Arthur Fitz Albini," a novel; "Theatrum Poetarum Anglicanorum," being a new edition, with additions, of a work under the same title by Philips, nephew of Milton; "Memoirs of the Peers of England during the reign of James I."; "Censura Literaria"; "The British Bibliographer"; "Restituta"; an edition of Collins's Peerage, 9 vols. 8vo.; "The Ruminator, a Series of Moral, Critical, and Sentimental Essays"; "Occasional Poems"; "Coningsby," a novel, 1819; "Letters on Lord Byron"; "Recollections of Foreign Travel"; "Lex Terræ, with regard to the descent of English Peerages"; "The Anglo-Genevan Critical Journal for 1831"; "Imaginary Biography"; and his "Autobiography, Times, Opinions, and Contemporaries," 1834. He was also a large contributor to periodical publications.—*Cooper's Biog. Dict.*

labor, while I was more fitful, flighty, and enthusiastic. He knew the rules of grammar better, and was more sure in any examination or task. He wrote Latin verses and prose themes with more correctness, while I was more ambitious and more unequal. There was the same difference in our tempers and our tastes. He was always prudent and calm; I was always passionate and restless. Each knew well wherever the other's strength lay, and yielded to it."

"I remember him well," added another contemporary, who rose to high preferment in the Church,— "grave, silent, and demure; always studious, and well behaved; reading his book instead of accompanying us to play, and recommending himself to all who saw and knew him by his quiet and decent demeanor. I think his first rise in life was owing to a boy of the name of Thurlow, an illegitimate son of the Lord Chancellor, who was at Canterbury school with us. Abbott and this boy were well acquainted, and when Thurlow went home for the holidays he took young Abbott with him. He thus became known to Lord Thurlow, and was a kind of helping tutor to his son; and I have always heard and am persuaded that it was by his Lordship's aid he was afterwards sent to college. The clergy of Canterbury, however, always took great notice of him, as they knew and respected his father."

Danger he ran in his fourteenth year. In his fourteenth year our hero ran a great peril, and met with a deep disappointment,—which may be considered the true cause of his subsequent elevation. The place of a singing-boy in the Cathedral becoming vacant, old Abbott started his son Charles as a candidate to fill it. The appointment would have secured to him a present subsistence, with the prospect of rising to 70l. a year, which he and his family considered a wealthy independence for him. His father's popularity among the members of the Chapter was so great that

his success was deemed certain, but from the huskiness
of his voice objections were made to him, and another
boy was preferred, who grew old enjoying the stipend
which young Abbott had eagerly counted upon. Mr.
Justice Richardson,[1] the distinguished Judge, used to

CHAP.
LII.

1. John Richardson was the third son of Anthony Richardson, a
merchant of London, and was born in Copthall Court, Lothbury, on
March 3, 1771. He commenced his education at Harrow, and
finished it at University College, Oxford, where he took his degree
of M.A. in 1795, having been assisted in his progress through the
university by the benevolent aid and steady patronage of Mr.
Stevens, the worthy treasurer of Queen Anne's Bounty. He aided
his patron in procuring the repeal of the penal statutes against the
episcopal clergy of Scotland, and was highly instrumental in forming
a club to Mr. Stevens's honor, called "Nobody's Club," from the
pseudonym under which that gentleman's various writings were published. The club still exists, and has numbered among its members
men the most famous in literature, theology, and law. Having been
entered at Lincoln's Inn in June, 1773, he practised as a special
pleader for several years, and was not called to the bar till June, 1803.
In the very next year he appeared as counsel for William Cobbett,
who was defendant in an action brought by Mr. Plunkett, and again
for him when indicted for publishing a libel against the lord lieutenant and lord chancellor of Ireland, which was written by Mr. Justice
Johnson of that country. He also soon after argued ably, though
unsuccessfully, in support of the plea filed by that judge against the
jurisdiction of the Court of King's Bench, and afterwards on his trial
in that court. (*State Trials*, xxix. 1, 53, 394, 423.) Joining the Western
Circuit, both there and in Westminster Hall he soon established such
a character for industry and legal learning as secured to him competent encouragement. When to this was added experience and observation, he obtained the laborious and responsible office of adviser
to the attorney and solicitor general, commonly denominated their
"devil." So efficient did he prove himself in this capacity, and so
universally acnowledged were his superior attainments, that in November, 1818, he was selected with the approbation of all to supply
the vacant seat in the Court of Common Pleas, and in June following
he was knighted. After filling this post with the reputation of one
of the soundest lawyers of the time, he was compelled by ill health
to retire from its labors in May, 1824. He lived nearly seventeen
years after his resignation, several of which he spent in Malta, where
he composed a code of laws for that island. He died on March 19,
1841. That excellent judge, Sir John Coleridge, describes him in a
lecture he delivered in 1859 as "a thoroughly instructed lawyer, an
accomplished scholar, and a man of the soundest judgment—a
tender-hearted, God-fearing man." (*Life of Stevens; Gent. Mag.*
July, 1841.)—*Foss's Lives of the Judges.*

relate that going the Home Circuit with Lord Tenterden, they visited the Cathedral at Canterbury together,
when the Chief Justice, pointing to a singing man in
the choir, said, "Behold, Brother Richardson, that is
the only human being I ever envied : when at school
in this town we were candidates together for a chor-
ister's place ; he obtained it ; and if I had gained my
wish, he might have been accompanying you as Chief
Justice, and pointing me out as his old schoolfellow, the
singing man."

However, the disappointed candidate, instead of
abandoning himself to despair, applied with still greater
diligence to his studies, and his master, proud of his
proficiency, showed his verses to all the clergy in the
neighborhood, and to others whom he could prevail
upon to read them, or to hear them recited—boasting
that the son of the Canterbury barber was qualified to
carry off a classical prize from any aristocratic versifier
at Westminster, Winchester, or Eton.

Q.Whether
he was to
be a hair-
dresser or
a Chief
Justice ?
The crisis of the young man's fate occurred as he
reached the age of seventeen.   He was then Captain of
the school, and it was necessary that some course
should be determined upon by which he was to earn
his bread.   His father proposed that he should be
regularly bound apprentice to the trade in which he
had been initiated from his infancy, and for which his
capacity could no longer be questioned.   This not only
horrified Dr. Beauvoir, but caused a shock to the whole
Chapter and to all the more cultivated inhabitants of
Canterbury who had heard of the fame of their young
townsman,—and a general wish was entertained that
he might be sent to the University.   A sum sufficient
for his outfit was immediately collected in a manner
calculated to prevent his feelings being hurt by hearing
of the assistance thus rendered to him ; and the trustees
of his school unanimously conferred upon him a small

exhibition in their gift, which happened to be then HAP.
CLII. vacant: but this was not sufficient for his maintenance while he remained an undergraduate, and a delicacy existed about the supply being raised by an annual sub- scription of individuals. For some days there was a danger of the plan so creditable to Canterbury being entirely defeated, and the indenture binding the future Chief Justice to the ignoble occupation of shaving being signed, sealed, and delivered,—when the trustees of the school came to a vote, that they had power to increase the exhibition from the funds of the school—and they did prospectively raise it for three years to a sum which, with rigid economy, might enable the object of their bounty to keep soul and body together till he should obtain his Bachelor's degree; then, by taking pupils or some other expedient, it was hoped that he might be able to provide for himself.

The bounty of individuals was carefully concealed from him, but at a subsequent period of his life, when he had been placed as a Judge on the Bench, he showed that he well knew the obligation under which he lay to the trustees. Attending a meeting of that body of which he had been elected a member, among the " AGENDA," there was " to consider the application from an exhibitioner of the school now at Oxford for an in- crease of his allowance." The Secretary declared that after a diligent search for precedents only one could be found, which had occurred many years before. " That student was myself," said the learned Judge, and he immediately supplied the required sum from his own private purse.

When it was announced to him that he was to be A.D. 1781. sent to the University he was much pleased, without He is sent to the Uni- being elated; for while he escaped the drudgery and versity. degradation of a trade not considered so reputable as that of a grocer, from which Lord Eldon had shrunk when in a very destitute condition, he foresaw that there might be much mortification in store for him, and that although all knowledge was to be within his reach, he might ere long find it difficult to provide for the day passing over him. He had likewise serious misgivings as to how he should appear as a gentleman among gentlemen. Hitherto he had only been noticed as the barber's son, and in the pressure of business on a Saturdry night, when he carried home any article to a customer, he had been well pleased to receive by way of gratuity a shilling or even a smaller coin. Not entering as a servitor, he was now to sit at table and to associate on a footing of equality with the sons of the prime nobility of England. While struggling forward in life he used to dread any allusion to such topics, but in his latter days he would freely talk of his first journey from Canterbury to Oxford, and the suddenness of his transition into a new state of existence. He was, on this occasion, accompanied by a prebendary of the Cathedral, who was a *Corpus* man, and who acted the part of a father to him.[1]

The following is a copy of his admission to his college, and of his matriculation:

" March 21st, 1781.　Charles Abbott, Kent Scho."
" Termino Sti. Hilarii, 1781.
　　Martii 24°.
　　" C. C. C. Carolus Abbott, 18, Joannis de Civitate Cantuariensi Pleb. Fil." [2]

He obtains
a scholar-
ship at
Corpus.
He tested his proficiency in classical literature by becoming a candidate for a vacant scholarship. Of this.

1. Samuel Pepys, the famous Diarist, who was the son of a tailor, describes his great embarrassment when, become Secretary to the Admiralty and a favorite of the King and Duke of York, he met a gentleman in reduced circumstances to whom, when a boy, he used to carry home fine suits of clothes.　　　　　　　　　　　Lord.
2. A true copy,
　　　　　　　　　　" PHILIP BLISS,
　　　　　　" Keeper of the Archives of the University."

contest we have an interesting account in a letter writ- ten by him to his schoolfellow, Sir Egerton Brydges, who was then entered at Queen's College, Cambridge:

"Oxford, Sunday, March 18, 1781.

"DEAR EGERTON,

"I have been a week in Oxford, and almost finished the examination; the day of election is next Tuesday. I cannot look forward without great dread, for my expectations of success are by no means sanguine. . . . . As yet I have kept to my resolution of drinking nothing. How long further I shall I know not, but I hope my pride will soon serve to strengthen it. I wish Tuesday were over."

"Monday Night.

"This has been a heavy day indeed. I would not pass another in such anxiety for two scholarships. Disappointment would be easier borne than such a doubtful situation. It is a great pleasure to me to be able to reflect that there is one person who will feel for me. What happiness would it have been to me had we had the good fortune to be both of the same university! Our examination has been very strict. . . . . Good night."

Tuesday, 12 o'clock.

"At last it is all over, and——Now your expectations are at the highest——I am——Guess——elected. You will see from my manner of writing that I am very much pleased—and so in truth I am. The President said to me (but don't mention it to any one) that I had gained it entirely by my merit—that I had made a very good appearance, and so had all the other candidates.

"Yours most affectionately,

"C. ABBOTT."

The following shows that he then felt much more exultation than on the day of his being made Chief

Justice of England, when I myself observed him repeatedly yawn on the bench from listlessness:

C. C. C., April 3, 1781.

" Yes, my dear Egerton, it does give me the most heartfelt pleasure to hear how kindly my friends rejoice in my success. Believe me, Egerton, the chief pleasure that I feel on this occasion is reading my letters of congratulation. I needed nothing to assure me of your friendship. Had any proof been wanting, your kind letter would have been sufficient. The examination was indeed a tedious piece of work, but I would undergo twice the trouble for the pleasure of knowing that I had answered the expectations of my friends. I have received two letters from my dearest mother, in which she gives me an account how sincerely all my friends at Canterbury have congratulated her on my success—and friends so much superior to our humble condition, that she says, ' such a universal joy as appeared on the occasion I believe hardly ever happened in a town left by a tradesman's son.' Who would not undergo any labor to give pleasure to such parents? . . . . You have heard me wish that I had never been intended for the university. It was impious ; it was ungrateful : I banish the thought for ever from my heart. Not that I foresee much pleasure in a college life, but I know that my present situation is perhaps the only comfort to those whose age and misfortunes have rendered some alleviation of care absolutely necessary. Pardon the expression of these sentiments to you, and consider that they flow from the breast of a son.

" What a dissatisfied wretch I am ! But a little while past to be a scholar of Corpus was the height of my ambition ; that summit is (thank Heaven) gained— when another and another appears still in view. In a

word, I shall not rest easy till I have ascended the rostrum in the theatre."

His conduct during the whole of his academical career was most exemplary. Avoiding all unnecessary expense he contrived always to preserve a decent appearance, and he gradually conquered the prejudice created against him by the whispers circulated respecting his origin and early occupations. The college tutor was Mr. Burgess,[1] afterwards Bishop of Salisbury, who speedily discovered his merit and steadily befriended him.

In the latter part of the eighteenth century Oxford education was at the lowest ebb, and a respectable degree might be taken by answering to the question, "Who was the founder of this university?" ALFRED THE GREAT! The study of mathematics had fallen into desuetude like that of alchymy. Young Abbott, therefore, had no opportunity of crossing the Asses' Bridge, and through life he remained a stranger to the exact sciences. But he was saved by the love of classical lore which he brought with him from Canterbury, and in which he found that a few choice spirits voluntarily participated. There being yet no tripos, the only academical honors that could be gained were the Chancellor's two medals for Latin and English compo-

1. Thomas Burgess, an English prelate, was the son of a grocer at Odiham, Hampshire, where he was born Nov. 19, 1756. After passing through Winchester School and Corpus Christi College, Oxford, he was collated by his patron, Dr. Shute Barrington, bishop of Salisbury, to a prebend in his cathedral 1787. After Dr. Barrington's translation to Durham, he gave Mr. Burgess a prebend in that church 1791. In 1803 he was promoted to the see of St. David's. Here he displayed the most exemplary attention to the affairs of his diocese, and formed a society for the foundation of a provincial college for the instruction of ministers for the Welsh church who have not the means to obtain a university education. He was translated to Salisbury 1825; and died Feb. 19, 1837. He published a number of works on classical learning and divinity, a list of which will be found in the Gentleman's Magazine for May, 1837.—*Cooper's Biog. Dict.*

sition, and these young Abbott was resolved to try for. The siege of Gibraltar[1] had then effaced all the disasters and disgraces of the American war, and was eagerly exchanged for the capitulation of Saratoga. Under date March 5, 1783, Abbott writes to his dear friend:

His prize poem.
" The subjects of our prizes were given out yesterday—for the Bachelors, THE USE OF HISTORY—for the Undergraduates, THE SIEGE OF GIBRALTAR—CALPE OBSESSA. I am very much displeased with the latter,

1. Gibraltar, a promontory at the entrance to the Mediterranean, is situated in the Spanish province of Andalusia. The natural strength of the position—it is, in fact, the key of the Mediterranean —attracted attention at a very early date. From 712 to the beginning of the fourteenth century it was in the hands of the Saracens, by whom it was again retaken from the Spaniards, in 1333. In 1410 the rock was taken by the Moorish King of Granada, and in 1462 fell into the hands of the Spaniards, by whom it was formally annexed, 1502. In 1704 a combined English and Dutch fleet, under Sir George Rooke, compelled the governor, the Marquis de Salines, to surrender, and Gibraltar has ever since remained in the possession of the English, sustaining a well-conducted siege in 1705. In 1713 it was formally ceded to Great Britain by the Treaty of Utrecht. Many attempts have been made by the Spaniards to recover so important a position. In 1718 Stanhope was almost induced to surrender what he regarded as of little value and an insuperable obstacle to peace with Spain. In 1720 a projected attack, under the Marquis of Leda, came to nothing, and in 1727 the Count de la Torres and 20,000 men also failed to take the rock. In 1757 Pitt was willing to surrender the rock if the Spaniards would help in the recapture of Minorca from the French ; but they persevered in neutrality, and in 1761 joined the Family Compact largely in consequence of the desire to win it back. The most famous siege of Gibraltar was one lasting from 1779 to 1783, by a combined force of Spaniards and French, which was successfully withstood by the English under General Elliot, afterwards Lord Heathfield ; a siege almost unparalleled in the annals of ancient or modern warfare. The English were more than once reinforced or revictualled by sea ; but the investment continued, and a very severe bombardment and powerful floating batteries were tried in vain against it. The possession of Gibraltar gives England a commanding attitude at the Atlantic entrance of the Mediterranean, which enables it to dispense with the continued presence of a large maritime force on that sea. The administration is in the hands of a military governor. As a " free port " Gibraltar is the seat of extensive smuggling.—*Dict. of Eng. Hist.*

for it appears to me to be at once unclassical and commonplace—

     ' Gun, drum, trumpet, blunderbuss, and thunder !"

But it will not do to set oneself against it. So I must
endeavor to make the most of it. Yet I feel my mind
labor with omens of ill success. It is certainly a noble
and splendid action. The difficulty will be in separat-
ing the circumstances peculiar to it from the common
occurrences which are to be found as well in all other
actions as in this."

Our aspirant's first attempt was not crowned with
the success he hoped for; but he was encouraged to
persevere by reading on his verses when returned to
him, " *quàm proximè accessit* "—the mark of approbation
bestowed on the second best. More than forty years
after, when a Judge on the circuit at Salisbury, he met
the Rev. W. L. Bowles,' the poet, who had carried off

    1. William Lisle Bowles, an eminent English poet, born at King's
Sutton, on the border of Northamptonshire, in September, 1762. He
was educated at Trinity College, Oxford, and chose the clerical profession. After he had been disappointed in love by the death of a
lady to whom he was engaged, he composed, in 1789, "Fourteen
Sonnets," which were remarkable for grace of expression and an air
of melancholy tenderness. He became rector of Dumbleton in 1797,
married a daughter of the Rev. Dr. Wake, and obtained the valuable
living of Bremhill, Wiltshire, in 1805. He published in 1804 "The
Spirit of Discovery," which is his longest poem. Among his numerous other poems are "The Grave of Howard" (1790), "The Missionary of the Andes" (1822), and "Saint John in Patmos" (1832).
In 1828 he became a canon of Salisbury Cathedral. He edited the
works of Pope (1807), and made some criticisms on that author
which provoked a long controversy between himself and the two
poets Byron and Campbell. He published in 1825 his "Final Appeal
to the Literary Public relative to Pope." Died in 1850. The poems
of Bowles were admired by Coleridge. Wordsworth, and Southey,
the last of whom wrote to a friend, "My poetical taste was much
meliorated by Bowles." "The Sonnets of Bowles," says Hallam,
"may be reckoned among the first-fruits of a new era in poetry.
They came in an age when a commonplace facility in rhyming, on
the one hand, and an almost nonsensical affectation in a new school,
on the other, had lowered the standard so much that critical judges
spoke of English poetry as of something nearly extinct." ("Address
before the Royal Society of Literature.")—*Thomas' Biog. Dict.*

the prize.   His Lordship immediately reverted to the literary contest in which they had been engaged, and very frankly confessed that the rule had been observed, DETUR DIGNIORI.[1]

The subject of the prize poem for the following year was GLOBUS AEROSTATICUS,—Lunardi's voyages in his balloon having made many people believe that this vehicle, although its moving power be the medium in which it floats, might be guided like a ship impelled by the wind across the ocean, and that a method had been discovered of establishing an easy intercourse, to be reckoned by hours, between the most distant nations.[2] Abbott having again invoked the Cantuarensian muse, by her inspiration he was successful, and as victor mounting the rostrum in the theatre, amidst loud plaudits, recited the following beautiful lines:

1. The poem may be seen at full length in 'Poemata Præmiis Cancellarii Academicis Donata,' &c., Oxoniæ, 1810, vol. i. p. 123. As a specimen I offer a short extract, giving an account of the state of things after the failure of the grand assault :

> "Nec vero, ut retulit nox exoptata tenebras
> Cessavit furor, ardenti conjecta ruina
> Sævit adhuc longe missi vis flammea ferri.
> Continuo exustæ dant mœsta incendia naves,
> Umbrosumque vadum fumanti tramite signant.
> Securi Britones geminata tonitrua torquent ;
> Ipse inter medios, altoque serenior ore,
> Dux late Martem spectat sublimis opacum,
> Seu quondam proprio vestitum fulmine numen
> Arma tenens, fatique velut moderatur habenas.
> Audiit insolitum sola sub nocte fragorem
> Adversum Libyæ littus, longeque tremescit
> Montanas inter latebras exsomnis hyæna !"

2. I have often heard my father relate the consternation excited by this same Lunardi in the county of Fife. He had ascended from Edinburgh, and the wind carried him across the Firth of Forth. The inhabitants of Cupar had observed a speck, which was at first supposed to be a bird, grow into a large globe, and pass at no great height over their heads, with a man in a boat depending from it. Some thought they could descry about him the wings of an angel, and believed that the day of judgment had arrived.

GLOBUS AEROSTATICUS.

Pondere quo terras premat aër, igneus ardor
Quam levis, et quali raptim nova machina nisu
Emicet in cœlum, et puro circum æthere ludat,
Pandere jam aggrediar ; juvat altas luminis oras
Suspicere, et magni rationem exquirere mundi.
   Quippe etenim, ut facili cura, certoque labore
Hæc lustrare queas, miro en ! spectacula ritu
Circum ultro tibi mille adsunt, rerumque recludens
Dat natura modum, et primordia notitiaï.
Namque ubi sulphureis concocta bitumina venis,
Ausa ultro mediæ penetrare in viscera terræ,
Gens hominum effodit, fundo illic semper ab imo
Exsudare leves æstus, summisque sub antris
Se furtim glomerare ferunt, quin sæpe repenti
Cum sonitu accensos, et diræ turbine flammæ,
Rumpere vi montem, superasque effervere in auras.
At vero angustus si terræ inclusa cavernis
Ignea vis longum subter duraverit ævum,
Quas ibi mox clades eheu ! quantasque videbis
Faucibus eruptis volvi super æthera flammas !
Quid repetam Ausoniis quoties tibi nuper in oris
Concussæ cecidere urbes ? quot corpora letho
Ipsa etiam horrendis suter distracta ruinis
Terra dedit ? dum jam luctantem funditus æstum,
Collectosque vomens ad cœlum efflaverat ignes.
Usque adeo est quædam subtilis cæca animaï
Materies, alti quæ vulgo ad sidera cœli
Vi propria volat, et terras contemnit inertes
   Ergo etiam hos æstus si quis finxisse per artem
Noverit, et levibus poterit concludere textis,
Continuo e terris volucrem miro impete cernas
Ire globum, aëriisque ultro secredere ventis,
Et jam jamque magis liquidas conscendere nubes
Altius, atque atro penitus se condere cœlo.
Verum ubi jam longo in spatio eluctatus abivit
Auraï levis æstus, et igneus exiit ardor,
Tum demum ætheriis idem se rursus ab oris
Demittet sensim, et mortalia regna reviset.
   Quare age, et hæc animo tecum evolvisse sagaci
Cura sit, et cæcas meditando exquirere causas.
Nec sine consilio fieri hæc, sine mente rearis,
Aut rebus non jura dari, verum omnia volvi
Lege una, et certo sub fœdere labier orbem.
   Principio hanc omnem cœli spirabilis auram,
Terraïque oras et lati marmora ponti,
Vis eadem regit, ac uno omnia corpora ritu
In medium, magna connixa cupidine tendunt,
Pondere quidque suo ; firmis ita nexibus orbis

Scilicet, et tuto circum se turbine versat,
Proinde, magis gravibus, densisque ut corpora cuncta
Seminibus constant, ita per leviora necesse est
Subsidisse magis ; queis ergo rarior intus
Textura, et levibus constant quæcunque elementis ;
Hæc contra e medio, sursum eluctata videntur
Volvere se supra, et magno circum æthere labi.
Quinetiam hic, tenuis quanquam et difusilis, aër,
Mollia qui rebus dat vitæ pabula, et omnem
Herbarumque fovet prolem, gentemque animantûm,
Ipse etiam, immani descendens pondere, terris
Incumbit, gravibusque urget complexibus orbem.
At vero insolitus si qua sibi parte calores
Hauserit, hac ultro se latius ipse relaxans
Rarescensque aër, leviori ita corpore, longe
Emicat e terra, et cœlo spatiatur in alto.
Hinc adeo expressos nimio sub sole vapores
Arida se per trata ferunt atpollere, et alte
Cœruleam nitidis variare coloribus æthram ;
Sæpe itaque et subitis incendi ardoribus auras
Per noctem, et longos in nubila spargier ignes.
Nonne vides etiam taciti per devia ruris,
Agricolæ ut parvo glomeratus de lare fumus
Avolat, et tenuem rotat alte in sidera nubem ?
Quare etiam, atque etiam commixto semper ab igni
Mutaturque aër, alienaque fœdera discit,
Et varium exercet, conversa lege, tenorem.
   Scilicet has rerum species, hæc fœdera, secum
Contemplata diu, et vigilanti mente secuta,
Hinc etiam ipsa novum simili sub imagine cœptum
Gens humana movet, curruque evecta per auras
Torquet iter, cœlumque audet peragrare profundum.
   Ergo etiam hanc ipsam versu me attingere partem
Ne pigeat ; tenues nec dedignere monendo
Tu didicisse artes ; quippe ultro carbasa Persæ
Dant levia, et viridi glomerata sub arbore bombyx
Vellera suspendit; tu lento tenuia fuco
Texta line, exiguoque liquescens adsit ab igni
Et cera, et spissum Panchaio e cortice gluten.
Maximus hic labor est, hæc alti gloria cœpti.
Ni facias, laxi per aperta foramina veli
Heu! tibi mox raræ nimium penetrabilis auræ
Vis ibit, frustraque artem tentabis inanem.
   Quod superest, seu jam piceas secta abiete tædas,
Et stipulam crepitantem, et olentis vellera lanæ,
Supponi, rapidumque velis advertier ignem,
Seu magis ardenti succensas subter olivo
Lampadas admota placeat suspendere flamma,
Quicquid erit, pariter raros bibet ipsa calores,
Ingentemque tumens se machina flectet in orbem.

Quid dicam, et quales novit tibi chymicus artes?
Quove modo effusum resoluto e sulphure acetum,
Et chalybis ramenta, levesque a flumine rores
Ille docet miscere, atrumque exsolvere in ignem?
Nempe ea cum proprio jam collabefacta calore
In sua se expediunt iterum primordia, et arctos
Dissolvunt nexus, et vincla tenacia laxant:
Ignea tum subito rapidæ tibi vis animal
Exagitata foras, validis exæstuat ultro
Vorticibus, clausaque arcte fornace remugit ;
Hanc ipse appositis effunde canalibus, ipse
Pendentem immissis distende vaporibus orbem.
Quin age, nec pigro Britonum depressa veterno
Corda diu jaceant, dum late ingentibus ausis
Gallia se in meritos attollit sola triumphos.
Illa quidem positis ultro pacatior armis,
Hanc ipsam in laudem, et potioris munera palmæ
Advocat, illa etiam faustos jam experta labores
Omina magna dedit, certæque exempla vial.
Attonitam quoties tremefacto pectore gentem
Vidit arundinea prælabens Sequana ripa
Stare, laborantes volventem in corde tumultus,
Audax dum ante oculos magni moliminis auctor
Avolat in cœlum, et spissa sese occulit umbra ;
Aut late aërium faustis aquilonibus æquor
Tranat ovans, validasque manu moderatur habenas.
Tum primum superi patefacta in regna profundi
Mortales oculi, mediæ e regionibus æthræ,
Convertere aciem, densis dum obducta tenebris
Sub pedibus terra atque hominum spatia ampla recedunt.
Nam neque per totum cessabant nubila cœlum
Densari, et vastos umbrarum attollere tractus,
Nec cuncti se circum ultro variare colores,
Cuncta figurarum late convolvier ora ;
Præsertim extremo cum jam pendebat Olympo
Sol, transversa rubens ; aut primum candida Phœbe
Monstrâratque ortum, et cœlo se pura ferebat.
Atqui illic vacuas nec jam vox, nec sonus, aures
Attingit, sed inane severa silentia regnant
Undique per spatium, et vario trepidantia motu
Corda quatit pavor, atque immixto horrore voluptas.
Hæc adeo, hæc præclara novæ primordia famæ
Gallia, tu posuisti ; hoc jam mortalibus unum
Defuit, excussis dudum patefacta tenebris
Alta animi ratio, et vital norma severæ
Eluxere ; patent terræque, atque æquora ponti,
Astrorumque viæ, atque alti lex intima mundi.
Jamque adeo et liquidæ quæ sit tam mobilis auræ
Natura, et superi passim per inania cœli
Qua ratione gerant se res, et fœdera nectant,

Explorare datur ; quo pacto rarior usque
Surgat, et in vacuum sensim se dissipet aër ;
Frigora quæ, qui ignes lateant ; quanto impete venti
Huc superis, illuc infernis, partibus instent,
Convulsumque agitent transverso flamine cœlum,
   Ergo etiam humanam, concepto hinc robore, mentem,
Insolito tandem nisu, et majoribus ausis,
Tollere se cernes, penitusque ingentia lati
Aëris in spatia, et magni supera alta profundi
Moliri imperium ac multa dominarier arte.

He thus announced his success to his friend Egerton :

"C. C. C., June 16, 1784.

"I have delayed writing to you for some time,
partly because I waited for the decision of the prizes,
but principally because I have been constantly employed in endeavoring to escape my own thoughts by
company and every means I could. I am now, however, repaid for my anxieties. They say it was a hard
run thing. There were sixteen compositions sent in.
. . . . All that has happened this morning appears a
dream."

Soon after this his joy was turned into mourning by
the death of his father. His mother continued to keep
the shop at Canterbury for the sale of perfumery, and
he devotedly strove to comfort and assist her. For
her sake he declined an advantageous offer to go to
Virginia, as tutor to a young man of very large fortune
there. He was willing to forego a considerable part
of his own salary, so that 50l. a year might be settled
on his mother for life. "This," he wrote, "with the
little left her by my father, would afford her a comfortable subsistence without the fatigue of business,
which she is becoming very unable to bear." [1] But
this condition being declined, the negotiation went off.

The English Essay was still open to him, and the
next year he likewise carried off this prize. If his per-

1. Letter to Sir Egerton Brydges, 2d June, 1785.

formance was less dazzling, it gave more certain proof
of his nice critical discrimination, and, from the exquisite good sense which it displayed, of his fitness for the business of life. The subject was THE USE AND ABUSE OF SATIRE.

In this composition he showed that he had already acquired (whence it is difficult to conjecture) that terse, lucid, correct, and idiomatic English style which afterwards distinguished his book on the LAW OF SHIPS, and his written judgments as Chief Justice of the King's Bench. The following is his analytical division of the subject, evincing the logical mind which made him a great judge:

"Early use of panegyrical and satiric composition; gradual increase of the latter with the progress of refinement.

"Different species of satire, invective, and ridicule.

"General division of satire into personal, political, moral, and critical.

"I. 1. Personal satire necessary to enforce obedience to general instructions. 2. Its abuse when the subject is improperly chosen, when the manner is unsuitable to the subject, and when it proceeds from private animosity.

"II. 1. Political satire, necessary for the general support of mixed governments. 2. Its abuse, when it tends to lessen the dignity of the supreme authority, to promote national division, or to weaken the spirit of patriotism.

"III. 1. Moral satire, its use in exposing error, folly, and vice. 2. Its abuse, when applied as the test of truth, and when it tends to weaken the social affections.

"IV. 1. Critical satire, its use in the introduction and support of correct taste. 2. Its abuse, when directed against the solid parts of science, or the correct productions of genius.

"Conclusion. Comparison of the benefits and disadvantages derived from satire. Superiority of the former."

His reflections on Personal Satire will afford a fair specimen of his manner:

" Personal satire has been successfully directed in all countries against the vain pretenders to genius and learning, who, if they were not rendered contemptible by ridicule, would too often attract the attention, and corrupt the taste, of their age. By employing irony the most artful, and wit the most acute, against the unnatural and insipid among his contemporaries, Boileau [1] drew the affections and judgment of his nation to the chaste and interesting productions of Molière [2]

1. Nicholas Boileau-Despreaux, a celebrated French poet, born Nov. 1, 1636. Studying the law, he was admitted advocate in 1656; but he did not possess the patience requisite for the bar, and exchanging his pursuits for divinity, he at last discovered that a degree at the Sorbonne was not calculated to promote the bent of his genius. In literature he now acquired eminence and fame. The publication of his first Satires, in 1666, distinguish him above his predecessors, and he became the favorite of France. His "Art of Poetry" added to his reputation. It is a monument of his genius and judgment, and he far surpasses the "Ars Poetica" of Horace in the happy arrangement of his ideas, the harmony of his numbers, and the purity of his language. His "Lutrin" was written in 1674, at the request of Lamoignon, and the insignificant quarrels of the treasurer and ecclesiastics of a chapel are magnified by the art of the poet into matters of importance, and every line conveys, with the most delicate pleasantry, animated description and refined ideas. Boileau became a favorite at the court of Louis XIV.; a pension was settled on him, and the king declared he wished his subjects to partake the same intellectual gratification which he himself enjoyed. As a prose writer Boileau possessed superior merit, as is fully evinced by his elegant translation of Longinus. After enjoying the favors of his sovereign, and the honors due to his merits, Boileau retired from public life, and spent the remainder of his days in literary privacy in the society of a few select friends. Died Mar. 11, 1711. He wrote, besides the works already mentioned, odes, sonnets, fifty-six epigrams, critical reflections, and some Latin pieces. As a poet Boileau has deservedly obtained universal applause.—*Cooper's Biog. Dict.*

2. Molière is the name which Jean Baptiste Poquelin assumed on becoming a player, and by which he is celebrated as the best comic writer of France. He was born in 1622, in Paris, where his father

and Racine.[1]

was a "tapissier," or upholsterer, holding also an appointment in the royal household. The poet, designed for his father's trade, was poorly educated till was fourteen years old; after which, having been inspired by his grandfather with a love both for reading and for plays, he obtained from his parents, with difficulty, the means of studying in the Collége de Clermont; and there, besides making other acquaintances that gained patronage far him, he attracted the notice and approbation of the philosopher Gassendi. In his nineteenth year, having been appointed to fill his father's place as "valet-de-chambre tapissier" to the king, he began to attend at court; his taste for the drama was now confirmed by the fashion which had been set by Cardinal Richelieu; and he put himself at the head of a few young persons who, playing at first as amateurs, soon became actors by profession.—From about 1645 Molière's history is lost amidst the wars of the Fronde; but he appears to have wandered in the provinces with his troop, and to have composed slight pieces for them, till 1653, when his first regular comedy, "L'Etourdi," was played at Lyons with great success. In Languedoc, next year, he produced "Le Dépit Amoureux," and, bent on his favorite pursuits, refused to become the secretary of his old school-fellow, the Prince de Conti. In 1658 Molière and his company, finding their way to Paris, received the patronage of the court; he was by this time an excellent actor; and he immediately showed that he possessed both a power of observation and of original invention, and a skill in dramatic construction, much exceeding anything that had appeared in his two earlier pieces. His clever satire on literary and accomplished ladies, called "Les Précieuses Ridicules," was followed by his humorous farce, "Le Cocu Imaginaire"; ' L'Ecole des Maris" and "Les Fàcheux" made him still more famous as a witty and correct painter of life and manners: and the series of his plays continued to be rapidly increased till 1673, when it was ended with his life, by "Le Malade Imaginaire." Some of his comedies, such as that last named, "Le Médecin Malgré Lui," "Le Bourgeois Gentil-homme," and "George Dandin," are chargeable, notwithstanding their liveliness, with degenerating into broad farce. But several of his comedies, though they do not indeed support his fame at the extravagant height to which his countrymen raise it, are yet fully sufficient to justify his rank as at once one of the most brilliant and skilful of all comic dramatists, and as the very best of those that have written comedies on the formal French model. Such praise belongs especially to "L'Ecole des Femmes" (1662), in which is his famous character of Agnes; "Le Misanthrope" (1666), of which Wycherly's "Plain-Dealer" is an imitation, with improvement in management and degradation in morality; "Le Tartuffe" (1667), so deservedly celebrated for its powerful picture of hypocrisy in person of the hero; and "Les Femmes Savantes" (1672), in which groundless pretensions are ridiculed with great force of humor. In

---

1. See note 1, on next page.

"Such have been the advantages derived from personal satire, but so great on the contrary are the injuries resulting from its misapplication, that the legisla-

1662, being forty years old, he married an actress of seventeen, whose light-minded coquetry embittered his comfort. He is described as having been a thoughtful, generous, and good-hearted man, and more popular with his players than managers are wont to be. He prided himself on his skill in playing low comedy, as much at least as on the fame he won as a dramatic poet. And he all but died on the stage. In acting "Argan" on one of the earliest appearances of his own last comedy, he was seized with convulsions and soon suffocated by blood from the chest. His body was refused admission to consecrated ground, till the king prevailed on the Archbishop of Paris to allow a private funeral.—*Univ. Biog. Dict.*

1. Jean Racine, an excellent French dramatic poet, born at Ferté-Milon (Aisne) December 31, 1639. His parents, who were *bourgeois*, died before he was four years old. He studied at the College of Beauvais, and afterwards at the famous school at Port-Royal, in which he passed three years (1655–58). He became a good Latin and Greek scholar. He began his poetical career by "La Nymphe de la Seine" (1660), an ode on occasion of the marriage of Louis XIV., which procured for him a small pension. Having become disgusted with the study of theology, which an uncle had persuaded him to pursue, he went to Paris, and formed friendships with Boileau and Molière. He produced in 1664 the tragedy of "La Thébaïde, ou les Frères ennemis," which had some success. The first work which revealed the power and peculiar character of his genius was "Andromaque" (1667). In 1668 he surprised the public by a comedy called "The Litigants" ("Les Plaideurs"), which was very successful. He afterwards produced the tragedies of "Britannicus" (1669), "Bérénice" (1670), "Bajazet" (1672), "Mithridate" (1673), "Iphigénie" (1674), and "Phèdre" (1677). "I avow," says Voltaire, "that I regard 'Iphigénie' as the *chef d'œuvre* of the stage." He was admitted into the French Academy in 1673.

At the age of thirty-eight he resolved to renounce dramatic composition. This resolution is variously ascribed to religious scruples, wounded sensibilities, or disgust excited by envious intrigues and malicious criticisms. He married in 1677 a pious young woman of Amiens, named Catherine Romanet, and was appointed historiographer by Louis XIV. In compliance with the wish of Madame de Maintenon, Racine wrote "Esther" a drama (1689), and "Athalie" (1691), which was his last, and, in the opinion of Boileau, his best drama. In the latter part of his life he was gentleman-in-ordinary to the king, who often conversed with him, and treated him with favor. Among his intimate friends were Boileau, La Fontaine, and La Bruyère. Racine wrote about 1695 a "History of Port-Royal," the style of which is so neat and perspicuous that it entitles him to rank in the list of those authors who have succeeded both in verse and prose. His natural disposition was rather melan-

ture of all nations has been exerted to restrain it. For if they, whose failings were unknown and harmless, be brought forth at once to notice and shame, or if, from the weakness common to human nature, illustrious characters be made objects of contempt, the triumphs of vice are promoted by increasing the number of the vicious, and virtue loses much of its dignity and force by being deprived of those names, which had contributed to its support. Not less injurious to science is the unjust censure of literary merit, which tends both to damp the ardor of genius, and to mislead the public taste. The most striking examples of the abuse of personal satire are furnished by that nation in which its freedom was the greatest. The theatres of Athens once endured to behold the wisest of her philosophers, and the most virtuous of her poets, derided with all the grossness of malicious scurrility. Nor has modern poetry been altogether free from this disgrace. Fortunate, however, it is that, although the judgment of the weak may be for a time misguided, truth will in the end prevail: the respect and admiration due to the names of Burnet and of Bentley, of Warburton and of

---

choly and tender. During the last twenty years of his life he was a devout member of the Church. He died on the 21st of April, 1699.

It is usual to compare Racine with Corneille as a rival poet. "Voltaire, La Harpe, and in general the later French critics," says Hallam, " have given the preference to Racine. I presume to join my suffrage to theirs. Racine appears to me the superior tragedian; and I must add that I think him next to Shakespeare among all the moderns. The comparison with Euripides is so natural that it can hardly be avoided. Certainly no tragedy of the Greek poet is so skillful or perfect as ' Athalie ' or ' Britannicus.' * * * The style of Racine is exquisite. Perhaps he is second only to Virgil among all poets. But I will give the praise of this in the words of a native critic : ' If we consider that his perfection in these respects may be opposed to that of Virgil, and that he spoke a language less flexible, less poetical, and less harmonious, we shall readily believe that Racine is, of all mankind, the one to whom nature has given the greatest talent for versification ' (Harpe)."—*Thomas' Biog. Dict.*

Johnson, are now no longer lessened by the wit of Swift, or the asperity of Churchill.[1]

"Even where the subject or design is not improperly chosen, abuse may still arise from the disposition and coloring of the piece. When bitterness and severity are employed against men whose failings may be venial and light, or ridicule degenerates either into the broad attacks of sarcastic buffoonery, or the unmanly treachery of dark hints and poisonous allusions, not only the particular punishment is excessive and unjust, but also general malice is fostered by new supplies of slander."

In conclusion he thus strikes the balance between

---

1. Charles Churchill, a popular English poet and satirist, born at Westminster in 1731. At school he was the fellow-student and friend of William Cowper. He married a Miss Scott privately when he was about seventeen, and soon after applied for a studentship at Oxford, but was rejected. Against his own inclination, he unwisely adopted the profession of his father, who was a curate. In 1756 he was ordained priest, and began to officiate at Rainham. Two years later he succeeded his father as curate and lecturer of Saint John's, Westminster. It is usually stated that a sudden or total change occurred in his habits at this period, after which he became dissipated and licentious. Macaulay, who dissents from this opinion, thinks he never was or professed to be religious, and intimates that, "with violent recoil from the hypocrisies, he outraged the proprieties of life," because his youth had been misdirected to a profession from which his heart was estranged.

Resolving to abandon that profession, he produced, about 1760, two poems, "The Bard" and "The Conclave." His "Rosciad," a pungent satire on the performers and managers of the stage, appeared in 1761, and was successful beyond his most sanguine hopes. He vindicated himself against the malice of the "Critical Reviewers" by the "Apology," a poem, which is much admired. He became very intimate with John Wilkes, the profligate pseudo-patriot, whom he assisted in "The North Briton." In 1763 he produced "The Prophecy of Famine," a political satire on the Scotch, which was immensely popular. "The Conference," a poem, is one of his masterpieces. While on a visit to France, he died in 1764. "His vices were not so great as his virtues," says Macaulay. Besides the works already noticed, he wrote "The Author," "Gotham," and other poems. Cowper was a warm admirer of his poetry, and said that "he well deserved the name of 'the great Churchill.'"— *Thomas' Biog. Dict.*

the evils inflicted by satire, and the benefits which it confers:

" From this general representation of the good and ill effects of satire, we may be enabled to form a comparison of their respective importance. By the improper exercise of satire individuals have sometimes been exposed to undeserved contempt ; nations have been inspired with unjustifiable animosity; immoral sentiments have been infused; and false taste has received encouragement. On the contrary, by the just exertions of satire personal licentiousness has frequently been restrained ; the establishments of kingdoms have been supported, and the precepts of morality and taste conveyed in a form the most alluring and efficacious. The success, however, of all those productions that have not been directed by virtue and justice, has been confined and transient, whatever genius or talents might be employed in their composition ; by the wise among their contemporaries they have been disregarded, and in the following age they have sunk into oblivion. But the effusions of wit, united with truth, have been received with universal approbation, and preserved with perpetual esteem, their influence has been extended over nations, and prolonged through ages. Hence, perhaps, we need not hesitate to conclude that the benefits derived from satire are far superior to the disadvantages with regard both to their extent and duration ; and its authors may therefore deservedly be numbered among the happiest instructors of mankind."

In 1785 he became B. A. If the modern system of honors had been then established, he would no doubt have taken a double first class; but when this degree was conferred upon him and others, there was nothing in the proceeding to distinguish him from the greatest dunce or idler in the whole university. By his prize compositions and college exercises his fame was established, and his fortune was made. All that followed in his future career was in a natural sequence, and with the exception of the deafness of Sir Samuel Shepherd when Attorney General, which led to Abbott being CHIEF JUSTICE instead of remaining a

His Bachelor's degree.

puisne judge, there appeared nothing of accident or extraordinary luck in his steady advancement.

From the completion of his second year he had begun to have private pupils in classics, whose fees eked out sufficiently his scanty allowance. He neither gave nor accepted invitations to wine-parties; his apparel was ever very plain, though neat; and instead of getting in debt by buying or hiring hunters, it is a curious fact that he never once was on horseback during the whole course of his life. In the declining state of his health, shortly before his death, he was strongly recommended to try horse exercise; but, as he related to his old friend, Philip Williams (who told me), he objected "that he should certainly fall off like an ill-balanced sack of corn, as he had never crossed a horse any more than a rhinoceros, and that he had become too stiff and feeble to begin a course of cavaliering." He added, with a sort of air of triumph, " My father was too poor ever to keep a horse, and I was too proud ever to earn sixpence by holding the horse of another." [1]

His horsemanship.

Abbott's college was very desirous of securing his services, and soon after taking his degree he was elected a fellow and appointed junior tutor along with Mr. Burgess, who was delighted to have him as a colleague. Under them CORPUS rose considerably in reputation, and it was selected by careful fathers who anxiously looked out for a *reading college*.

He is appointed College tutor.

While fellow and tutor Abbott was intended for the Church, and the time now approached when he ought to go into orders. His destination was again changed by his having become private tutor to a son of the famous Mr. Justice Buller. In a letter to his

His acquaintance with Judge Buller.

1. Yet so gained his livelihood on his arrival in London, a still greater man—WILLIAM SHAKESPEARE!

friend Egerton Brydges, dated 22d June, 1785, he CHAP.
LII.
says:

"I had received a slight hint that the President had
another offer to make to me. This is the tuition of Judge
Buller's son, who will come from the Charterhouse to enter at
this College next term. I was desired to fix the salary ; but,
upon consultation with Sawkins, declined it. The President
and Dr. Bathurst,[1] canon of Christ Church (who recommended
the College to the Judge), are disposed to think of 200*l.* a year
exclusive of travelling expenses ; but whether they will propose this to the Judge, or desire him to name, I am not certain. Mr. Yarde has a large fortune independent of his father,
for which he changed his name. Sawkins advised me (and
the President approved) to refuse one hundred guineas. Between the two offers there could be no hesitation; and indeed
my friends here thought the American place unworthy of my

1. "Henry Bathurst (1744-1837), bishop of Norwich, seventh son
of Benjamin, younger brother of Allen, first Earl Bathurst, was born
at Brackley, Northamptonshire, on Oct. 16, 1744, and was educated
at Winchester, and New College, Oxford. He became rector of
Witchingham in Norfolk ; in 1775 was made canon of Christ Church,
Oxford ; and in 1795 prebendary of Durham. In 1805, on the translation of Dr. Manners-Sutton to Canterbury, he was consecrated
bishop of Norwich. Dr. Bathurst died in London, 1837, and was
buried at Great Malvern. He was distinguished throughout his life
for the liberality of his principles, and for many years was considered to be 'the only liberal bishop' in the House of Lords. He
warmly supported Roman Catholic emancipation, both by his speeches
in the house, and by his presentation of a petition in favor of that
movement from the Roman Catholics of Tuam. In 1835, when over
ninety years of age, he went to the house to vote in support of Lord
Melbourne's government. Though his published writings were but
scanty, comprising only a few sermous, two of his charges (1806,
1815) and a 'Letter to the late Mr. Wilberforce on Christianity and
Politics, how far they are reconcilable' (1818), Dr. Bathurst's love of
literature was great, and his literary instinct just : he refused to
believe in the authenticity of the Rowley poems, which, he said, had
no mark of antiquity, but might pass for a modern work if the spelling and obsolete words were taken away. The bishop married a
daughter of Charles Coote, dean of Kilfenora, and brother of Sir
Eyre Coote. His eldest son, Henry Bathurst, was fellow of New
College, Oxford, became chancellor of the church of Norwich in 1805;
held the rectories of Oby (1806), North Creake (1809), and Hollesley
(1828); and was appointed archdeacon of Norwich in 1814."—*Nat.
Biog. Dict.*

acceptance. If we agree upon terms, I propose to spend this summer in France, if the Judge wishes his son's tutor to be able to speak French. I am particularly pleased with the appearance of this offer, as it will give me an opportunity of being much in London."

In a letter of July 10th, 1785, he adds:

" The plan which I mentioned to you in my last respecting Mr. Yarde has been so altered by the Judge, that the parts of it from which I promised myself most pleasure and advantage are gone. Still the offer is too good to be refused. It is to attend him in college only. Family circumstances make the Judge wish to have his son at home in London as little as possible. The matter is not entirely settled; but for residence with him here during the terms I shall have, I believe, a hundred guineas a year. If he stays here any vacation, or if I accompany him out (which it seems I shall sometimes do), a consideration is to be made for it. Mr. Willoughby, a particular friend of the Judge, and an acquaintance of the President, is commissioned to settle the affair."

The affair was at last settled satisfactorily, and Abbott did act as Mr. Yarde's private tutor for two or three years, sometimes accompanying his pupil to the family seat in Devonshire. The quick-sighted Judge soon discovered Abbott's intellectual prowess, and his peculiar fitness for law. He therefore strongly advised him to change his profession, and, somewhat profanely, cited to him a case from the Year Books, in which the Court laid down that " it is actionable to say of an attorney that he is a d——d fool, for this is saying that he is unfit for the profession whereby be lives; but *aliter* of a parson, *par ce que on poet estre bon parson et d——d ?fool.*" In serious tone the legal sage pronounced, that with Abbott's habits of application and clear-headedness his success was absolutely certain—saying to him, " You may not possess the garrulity called *eloquence*, which sometimes rapidly forces up an impudent pretender, but you are sure to get early into respectable business at the bar, and you may count on becoming in due time a puisne Judge." [1] Although Abbott had been contented with the prospect of obscurely continuing a college tutor till he succeeded to a country living, where he might tranquilly pass the remainder of his days, he was not without ambition; and when he looked forward to his sitting in his scarlet robes at the Maidstone assizes, while citizens of Canterbury might travel thither to gaze at him, he was willing to submit to the sacrifices, and to run the risks which, notwithstanding the sanguine assurances of his patron, he was aware must attend his new pursuit. He was now in his twenty-sixth year, and he had resided seven years in his college. His only certain dependence was his fellowship, the income of which was not considerable; but from the profits of his tutorship he had laid by a little store, which he hoped might not be exhausted before it was replenished by professional earnings.

In much perplexity as to the course of study he should adopt to fit himself for the bar, he thus addressed his faithful friends:

"C. C. C., June 13th, 1787.

". . . I can never sufficiently thank you for the offer of your house in town. There are two modes in which I might enter the profession of the law—that which you propose, of residing chiefly in Oxford till I am called to the bar, which would be the line of study

---

1. Sir Egerton Brydges, after mentioning how Abbott's destiny depended on his being tutor to Buller's son, merely adds: "That learned and sagacious Judge immediately appreciated his solid and strong talents, and recommended him to embrace the profession of the law, rather than of the Church, for which he had hitherto designed himself." The language in which the advice was given rests on tradition.

which I should chose ; but then what am I to do when
called to the bar with the enormous expense of going
circuits, &c.?—and that of going at once to a special-
pleader, and practising first below the bar.   As far,
however, as I am able to comprehend this line of practice, which seems to me to consist in a knowledge of
forms and technical minutiæ, it would be very unpleasant
to me, and the necessity of sitting six or eight hours a
day to a writing-desk renders it totally impracticable,
as from the peculiar formation of the vessels in my head,
writing long never fails to produce a headache.   Indeed
any great exertion has always the same effect, so that
on this account alone I think it will be wiser to choose
a more quiet profession."

However, his misgivings were much quieted by a
conference he had with his namesake Abbott, afterwards elected Speaker of the House of Commons, and
created Lord Colchester.   Thus, in a letter dated 13th
October, 1787, he writes to Sir Egerton:

"I received a visit from Abbott this morning, and
we held a long conversation together.   He spent a year
in a Pleader's office, and another in a Draughtsman's,
and now practises in equity.   Very particular reasons
determined him to the Court of Chancery ; but he
would advise me to adopt the common law, and chiefly
on this account : the practice of the Court of Chancery
being necessarily confined to certain branches of the
law in exclusion of certain others, a man's general professional connections can contribute less to his assistance, and he has less opportunity of distinguishing
himself.   At the same time a person who begins and
goes forward in equity seldom is able to make himself
a perfect master of his profession, or qualify himself for
many of its highest offices.   With regard to my own
particular case, Abbott thinks that, even if no connection determined me, it would be better to take one year

to look into books and courts a little, than to enter at once into an office where I could not possibly understand the business without previous knowledge. This, you know, is exactly what I have always thought, and wished others to think. He thinks too, that with proper application, I might get sufficient knowledge by working one year in an office to enable me to proceed afterwards by myself, and doubts not that by the help of two or three introductions to men in business, such as Foster, &c., I should make my way without expending so much as six hundred pounds. This, you see, is all very flattering. I wish it be not too flattering."

Being thus reassured, on the 16th day of November, 1787, he was admitted a student of the Middle Temple;[1] and he soon after hired a small set of chambers in Brick Court. By Judge Buller's advice, to gain the knowledge of writs and practice, for which in ancient times some years were spent in an Inn of Chancery, he submitted to the drudgery of attending several months in the office of Messrs. Sandys and Co., eminent attorneys in Craig's Court, where he not only learned from them the difference between a Latitat, a Capias, and a Quo Minus, but gained the good will of the members of the firm and their clerks,[2] and laid the groundwork of his

CHAP.
LII.

He is entered of the Temple.

"Die 16 Novembris 1787.

"Ma'. Carolus Abbott Collegii Corporis Christi apud Oxonienses Scholaris, Filius natu secundus Johannis Abbott, nuper de Civitate Cantuariensi, defuncti, admissus est in Societatem Medij Templi Londini specialiter.

"Et dat. pro fine . . . 4 : 0 : 0"

From the following entry in the books of C. C. C., it appears that at this time he had leave of absence from his College:

"1787. Nov. 13th. Abbott, A Bachelor of the House, applied for leave of absence to keep the London Law Terms. The same was granted (conformably to Statute) by the President, one Dean, one Bursar, and two other Fellows *Promotionis causâ.*"

2.   " Nor did I not their Clerks invite
                To taste said venison hashed at night."
                                        Pleader's Guide.

CHAP.
LII.
reputation for industry and civility which finally made
him Chief Justice.

His indus-
try as a law
student.
His next step was to become the pupil of George
Wood, the great master of Special Pleading, who had
initiated in this art the most eminent lawyers of that
generation. Resolved to carry away a good penny-
worth for the 100 guinea fee which he paid, he here
worked night and day ; he seemed intuitively to catch
an accurate knowledge of all the most abstruse mysteries of the DOCTRINA PLACITANDI, and he was supposed
more rapidly to have qualified himself to practise
them than any man before or since. The great model
of perfection in this line, in giving an account of his
status pupillaris under the eminent special pleader,
TOM TEWKESBURY,[1] sings

> " Three years I sat his smoky room in,
> Pens, paper, ink, and pounce consumin'."

But at the end of one year Abbott was told that he
could gain nothing more by quill-driving under an instructor.

With characteristic prudence he resolved to practise as a special pleader below the bar till he had established such a connection among the attorneys as should
A.D. 1788. render his *call* no longer hazardous, citing Mr. Law's
splendid success from following the same course. He
He prac-
tices as a
pleader
under the
bar.
accordingly opened shop, hired a little urchin of a
clerk at ten shillings a week, and let it be understood
by Messrs. Sandys and all his friends that he was now
ready to draw Declarations, Pleas, Replications, and
Demurrers with the utmost despatch, and on the most

---

1. Hero of ANSTEY'S, ' *Pleader's Guide*,' a poem which is, I am
afraid, now antiquated, and which will soon become almost unintelligible from the changes in our legal procedure, but the whole of
which I have heard Professor Porson, at the Cider Cellar in Maiden
Lane, recite from memory to delighted listeners. He concluded by
relating, that when buying a copy of it and complaining that the
price was very high, the bookseller said, " Yes Sir, but you know
Law-books are always very dear."

reasonable terms. Clients came in greater numbers than he had hoped for, and no client that once entered his chambers ever forsook him. He soon was, and he continued to be, famous for "the ever open door, for quick attention when despatch was particularly requested, for neat pleadings, and for safe opinions."[1]

Seven years did he thus go on, sitting all day, and a great part of every night, in his chambers,—verifying the old maxim inculcated on City apprentices, "Keep your shop and your shop will keep you." He was soon employed by Sir John Scott, the Attorney General, in preparing indictments for high treason and criminal informations for libel in the numerous state prosecutions which were going on during "the reign of terror," and by his pupils and his business he was clearing an annual income of above 1000*l.* He had now reached the age of thirty-three, which, although it is considered in our profession as early youth, the rest of the world believe to smack of old age.[2] He exclaimed, "Now or never must I take the leap into the turbid stream of forensic practice, in which so many sink, while a few—*rari nantes in gurgite vasto*[3]—are carried successfully along to riches and honor."

Accordingly he was called to the bar in Hilary Term, 1796, by the Society of the Inner Temple,[4] and

He is called to the bar.

1. Townsend's Twelve Judges, Vol. I. 243.

2. I remember Mr. Topping giving great offence to the junior members of the bar, who expected to be considered young men till fifty-five, by observing, when counsel for the plaintiff in a crim. con. cause, that the defendant's conduct was the more excusable, "as the heyday in the blood was over with him, and he had reached the mature age of thirty-three." According to Lord Byron, a lady thinks she has married an aged husband, although he may be several years younger than that :

"Ladies even of the most uneasy virtue
Prefer a spouse whose age is under *thirty.*"

3. "A few here and there swimming in the vast whirlpool."

4. The following is a copy from the books of that Society of his admission and of his call :

CHAP.
LII.
His success
on the Ox-
ford Cir-
cuit.
a few weeks after he started on the Oxford Circuit. I myself joined that circuit about fourteen years later, when I formed an intimacy with him, which continued till his death. I then found him with a junior brief in every cause tried at every assize town; and I heard much of his rapid progress and steady success, with a good many surmises, among his less fortunate brethren, that it was not from merit alone that he had surpassed them. He had at once stepped into full business, and this they ascribed to the patronage of an old attorney called Benjamin Price, who had acted as clerk of assize for half a century, and was agent in London for almost all the country attorneys in the eight counties which constituted the Oxford Circuit. But in truth Abbott was greatly superior to all his rivals as a junior counsel; and this superiority was quite sufficient to account for his success, although he certainly had been very civil always to old Ben, and old Ben had been very loud in sounding his praise. He was most perspicacious in advising on the bringing and defence of actions; he prepared the written pleadings on either side very skilfully, and without too much finesse; he was of admirable assistance at the trial to a shallow leader; he acknowledged that he was an indifferent hand at cross-examining adverse witnesses, but he never brought out unfavorable facts by indiscreet questions; he had great weight with the Judge by his

"INNER TEMPLE.

"Charles Abbott, second son of John Abbott, late of the City of Canterbury, deceased (who was admitted to the Society of the Middle Temple the sixteenth day of November, in the year of our Lord 1787, as by Certificate from the Middle Temple appears), admitted of this Society the eighth day of May in the year of our Lord 1793.

" *Calls to the Bar.—Hilary Term*, 1796.

" Mr. John Fuller,
" Mr. Charles Abbott,
" Mr. William Lloyd,
" Mr. John Wadman,
} 15th Feb. 1796."

quiet and terse mode of arguing points of law arising at nisi prius, and if a demurrer, a motion in arrest of judgment, a special case, a special verdict, or a writ of error was to be argued in banc, he was a full match for Holroyd, Littledale,[1] or Richardson.

1. "Descended from an ancient Cumberland family, Sir Joseph Littledale was the eldest son of Henry Littledale, Esq., of Eton House, Lancashire, and of Mary the daughter of Isaac Wilkinson, Esq., of Whitehaven. He was born in 1767, and completed his education at St. John's College, Cambridge, in 1787, with the honorable distinction of senior wrangler and first Smith's prizeman. Entering Gray's Inn he practised for some years as a special pleader under the bar till 1798. Being then called, from that time till 1824, a period of twenty-six years, his intimate knowledge of the law and patient industry insured the confidence of all who had the management of business, and gave him very extensive employment. In 1822 he was sent into Scotland with Mr. Hullock (afterwards elevated to the bench) for the purpose of arranging some government prosecutions. He never accepted a silk gown, nor took the common course of seeking advancement by obtaining a seat in parliament, and was indeed so little of a party man and so entirely a lawyer, that when he was asked by a friend what his politics were, he is said to have answered, "Those of a special pleader." His professional merits alone pointed him out as the most worthy successor of Mr. Justice Best in the Court of King's Bench. He received his appointment on April 30, 1824, with the usual honor of knighthood. With such colleagues as Chief Justice Abbott, Mr. Justice Bayley, and Mr. Justice Holroyd, the court presented for many years as perfect a phalanx of learned and efficient men as had ever been united in the administration of justice. For the remaining years of the reign of George IV., for the whole of that of William IV., and for nearly four years of the present reign, a period altogether of seventeen years, Sir Joseph Littledale performed the duties of his office to the admiration not only of lawyers but of the public in general. Lord Campbell, who practised under him during the whole time, calls him 'one of the most acute, learned, and simple-minded of men'; and there was scarcely a barrister who did not regard him as a judicial father, and none could recall an unkind word of his utterance, or an impatient expression of his countenance. He was so devotedly attached to his profession that he heartily enjoyed the discussion of the legal points before him. Once when the author of these pages ventured to express a hope that he was not fatigued with the labors of a heavy day, he answered, 'Oh no, not at all; I like it.' Having attained the age of 74, he felt that it was time for him to quit active life, and therefore at the end of Hilary term, 1841, he resigned his seat, to the regret of his colleagues, and also of an admiring bar; who paid him the well merited compliment of an affectionate address, expressive of their sorrow at parting, and of good

In about two years after his call a deep sensation was produced by the unexpected prospect of an opening for juniors on the Oxford Circuit. It was the custom in those days, that while the Judges went all the way round in their coaches and four, the counsel journeyed on horseback. Abbott refused to cross the most sedate horses which were offered to him, from the certain knowledge that he must be spilt ; but he took it into his fancy that it would be a much more easy matter to drive a gig, although to this exercitation he was equally unaccustomed. As far as Gloucester, after some hair-breadth escapes, he contrived to get, without fracture or contusion ; but in descending a' hill near Monmouth his horse took fright, he pulled the wrong rein, he was upset, and, according to one account, " he died immediately from a fracture of the skull," and, according to another, " he was drowned in the Wye." The news was brought to the assembled barristers at their mess, and all expressed deep regret. Nevertheless the brightened eyes and flickering smiles of some led to a suspicion that the dispersion of briefs might be a small recompense for their heavy loss. It turned out that there had been considerable exaggeration as to the fatal effect of Abbott's overturn ; but in truth his leg was broken in two places, and he had received very severe injury in other parts of his body— so that from this accident he was permanently lame, and he had a varicose vein on his forehead for the rest of his days. Although he was able in a few weeks to return to business, his constitution materially suffered

wishes for his future welfare, orally delivered by the Attorney General (Sir John Campbell) on his taking leave of the court on February 6. Though he was immediately called to the Privy Council, he had very little opportunity of aiding in the hearings before its judicial committee ; for in less than a year and a half the infirmities that had warned him to retire made rapid way, and he died at his house in Bedford Square on June 26, 1842."—*Foss's Judges of England.*

from this shock, and the inability to take exercise
which it superinduced.

While flourishing on the circuit he had as yet very
slender employment at Guildhall, and he felt a great
desire to participate in the commercial business there,
which is considered the most creditable and the most
lucrative in the courts of common law. With this view,
in spite of the sneers of Lord Ellenborough at book-
writing lawyers, by the advice of Sir John Scott, who
had become his avowed patron, he composed and published a treatise 'ON MERCHANTS' SHIPS AND SEA-
MEN.' In no department does English talent appear
to such disadvantage as in legal literature ; and we
have gone on from bad to worse in proportion as
method and refinement have advanced elsewhere.
Bracton's work, ' De Legibus et Consuetudinibus
Angliæ,' written in the reign of Henry III., is
(with the exception of ' Blackstone's Commentaries ')
more artistically composed and much pleasanter to
read, than any law-book written by any Englishman
down to the end of the reign of George III.—while we
were excelled by contemporary juridical authors not
only in France, Italy, and Germany, but even in
America.   Abbott did a good deal to redeem us from
this disgrace.   Instead of writing all the legal dogmas
he had to mention, and all the decisions in support of
them, on separate pieces of paper, shaking them in a
bag, drawing them out blindfold, and making a chapter
of each handful, connecting the paragraphs at random
with conjunctives or disjunctives (" And," " So," " But,"
" Nevertheless "),—he made an entirely new and mas-
terly analysis of his subject ; he divided it logically
and lucidly ; he laid down his propositions with precision ; he supported them by just reasoning, and he
fortified them with the dicta and determinations of
jurists and judges methodically arranged.   His style,

clear, simple, and idiomatic, was a beautiful specimen
of genuine Anglicism.   The book came out in the
year 1802, dedicated (by permission) to the man who
had suggested the subject to him,—now become Lord
Chancellor Eldon. Its success was complete. Not
only was it loudly praised by all the Judges, but by all
the City attorneys, and, ever after, the author was employed in almost all the charterparty, policy, and other
His busi- mercantile causes tried at Guildhall. Nay, the fame of
ness at
Guildhall. the book soon crossed the Atlantic, although it was for
some time ascribed to another ; for, as I have heard
the true author relate with much glee, the first edition,
reprinted at New York, was announced in the title-
page to be by "the RIGHT HONORABLE CHARLES
ABBOTT, SPEAKER OF THE HOUSE OF COMMONS IN
ENGLAND."   This was his distinguished namesake,
Lord Colchester, who had been at the bar, and who
was complimented by the American editor for employing his time so usefully during the recess of parliament.[1]

Our hero was now as eminent and prosperous as a
counsel can be at the English bar, who is not a leader
—either with a silk gown as the ordinary testimonial of
his eminence—or, if this for any reason be withheld
from him, dashing into the lead in bombazeen, like
Dunning, Brougham, and Scarlett.[2] Abbott wore
the bombazeen quite contentedly, and shrunk from
everything that did not belong to the subordinate
duties of the grade of the profession to which this
costume is supposed to be appropriated. Yet both for

1. Our legal literature has likewise been greatly indebted to the
admirable works of Lord St. Leonards on " Vendors and Purchas-
ers " and on " Powers."

2. Dunning always wore stuff, except during the short time when
he was Solicitor General. The two others were in the full lead long
before they were clothed in silk. I myself led the Oxford Circuit in
bombazeen for three years.

·profit and position he was more to be envied than most
of those who sat within the bar, and whose weapon was
supposed to be eloquence. He was a legal pluralist.
His best appointment was that of counsel to the Treasury, or rather "Devil to the Attorney General"—by
virtue of which he drew all informations for libel and
indictments for treason, and opened the pleadings!in
all Government prosecutions. Next he was counsel
for the Bank of England, an office which, in the days of
one pound notes, when there were numerous executions
for forgery every Old Bailey Session, brought in enormous fees. He was likewise standing counsel for a
number of other corporations and chartered companies, and being known to be a zealous churchman as
well as good ecclesiastical lawyer, he had a general
retainer from most of the Prelates, and Deans and
Chapters in England. Erskine in all his glory never
reached 10000*l.* a year; yet Abbott, "Leguleius qui-
dam," is known in the year 1807, to have made a return His large
to the income-tax of 8026*l.* 5*s.* as the produce of his income.
professional earnings in the preceding year, and he is
supposed afterwards to have exceeded that amount.

I believe that he never addressed a jury in London His incom-
in the whole course of his life. On the circuit he was an advo-
now and then forced into the lead in spite of himself, cate.
from all the silk gowns being retained on the other
side,—and on these occasions he did show the most
marvellous inaptitude for the functions of an advocate,
and almost always lost the verdict. This partly arose
from his power of discrimination and soundness of
understanding, which, enabling him to see the real
merits of the cause on both sides, afterwards fitted him
· so well for being a Judge. I remember a Serjeant-at-
law having brilliant success at the bar from always sincerely believing that his client was entitled to succeed,
although, when a Chief Justice, he proved without any

exception, and beyond all comparison, the most indifferent Judge who has appeared in Westminster Hall in
my time. Poor Abbott could not struggle with facts
which were decisive against him, and if a well-founded
legal objection was taken, recollecting the authorities
on which it rested, he betrayed to the presiding Judge
a consciousness that it was fatal. His physical defects
were considerable, for he had a husky voice, a leaden
eye, and an unmeaning countenance. Nor did he ever
make us think only of his intellectual powers by any
flight of imagination or ebullition of humor, or stroke
of sarcasm. But that to which I chiefly ascribed his
failure was a want of boldness, arising from the recollection of his origin and his early occupations. "He
showed his blood." Erskine undoubtedly derived
great advantage from recollecting that he was known
to be the son of an Earl, descended from a royal stock.
Johnson accounts for Lord Chatham's overpowering
vehemence of manner from his having carried a pair
of colors as a cornet of horse. Whether Abbott continued to think of the razor-case and pewter basin I
know not; but certain it is there was a most unbecoming humility and self abasement in his manner,
which inclined people to value him as he seemed inclined to value himself. Called upon to move in his
turn when sitting in court in term time, he always
prefaced his motion with "I humbly thank your Lordship." I remember once when he began by making
an abject apology for the liberty he was taking in
contending that Lord Ellenborough had laid down
some bad law at nisi prius, he was thus contemptuously reprimanded :—" Proceed, Mr. Abbott, proceed ;
it is your right and your duty to argue that I misdirected the jury, if you think so."

He had apprehensions that he could not remain
much longer stationary at the bar. He said to me that

if he were sure of having the second brief in a cause he would never wish to have the first, but that he might be driven to hold the first if he could not have the second. Soon after this display of rising spirit he had a great opportunity of gaining distinction, for he was called upon to lead a very important Quo Warranto cause at Hereford, on which depended the right of returning to parliament a member for a Welsh borough. But nothing could rouse him into energy, and he had a misgiving that the proper issue was not taken on the 7th replication to the 10th plea. When he had been addressing the Jury as leader for half an hour a silly old barrister of the name of Rigby came into Court, and when he had listened for another half hour, believing all this was preliminary to Dauncey or Serjeant Williams acting the part of leader, and explaining what the case really was about, he innocently whispered in my ear, " How long Abbott is in opening the pleadings in this case! " The verdict going against him, a new trial was to be moved for next term,—when he had not the courage to make the motion himself, but insisted that it should be made by Scarlett of the Northern Circuit, who was still practising without the bar in a stiff gown like himself.

His chief effort in oratory.

. In 1808, when Mr. Justice Lawrence differed with Lord Ellenborough, and retired into the Common Pleas, Abbott had declined the offer of being made a Puisne Judge, on account of the diminution of income which the elevation would have occasioned to him— but soon after I joined the Circuit I found that he earnestly longed for the repose of the Bench, and he was much chagrined that his patron, Lord Eldon, did not renew the offer to him. Sir Egerton Brydges, who was still more in his confidence, thus writes: " For twenty years he worked at the bar with steady and progressive profit and fame, but with no sudden bursts

and momentary blaze, till his health and spirits began
to give way. I well remember, in the year 1815, his
lamenting to me in a desponding tone that his eye-sight
was impaired, and that he had some thoughts of retiring
altogether from the profession. I dissuaded him, and
entreated him not to throw away all the advantages he
had gained by a life of painful toil, at the very period
when he might hope for *otium cum dignitate.* I left him
with regret, and under the impression that his health
and spirits were declining."

While in Court upon the Circuits he betrayed a
languor which showed that he was sick of it, but in society, and in travelling from assize town to assize town,
His con-
duct as
Attorney-
General in
the Grand
Circuit
Court. he was lively and agreeable. No one relished a good
dinner more, although he never was guilty of any excess. He still filled the office of Attorney General in
the Grand Circuit Court, held at Monmouth, which I
regularly opened as crier, holding the poker instead of
a white wand ; and being so decply versed in all legal
forms, he brought forward his mock charges against
the delinquents whom he prosecuted with much
solemnity and burlesque effect—so as for the moment
to induce a belief that notwithstanding his habitual
gravity, Nature intended him for a wag.[1]

I ought to have mentioned that as early as the year
1795, he was so confident of increasing employment that
he ventured to enter the holy state of matrimony, being
united to Mary, eldest daughter of John Lamotte, Esq.,
a gentleman residing at Basildon.

1. Before the public he was always afraid of approaching a jest
lest his dignity might suffer, and in his book on Shipping he would
not, without an apology, even introduce a translation of a passage
from a foreign writer which might cause a smile : "If mice eat the
cargo, and thereby occasion no small damage to the merchant, the
master must make good the loss, because he is guilty of a fault ; yet
if he had cats on board he shall be excused (Roccus, 58). The rule
and exception, *although bearing somewhat of a ludicrous air,* furnish a
good illustration of the general principle."

There had been a mutual attachment between them some years before it was made known to her family, and he had received as a *gage d'amour* from her, a lock of her hair. This revived his poetical ardor, and in the midst of Declarations, Demurrers, and Surrebutters, he *drew and settled*—

"The Answer of a Lock of Hair to the Inquiries of its former Mistress."

The reader may like to have two or three of the stanzas (or counts) as *a precedent :*

> " Since first I left my parent stock,
>   How strangely alter'd is my state !
> No longer now a flowing lock,
>   With graceful pride elate,
> Upon the floating gale I rise
>   To catch some wanton rover's eyes.

> " But close entwin'd in artful braid,
>   And round beset with burnish'd gold,
> Against a beating bosom laid,
>   An office now I hold :
> New powers assume, new aid impart,
>   And form the bulwark of a heart."

The Lock goes on to describe a great discovery it had made while guarding the heart of her lover :

> " For in this heart's most sacred cell,
>   By love enthron'd, arry'd in grace.
> I saw a fair enchantress dwell
>   The sovereign of the place :
> And as she smil'd her power to view,
>   I straight my former mistress knew.

> " Then, lady, cease your tender fears ;
>   Be doubt dismiss'd ! Adieu to care !
> For sure this heart through endless years
>   Allegiance true will bear,
> Since I all outward foes withstand,
> And you the powers within command."

It is said that while still practising as a special pleader under the bar he at last ventured to mention the proposal to the lady's father. The old gentleman asking him " for a sight of his rent-roll," not yet being able to boast of "a rood of ground in Westminster Hall," he exclaimed, " Behold my books and my pupils."

The marriage took place with her father's consent, and proved most auspicious. The married couple lived together harmoniously and happily for many years, although of very different dispositions. While he was remarkably plain and simple in his attire, she was fond of finery, and according to the prevailing fashion, she His wife. habitually heightened her complexion with a thick veneering of carmine. So little suspicious was he on such subjects that I doubt whether he did not exult-ingly say to himself, " her color comes and goes." Once, while paying me a visit in my chambers, in Paper Buildings, the walls of which were of old dark oak wainscot, he said, " Now, if my wife had these chambers, she would immediately *paint* them, and I should like them the better for it."

In the collection of his letters intrusted to me I find only one addressed to his wife, and this I have great pleasure in copying for my readers, as it places him in a very amiable point of view. Some years after his marriage, when he had been blessed with two hopeful children, being at Shrewsbury upon the Circuit, he thus addressed her :

" Shrewsbury, March 27th, 1798.

" MY DEAREST LOVE :

" I have just received and read your kind letter, which I had been expecting near half an hour. The inhabitants of any country but this would be astonished to hear that a letter can be received at the distance of 166 miles on the day after its date, and its arrival cal-culated within a few minutes.[1] As the invention of *paper* has now ceased to be a theme of rejoicing among

1. The rapidity of communication by the mail coach, then lately established, so much exciting his astonishment, what would he have said had he lived to see *Railroads* and the *Electric Telegraph?*

poetical lovers, I recommend them to adopt the subject of *mail coaches*. They have only to call a turnpike road a velvet lawn, and change a scarlet coat into a rosy mantle, and they may describe the vehicle and its journey in all the glowing colors of the radiant chariot of the God of Day. And that no gentleman or lady may despair of success in attempting to handle this new sub_ ject, I have taken the pains to write a few lines, which a person of tolerable ingenuity may work out into a volume:

> ' In rosy mantle clad, the God of Day
> O'er heaven's broad turnpike wins his easy way ;
> Yet soon as envious Night puts out his fires,
> The lazy deity to rest retires.
> But sure *his* robes with brighter crimson glow,
> Who guides the mail-coach through the realms below
> And greater *he* who, fearless of the night,
> Drives in the dark as fast as in the light.
> Sweet is the genial warmth from heaven above ;
> But sweeter are the words of absent love.
> Then cease, ye bards, to sing Apollo's praise,
> And let mail-coachmen only fill your lays.'

" You see my verses are very stiff, but recollect that husbands deal more in truth than in poetry. In truth then, I am very happy to hear that you, my dearest Mary, and our beloved little John, are so much better, and in truth I am very happy to think that the circuit is almost over, and that in a few days I shall embrace you both. Unless I am detained beyond my expectation I shall certainly have the pleasure of dining with you on Monday. Indeed I hope to get to Maidenhead on Sunday afternoon, and there step into one of the Bath coaches that arrive in town about eleven at night. I have brought a box of Shrewsbury cakes to treat the young gentleman when he behaves well after dinner.

" Adieu, my dearest Mary,
" Your faithful and affectionate husband,
" C. ABBOTT."

The following verses, which I find in his handwriting, were probably enclosed in a letter from him to Mrs. Abbott, while on the Circuit at Hereford:

" In the noise of the bar and the crowds of the hall,
 Tho' destined still longer to move,
Let my thoughts wander home, and my memory recall
 The dear pleasures of beauty and love.

" The soft looks of my girl, the sweet voice of my boy,
 Their antics, their hobbies, their sports ;
How the houses he builds her quick fingers destroy,
 And with kisses his pardon she courts.

" With eyes full of tenderness, pleasure, and pride,
 The fond mother sits watching their play ;
Or turns, if I look not, my dulness to chide,
 And invites me like them to be gay.

" She invites to be gay, and I yield to her voice,
 And my toils and my sorrows forget ;
In her beauty, her sweetness, her kindness rejoice,
 And hallow the day that we met.

" Full bright were her charms in the bloom of her life,
 When I walked down the church by her side ;
And, five years past over, I now find the wife
 More lovely and fair than the bride.

" Hereford, Aug. 6, 1800."

His affection for her was warmly returned, and she continued very tenderly attached to him. Shortly before his assumption of the ermine, she expresssd to me the deep anxiety she felt from a weakness in his eyes, discontent with the tardiness of Eldon in fulfilling the promise to make him a Judge, and the pleasure she should have in consenting to his retirement from the profession altogether, if this would contribute to his comfort. They had lived ever since their marriage in a small house in Queen Square, Bloomsbury, giving a dinner to a few lawyers now and then,[1] and seeing no other company. He always contributed a dish to his own dinner table ; for passing the fishmonger's on his

His desire
to be made
a Judge.

---

1. One of the wise *saws* which I have heard him recite was, " A good dinner, given to guests judiciously selected, is money well spent."

way to Westminster, he daily called there and sent HAP. home what was freshest, nicest, and cheapest—trusting CLII. all the rest to her. Their union was blessed with four children—two sons and two daughters, and the whole household was ever remarkable for all that is excellent and amiable.

On the resignation of Mr. Justice Chambre,[1] it He is dis-was thought that Abbott's well-known desire to be appointed.

1. The family of De la Chambré, De Camera, or Chaumberay, was of Norman origin, and the name of one of its members occurs on the roll of Battle Abbey. Hugh De Chambré, or De Camera, in the reign of Henry III., settled in Westmoreland, where his descend-ants have flourished in an uninterrupted lineal succession till the present time. Halhead Hall in the parish of Kendal was acquired by them by marriage in the reign of Henry VIII., and still remains in their possession. Four successive generations became eminent in the law ; this judge's great-grandfather and grandfather (both named Alan) having been benchers of the Middle Temple, and the latter recorder of Kendal, to which his son, Walter Chambré, was elected on his father's resignation. The judge was the eldest son of this Walter, by his marriage with Mary, daughter of Jacob Morland of Capplethwaite Hall in the same county. Alan Chambré was born on October 4, 1739, and, of course, was destined to the profes-sion which his progenitors had pursued. With this view, reviving an ancient custom which had been long discontinued, he first resorted to an inn of Chancery, and paid the customary dozen of claret on admission into the society of Staple Inn. He was a member of that society in 1757, and his arms are emblazoned on a window in the Hall. From this inn he removed to the Middle Temple in February, 1758, but transferred himself to Gray's Inn in November, 1764, and was called to the bar in May, 1767. The diligence with which he had devoted himself to his studies was proved by the success which he achieved; and his independent and upright conduct and amiable disposition may be estimated by his popularity among his colleagues. He selected the northern circuit and soon became one of its leaders. In June, 1781, he was chosen bencher and in 1783 treasurer of his inn ; and in November, 1796, he was elected recorder of Lancaster. On the resignation of Mr. Baron Perryn in 1799, he was named as his successor; the announcement of which was received by the cir-cuit bar with "acclamations quite unprecedented." It was, of course, necessary, in order to enable him to be appointed, that he should be made a serjeant : and as Baron Perryn's retirement took place in vacation, and serjeants could not be called except in term, a short Act of Parliament was passed on July 1, 1799, authorizing, for the first time, a serjeant to receive his degree in the vacation, so that the vacant office might be immediately granted to him. In June of the following year he was removed from the Court of Exchequer

made a Judge would have been gratified ; but James
Allan Park had been conducting very successfully
some Government prosecutions on the Northern Circuit, to which much importance was attached, and his
claims were pressed upon the Chancellor so impor-
tunately by Lord Sidmouth, that they could not be
resisted. Abbott and his family were deeply disappointed, and his health then rapidly declining, there
were serious apprehensions that he would not be able
to stand the fatigue of bar practice any longer, and
that he must retire upon the decent competence which
he had acquired. It is said that he himself was de-
liberating between Canterbury and Oxford as his retreat, and that he had fixed upon the latter city, where
he had always passed his time agreeably, whereas the
recollections of the former were not the unmixed
" pleasures of memory."

to the Common Pleas on the death of Mr. Justice Buller. In that
court he remained till his resignation in Michaelmas vacation, 1815;
when having filled the judicial office for more than fifteen years, he
resigned his seat and became entitled to a retiring annuity of 2000*l*,
under the Act of Parliament passed in the year in which he was
appointed. In the exercise of his functions he merited and received
universal praise both for his learning and urbanity. Lord Brougham
alludes to him in his sketch of Lord Mansfield as " among the first
ornaments of his profession and among the most honest and amiable of men." So extremely careful was he of doing anything that
could by possibility be misinterpreted, that on one occasion he declined the invitation to a house at which the judges had been accustomed to be entertained during the circuit, because the proprietor
was defendant in a cause at that assize. Sir Alan lived seven
years after his retirement, and, dying at Harrogate on September
20, 1823, was buried in the family vault at Kendal. He was never
married and was succeeded in his estates by his nephew, Thomas
Chambré."—*Foss's Judges of England.*

CHAPTER LIII.

CONTINUATION OF THE LIFE OF LORD TENTERDEN
TILL HE WAS ELEVATED TO THE PEERAGE.

OPPORTUNELY another vacancy in the Court of Common Pleas soon after arose from the sudden death of Mr. Justice Heath, who, considerably turned of eighty, made good his oft-declared resolution "to die in harness."[1] Abbott was named to succeed him, and

CHAP.
LIII.

A.D. 1816.
He is a
puisne in
the Com-
mon Pleas.

1. Another peculiarity about him was, that he never would submit to be knighted ; being likewise resolved to die, as he did, " JOHN HEATH, Esq."

The father of this estimable judge was Thomas Heath, an alderman of Exeter ; and his uncle was Benjamin Heath, town-clerk and a lawyer of eminence in that city, who was the father of Dr. Benjamin Heath, the head master of Eton. Both the brothers were learned men, and several works were published by them, among which was an Essay on the Book of Job by the judge's father. The judge himself for a time filled the office of town-clerk of his native city ; and on his death bequeathed nearly 20,000*l.* to his friend Mr. Gatty, who held the office after him. He was a member of the Inner Temple, to which he was admitted in May, 1759, and was called to the bar in June, 1762. In 1775 he was graced with the dignity of the coif, and had a certain prospect of promotion in the friendship of Mr. Thurlow, who when he became Lord Chancellor recommended him for the first vacancy on the bench that occurred. Accordingly, on the death of Mr. Justice Blackstone, Mr. Heath was appointed to supply his place in the Common Pleas on July 19, 1780. . . . His age at his death is recorded in the parish register to have been eighty, but on his monument in the church of Hayes in Middlesex, where he lived with his sister, he is stated to have been eighty-five. That the latter was incorrect is rendered more probable from another blunder on the stone, representing his death to have taken place on January 23, 1817, when in fact it occurred on January 16, 1816. That he was somewhat eccentric may be surmised from his refusal to accept the honor of knighthood, at that time and now

being obliged to submit to the degree of Serjeant at-
Law, he took the same motto which he had modestly
adopted for his shield when he first indulged his fancy
in choosing armorial bearings—LABORE.

The following letter was written by him in answer
to congratulations from his old school-fellow—but it
cannot be trusted as disclosing the whole truth; for he
was ever unwilling to breathe any complaint against
Lord Eldon, even when he thought himself deeply
aggrieved by the selfishness of his patron:

"Serjeants' Inn, Feb. 15th, 1816.

"MY DEAR FRIEND,

"I have felt highly gratified by the receipt of your
kind letter and the warmth of your congratulations on
my promotion to the Bench. I can never forget how
much my present station is owing to your early friendship. The great object of my desire and ambition is
now attained: it has been attained at a time when I

almost invariably conferred on the occupiers of the judicial bench.
. . . But his excellence in performing the functions of a judge is
allowed by all who were witnesses of his career. Lord Eldon, who
was part of the time chief justice of that court, took occasion to
remark with admiration and surprise on the extent of his professional
knowledge. Many also are the testimonies to his private worth and
to the universality and accuracy of his general knowledge. He was
strictly impartial, and on the trial of the Bishop of Bangor and
others for a riot he stated that the evidence proved the case, and
summed up strongly against them. But their compassion for the
bishop more than the eloquence of Erskine induced the jury to
bring in a verdict of acquittal. He was considered a severe judge,
and Lord Campbell says (Chancellors, vi. 154) that he used to hang
in all capital cases on principle, because he knew of no good sec-
ondary punishments. Though capital punishments were then carried to an outrageous extent, the failure of the ticket-of-leave
system which too frequently follows the penalties since substituted
forcibly confirms the judge's opinion that "the criminal is soon
thrown upon you again, hardened in guilt." Though he is said to
have held this opinion, in his private intercourse he was kind, charitable, and good natured ; and Mr. Serjeant Shepherd took an opportunity of expressing the sentiments of the bar and his own, in
paying respect to his memory as an able and upright judge and a
worthy and valuable man. He died unmarried.—*Foss's Judges of
England.*

had begun to be solicitous about it, as well on account
of my advancing age as of a complaint that has for some months affected my eye-lids and made reading by candle light very inconvenient. The comparative leisure I now enjoy has, I think, already been attended with some beneficial effect and an abatement of the complaint. If the offer had not come now, it might have come too late; if it had come much sooner, pecuniary considerations would not have allowed me to accept it. But, like all other men who have obtained the object of their pursuit, I am now beginning to feel the difficulties that belong to it—to tremble lest I should be found unequal to the discharge of the duties of my station from want of learning, or talents, or temper, or lest the *res* still *angusta domi* should not enable me to keep up the outward state that so high a rank in society requires, without injury to my family. These difficulties, small at a distance, like all others, now appear large to my view—the last of them larger, perhaps, than it ought, though the transition from an income exceeding present calls and daily flowing in, to one receivable at stated periods and of which the sufficiency is not quite certain, is attended with very unpleasant sensations. The employment of the mind, however, so far at least as my very short acquaintance with it enables me to judge, is far more agreeable. The search after truth is much more pleasant than the search after arguments. Some time may also be allowed to those studies which are the food of youth and the solace of age, but to which a man actively engaged in the profession of the law can only give an occasional and almost stolen glance. And some time may be allowed, too, for the discharge of the duties of domestic life, for the calls and the pleasures of friendship, and for that still more important task, the preparation for another world, to which we are all hastening. I have

been told that some persons, on their promotion to the
Bench, have found their time hang heavy on their
hands; but I cannot think this will ever be my own
case.

"I have another subject of congratulation, for I am
to go the Home Circuit, which I shall not have another
opportunity of doing for many years. C. Willyams
has promised to be at Maidstone during the assizes. I
hope he will not be the only old friend I shall meet
there.[1]

"With best respects to Lady Brydges,
"I remain,
"My dear Sir Egerton,
"Your very faithful and affectionate friend,
"C. ABBOTT."

He sat for a very short time as Judge in the Court
of Common Pleas; but not a word which fell from him
there has been recorded, and had he remained there
we should probably have known little more of him
than the dates of his appointment and of his death in
'*Beatson's Political Index.*' But he was unexpectedly
transferred to another sphere, where he gained himself

He is trans-
ferred to
the King's
Bench.
a brilliant and a lasting reputation. Of this change he
gives an account in the following letter:

"Queen Square, May 5th, 1816.
"MY DEAR SIR EGERTON,

"You have probably been already informed that
I have been removed from the Common Pleas to the
King's Bench. The change was greatly against my
personal wishes on account of the very great difference in the labor of the two situations, which I estimate
at not less than 400 hours in a year. I had hoped to
pass the remainder of my life in a situation of compara-

1. The vision of his fellow townsmen coming over from Canterbury to see him in the Crown Court, habited in scarlet and ermine,
was about to be fulfilled.

tive ease and rest; but the change was pressed upon me in a way that I could not resist, though very unwilling to be flattered out of a comfortable seat. I hope you will not think I have done wrong.

"I remain,

"My dear Sir Egerton,

"Yours most sincerely,

"C. ABBOTT."

In his DIARY, begun November 3d, 1822, but taking a retrospect of his judicial life, he explains that the true reason of his removal was that Lord Eldon wished to make a Judge of Burrough,[1] who, from age and other defects, was not producible in the King's Bench, but might pass muster in the Common Pleas. Having stated how he at first refused and how Lord Ellenborough pressed him to agree, he proceeds: "Upon this I went to Lord Chief Justice Gibbs, at his house at Hayes, in Kent, to consult him. I spoke of the state of my eyes. He said, 'If a higher situation were offered to you, would you refuse it on that account?' I answered, 'I should not think myself justified toward my family in doing so, but my own ambition is quite satisfied' (as in truth it was). He replied, 'Then you must

1. Sir James Burrough (1750–1839), judge, third son of the Rev. John Burrough of Abbots-Anne, Hampshire, was born in 1750. Entering the Inner Temple in February, 1768, he was called to the bar by that society in November, 1773, but was not elected a bencher until 1808. He joined the western circuit, and after many years' practice was in 1792 appointed a commissioner of bankruptcy, in 1794 Deputy Recorder of Salisbury, and afterwards Recorder of Portsmouth. In May, 1816, being then sixty-six years of age, he was raised to the bench of the Common Pleas, and received the customary knighthood, a promotion he owed to the steady friendship of Lord Eldon. In that court he sat until the end of 1829, when increasing infirmities obliged him to retire. He survived nearly ten years, and, dying on March 25, 1839, was buried in the Temple Church. His daughter Anne, his only surviving child, erected a monument to his memory in the church of Taverstock, Wiltshire, in which county and in Hampshire he possessed considerable property.—*Nat. Biog. Dict.*

not let that excuse prevent your removal.' After some further conference, in the course of which he expressed himself with great kindness in regard to losing my assistance in the Common Pleas, it was resolved that I should remove, and upon my return from Hayes I communicated to the Lord Chancellor that I was willing to remove. This account of my removal to the King's Bench may serve as an example of the maxim that to do right is the greatest wisdom—even the greatest worldly wisdom. It was right that I should remove into the King's Bench, and I ought to have done so at the first proposal from the Lord Chancellor; but I preferred Gibbs, C. J., to Lord Ellenborough, as I had a right to do from long acquaintance and many acts of kindness. I preferred my ease to the wish of the Chancellor, for I might have understood his proposal to contain his wish, though he would not tell me so. This I had no right to do, for I owed everything to him and his kindness. As soon as I removed I felt satisfied with myself, though I may truly say I did not by any means expect the consequence that followed two years and a half afterwards. But if I had not removed into the King's Bench, I think it certain that I should not have been placed at the head of that Court."

On Friday, the 3d of May, 1816, Mr. Justice Abbott took his seat in the Court of King's Bench along with Lord Ellenborough, Mr. Justice Bayley, and Mr. Justice Holroyd [1]—and he officiated there as a puisne Judge till Michaelmas Term, 1818. Never having led at *Nisi Prius*, and having been accustomed to attend to detached points as they arose, rather than to take a broad and comprehensive view of the merits of the cause, he at first occasioned considerable disappointment among those who were prepared to admire him; but he gradually and steadily improved, and

1. 6 Taunton, 516; 5 Maule and Selwyn, 2.

ROBERT PEEL.

before the expiration of the second year he gave de- CHAP.cided proof of the highest judicial excellence.   The LIII.complaints made against him were, that in spite of
efforts at self-control, his manner to *boring* barristers
was sometimes snappish ; that he showed too much
deference to the Chief Justice ; above all, that in some
political prosecutions, although his demeanor was
always decorous, and he said nothing that could be laid
hold of as misdirection or misrepresentation, he betrayed
an anxiety to obtain a verdict for the Crown.   Lord
Ellenborough's health was seriously declining, and in
those days there was still a strong disposition in the
Government to repress free discussion and to preserve
tranquillity by a very rigorous enforcement of the
criminal law—a disposition which soon after ceased,
when Peel[1] became Home Secretary and Copley At-

1. Sir Robert Peel (*b.* Feb. 5, 1788, *d.* July 2, 1850) was the son
of Sir Robert Peel, an enormously wealthy Lancashire cotton manu-
facturer.   Educated at Harrow and Christ Church, Oxford, Peel,
after a very brilliant university career, entered parliament for
Cashel in 1809, as a supporter of Mr. Perceval.   In 1810 he was
made Under-Secretary for the Home Department.   In 1812 he was
Chief Secretary for Ireland under Lord Liverpool.   In 1817 he was returned as member for Oxford University, and in 1819 he was
chosen chairman of the committe on the currency, in which capacity
he was mainly instrumental in bringing about the return to cash
payments.   From 1822 to 1827 Peel was Home Secretary : but on the
accession of Canning (April, 1827), he retired, being unable to agree
with that minister on the subject of Catholic Emancipation.   In 1828
he returned under the Duke of Wellington ; and in March, 1829,
having become convinced of the necessity of granting the demands
of the Catholics, he moved the Catholic Relief Bill in the House of
Commons.   In May, 1830, Peel succeeded his father in the baronetcy,
and, having been rejected the previous year by the University of
Oxford, re-entered parliament as member for Tamworth.   During
the discussion on the Reform Bill, Peel, who resigned with his colleagues (Nov., 1830), strenuously opposed the measure.   In 1834 he
was recalled to office during the brief Conservative ministry of William IV.   On May 5, 1839, on the resignation of the Melbourne ministry, Sir Robert Peel was sent for by the queen ; but his request for
the removal of certain of her majesty's ladies of the bed-chamber
who were connected with Whig leaders being refused, he declined to
form a ministry, and the Whigs returned to office.   In Aug., 1841,
they resigned, and Sir Robert Peel became Prime Minister, holding

torney General. The malicious insinuated that an aspiring puisne was trying for the Collar of SS by "a mixture of good and evil arts." He himself was so profoundly reserved that he might have been acting upon this plan without having disclosed it to his own mind.

I happened to be much in his company during the long vacation of 1816. In consequence of a serious illness, then being a desolate bachelor, I had retired to a lonely cottage at Bognor, on the coast of Sussex, and Mr. Justice Abbott taking up his residence there with his family, he was exceedingly kind to me. In our walks he talked of literature much more than of law, and he would beautifully recite long passages from the Greek and Latin classics, as well as from Shakespeare, Milton, and Dryden. For all modern English poetry he expressed infinite contempt. When I ventured to stand up for brilliant passages in Byron, he only exclaimed

" Unus et alter
Assuitur pannus ! "[1]

office till June, 1846. His *régime* was marked by some important financial changes, including the Bank Charter Act of 1844. But it was specially marked by the repeal of the Corn Laws and the removal of protectionist restrictions on trade. Sir Robert, with the bulk of his followers, was altogether opposed to the removal of the corn duties, and vigorously resisted the Anti-Corn Law agitators. But he at length became convinced of the justice of their cause, and, to the intense disgust of many of his followers, himself brought in the bill for the repeal of the duties on corn. But a large portion of the Conservatives abandoned him, and the Liberals gave him little support, and in June, 1846, he resigned. During the remaining years of his life he gave a general support to the home and commercial policy of the Whig ministers, though he opposed their foreign policy. He died from the effects of a fall from his horse while riding in St. James's Park. Peel's public action, especially in the matter of the Catholic Claims and the Corn Laws, exposed him to much misconstruction in his lifetime. But his honesty, his zeal for the welfare of the country, his moral courage and independence of character, have been amply acknowledged by the succeeding generations. And whatever exception might be taken to his general statesmanship, no one has doubted that his talents as an administrator and a financier were of the highest possible order.—*Dict. of Eng. Hist.*

1. " One and another patch is sewed on."

ROBERT BARON GIFFORD.

Yet he was himself still sometimes inspired by the
Muse. While we remained at Bognor, the Channel was visited by a tremendous tempest, which he celebrated by the following

> " *Sonnet to the South-West Gale.*
>
> " Perturbed leader of the restless tide,
>   That from the broad Atlantic swept away,
>   Here mingles with the clouds its lofty spray.
> As if it would the narrow limits chide
> That Albion from her neighbor Gaul divide—
> Relentless SOUTH-WEST ! curb thy angry sway,
> Ere yet the swelling billows' fierce array
> Close o'er yon shattered bark's devoted side !
> The melancholy signal sounds in vain;
>   The crew, desponding, eye the distant shore;
> Calm, ere they perish, calm the troubled main,
>   The placid sea and sky serene restore;
> And be thou welcom'd in the poet's prayer,
> God of the balmy gale and genial air!"

In the autumn of 1818 there was a great excitement in the legal world. Lord Ellenborough had had a paralytic seizure, and it was certain that he could never sit again. Sir Samuel Shepherd, the Attorney General, although an excellent lawyer as well as a very able and honorable man, was so deaf that he could not with propriety accept any judicial office which required him to listen to parol evidence, or to *vivâ voce* discussion. Sir Robert Giffard[1] had been recently promoted to be Solicitor General, from a rather obscure position in the profession, and he could not as yet with propriety be placed at the head of the common law. Sir Vicary Gibbs was looked to, having a great legal reputation, and being in the highest favor with the Government; for from Attorney General, he had successively been made a puisne Judge, Chief Baron of the Exchequer,

---

1. Robert Giffard, Baron Saint Leonards, an able English lawyer, born at Exeter in 1779. He was appointed Solicitor General in 1817, and Attorney General in 1819. In this capacity he conducted the prosecution of Queen Caroline in 1820, after which he received the title of baron. He became master of the rolls and chief justice of common pleas in 1824. Died in 1826.—*Thomas' Biog. Dict.*

and Chief Justice of the Common Pleas; but the hand
of death was now upon him. Who was to be Chief
Justice of England? Lord Ellenborough strongly recommended Mr. Serjeant Lens, a most honorable man,
an accomplished scholar, and a very pretty lawyer,—
and he was for some time the favorite.

I well remember one morning in the end of October,
1818, about a fortnight after Lord Ellenborough's death,
when the puisne Judges of the King's Bench were assembled at Serjeants' Inn for the hearing of special
arguments in what was called the " Three Cornered
Court," it was announced that Abbott was certainly to
be Chief Justice. Nothing discredited the assertion
except that his own manner was tranquil and listless,
and that he was observed several times to yawn, seem-
ingly against his will. Some alleged that the news
might be true, as he was only acting a part—and
others, who knew him better, explained what they be-
held by his habitual want of animal spirits and the collapse after long and painful anxiety.

At the rising of the Court he accepted our congratulations on his appointment, and on the 4th of
November, fourteen years to a day before his own
death, he actually appeared in Court at Westminster
wearing the Chief Justice's golden chain.

His family expected to see at the same time his
brows encircled with a coronet, for ever since Lord
Mansfield's elevation in 1756, the Chief Justice of the
King's Bench had been ennobled on his appointment.
This distinction was withheld from Chief Justice Abbott for nine years; but without such adventitious aid
he won the highest respect of the public (as Holt had
done) by the admirable discharge of his judicial duties.

The following letter from him to Sir Egerton
Brydges, who had calculated upon a peerage being at

once conferred upon him, fully explains what then took place, and his own views upon the subject:

"Russell Square, Jan 17th, 1819.

"MY DEAR SIR EGERTON,

"I thank you most heartily for your very affectionate letter, and assure you I do not doubt the sincerity of your warm and kind expressions. It is well that you waited no longer in expectation of seeing my promotion to the peerage announced. Such an event is neither probable nor desirable. When the Lord Chancellor told me he was authorized by the Prince Regent to propose the office of Chief Justice to me, he said he was also directed by His Royal Highness to acquaint me that it was not the intention of His Royal Highness to confer a peerage upon the person who should take the office, whoever he might be. My answer was, that the latter part of his sentence relieved me from the only difficulty I could have had in answering the first. I was willing to take the office, but neither the state of my fortune nor that of the office would allow me to take a peerage, according to my views of expediency and justice to my family. All the offices in the gift of the Chief Justice, and which make his office a means of providing for a family, are now held by the families of my predecessors upon lives which I can never expect to survive. My emoluments will fall far short of two-thirds of those which Lord Ellenborough enjoyed for many years past. Under such circumstances I should be most unwilling to accept an hereditary honor, and I think myself fortunate in having a family, of which no one member is desirous of such a distinction. I have written so much about myself and my own situation, because I know that you wish to hear of them. It is a subject of deep regret to me that I receive your congratulations on my promotion from a distant country.

"Wherever you are and whatever you do, may health and comfort attend you!"

Extraor-
dinary ex-
cellence of
the King's
Bench as a
Court of
Justice
while he
presided
over it.

The far happiest part of my life as an advocate I passed under the auspices of Chief Justice Abbott. From being a puisne, it was some time before he acquired the ascendency and the *prestige* which, for the due administration of justice, the Chief ought to enjoy, —and while Best [1] remained a member of the Court,

1. While this judge was an actor on the legal stage he was only known by his patronymic, his title of Lord Wynford not having been given to him till he had retired from the bench. He was born on December 13, 1767, at Hasselbury Plunknett in Somersetshire, the third son of his father Thomas Best, Esq., by a daughter of Sir William Draper, well known as the antagonist of 'Junius.' Left an orphan in infancy he was sent to the school of the neighboring town of Crewkerne, and at the age of fifteen was removed to Wadham College, Oxford, where he was educated with the view of entering the Church. This plan he was induced to relinquish in consequence of coming into possession by the death of a near relation, of a considerable estate. Then selecting the law as his profession he entered the Middle Temple on October 9, 1784 ; and being called to the bar on November 6, 1789, joined the Home Circuit. Very early in his career he had the good fortune to extract a flattering eulogium from Lord Kenyon in a case which he argued in the Court of King's Bench. This was so unwonted in the Chief Justice that it was sure to attract attention ; and he consequently soon received ample employment. Though superficial in legal knowledge, his readiness of comprehension and fluency of speech enabled him to avail himself of his early success, and his increase of business warranted him in accepting the degree of the coif in 1800. His services were in great requisition, not only in his own Court of Common Pleas but in the other courts of Westminster Hall ; and he sometimes appeared on important criminal trials. He succeeded for William Macfarlane, charged in 1802 with destroying the brig *Adventure*, upon a point of law taken by him and Mr. Erskine. In the case of Colonel Despard, whom in the next year he defended, the evidence of high treason was too clear to leave a hope for acquittal. He entered parliament in 1802 as member for Petersfield, and took a prominent part in its proceedings ; particularly in reference to naval affairs and public accounts. He was one of the acting managers on the impeachment of Lord Melville, and, with Sir Samuel Romilly, answered the legal objections taken by the counsel for the defence. A bill for the improvement of the livings of the London clergy was originated by him, for which that reverend body showed their gratitude by presenting him with a valuable piece of plate. In 1814 he represented Bridport ; and from that time till his death, leaving the Liberal party with whom he had hitherto acted, he was a zealous

he frequently obstructed the march of business. But

supporter of Conservative principles. In his professional capacity he showed cause against the rule for filing a criminal information against Colonel Draper in May, 1806, for a libel on Mr. Sullivan; but did not appear for him on his trial in June, 1807; though he did in the subsequent proceedings against the colonel for the libel on Colonel Fullarton. In the meantime he had been appointed one of the King's Serjeants, and recorder of Guildford; and in Michaelmas, 1813, he was selected as Solicitor General to the Prince of Wales, then Regent, succeeding in 1816, to the Attorney Generalship to his Royal Highness. With that prince he was a great favorite; and by the royal patronage he became successively Chief Justice of Chester and a Judge of the King's Bench; the latter promotion taking place in December, 1818. He was knighted in the following June. After sitting in that court rather more than five years he was advanced in April, 1824 to the head of the Court of Common Pleas, from which in five years more his increasing infirmities obliged him to retire in June, 1829. By the continuance of royal favor he was then raised to the peerage as Baron Wynford, the title being taken from an estate he had purchased in Dorsetshire; and at the same time he was appointed a deputy speaker of the House of Lords. In that House and in the Privy Council he took his due proportion of labor in the judicial business, as often as his violent attacks of the gout enabled him to attend. In the debates he strenuously opposed the reform bill through all its stages; and was always found in opposition to the party who supported it. He lived for sixteen years after his retirement, and died at his seat called Leesons in Kent on March 3, 1845. Lord Wynford's countenance, though not handsome was very attractive. It indicated great cordiality and good humor, with much intelligence; but it also showed something of a hasty temperament. As an advocate he was fluent if not eloquent, acute if not learned, and his zeal for his clients left no means untried for ensuring their success. Sometimes in the ardor of his exertions he would disturb the dignity of his court, and excite the temper of the Chief Justice. But he was a favorite not only with his colleagues at the bar, but also with the attorneys and the litigating public; and consequently commanded a large business both in the Common Pleas and on the circuit. As a judge he was apt to form hasty and questionable opinions, and when presiding at *Nisi Prius*, to lean in his summing up so much to one side that he was nicknamed the "judge advocate." Though he was remarkable for the clearness and terseness of his decisions, he was considered by the profession as an indifferent judge, and brought himself into bad odor, as well by the political bias he often displayed, as by his occasional irritability and intemperance on the bench. His disposition as a man was essentially kind, amiable, and charitable. He married very early in life Mary Anne, the daughter of Jerome Knapp, Esq., of Haberdashers' Hall, London; and had by her ten children. The title is now borne by his son, the second baron.—*Foss's Judges of England.*

when this very amiable and eloquent, although not very logical, Judge had prevailed upon the Prince Regent to make him Chief Justice of the Common Pleas, the King's Bench became the *beau idéal* of a court of justice. Best was succeeded by Littledale, one of the most acute, learned, and simple-minded of men. For the senior puisne we had Bayley. He did not talk very wisely on literature or on the affairs of life, but the whole of the common law of this realm he carried in his head and in seven little red books. These accompanied him day and night; in these every reported case was regularly posted, and in these, by a sort of magic, he could at all times instantaneously turn up the authorities required. The remaining puisne was Holroyd, who was absolutely born with a genius for law, and was not only acquainted with all that had ever been said or written on the subject, but reasoned most scientifically and beautifully upon every point of law which he touched, and, notwithstanding his husky voice and sodden features, as often as he spoke he delighted all who were capable of appreciating his rare excellence. Before such men there was no pretence for being lengthy or importunate. Every point made by counsel was understood in a moment, the application of every authority was discovered at a glance, the counsel saw when he might sit down, his case being safe, and when he might sit down, all chance of success for his client being at an end. I have practised at the bar when no case was secure, no case was desperate and when, good points being overruled, for the sake of justice it was necessary that bad points should be taken; but during that golden age law and reason prevailed—the result was confidently anticipated by the knowing before the argument began,—and the judgment was approved by all who heard it pronounced,—including the vanquished party. Before such a tribunal the advocate becomes dearer to himself by preserving his own esteem, and feels himself to be a minister of justice, instead of a declaimer, a trickster, or a bully. I do not believe that so much important business was ever done so rapidly and so well before any other Court that ever sate in any age or country.

Although the puisnes deserve all the praise that I have bestowed upon them, yet the principal merit is, no doubt, due to Abbott, and no one of them could have played his part so well. He had more knowledge of mankind than any of them, and he was more skilful as a moderator in forensic disputation. He was not only ever anxious, for his own credit, that the business of the Court should be despatched, but he had a genuine love of law and of justice, which made him constantly solicitous that every case should be decided properly. His pasty face became irradiated and his dim eye sparkled if a new and important question of law was raised; and he took more interest in its decision than the counsel whose fame depended upon the result. Though a most faithful trustee of the public time, insomuch that he thought any waste of it was a crime and a sin, he showed no marks of impatience, however long an examination or a speech might be, if he really believed that it assisted in the investigation of truth, and might properly influence the jury in coming to a right verdict.

The language in which he clothed his statements and decisions was always correct, succinct, idiomatic, and appropriate, and he would not patiently endure conceit or affectation in the language of others. He was particularly irate if a common *shop* was called a *warehouse* by its owner, or the *shopman* dubbed himself an *assistant*. A gentleman pressing into a crowded court, complained that he could not get to his counsel. *Lord Tenterden:* "What are you, Sir?" *Gentleman :*

" My Lord, I am the plaintiff's solicitor." *Lord Tenterden :* "We know nothing of *solicitors* here, Sir. Had
you been in the respectable rank of an *attorney*, I
should have ordered room to be made for you." [1]   A
country apothecary, in answer to some plain questions,
using very unnecessarily high-sounding medical phrase-
ology, the Chief Justice roared out, " Speak English,
Sir, if you can, or I must swear an interpreter."

There were heavy complaints against him at *nisi
prius,* that when a fact had been proved by one witness, he reprimanded the counsel for calling another to
prove it over again,—that he was angry when a witness was cross-examined as to the facts sworn by him
when examined in chief,—and that he appealed to the
evidence he had written down in his note book as if it
were a special verdict upon which the cause was to be
decided,—forgetting that everything might depend
upon the impression made by the evidence upon the
minds of the jury and the credit they might give to the
witnesses.   There is no denying that occasionally he
was rather irritable and peevish, and showed in his
manner a want of good taste and of good breeding.
When a third or fourth counsel rose to address him,
following able leaders, he would sneeringly exclaim,
" I suppose we are now to hear what is to be said *on
the other side,*" although it might be the maiden effort
of a trembling junior ; and he too often forgot the remark of Curran,[2] when reproached for too much for-

1. When in 1850 I returned to Westminster Hall, after an absence
of nine years, I found that the *Attorneys* had almost all grown into
SOLICITORS ; and the more expedient course now would probably be
entirely to abolish the word *attorney*, although it denotes the representative character of the forensic agent much more appropriately
than the favored word *Solicitor*.

2. John Philpot Curran was born at Newmarket, near Cork, in
1750.   He received a grammatical education, and was afterwards
admitted a sizar of Trinity College, Dublin, from whence he removed
to one of the inns of court in England, where in regular course he
was called to the bar.   He did not, however, succeed in practice for

bearance on becoming Master of the Rolls, "I do not like to appear in the character of a drill-serjeant, with my cane rapping the knuckles of a private, when I am raised from the ranks to be a colonel."

Although he behaved very courteously to the other puisnes, he could not always conceal his dislike to brother Best. That learned Judge, in trying a defendant for a blasphemous libel, had thrice fined him for very improper language in addressing the jury—20*l.* for saying to the Judge when reproved, "My Lord, if you have your dungeon ready, I will give you the key"—40*l.* for saying that "the Scriptures were ancient tracts containing sentiments, stories, and representations totally derogatory to the honor of God, destructive to pure principles of morality, and opposed to the best interests of society"—and the like sum of 40*l.* for saying very irreverently, but one would have thought less culpably, "The Bishops are generally sceptics." A motion being made for a new trial on the ground that the defendant had been improperly interrupted in making his defence, Abbott, C. J., recognized the power of fining for a contempt, and intimated an opinion that the exercise of it on this occasion had not really debarred the defendant from using any arguments which could have availed him, but sneered at the tariff of pecuniary mulcts, and pretty plainly intimated that he himself should have pursued a different course.[1]

a considerable time; but in the administration of the Duke of Portland he obtained a silk gown and a seat in parliament. His popularity now rose rapidly, and he was retained in all great causes, especially those of a public nature. In 1806 he was made Master of the Rolls in Ireland, which office he resigned in 1814. He died at Brompton Nov. 13, 1817. Mr. Curran was a man of great wit and flowing eloquence. Some of his poetical pieces possess merit.— *Cooper's Biog. Dict.*

1. *Rex* v. *Davison*, 4 B. & A. 33. It should be noted that Best, who, though a passionate, was an exceedingly good-natured man, had himself remitted the fines before the Court rose.

CHAP.
LIII.
His sub-
jection
under a
favorite
counsel.

The only grave fault which could be justly imputed to Chief Justice Abbott was, that he allowed himself to fall under the dominion of a favorite. A judge is in danger of having such a charge brought against him from one counsel in his court being much more em- ployed than any other, and being almost always retained by plaintiffs, who in a large proportion of causes succeed. This may prove a palliation for Abbott, but by no means an entire exculpation. Sir James Scarlett had been his senior at the bar, and when they were in the same cause on the same side had often snubbed him, without permitting him to examine an important witness, and hardly even to open his mouth upon a point of law. The timid junior, become Chief Justice, still looked up to his old leader with dread, was afraid of offending him, and was always delighted when he could decide in his favor. The most serious evil aris- ing from this ascendency was when Scarlett conducted criminal prosecutions before Abbott, and, above all, prosecutions for conspiracy. In a long sequence of these in which there had been convictions, the Court granted new trials, on the ground that the verdict was not supported by the evidence.

" This acute and dexterous lawyer," it has been said, " used to confirm his influence by well-timed delicate flattery. Having moved for a new trial for misdirec- tion, he prefaced his motion with the explanatory re- mark that he had taken an accurate note of the summing up, which he only did when he conceived there was a misconception on the part of the Judge—which did not happen with regard to his Lordship three times a year. The Chief Justice was evidently gratified, and observed with a smile, ' I fear, Mr. Scarlett, that you do not take notes as often as you ought to do.' "[1]

The bar evinced a jealous sense of the ascendency

1. Townsend's Lives, ii. 263.

of the favorite. On one occasion when, with the seeming approbation of the Chief Justice, Scarlett had said,
in an altercation with Mr. Adolphus,[1] who practised
chiefly in the Criminal Courts, "There is a difference
between the practice here and at the Old Bailey," his
antagonist retorted, to the delight of his brethren, "I
know there is. The Judge there rules the advocate;
here, the advocate rules the Judge."

The following letter from the Chief Justice to Sir
Egerton Brydges, after some remarks upon Lord Eldon, Lord Giffard (then Attorney General), and Lord
Lyndhurst (then Solicitor General), enters with extraordinary freedom into his own judicial character:

"The Chancellor, who has done more work than any
living lawyer, perhaps than any deceased, is, I verily
believe, and has for some time been, desirous of resign-
ing, but kept in his place from the difficulty of filling
it up, and from the King's personal desire. The
present Attorney General will probably be his successor: he is a good lawyer and a sound-headed man;
warm rather than vigorous, and without dignity of person or manner. Yet I think he is the fittest man living
to succeed one for whom a successor must soon be

---

1. John Adolphus, F.S.A., an historical writer, born in London
1764 or 1765. He was first admitted an attorney, but afterwards he
went to the bar, and gained a large practice and much reputation as
an advocate. His speech in defence of Thistlewood the conspirator
was regarded as an admirable effort of eloquence. Died July 16,
1845. Among Mr. Adolphus's writings are "Biographical Anecdotes of the Founders of the French Revolution"; "The British
Cabinet, containing Portraits of Illustrious Personages, with Biographical Memoirs"; "The History of England from the Accession
of George III. to the Peace of 1783"; "The History of France from
1790 to the Peace of 1802"; "The Political State of the British
Empire"; "Observations on the Vagrant Act and some other Statutes, and on the Powers and Duties of Justices of the Peace";
"Memoirs of John Bannister, Comedian"; and "History of the
Reign of George III." He also assisted the historian Coxe in preparing for the press the "Memoirs of Lord Burghley."—*Cooper's
Biog. Dict.*

found—though perhaps an equal never will be. The
Solicitor General is probably very little known to you,
though I think you have sat with him in the House of
Commons. He has less learning than the Attorney
General, but a much better person, countenance, and
manner; a good head and a kind heart, and not deficient in learning. I suppose he will soon fill one of our
high offices in the law.

"Of myself I have really scarce any thing to say.
My health is good, and my spirits are generally good.
I go through my work as well as I can, though certainly
not without some anxieties and some crosses. I
scarcely know whether the extreme caution that the
prevailing spirit of cavil and misrepresentation imposes
on a Judge be fortunate or unfortunate for his future
reputation—it is certainly unfortunate for his comfort :
a bridle in the mouth with a sharp curb is not a very
pleasant attire, yet in these times at least it is very
necessary. I generally study to say as little as possible
from the Bench, and to confine myself closely to the very
point before me, not hazarding allusions or illustrations
in which I know much wiser men have often failed. How
far I succeed others may better judge. I am sure many
of my decisions, when I read them in the Reports, are at
least as dry and jejune as may well be tolerated. Lord
Mansfield indulged himself in allusions and illustrations : his opinions are said to have produced a great
effect on the majority of those who heard him ; they
are not well reported by Burrow—at least, few of them
read well to a lawyer. His taste for illustration was
not fortunate. His opinion is often right when his
illustrations are not right. Dr. Jackson [1] (Dean of

1. Cyril Jackson, D.D., was the son of a physician at Halifax.
He received his academical education at Christ Church, Oxford
(B.A., 1768 ; M.A. 1771 ; B.D. 1777 ; D.D. 1781). He held the post
of sub-preceptor to the prince of Wales, afterwards George IV., and
eventually became dean of Christ Church, which office he filled for

Christ Church) knew him well and privately, and often HAP.
CLIII. talked with me about him. We agreed upon his talents and character. They were plausible and showy, and not unsuited to the age. He certainly did much for the mercantile law, and not a little for the law in general, by breaking down the barrier of what are usually called forms; but in this he sometimes went too far. The preservation of forms, however unpopular, is of the essence of all establishments—of the judicial in particular—for if Judges disregard them, they become authors and not expounders of law. The great art of a lawyer is to understand them. If a Judge does not understand them, he will violate the law in a few instances by breaking them ; and if of a cautious temper, do injustice in many by a mistaken adherence to their supposed effect: the latter has been the most common error. The less a Judge knows of special pleading, the more nonsuits take place under his direction. Buller told me so many years ago, and experience has shown the truth of his assertion. You must forgive all this from an old Special Pleader."

I have anxiously looked through this Chief Justice's judgments with a view to select some which might interest the general reader, but have met with sad disappointment. They are all excellent for the occasion, but I find none that are very striking. It so happened, that while he presided in the Court of King's Bench there were hardly any State trials, and no great constitutional question arose, such as " general warrants," or " the right of juries to consider the question of libel or no libel," or " whether a court of law is to limit the

His discretion in avoiding disputes about jurisdiction.

twenty-six years. At the end of that period he retired to his favorite village of Felpham, Sussex, where he died Aug. 31, 1819, aged 76. Dr. Jackson published nothing, though he had a high reputation for scholarship. His brother, *William Jackson*, D.D., became Greek professor at Oxford 1783 ; bishop of Oxford 1811 ; and died Dec. 2, 1815, aged 64.—*Cooper's Biog. Dict.*

privileges of the two Houses of Parliament." With
admirable tact and discretion he avoided any attempt
to extend the jurisdiction of his own Court; and he
never once got into collision with any other Court or
any other authority in the State. He was cautious
likewise in restraining the prerogative writs to their
proper purposes.

A motion being made before him for a prohibition
to the Lord Chancellor sitting in bankruptcy : after
showing that upon the facts disclosed, the Lord Chancellor had done nothing amiss, he added, " We wish not
to be understood as giving any sanction to the supposed
authority of this Court to direct such a prohibition. It
will be time enough to decide the question when it
arises—if ever it shall arise, which is not very probable,
as no such question has arisen since the institution of
proceedings in bankruptcy—a period little short of
three hundred years. If ever the question shall arise,
the Court, whose assistance may be invoked to correct
an excess of jurisdiction in another, will without doubt
take care not to exceed its own." [1]

His deci-
sions.—
The public
have no
common
law right
to the use
of the sea-
shore for
bathing.
I know not that I can offer a fairer specimen of his
judgment than that given by him in *Blundell* v. *Catterall*,
where the question arose, whether there be a common-
law right for all the King's subjects to bathe in the sea ;
and, as incident thereto, of everywhere crossing the
sea-shore on foot or in bathing-machines for that purpose. Best, J., strenuously supported the right, and
thus was he answered :—*Abbott, C. J.:* " I have considered this case with very great attention, from the respect I entertain for the opinion of my brother Best,
though I had no doubt upon the question when it was
first presented to me ; nor did the defendant's counsel
raise any doubt in my mind by his learned and ingenious argument. This is an action of trespass brought

1. Ex parte *Cowan*, 3 B. and A. 123.

against the defendant for passing with carriages from some place above highwater-mark across that part of the shore which lies between the high and low watermark, for the conveyance of persons to and from the water for the purpose of bathing. The plaintiff is the undoubted owner of the soil of this part of the shore, and has the exclusive right of fishing thereon with stake-nets. The defendant does not rely on any special custom or prescription for his justification, but insists on a common-law right for all the King's subjects to to bathe on the sea-shore, and to pass and repass over it for that purpose on foot, and with horses and carriages. Now, if such a common-law right existed, there would probably be some mention of it in our books; but none is found in any book, ancient or modern. If the right exist now, it must have existed at all times; but we know that sea-bathing was, until a time comparatively modern, a matter of no frequent occurrence, and that the carriages, by which the practice has been facilitated and extended, are of very modern invention.

" There being no authority in favor of the affirmative of the question in the terms in which it is proposed, it has been placed in argument at the bar on a broader ground; and as the waters of the sea are open to the use of all persons for all lawful purposes, it has been contended, as a general proposition, that there must be an equally universal right of access to them for all such purposes overland, such as the plaintiff's, on which the alleged trespasses have been committed. If this could be established, the defendant must undoubtedly prevail, because bathing in the waters of the sea is, generally speaking, a lawful purpose. But in my opinion there is no sufficient ground, either in authority or in reason, to support this general proposition. Bracton, in the passage referred to, speaks not of the waters of the sea generally, but of ports and navigable rivers;

and as to ports, Lord Hale distinguishes between the interest of property and the interest of franchise; and says, that if A. hath the *ripa* or bank of the port, the King cannot grant liberty to unlade on the bank or *ripa* without his consent, unless custom hath made the liberty thereof free to all, as in many places it is. Now, such consent, as applied to the natural state of the *ripa* or bank, would be wholly unnecessary if any man had a right to land his goods on every part of the shore at his pleasure. If there be no general right to unlade merchandise on the shore, there can be no right to traverse the shore with carriages or otherwise for the purpose of unlading; and consequently, the general proposition to which I have alluded cannot be maintained as a legitimate conclusion from the general right to navigate the water. One of the topics urged at the bar in favor of this supposed right was that of public convenience. Public convenience, however, is in all cases to be viewed with a due regard to private property, the protection whereof is one of the distinguishing characteristics of the law of England. It is true, that property of the description of the present is in general of little value to its owner; but I do not know how that little is to be respected, and still less how it is ever to be increased, if such a general right be established. How are stake-nets to be lawfully fixed on the beach? By what law can any wharf or quay be made? These, in order to be useful, must be below the high-water mark. In some parts of the coast where the ground is nearly level the tide ebbs to a great distance, and leaves dry very considerable tracts of land. In such situations thousands of acres have, at different times, been gained from the sea by embankments, and converted to pasture or tillage. But how could such improvements have been made, or how can they be made hereafter, without the destruction or infringe-

ment of this supposed right? And it is to be observed,
that wharfs, quays, and embankments, and in-takes from the sea, are matters of public as well as private benefit. I am not aware of any usage in this matter sufficiently extensive or uniform to be the foundation of a judicial decision. In many places, doubtless, nothing is paid to the owner of the shore for leave to traverse it. In many places the King retains his ownership, and it is not probable that he should offer any obstruction to those who, for recreation, wish to walk, or ride, or drive along the sands left by the receding tide. Of private owners, some may not have thought it worth while to advance any claim or opposition; others may have had too much discretion to put their title to the soil to the hazard of a trial by an unpopular claim to a matter of little value; others, and probably the greater number, may have derived or expected so much benefit from the increased value given to their enclosed land by the erection of houses and the resort of company, that their own interest may have induced them to acquiesce in, and even to encourage the practice as a matter indirectly profitable to themselves. Many of those who reside in the vicinity of inland wastes and commons walk and ride on horseback in all directions over them for health and amusement, and sometimes even in carriages, deviate from the public paths into those parts which may be so traversed with safety. In the neighborhood of some frequented watering-places this practice prevails to a very great degree; yet no one ever thought that any right existed in favor of this enjoyment, or that any justification could be pleaded to an action at the suit of the owner of the soil. The defendant finally says, that the right may be considered as confined to those localities where it can be exercised without actual prejudice to the owner of the shore, and subject to all modes of present use or future

improvement on his part. No instance of any public right so limited and qualified is to be found. Every public right to be exercised over the land of an individual is *pro tanto* a diminution of his private rights and enjoyments, both present and future, so far as they may at any time interfere with or obstruct the public right. But shall the owner of the soil be allowed to bring an action against any person who may drive a carriage or walk along any part of the sea-shore, although not the minutest injury is done to the owner? The law has provided suitable checks to frivolous and vexatious suits, and experience shows that the owners of the shore do not trouble themselves or other about such trifles. But where one man endeavors to make his own special profit by conveying persons over the soil of another, and claims a public right to do, as in the present case, it does seem to me that he has not any just reason to complain, if the owner of the soil shall insist on participating in the profit, and endeavor to preserve the evidence of the private right which has belonged to him and his ancestors. For these reasons I am of opinion that there is not any such common-law right as the defendant has claimed; and my brothers Bayley and Holroyd agreeing with me, there must be judgment for the Plaintiff." [1]

No action
lies for
pirating an
obscene
book.
In the following judgment Chief Justice Abbott held that the author or publisher of an immoral book cannot maintain an action for pirating it. "This was an action brought for the purpose of recovering a compensation in damages for the loss alleged to have been sustained from the publication of a copy of a book which had been first published by the plaintiff. At the trial it appeared that the work professed to be a history of the amours of a courtezan, that it contained in some parts matter highly indecent, and in others

1. *Blundell* v. *Cattersall*, 5 Barn. and Ald., 268-316.

matter of a slanderous nature upon persons whose supposed adventures it narrated. The question, then, is
whether the first publisher can claim a compensation
in damages for a loss sustained by an injury done to
the sale of such a work. In order to establish such a
claim he must in the first place show a right to sell, for
if he has not that right, he cannot sustain any loss
which the law will recognize by an injury to the sale.
Now, I am certain no lawyer can say that the sale of
each copy of this work is not an offence against the
law. How, then, can we hold that by the first publication of such a work a right of action can be given
against any person who afterwards publishes it? It is
said that there is no decision of a court of law against
the plaintiff's claim. But upon the plainest principles
of the common law, founded as it is, where there are
no authorities, upon common sense and justice, this
action cannot be maintained. It would be a disgrace
to the common law if a doubt could be entertained
upon the subject; but I think no doubt can be entertained, and I want no authority for pronouncing such a
judicial opinion." [1]

Thus he pointedly defended our peculiar doctrine His defence
of high treason, which constitutes the offence in the lish doc-
intention, but requires this intention to be manifested trine of
by an *act*. "The law has wisely provided (because the treason.
public safety requires it) that in cases of this kind
which manifestly lead to the most extensive public
evil, the intention shall constitute the crime; but the

1. *Stockdale* v. *Onwhyn*, 5 Barn. and Cr. 175. This principle is
perfectly sound, but there must be great difficulty in acting upon it.
Judges and juries may be much divided as to whether the authors of
such novels as 'Tom Jones' and 'Peregrine Pickle' ought to be
allowed to maintain an action for pirating their works. Lord Eldon
refused an injunction against the piracy of a poem dedicated by
Lord Byron to Walter Scott, on the ground of its being atheistical,
although it is generally considered to be no more liable to that
charge than 'Paradise Lost.'

law has at the same time with equal wisdom provided (because the safety of individuals requires it) that the intention shall be manifested by some act tending towards the accomplishment of the criminal object."[1]

Libellous
to say
falsely that
the Sover-
eign is af-
flicted with
insanity.
Although he saw more distinctly the evils than the benefits arising from the freedom of the press, he laid down the law of libel always with calmness and decorum. Soon after the accession of George IV. a criminal information was filed by the Attorney General (not very discreetly) against the proprietor and printer of a newspaper for the following paragraph : " Attached as we sincerely and lawfully are to every interest connected with the Sovereign or any of his illustrious relatives, it is with the deepest concern we have to state that the malady under which his Majesty labors is of an alarming description, and may be considered hereditary. It is from authority we speak." At the trial before Abbott, C. J., at Guildhall, the counsel for the defendants admitted that the paragraph complained of imported that the King labored under insanity, and that this assertion was untrue, but insisted that the defendants believed the fact to be as they stated it, and that they were not criminally answerable, as there had previously been strong public rumors to the same effect.

Abbott, C. J.: " To assert falsely of his Majesty or of any other person that he labors under the infliction of mental derangement is a criminal act. It is an offence of a more aggravated nature to make such an assertion concerning his Majesty than concerning a subject, by reason of the greater mischief which may thence arise. It is distinctly admitted by the counsel for the defendants that the statement in the libel was false in fact, although they allege that rumors to the same effect had been previously circulated in other

1. State Tr. vol. xxxiv.—Thistlewood's Case.

newspapers. Here the writer of this article does not seem to found himself upon existing rumors, but purports to speak from authority ; and inasmuch as it is now admitted that the fact did not exist, there could be no authority for the statement. In my opinion the publication is a libel calculated to vilify and scandalize his Majesty, and to bring him into contempt among his subjects. But you have a right to exercise your own judgment upon the publication, and I invite you to do so."

After the jury had retired about two hours, they returned into Court and said they wished to have the opinion of the Lord Chief Justice " whether it was or was not necessary that there should be a malicious intention to constitute a libel ? "

Abbott, C. J. : " The man who publishes slanderous matter in its nature calculated to defame and vilify another, must be presumed to have intended to do that which the publication is calculated to bring about, unless he can show the contrary, and it is for him to show the contrary."

The jury, having again retired for three hours, returned a verdict of GUILTY, but recommended the defendants to mercy. Brougham and Denman moved for a new trial on account of the Judge's direction, and more particularly for his having told the jury that they (the counsel) had admitted the statement in the libel to be *'false in fact*, using that word to denote a criminal untruth ; whereas they had only admitted the statement to be untrue, the defendants believing it to be true, and an untrue statement may be made with perfect innocence and good faith. Bayley and Holroyd having said that the direction was unexceptionable, Best added, " Whether a publication be true or false is not the subject of inquiry in the trial of an information for a libel, but whether it be a mischievous or innocent paper.

We are not called upon to decide whether the defendants would have been justified had the statement been
true.   But it must not be taken for granted that if such
a dreadful affliction had happened to the country as the
insanity of the King, the editor of a newspaper would
be justified in publishing an account of it at any time
and in any manner that he thought proper.   It is fit
that the time and mode of such a communication should
be determined on by those who are best able to provide
against the effects of the agitation of public feeling
which it is likely to produce.   Such a communication
rashly made, although true, might raise an inference of
mischievous intention, for truth may be published
maliciously."

Abbott, C.J. : " My learned brothers having delivered
their opinion that nothing which fell from me in my
address to the jury furnishes sufficient ground for
granting a new trial, I will merely add that unless
malicious intent may be inferred from the publication
of the slander itself in a case where no evidence is given
to rebut that inference, the reputation of all his Majesty's subjects, high and low, would be left without
that protection which the law ought to extend to them.
I will say further, with regard to the particular expression contained in this publication, that if any writer
thinks proper to say that *he speaks from authority* when
he informs his readers of a particular fact, and it shall
turn out that the fact so asserted is untrue, I am of
opinion that he who makes the assertion in such a form
may be justly said to make a false assertion.   I am not
a sufficient casuist to say that to call it *an untrue assertion* would be a more proper form of expression." [1]

After the transfer of Best to preside in the Common
Pleas there was hardly ever a difference of opinion
among the Judges of the King's Bench, but strange to

[1]. *Rex.* v. *Harvey* and another, 2 Barn. and Cr., 257.

say, on one question which seems very plain and easy, they were divided equally, although all actuated by singleness of purpose to decide rightly. A gentleman residing in London hired of a public stable-keeper a pair of horses to draw his carriage for a day, and the owner of the horses provided the driver. Through the negligence of the coachman in driving, the carriage struck a horse belonging to a stranger. The question was whether the owner of the carriage was liable to be sued for this injury? The Chief Justice, before whom the cause was tried, thought that he was not, and directed a nonsuit. On an application to the Court to set aside the nonsuit, Bayley and Holroyd held that the driver was *pro hac vice* the servant of the owner of the carriage, although let for the day, with the horses, by the owner of the horses.

Abbott, C. J.: " I must own that I cannot perceive any substantial difference between hiring a pair of horses to draw my carriage about London for a day, and hiring them to draw it for a stage on a road I am travelling, the driver being in both cases furnished by the owner of the horses in the usual way, although in the one instance he is called a coachman and in the other a post-boy. Nor can I feel any substantial difference between hiring the horses to draw my own carriage on these occasions and hiring a carriage with them of their owner. If the temporary use and benefit of the horses will make the hirer answerable, and there being no reasonable distinction between hiring them with or without a carriage, must not the person who hires a hackney-coach to take him for a mile or other greater or less distance, or for an hour or longer time, be answerable for the conduct of the coachman? Must not the person who hires a wherry on the Thames be answerable for the conduct of the waterman? I believe the common sense of all men would be shocked if any

CHAP. LIII.

Q. Whether the person who hires horses, with a driver, to draw his carriage for a day, is liable for the negligence of the driver?

one should affirm the hirer to be answerable in either of these cases."

Littledale, J., concurred in this opinion, and the nonsuit stood.[1]

The Cato Street conspiracy.

Chief Justice Abbott in his addresses from the Bench never aimed at eloquence or epigram, but he showed himself master of a nervous style which rose in dignity with the occasion. In opening the commission for the trial of the Cato Street conspirators,[2] a set of low desperate men who had laid a plot to assassinate all the Cabinet Ministers, and then to seize upon the government, he thus cautioned the Grand Jury against incredulity on account of the improbability of the statements which might be made by the witnesses:

" Such ulterior designs, if they shall appear to be of the nature to which I have alluded, and to relate to the

1. *Laugher* v. *Pointer*, 5 B. and C. 547. By the Common Law Procedure Act, where the Judges are divided, the case now goes by appeal to a Court of Error.—Lord Abinger, Chief Baron, afterwards ruled that the liability under such circumstances is not a question of law, and that it is for the jury to say whether the driver, when the accident happened, was the servant of the person who has taken the horses to hire, or has let them·to hire. *Brady* v. *Giles*, 1 Moody and Robinson, 494.

2. Cato Street Conspiracy (1820) was the name given to a wild plot formed by a number of desperate men, having for its chief object the murder of Lord Castlereagh and the rest of the ministers. The originators were a man named Arthur Thistlewood, who had once been a subaltern officer ; Ings, a butcher ; Tidd and Brunt, shoemakers ; and Davidson, a man of color : and they had arranged to murder the ministers at a dinner at Lord Harrowby's on the night of the 23d February, to set fire to London in several places, seize the Bank and Mansion House, and proclaim a provisional government. The plot, however, had been betrayed to the police by one of the conspirators, named Edwards, some weeks before. The conspirators were attacked by the police as they were arming themselves in a stable in Cato Street, near the Edgware Road. A scuffle ensued, in which one policeman was stabbed and several of the criminals escaped. Thistlewood was among these, but he was captured next morning. He and four others were executed, and five more were transported for life. A good deal of discussion took place in the House of Commons on the employment of the informer Edwards by the authorities.—*Dict. of Eng. Hist.*

usurpation of the government in opposition to the con- stituted authorities of the realm even for a season, will appear to the calm eye of sober reason to be wild and hopeless. But you, gentlemen, know that rash and evil-minded men, brooding over their bad designs, gradually lose sight of the difficulties that attend the accomplishment of their schemes, and magnify the advantage to be derived from them. And as it is the natural propensity of the vicious to think others no less vicious than themselves, those who form wicked plans of a public nature easily believe that they shall have numerous supporters, if they can manifest at once their designs and their power by striking some one important blow."

To prepare the minds of the Grand Jury for the evidence of spies and accomplices, he added: " This belief leads in some instances to a rash and hasty communication of the wicked purpose to others who are thought likely to adopt it and join in its execution, but who, in fact, are not prepared to do so, and thereby occasionally furnishes the means of detection. Dark and deep designs are seldom fully developed except to those who consent to become participators in them, and can therefore be seldom exposed and brought to light by the testimony of untainted witnesses. Such testimony is to be received on all occasions with great caution; it is to be carefully watched, deliberately weighed, and anxiously considered. He who acknowledges himself to have become a party to a guilty purpose does by that very acknowledgment depreciate his own personal character and credit. If, however, it should ever be laid down as a practical rule in the administration of justice that the testimony of accomplices should be rejected as incredible, the most mischievous consequences must necessarily ensue; because it must not only happen that many heinous crimes must pass unpunished, but great encouragement will be given to bad men by withdrawing from their minds the fear of detection and punishment through the instrumentality of their partners in guilt, and thereby universal confidence will be substituted for that distrust of each other which naturally possesses men engaged in wicked projects, and which often operates as a restraint against the perpetration of offences to which the co-operation of a multitude is required."

In passing sentence of death upon the prisoners, he thus moralized the same theme :

" It has happened to you on the present occasion, as to many others before you, that the principal instruments by which you were brought to justice are persons who have partaken in your own guilty design. I trust that this circumstance will have its due weight in the consideration of all who shall become acquainted with your fate, and that they will ever for the sake of their own personal safety, if they cannot be influenced by any higher consideration, be induced to abstain from those evil combinations which have brought you into the melancholy situation in which you now stand. That Englishmen, laying aside the national character, should assemble to destroy in cold blood the lives of fifteen persons unknown to them, except from their having filled the highest offices in the state, is without example in the history of this country, and I hope will remain unparalled for atrocity in all future times."

Improper proceeding in trying to forbid the publication of trials for treason till they are all concluded. Our Chief Justice, however, tarnished the fame which he might have carried off without a shade from his dignified, impartial, and firm demeanor during these trials, by imprudently making an order that there should be no publication of any part of the proceedings till they were all concluded, and by fining the proprietor of a newspaper 500l. for publishing an account of the first trial before the second had begun. The courts upheld the power to make the order and to enforce it CHAP. LIII. by fine, but such a mode of proceeding has never since been attempted, the sound opinion being that the delay of publication is not desirable, even if it could practically be insured, and that the newspapers may be considered as indefinitely enlarging the dimensions of the Court so as to enable the whole nation to see and hear all that passes—between the arraignment of the prisoner and his condemnation or acquittal.

I ought to record for the credit of this Chief Justice and for the imitation of his successors, that while he maintained forms necessary to guard against fraud and to protect innocence, he had not the passion for technical objections by which justice is sometimes defeated. An indictment charged " that Mary Somerton, on a day and at a place named, being then and there servant to one Joseph Hellier, on *the same day* there stole his goods." The prisoner being convicted and sentenced to transportation fourteen years, the record was removed by writ of error, and error assigned that it did not sufficiently appear from the indictment that she was servant to the owner of the goods at the time when the larceny was committed, although she might have been so at some moment of the same day. *The Chief Justice's dislike of technical niceties.*

Lord Tenterden, C. J.: " If we were to hold that the allegation ' that on such a day the prisoner being the servant of Joseph Hellier did on the same day steal his goods,' does not import that she stole the goods at the same time when she was his servant, we should expose ourselves to the reproof expressed by a very learned and very humane judge, that it is disgraceful to the law when criminals are allowed to escape by nice and captious objections of form." [1]

Although generally so sound in his decisions, he did not reach the reputation of infallibility. He shocked *Doubtful decisions by him.*

1. *Rex* v. *Somerton*, 7 B. and C. 465.

the conveyancers exceedingly by holding that a jury might presume the surrender of a term assigned to attend the inheritence where it had not been dealt with for a number of years in subsequent conveyances,[1] and he got into some discredit by broadly laying down that a mortgagor allowed to remain in possession of the mort- gaged premises is tenant to the mortgagee.[2] I must be permitted likewise to doubt the soundness of his decision that a native of Scotland born out of wedlock, but rendered legitimate according to the law of the country by the subsequent marriage of his parents, is not inheritable to freehold property in England. It was confirmed by the House of Lords, but I cannot help thinking that it proceeded on a narrow-minded and erroneous principle. The admission was freely made that the claimant, having the status of legiti- macy in the country of his birth, was to be considered legitimate in England for every other purpose, and the *conundrum* arising from the definition of a " bas- tard " in the Statute of *Merton* might easily have been got over by the supposition of law upon which such legitimation proceeds—that a prior marriage had been contracted though not declared till after the birth of the child. The notion that there is some peculiarity in the tenure of common soccage land whereby it must descend to a son *de 'facto* born in wedlock, as borough English land goes to the youngest son, is in my opinion a fiction to support a miserable technicality.[3]

His pro- pensity to suspect fraud.   The bias which chiefly carried Abbott's mind astray when it missed the object to which it was directed was a suspicion of fraud. He had a very indifferent opinion of human nature, and at times he seemed to believe all

1. *Doe* v. *Hilder*, 2 B. and A. 784.
2. *Partridge* v. *Beer*, 5 B. and A. 604.
3. *Doe* v. *Barthwistle* v. *Vardill*, 5 B. and C. 438. This decision lowered us terribly not only in the opinion of Scotch but of French and American lawyers. Professor Storey was very strong against it.

mankind to be rascals. He delighted in discovering what he considered a fraudulent contrivance on the part of the plaintiff or of the defendant and in unravelling it. I have heard Scarlett jocularly boast that he got many a verdict by humoring this propensity—" just giving the hint very remotely to the Chief Justice and allowing his Lordship all the pleasure and the éclat of exposing and reprobating the cheat." This dexterous advocate certainly did at last prevail upon him to lay down a rule which, while it was acted upon, materially obstructed the transfer of negotiable securities—that " where a bill of exchange has been lost or stolen, a subsequent holder, although he has given a valuable consideration for it, cannot maintain an action upon it if the jury should think that he took *it under circumstances which ought to have excited the suspicion of a prudent and careful man.*" The rule having before been that the title of the holder for value could only be impeached by proof of fraud,[1] the new doctrine was questioned and thus defended :

Abbott, C. J. : " I cannot help thinking that if Lord His doctrine about Kenyon had anticipated the consequences which have "care and caution" followed from the rule laid down by him in *Lawson v.* in taking negotiable *Weston*, he would have paused before he pronounced securities overruled. that decision. Since then the practice of robbing stage-coaches and other conveyances of securities of this kind has been very considerable. I cannot forbear thinking that this practice has received encouragement by the rule laid down in *Lawson v. Weston*, which gives a facility to the disposal of stolen property of this description. I should be sorry if I were to say anything, sitting in the seat of judgment, that either might have the effect or reasonably be supposed to have the effect of impeding the commerce of the country by preventing the due and easy circulation of paper. But it ap-

1. *Lawson v. Weston*, 4 Esp. 56.

pears to me to be for the interest of commerce that no person should take a security of this kind from another without using reasonable caution. I wish that doubts had been thrown on the case of *Lawson* v. *Weston* at an earlier time, and then this plaintiff would have conducted himself more prudently and would not have suffered."

The new fashion took amazingly. This rule of "circumstances to excite the suspicion of a prudent and careful man" was adopted by all the Judges, and was applied to all cases where the owner of any negotiable instrument had once been induced by improper means to part with the possession of it, as well as to cases of accidental loss and of robbery. But the rule died with its author. It was soon much carped at: some Judges said that *fraud and gross negligence* were terms known to the law, but of "the circumstances which ought to excite suspicion," there was no definition in Coke or in Cowell,—and the complaints of bill brokers resounded from the Royal Exchange to Westminster Hall, that they could no longer carry on their trade with comfort or safety. The consequence was that in the course of a few years by decisions in all the Courts at Westminster, the doctrine of "suspicion" was completely exploded, and the old rule restored that the claim of the holder of a negotiable security who gave value for it before it was due, although he may have received it from a person who could not have sued upon it, can only be defeated by proof of *mala fides* on his part.[1]

Notwithstanding these imperfections, failings, and errors, which it has been my disagreeable duty to allude to, I have pleasure in quoting and corroborating the testimony in the Chief Justice's praise of his contemporary and friend Sir Egerton Brydges, which

1. *Goodman* v. *Harvey*, 4 Ad. and Ell. 470.

shows the general estimation he enjoyed among his CHAP. LIII.
countrymen :—" With what admirable skill, honor, and
steadiness he fulfilled the most laborious, most difficult
and overwhelming duties of his high station is universally acknowledged."

I am reluctant to bring to a conclusion my observations upon Abbott as a great magistrate, for in this
capacity he excites almost unmixed admiration and respect. But in the last years of his life his destiny made
him a political character, and although he still acted
honorably and conscientiously, he by no means added
to his permanent fame. I cannot help wishing indeed
that like HOLT he had died a commoner. The coronet
placed on his brow might raise his consequence with
the vulgar, but in the eyes of those whose opinion was
worth regarding he was a much greater man when,
seated on his tribunal, with conscious mastery of all
that belonged to his high office, he distributed justice
to his admiring fellow subjects, than when he sought
to sway a legislative assembly with which he was
wholly unacquainted, and to which he was wholly unsuited.

Q. Whether it would have been for his reputation that he had died a commoner?

CHAPTER LIV.

CONCLUSION OF THE LIFE OF LORD TENTERDEN.

CHAP.
LIV.
A.D. 1827.
His degra-
dation to
the peer-
age. THE supposed elevation of the Chief Justice at this time, which exposed him to some censure, was no fault of his. He used confidentially to express surprise that his friend and patron Lord Chancellor Eldon, whose advice would have been implicitly followed by the Prime Minister and the King, had not raised him to the peerage when he became Chief Justice, but had actually resigned the Great Seal without making him such an offer. He concluded that at any rate Sir Charles Abbott ought to have had the refusal of the honor in 1824, when Sir Robert Giffard was created a Baron, having filled only the inferior offices of Chief Justice of the Common Pleas and Master of the Rolls. But he made no application or remonstrance by reason of what might have been considered a slight, and I believe that he would have been perfectly contented to remain Sir Charles Abbott, Knight, for the rest of his days. Lord Eldon's conduct is very inexplicable in withholding a peerage from one who from his high office had a fair claim to it, of whom he could have felt no jealousy, who had been many years his devil and dependant, and with whom his word in the House of Lords would have been law. Can we suppose that he was actuated by a disinterested study of Abbott's real good?[1]

1. Since writing the statement in the text respecting Abbott's peerage, I have been favored with a perusal of his DIARY, from

HON. GEORGE CANNING.

However, he was most unexpectedly made a peer on the *disgrace* of that patron in all whose notions respecting State and Church he fully coincided, by a Prime Minister whom he had never seen, and whose principles, although they were not altogether Whiggish, he considered dangerously latitudinarian.

Mr. Canning,[1] the warm friend of religious tolera-

which I make the following extract, showing that he had become more desirous of having his blood ennobled than could have been suspected from his usual moderation and good sense, and from sentiments which he himself had expressed in his letter to Sir Egerton Brydges :

"*April 7th*, 1824.—Lord Giffard took his seat in the House of Lords on the first day of the Session, and within a day or two afterwards a patent issued, appointing him to act as Speaker of the House of Lords in the absence of the Lord Chancellor. A few days afterwards, the Lord Chancellor, with some hesitation and appearance of difficulty in introducing the subject, asked me what my feelings had been on Lord G.'s promotion to the peerage? I told him I had felt very little as it regarded myself, but much as it regarded my office, being higher than Lord G.'s. He asked whether I should think it right to move in the matter myself or to leave it to him? I told him I certainly should not think it right to move in it myself. All that I could collect farther was that some of the Ministers had thought it not necessary to propose a peerage to me on the present occasion, because it was conferred on Lord G. for the special purpose of enabling him to sit in the House of Lords to hear appeals. I remarked that though I could not give my eldest son a fortune by any means suitable to the dignity, yet, under present circumstances, I should hardly think myself at liberty to refuse the honor, and should leave my son to make such advantage as he could of it, being sure he would never disgrace it by his conduct."

In a letter to the second Lord Kenyon, Lord Eldon professes to explain his sincere views respecting Abbott's peerage : " I agree with you that, generally speaking, the Chief Justice of the King's Bench should be a peer, even if there had been no usage on the subject. Now, as to Abbott, his practice has been behind the bar. He never had any office—I think not a silk gown. He enters therefore on the office in very moderate circumstances, with a considerable family. His health is tender, and his eyesight not in a very safe state. Upon the whole, his own difficulty about taking the office was the apprehension that peerage was to go with it. This determination appears to me to have been quite right."—*Lives of Chancellors*, vol. vii. p. 338, 3d ed.

1. George Canning, an eminent statesman, born in London April 11, 1770. From Eton School he went to Christ Church, Oxford, where he acquitted himself with great distinction. Afterwards he

tion, having agreed to form a balanced Cabinet with an anti-Catholic Lord Chancellor, Sir John Copley, still in dreadful apprehension of the Pope, although on the verge of a sudden conversion to Catholic emancipation, had agreed to take the Great Seal, and was to be raised

was entered of Lincoln's Inn, but soon abandoned law for politics. The opposition thought they had gained in him a powerful recruit; but as soon as he obtained a seat in the House of Commons, in 1793, he joined the ministerial party. In 1794, he delivered his first speech in favor of one of the measures of Mr. Pitt, who in 1796 appointed him under-secretary of state, which post he retained till Pitt went out of office in 1801. He then acted in opposition to the new ministry, and for his services was nominated treasurer of the navy on Pitt becoming prime minister in 1804. This office he held till 1806, when he again went into opposition. The next year he joined the administration of the duke of Portland, and was appointed foreign secretary. In the following year he defended the bombardment of Copenhagen. There was a split in the cabinet in 1809, when, in consequence of a misunderstanding, Mr. Canning fought a duel with Lord Castlereagh, at that time secretary for war, and was wounded in the thigh. The result was that both the ministers resigned their places. In Nov., 1814, Canning was despatched as ambassador extraordinary to Portugal, where he remained till after the battle of Waterloo. He then passed some time in the south of France, and towards the end of 1816 was appointed president of the Board of Control. He held this office till the scandalous proceedings took place about Queen Caroline in 1820, when he tendered his resignation, which was accepted. In 1822 he was appointed the successor of the marquis of Hastings, as governor-general of India, and was on the eve of his departure for that country when the marquis of Londonderry committed suicide, whereupon he was recalled and made secretary of state for foreign affairs. He fulfilled the duties of this office till April 12, 1827, when he succeeded Lord Liverpool as premier. Nearly all the old ministers then resigned, and for the first time in his life Canning received the support of the Whigs, some of whom joined his administration. He occupied this exalted post only a short time, dying Aug. 8, 1827. The principal measures which distinguish Canning's ministerial career are the recognition of the states of South America, the maintenance of the independence of Portugal, and the treaty concluded between England, Russia, and France, in favor of Greece. He was a constant and zealous advocate of Catholic Emancipation, though he did not live to see the triumph of that great cause. When a young man at Eton Canning projected " The Microcosm," a periodical work, and later in life he contributed several witty satirical poems to " The Anti-Jacobin." His widow was created a viscountess 1828, with remainder of the dignity to the heirs male of the body of her late husband.—*Cooper's Biog. Dict.*

to the peerage by the title of Baron Lyndhurst. Moreover Plunket, upon a slight show of opposition from the
bar, having renounced the office of Master of the Rolls
in England, and accepted the office of Chief Justice of
the Common Pleas in Ireland, was likewise to be made
a British peer by the family name, which his eloquence
had rendered illustrious. It was thereupon suggested
to the new premier by Scarlett, long his intimate private friend, and now his Attorney General elect, that
it would be a graceful act in public estimation, and
would throw some obloquy on Lord Eldon, whom they
both heartily hated and who heartily hated them both,
if a peerage were given to Lord Eldon's neglected
protégé, the Chief Justice of England. Accordingly
Mr. Canning, in a letter to him, dated 19th April, 1827,
after an introduction of polite eulogy, said—" As in the
approaching law promotions more than one peerage
will be conferred by his Majesty, it has occurred to Mr.
Canning as due to Lord Chief Justice Abbott, to his
Lordship's eminent services and to the dignity of the
Court over which he presides, that an opportunity
should be offered to the Lord Chief Justice to express
his willingness (if he entertains it) to accept a similar
honor, which his Majesty is ready graciously to bestow
upon him." The answer expressed humble and grateful acquiescence,—upon which immediately came a
notice from the Home Office that the inchoate peer
should notify his choice of a title, and that a sum of
money, about 800*l.*, should be deposited for the fees of
the patent. He was afraid of jest if he should become
" Lord Abbott," and he thought of the title of HENDON,
where he had a villa ; but he was advised to have something more sounding, and TENTERDEN being familiar to
him, as a Kentish man, from the well known connection
between the first appearance of its steeple and of the
Goodwin Sands, the Gazette announced that " his

Majesty had ordered letters patent to pass the Great Seal, to create Sir Charles Abbott, Knight, a Baron of the United Kingdom, by the name, style, and title of Lord Tenterden, of Hendon, in the County of Middlesex."

Ceremony of his taking his seat in the House of Lords.
On the 2d of May following there was a grand ovation in Westminster Hall, to do honor to the solemnity of his taking his seat in the House of Lords. Sir James Scarlett, the Attorney General, mustered an immense congregation of barristers, and we followed the new peer, as yet only in his judicial robes, from the Court of King's Bench to the room of the Earl Marshal. There he was habited in his peer's robes, and, marching between Lord Bexley[1] and Lord Kenyon, he entered the House, and presented his patent and writ to the Lord Chancellor. We all stood under the bar, and the space being too small for us, such a serried conglomeration of wigs never was seen before or since. We could hear nothing of the patent, the writ, or the oaths which were read, but we witnessed the procession through the House, headed by the Earl Marshal, and our Chief being seated by Garter King at Arms on the Barons' bench, we joyfully took our departure. Next morning

1. Nicholas Vansittart, Lord Bexley, son of Henry Vansittart, sometime governor of Bengal, was born April 29, 1766, and received his education at Mr. Gilpin's school at Cheam in Surrey, whence he removed to Christ Church, Oxford (M.A. 1791). He was subsequently called to the bar, and distinguished himself by the production of various political and financial pamphlets, which attracted general attention. He was first returned to parliament for Hastings in 1796. In 1801, he was sent to Denmark in the character of minister plenipotentiary, with the view of detaching that country from the Northern Alliance, but the negotiation failed. In the same year he was appointed joint secretary to the Treasury, and after filling other offices under the crown, he succeeded Mr. Perceval as chancellor of the exchequer 1812. This important office he occupied till Jan , 1823, and on his retirement he was raised to the peerage by the title of Baron Bexley. He had a great reputation for skill in financial matters. Died at Footscray Place, Kent, Feb. 8, 1851.—*Cooper's Biog. Dict.*

in Court the new peer threw down the following note, which was handed through all the rows till it reached the junior of our body :

" DEAR MR. ATTORNEY,

" I was indeed gratified yesterday by the flattering mark of attention which I received from the Bar. Assure them that it went to my heart.

" Ever most faithfully yours,
" TENTERDEN."

He continued to attend the House for some time very diligently, much pleased with his new honors, and afterwards as often as he entered it he wore his judicial *costume*, being the last Chief Justice who ever did so, when not officiating as Speaker. There was *franking* in those days, and he was pleased to say to me that " he considered this privilege to be conferred upon him for the benefit of the profession." He really was tickled when asked for a frank, and a glow of satisfaction might be descried on his countenance as he was writing, " Free—TENTERDEN." But he soon looked as if he considered it rather a liberty to ask him for a frank—particularly after he discovered that when on the circuit, sitting in Court, surrounded by country Justices, a graceless youth had made him frank a letter to a young lady of notoriously light character in London.

Lord Tenterden's maiden speech was his most successful (I might say his only successful) effort as a parliamentary orator. Luckily the subject was quite in his own line as a lawyer. A young heiress of 15 had been decoyed away from a boarding school by a profligate adventurer, whose object was her fortune, and had been induced to marry him. As he thought his scheme completely successful the moment the marriage ceremony had been performed, her friends had an op-

His maiden speech.

portunity to rescue her before any further injury had
been inflicted upon her. They prosecuted him for the
abduction, and he was convicted and sentenced to a
long imprisonment. They then presented a petition to
the House of Lords, with her concurrence, praying
that the marriage might be dissolved. He presented a
counter-petition praying that the House would make
an order for his being brought up to defend his marital
rights. The Earl of Lauderdale, who had been called
to the Scotch bar, possessed at the time great weight
as a "Law Lord," and he contended that although
there had been instances of dissolving by Act of Parliament the marriage of a young lady brought about
by force, the present marriage having been solemnized
with the consent of both parties could not be dissolved
without a violation of principle nor without establishing a very dangerous precedent.

Lord Tenterden recapitulated all the facts of the
case as if he had been summing up to a jury. He said
"the principal offender and his accomplices had been
convicted of a conspiracy originating in the basest
motives of lucre, and conducted by fraud and forgery.
He thought the House bound to afford the relief
prayed. The friends of the unfortunate girl had done
all in their power to vindicate the law, and now came
to the Legislature for that relief which the peculiar
nature of the case demanded. Although there had
been here no actual force, the law says that fraud supplies the place of force. Possibly the marriage might
be declared null and void by sentence of the Ecclesiastical Court, but if proceedings were to be instituted
for that purpose, their Lordships must recollect the
great delay which must take place and the anxiety and
distress to which the parties must be subjected in the
mean time. The pretended husband had the audacity
to complain of hardship, but his punishment had been

light compared with the enormity of his offence. CHAP. LIV. Their Lordships were bound to inform him and all others who possessed themselves of the persons of young women for the sake of base lucre, that they not only exposed themselves to the penalties which the Courts of law might inflict, but that there is a power in the country which will deprive them of all possibility of ever reaping any advantage from their crimes." [1]

Leave was given to bring in the Bill, and it afterwards quietly passed through both Houses and received the Royal assent.

Before Lord Tenterden again opened his mouth in the House of Lords, Mr. Canning had fallen a victim to the aristocratic combination against him; Lord Gooderich,[2] the most imbecile of prime ministers, after a few weeks of premiership had ingloriously resigned; the Duke of Wellington and Peel were at the head of affairs; and a Bill had come up from the House of Commons to repeal the Corporation and Test Acts. These our Chief Justice had been taught to believe, and did potently believe, to be the two main pillars of the Church, and he was absolutely horrified to find that they were in danger from a joint assault of Whigs and liberal Tories. The Earl of Eldon remained true to

He opposes the repeal of the Corporation and Test Acts.

1. 17 Parl. Deb. 882.

2. Frederick John Robinson, first Earl of Ripon, an English minister of state, born in London in 1782, was a younger son of Lord Grantham. He began public life as a moderate Tory. He became a member of the Board of Admiralty in 1810, and vice-president of the Board of Trade in 1812. In January, 1823, he was appointed Chancellor of the Exchequer. When Canning became Prime Minister, in 1827, he obtained the office of Colonial Secretary, and entered the House of Lords, with the title of Lord Gooderich. He was Prime Minister from the death of Canning, August, 1827, to January, 1828. In the Whig ministry, formed in 1830, he was Colonial Secretary and Lord Privy Seal. He was created Earl of Ripon about 1833, and resigned office in 1834. In 1841 he accepted the presidency of the Board of Trade from Sir Robert Peel, who appointed him president of the Indian Board in 1843. He resigned with Peel in 1846. Died in 1859.—*Thomas' Biog. Dict.*

his colors ; but, sad to relate, Lord Lyndhurst and the
Duke of Wellington himself meditated desertion.

The enemies of the Bill did not venture to attempt
to throw it out on the second reading, and confined
themselves to attempts to damage it in Committee.
Lord Tenterden finding that there was no chance of
retaining the "Test Act," which applied to all offices
and places of profit or power under the Crown, and if
strictly enforced prevented any member of the established church of Scotland from holding a commission
in the army or being an exciseman in any part of the
United Kingdom, made a desperate struggle in favor
of the "Corporation Act,"[1] whereby dissenters were
excluded from the offices of mayor, alderman, common
councillor, and all other offices in all municipal corporations in England.   Not meeting with any sympathy with his attachment to the Corporation Act in
its integrity, he moved an amendment whereby at least
the office of chief magistrate in towns should not be
polluted by being held by a dissenter.   He urged that
the Church was and ought to be supported as part of
the constitution ; consequently everything which upheld its dignity should be attended to ; and he therefore proposed that in the declaration to be made by the
mayor or chief magistrate of any municipal corporation these words should be inserted : " I entertain no
opinion on the subject of religion which may or can
prevent me attending the morning and evening service
of the Church of England, as set forth in the book of

1. The Corporation Act (1661) was passed by the first parliament
of Charles II., with the intention of destroying the power of the Dissenters in the towns.   By this statute it was enacted that all officers
of corporations should take the sacrament according to the rites of
the Church of England, within twelve months of their election to
office ; and on their election should take the oaths of supremacy,
allegiance, and non-resistance, and abjure the Solemn League and
Covenant.   The Corporation Act was repealed in 1828, though long
before that date it had become a dead letter.—*Dict. of Eng. Hist.*

Common Prayer." The Bishop of Chester asked
whether, as the law would still stand, a corporate magistrate would not be prevented from attending a dissenting place of worship in the insignia of his office? Lord Tenterden answered "that might be so, but still he thought that this amendment would be useful." Upon a division there were only 22 contents against 111 non contents.[1] He succeeded, however, by a suggestion which he offered, in excluding Jews from municipal corporations, till in the year 1844 they were admitted by an Act brought in by Lord Lyndhurst, and passed during the administration of Sir Robert Peel. The first form of declaration proposed by Lord Tenterden was: "I recognize the books of the Old and New Testament according to the authorized version as truly expressing the revealed will of God"; but to this the Duke of Wellington objected, as it would exclude Roman Catholic officers from the army. Thereupon Lord Tenterden prompted a bishop to move the introduction of the form used in the oath of abjuration—"on the true faith of a Christian," and this being considered unobjectionable was agreed to without a division.

The Bill, even with the substituted declaration, the Chief Justice still condemned as fatal to the Church. It is wonderful that a man of his religious feelings should have had no objection to the desecration of the most solemn rite of Christianity by requiring it to be administered for a political purpose[2]—and that a man of his shrewdness did not anticipate the certain declension

1. 18 Parl. Deb. 1609.

2. I well remember the time when barristers, who had not been at church for many years, on being appointed King's Counsel, used to go to St. Martin's Church (appropriated for this purpose), pay their guinea, and bring away a certificate of their having taken the Sacrament of the Lord's Supper according to the rites and ceremonies of the Church of England.

of the Dissenters as soon as they should be deprived of
this invaluable grievance.[1]

He opposes
the Bill for
Catholic
Emancipa-
tion.
If he disapproved of the conduct of the Government
in 1828, for supporting the Bill introduced by Lord
John Russell[2] in favor of Protestant Dissenters, what
must have been his sensations when, in 1829, he heard,
on authority which could no longer be distrusted,
that the Duke of Wellington and Sir Robert Peel were
about to introduce a Bill to remove all disabilities from

1. The Church has ever since been gaining ascendency over the
Dissenters. and has now only to fear internal divisions.

2. John, Earl Russell, (b. 1792, d. 1878), was the third son of
the sixth Duke of Bedford. He was educated at Edinburgh,
and entered parliament in 1813 as member for Tavistock in the
Whig interest. In 1818 he took up the question of Parliamentary
Reform and moved four moderate resolutions, henceforth specially
associating himself with the Reform movement, and annually
moving a resolution on the subject. In 1828 he carried a motion
for the repeal of the Test and Corporation Acts, and a bill was subsequently passed to that effect. In 1830 he became Paymaster of the
Forces under Lord Grey, and was entrusted with the presentation of
the Reform Bill to the House (March 1, 1831). His reputation was
greatly increased by the ability which he displayed in the passage
of the bill ; and when Peel gained office, Russell was recognized as
leader of the Opposition. In 1835 he became Home Secretary under
Melbourne, and in 1839 Secretary for War and the Colonies. At the
general election of 1841 Russell was returned for London, a seat
which he retained for twenty years. In 1845 he declared himself in
favor of the repeal of the Corn Laws, in a letter to his constituents,
and in 1846 he became Prime Minister. Four years later, in 1850, he
made the great mistake of countenancing the No Popery agitation
by his *Letter to the Bishop of Durham* upon the creation of a Catholic
episcopate in England, and by carrying the Ecclesiastical Titles Bill,
which, however, remained a dead letter. At the end of 1851 he
quarrelled with and dismissed Palmerston, who in the next year
brought about the fall of the Russell ministry. In Aberdeen's ministry Russell was at first Foreign Secretary, and afterwards President of the Council ; in 1855 he resigned, and came back to the
Foreign Office under Palmerston in 1859. In 1861 he was created
Earl Russell, and became again Prime Minister on Palmerston's
death in 1865. He was defeated in 1866 on the Reform Bill, and
resigned. He never afterwards held office, though he continued
to take an active part in politics, and in 1869 introduced a bill em-
powering the crown to confer life-peerages. Earl Russell was a
voluminous writer, and edited himself selections from his *Speeches*
and *Despatches* with introductions, 2 vols., 1870.—*Dict. of Eng. Hist.*

LORD JOHN RUSSELL.

Roman Catholics, and to allow them to sit in both
Houses of Parliament! On the second reading of the
Bill, Baron Tenterden made a speech, the beginning of
which was attentively listened to, and is said, from the
solemn tone and manner of the speaker, to have been
very impressive:

" My Lords," said he, " I would not now have offered
myself to your Lordships in my individual capacity;
but, thinking that it may be expected that a person in
my situation should not give a silent vote against this
portentous measure, I am induced to stand up and express my sentiments upon it. Several noble Lords who
have supported it have denominated themselves 'the
friends of civil and religious liberty.' If by assuming
that title they mean to insinuate that those who differ
from them as to the fitness of the proposed innovation
are not the friends of civil and religious liberty, I for
one must enter my protest against such an imputation.
Every man may be mistaken in his opinion—he may
even be mistaken in the motives on which he is acting
—but, for myself, I have no hesitation in asserting
that the very reason for my opposition to the present
measure is derived from an attachment to civil and
religious liberty. I have all my life admired the Protestant Church of England. I should have been the
most ungrateful of men if I had not done so. My
esteem for that church, which grew with my growth
and strengthened with my strength, has not declined
since the bodily feebleness of age has been stealing upon
me, but is increased by the perils to which she is now
exposed. Not only am I actuated by religious considerations, but by the fixed conviction that our Protestant
church is more favorable to civil and religious liberty
than any other established church which either does
at present exist, or has ever before existed in the
world. Can I support a measure which I am sure

by a broad and direct road leads to the overthrow of
this Protestant church? We have been told of countries in Europe in which Roman Catholics and Protestants have been found to go on very amicably
together. But is there any other country in Europe
or elsewhere which bears any resemblance to Ireland?
In Ireland there is an acknowledged Popish hierarchy,
assuming to themselves the names and titles of those
dioceses which by law belong to Protestant prelates.
And is it to be supposed that any hierarchy—let alone
a Popish hierarchy—would be content to leave others
in the enjoyment of those honors and emoluments
which were wrested from their ancestors of the same
faith with themselves? Is it possible that there should
not exist in the human mind an earnest and anxious
desire to obtain the restitution of these privileges?
And will not strength be given to persons of the
Roman Catholic persuasion to effect their object by
granting them political power? By political power
I mean a power exercised according to legitimate
means; I cannot consent to give that designation to
mere physical force or the power of numbers, which,
if properly resisted, I do not dread."

He then went into a long, tiresome enumeration of
all the acts passed against Roman Catholics, since the
Reformation down to the Union with Ireland, and set
the peers on both sides of the House a yawning, although they were too well bred to cough, or in any
way intentionally to interrupt him. He concluded by
declaring his conviction that, although the measure
might for a time produce tranquillity, such tranquillity would not be of long duration—and would only
be the deceitful stillness which precedes the storm, and
that hereafter the combination of physical force and
political power would be fatal to the empire.

Earl Grey spoke next, and thus began in a strain something between compliment and sneer:

"I too, my Lords, am very reluctant to offer myself to your notice. I rise with a considerable degree of fear lest presumption should be imputed to me for attempting to follow the noble and learned Lord, the Chief Justice of England, who has just delivered his opinion, and who has rested the greater part of the argument which he addressed to your Lordships on a review of the laws which bear upon the situation of his Majesty's Roman Catholic subjects, and whose great learning, professional habits, and high authority give him claims to your Lordships' attention to which I cannot pretend."

He commented upon all the statutes which had been quoted, contending that none of them presented a permanent bar to the claims of the Roman Catholics. When he came to the Bill of Rights, and alluded to the declaration, that to keep and carry arms was the right of the subjects of this realm, Lord Tenterden interjected, " being Protestants." *Earl Grey:* " Well, my Lords, *of the Protestant subjects*—it makes no difference in my argument : among all the provisions of the Bill of Rights the noble and learned Lord does not find it anywhere stated that Roman Catholics are to be for ever excluded from the enjoyment of the rights of the British constitution."

The Chief Justice fared no better when, on Lord Grey's statement that parliament had enacted in the reign of William and Mary that every officer of the army and navy shall take the oath of supremacy before receiving his commission, he exclaimed, " It was a separate Act." *Earl Grey:* " Yes, it was a separate Act (1 W. and M. c. 8, s. 10); but it was as much a part of the measures of the Revolution as the law which required that the members of both Houses of Parliament should take the oath of supremacy. Although an administration to which I belonged was overturned by an attempt slightly to modify that Act, it was afterwards totally repealed by the very men who raised against us the cry *that the Church was in danger,*—the Earl of Eldon from the woolsack giving the royal assent,—and both services were thrown open to Roman Catholics,—as both Houses of Parliament, I hope, will shortly be,—notwithstanding his opposition and that of the noble and learned Lord,—who perhaps was not fully aware of his apparent inconsistency."[1]

He opposes the Anatomy Bill.

I heard Lord Tenterden, without any diminution of my respect for him, oppose the Catholic Relief Bill,—which, though a necessary, was a perilous measure,—the ominous prophecies about which certainly have received some verification by subsequent Papal aggression. But I felt much disgust from his violent and vulgar opposition to a bill which I had materially assisted in carrying through the House of Commons, to put an end to the system of robbing churchyards of dead bodies, and to the crime of committing murder for the supply of subjects for dissection to schools of anatomy. He utterly misrepresented the Bill, by saying that all who went into hospitals hereafter must lay their account with their bodies being " dissected and anatomized, as if they were hanged for wilful murder." To excite prejudice and passion against that which must evidently be conducive to decency and humanity, he added, in a piteous tone, that " the poor justly felt an unconquerable aversion to the dissection of their bodies, which would not be overcome by the most solemn assurance that they would afterwards receive Christian burial." The practice of " Burking,"[2] which

1. 21 Parl. Deb., 300.
2. " Burking," a name applied to the murder of persons in order to obtain subjects for dissection—Burke being the name of the person practicing it.

had brought such disgrace upon Edinburgh, he declared might in future be prevented by a newly-discovered test, which enabled any skilful medical man to ascertain whether a person whose body was offered for sale had died by disease or by violence, and so, the market for murdered dead bodies being spoilt, murders to obtain them for sale would cease. These arguments, coming from a Chief Justice, made a considerable impression on the Episcopal bench and Conservative peers, and the Bill was lost. However, proof being given that, in spite of the continuing atrocities of resurrection-men, anatomy could not be taught under the existing system, the Bill was allowed to pass in the next session of parliament, and it has been found to operate most beneficially."[1]

Lord Tenterden likewise strenuously opposed the Bill for taking away the capital punishment from the crime of forgery, which had long been considered, even by enlightened men, indispensably necessary for our commercial credit. He said, " When it was recollected how many thousand pounds, and even tens of thousands, might be abstracted from a man by a deep laid scheme of forgery, he thought that this crime ought to be visited with the utmost extent of punishment which the law then wisely allowed."[2]

He opposes the Bill for taking away capital punishment for forgery.

Nevertheless he was by no means, like Eldon and Kenyon, a bigoted enemy to law reform. When commissions were issued by Peel, on the suggestion of Lord Brougham, for this laudable object, he allowed his own name to be introduced into that for inquiring into the procedure of the ecclesiastical courts; he assisted in pointing out proper commissioners for the others;[3] he encouraged their labors, and when they

His efforts for amending the law.

1. 21 Parl. Deb., 1749.   2. 25 Parl. Deb., 854.
3. By his advice I was myself placed at the head of the Real Property Commission.

had made their reports, he employed himself in drawing Bills to carry their suggestions into effect.

Thus he wrote in the summer of 1830 to his old
friend Sir Egerton: "You are probably aware that we
had three commissions, one on the practice and proceedings of the superior Courts of Common Law,
another on the Law of Real Property, and a third on
the Ecclesiastical Courts. Two reports have been
made by each of the two first—none by the latter, of
which I am a member. The reports contain recommendations and proposals for many alterations, some
of which I think useful and practicable. Something,
however, must be done by the Legislature to satisfy
the public mind; and under this impression I have employed myself since the circuit in preparing no fewer
than five bills, intended chiefly to give some further
powers to the common law courts, and make some
alteration in the practice, but without infringing on
any important principle, adopting some of the recommendations, with some alterations from the proposals.
I wish it were possible to cure the evil you so justly
complain of. Whatever shortens and simplifies will be
calculated to save expense; but Acts of Parliament
cannot make men honest. I doubt whether an act to
subject bills for conveyancing to taxation would effect
much. As I think they ought to be, I would willingly
promote such an act; but if I bring my five bills before
parliament, I shall have done at least as much as I
ought to do, and perhaps more, though, to say the
truth, I have one more bill on the anvil, and have had
for at least three years, without the courage to propose it. It has had much of the *limæ labor*. Indeed,
to say the truth, this *limæ labor* is an occupation by no
means disagreeable to my mind."

The Bills respecting the procedure of the Common
Law Courts, embodying the suggestions of the Com-

missioners, passed without opposition, and almost
without notice, but that on which the *limæ labor* had
been so long bestowed, and which was peculiarly his
own, caused a good deal of discussion. The object of
it was to define the periods of time which will confer a
title to certain rights by enjoyment, without a reference either to prescription or grant, and to rectify
the injustice which arose from claims to tithe being
brought forward, notwithstanding exemption from
payment of tithe, or the existence of a modus for cen-
turies, during which the advowson of the living and
the land in the parish had been sold upon the footing
of the exemption or the modus. In introducing his
Bill in the House of Lords he thus tried to make it
intelligible to his unwilling hearers: "Your Lordships
may be aware that many rights can only be established
on the supposition that they have existed 'for time
whereof the memory of man runneth not to the contrary;' and that this period denominated *legal memory*'
or '*prescription*' extends so far back as the commencement of the reign of Richard I., or as some say, only
to his return from the holy war. But it is hardly ever
possible to trace a right so far back by direct evidence,
and Judges are obliged to tell juries that from modern
enjoyment they may presume the existence of the
right in very remote times. This, however, leads to
great uncertainty, for Judges may differ as to what is
a reasonable ground for the presumption; and if evidence is offered, showing that during any reign since
Richard I. the right did not, or could not exist, it is
gone for ever. Again, some rights may be claimed by
grant from the owner of the land over which they are
to be exercised, and after an enjoyment of them for a
certain period of time, Judges have been in the habit
of calling upon juries to presume that such a grant has
been made, although it is not forthcoming, and in

truth never had existence. But besides the scruples of some Judges and some jurors against resorting to this fiction, it is occasionally insufficient from legal technicalities to protect long enjoyment. I conceive that it will be much better to follow the example of all other civilized nations, and to enact that after undisturbed enjoyment for periods to which direct and satisfactory evidence may be applied, the right shall be conclusively established, and I propose periods of sixty, forty, thirty, and twenty years, under different modifications and conditions according to the nature of the right—whether it be to take part of the profits of land, or only to exercise an easement over it. Thus the right to common of pasture, to common of estovers, to ways, to light, air, and water, will be respectively regulated and provided for. The next subject to which I have to draw your Lordship's attention is the claim to tithes. At present, under the maxim *nullum tempus occurrit ecclesiæ*, a modus, or small payment in lieu of tithes, may be challenged and set aside, unless it is supposed to have existed so far back as legal memory. Here again the doctrine of presumption is resorted to, but it will surely be much better that some reasonable time should be fixed, during which positive proof of the modus shall be required, and that then the modus shall be unchallengeable. Farther, non-payment of tithes for any length of time operates no exemption, unless the land can be proved to have belonged to a religious house before the Reformation, and thence much expensive and vexatious litigation ensues. I propose to make the payment of a modus or entire nonpayment for thirty years sufficient to establish the modus or exemption, unless a contrary practice can be distinctly proved at some antecedent time, and where the evidence extends to sixty years to make the right claimed by the occupier of the land to

pay a modus, or to be altogether exempt from payment, absolute and indefeasible. I am, my Lords,
most sincerely attached to the clergy of the Church of
England; I should be most ungrateful if I were not so:
but it is better for them as well as for their parish-
ioners that a permanent peace should be concluded
between the parties on the basis of *uti possidetis*. I
doubt not that the clergy have much oftener lost what
strictly belonged to them than gained by usurpation.
Having seen the bad effects of the warfare which has
been carried on, I must say PETO PACEM. Tithe suits
almost invariably cause personal dissensions in the
parish, and lessen the usefulness of the incumbent, but
they not unfrequently involve him in expense which
he can ill afford, and turn out disastrously for himself
and his family."

Lord Chancellor Brougham highly complimented
the Bill, and it was read a first time, but on account of
the speedy dissolution of parliament it was lost for that
Session. In the following year Lord Tenterden again
brought forward the measure, dividing it into two
Bills, one " For shortening the time of Prescription in
certain cases," and the other " For shortening the time
required in claims of modus decimandi, or exemption
or discharge of tithe." They both passed [1] exactly as
he framed them,—but I am sorry to say that although
they proceed on very good principles, they have by no
means established for him the reputation of a skilful
legislator. The Judges have found it infinitely difficult
to put a reasonable construction upon them, and, in

1. 2 and 3 Wm. IV. c 71, and 2 and 3 Wm. IV. c. 100. One of
his biographers has likewise given to him the credit of 3 and 4 Wm.
IV. c. 27, for abolishing real actions and making a uniform rule as to
the title to lands from enjoyment.—Townsend, vol. ii., 272. Having
drawn it myself, with the assistance of my brother Commissioners,
I can testify that he never saw it till it was in print.

adapting them to the cases which have arisen, have been obliged to make law rather than to declare it.[1]

His sound views respecting parliamentary privilege. An opportunity occurring to him of expressing his general opinion upon "Parliamentary privilege," he showed very plainly what his opinion would have been respecting the questions on this subject which arose after his death. Lord Brougham, the Chancellor, being rather hostile to Parliamentary privilege, had expressed a doubt respecting the power of the House to fine and imprison for a libel. *Lord Tenterden :* " All the Courts of Westminster Hall exercise this privilege, and how can it properly be denied to your Lordships? In what cases, under what circumstances, and to what extent your Lordships should exercise this privilege, it is for your Lordships to determine—but the privilege is clear, distinct, and indisputable—being conferred not for the protection of those who possess it, but for the sake of the public and for the good government of the nation. The very principle of our constitution requires that the two Houses of Parliament should possess all the powers necessary for enabling them to perform the functions which it assigns to them." [2]

He opposes the Reform Bill. Oct. 7, 1837. I now come to the measure which he considered fatal to the monarchy, which drove him from the House of Lords, and which probably shortened his days—the reform of the representation of the people in parliament. On the 5th night of the debate on the second reading of the Reform Bill of 1831,[3] he rose and spoke

1. On one question which arose respecting exemption from tithes, a case was sent by the Lord Chancellor successively to the Court of Common Pleas, the Court of Queen's Bench, and the Court of Exchequer, and in each Court the Judges were equally divided upon it.

2. 3 Parl. Deb., 3d Series, p. 1714. Lord Brougham imputed to him a blunder, by supposing that he had attributed to the House of Commons, as well as to the House of Lords, the power of fining and imprisoning for a time certain. He merely excused himself on the ground that he had never been a member of the Lower House.

3 Reform Bills. The question of Parliamentary Reform was first raised in a practical shape by Pitt, when he brought forward in

as follows: "I feel it necessary to address a very few
sentiments to your Lordships on this important ques-

1785 a motion, proposing to disfranchise thirty-six rotten boroughs returning two members each, and to give the members to the counties and to London. The motion was rejected by 248 to 174. The breaking out of the French revolution a few years afterwards, and the European war, diverted men's minds from the subject, and produced a disinclination towards the extension of popular liberty. In 1793 both Burke and Pitt opposed Mr. Grey's Parliamentary Reform motion, which was negatived by 232 to 41, and met with no better fate when brought forward again in 1797. The Fox ministry had no leisure, and the Portland ministry no inclination, to attend to the matter. In 1817 a motion of Sir Francis Burdett was lost by 265 to 77, and a bolder attempt of the same member to introduce manhood suffrage the following year found not a single supporter beside the mover and seconder. In 1820 Lord J. Russell carried a Bill for withholding writs from the rotten boroughs of Camelford, Grampound, Penryn, and Barnstaple, which was thrown out by the Lords. Each year from 1821 to 1829 Lord J. Russell or some other Whig introduced a motion for reform, which in each case was rejected. In Feb., 1830, the Marquess of Blandford moved an amendment to the address in favor of reform, which was rejected by 96 to 11. The same year Calvert's Bill to transfer the representation of East Retford to Birmingham, and Lord J. Russell's motion to enfranchise Leeds, Manchester, and Birmingham, were rejected. When Lord Grey became Prime Minister in this year the subject was at once taken up by the Cabinet. On March 1, 1831, Lord J. Russell introduced the Reform Bill. After most animated debates the second reading of the bill was carried (March 2) by a majority of one (302 to 301). On an amendment in committee for reducing the whole number of members the ministry were defeated. On April 22 parliament was dissolved, to meet again in June with the reformers in great majority. The Reform Bill was again carried, this time by 367 votes to 131. On Sept. 22 the bill finally passed the Commons, but was thrown out by the Lords (Oct. 8) by 199 to 158. In December a third Reform Bill was brought in and carried by a majority of 162. The Bill sent up to the Lords in 1832 passed the second reading on April 14 of that year. But on May 7 the Peers, by a majority of 35, postponed the disfranchising clauses of the Bill, thus virtually rejecting it. The king refused to create new Peers, the ministers resigned, and the Duke of Wellington attempted to form a Tory ministry. But the attempt was hopeless and the nation almost in a state of insurrection. On May 15 the Grey ministry returned to office, and the king was prepared to create new Peers if necessary. The Lords, however, at length gave way, and on June 4 the Bill was passed. The Reform Bill of 1832 disfranchised 56 boroughs, having less than 2000 inhabitants, and deprived 30 other boroughs of one member each. Of the 143 seats gained, 65 were given to the counties, 22 of the large towns received two members each, and 21 others one each. A uniform 10l household

tion. Many topics had occurred to me against this appalling Bill, but they have already been urged by others with more force and ability than I could have brought to the task. But there is one point on which I feel it my peculiar and sacred duty to address you —not so much in my character as a Peer, as in the character which the robes I wear remind me that I have to sustain. I find, my Lords, that the rights of almost all the corporate bodies in England, whether they are held by charter or prescription, are treated by this Bill, so far as I see, with absolute contempt. Many of them are to be annihilated, and the rest are to be despoiled of their privileges. I have listened in vain for any rea-

franchise was established in boroughs, and in the counties the franchise was given to copyholders, lease holders, and tenants-at-will holding property of the value of 50*l* and upwards. Reform Bills with analogous provisions were also passed for Scotland and Ireland in 1832. Between 1832 and 1850 motions for further extending the franchise were frequently made and lost. In 1852 and 1854 Lord J. Russell introduced Reform Bills, which were withdrawn. In 1859 Mr. Disraeli, on behalf of the Conservatives, introduced a Bill, which was defeated by 39 votes. In 1866 (March) a comprehensive Reform Bill was introduced by Mr. Gladstone. The "Adullamite" section of the Liberals had, however, seceded from their party, and the Bill, after fierce debate, was carried only by 5 votes, and in June the government were defeated by an amendment. The Liberals resigned and the Conservatives, in Feb., 1867, brought forward and passed (Aug.) Mr. Disraeli's Reform Bill of 1867. This bill conferred a household and lodger franchise in boroughs, though it still left a property qualification in counties [ELECTIONS]. Between 1872 and 1883 motions in favor of household franchise in the counties were moved (generally by Mr. G. O. Trevelyan) and rejected. In 1884 Mr. Gladstone introduced a Reform Bill intended to render the franchise uniform in England, Scotland, and Ireland, and to assimilate it in counties and boroughs. No provisions for the redistribution of seats were made, but the government undertook to bring in a bill dealing with the subject at an early date. After several amendments in favor of joining the Franchise Bill with a Redistribution Bill had been thrown out in the Commons, the bill passed its third reading in the lower House by a majority of 130. The Lords, however, declared by a majority of 51 that no bill would be satisfactory which did not deal with the two subjects of extension of the franchise and redistribution. The two bills were brought in the next Session and carried.—*Dict. of Eng. Hist.*

son for the extent to which this destruction and spoliation are carried. I should be ready to run the risk of
innovation were it intended only to transfer privileges
from some decayed parts of the constitution to other
more sound and healthy parts, which I believe in my
conscience is all that is desired by the reasonable portion of his Majesty's subjects, by the middle classes, for
whom I entertain as great a respect as any man (I may
tell your Lordships that I feel a respect and affection
for these classes, having sprung from them), but instead
of such a reasonable and moderate measure, reconcilable with the institutions of the country, I find one
going farther than the worst fears of alarmists had ever
anticipated. On what footing is the measure rested?
Expediency alone! My Lords, Expediency is a tyrant
whose will is made a pretext for every act of injustice.
Corporate rights, hitherto held sacred, are now reck-
lessly violated, and· I will tell those who despise them
that after this precedent the rights of property will be
equally disregarded, and liberty and life itself will be
sacrificed to expediency, or the appetite of the mob for
plunder and blood. I conclude with repeating that I
consider myself in the situation which I unworthily fill
peculiarly bound to uphold the chartered rights of the
people, and I hereby solemnly proclaim that the flagrant
violation of these rights is of itself an insuperable objection to this Bill.''

I happened to be standing on the steps of the throne
when this oracular denunciation was delivered, and I
am sorry to say that the effect was rather ludicrous.
The notion had never before entered the imagination
of any man that the Chief Justice of England is ex-
officio the Patron Saint of all municipal corporations,
and that when they are in danger he is bound to appear
Deus ex machinâ in their defence.

The doomed Tenterden was soon after snatched

CHAP.
LIV.
away (happily, perhaps) from the evil to come. How would he have comported himself when the "Municipal Corporation Reform Bill" was brought forward, which actually did sweep away every close corporation in the kingdom, made every ratepayer a burgess, and created by popular election a Mayor, Aldermen, and Councillors in every borough—"*all statutes, charters, and customs to the contrary in anywise notwithstanding?*"—On the present occasion he was in a triumphant majority of 199 to 158 against the second reading of the Parliamentary Reform Bill—and for some months longer he slept sound, corporate rights remaining untouched.[1]

A.D. 1832.
His last
speech in
the House
of Lords,
w¹th his
vow never
again to
enter the
House if
the Reform
Bill passed.
But in the month of April following, the Parliamentary Reform Bill again came up from the Commons; and although it now very improperly preserved the franchise of the corrupt freemen, Lord C. J. Tenterden's hostility to it was in no degree mitigated. Accordingly it was thus assailed by him in the last speech he ever delivered in parliament:—"A safe and moderate plan of reform I should not object to; but the question is, whether you will go further with the consideration of this bill—a bill which I have no hesitation in saying ought on no account to be permitted to pass into a law. The bill evinces a settled disregard of all existing rights. In its disfranchising clauses it does more than can be attempted with safety, and in its enfranchising clauses it goes infinitely beyond the wants and the wishes of the country. The right of sending representatives to parliament is to be lavished not merely on great populous towns which have recently risen into opulence, but on villages and hamlets which have sprung up around them. Moreover, the elective franchise is to be placed, if not entirely, at least in a preponderating degree, in the hands of one class. If this had been a class of well educated, well informed men,

1. Parl. Deb., 3d Series, 301.

still I should have objected to making it the sole depos-
itary of political power; but this class notoriously does
not consist of such persons as I have just described.
Those who belong to it are entitled to your Lordships'
superintending care and protection; but they are unfit
to become your masters. We are asked to go into a
committee on the bill, because there it may be amended.
In committee I should feel it my duty to move that the
whole be omitted after the word 'that,' for it cannot be
modified so as to be rendered innocuous. The principle
of the bill is precisely the same with that which you
have already rejected. It is said that we must not go
against the wishes of the people and a decided majority
of the House of Commons. But you must consider
whether the fulfilment of such wishes would not be per-
nicious to the people; and a majority of the House of
Commons, however much entitled to respect, ought
not to induce your Lordships to sanction a measure
which you believe in your conscience would involve
Lord and Commons in the general ruin. Let the bill
be immediately rejected, for any protracted consideration of it can only lead to the delusion as well as to the
disappointment of the public. We are threatened with
calamitous consequences which may follow the rejection of the bill; but I have no faith in such predictions.
I never have despaired, nor will now despair of the
good sense of the people of England. Give them but
time for reflection, and I am sure they will act both
wisely and justly. Of late they have been excited by
the harangues of ministers, by the arts of emissaries,
and by the inflammatory productions of the periodical
press. Let them have time to cool, and they will ere
long distinguish between their real and their pretended
friends. Already there is a growing feeling among the
people that they have been following blind guides, and
I believe there is a great majority of the nation ready

to adopt any measure of temperate reform.   This
measure, my Lords, leaves nothing untouched in the
existing state of the elective franchise.   It goes to vest
all the functions of government in the other House of
Parliament, and if it were to pass there would be
nothing left for this House or for the Crown, but to
obey the mandates of the Commons.   NEVER, NEVER,
MY LORDS, SHALL I ENTER THE DOORS OF THIS HOUSE
AFTER IT HAS BECOME THE PHANTOM OF ITS DEPARTED
GREATNESS."

There was still a decided majority of the Peers
determined that the bill should not pass.   Nevertheless
the expedient course was considered to be, that it
should not again be thrown out in this stage, and the
second reading was carried by a majority of 184 to
175.[1]

For a few days there seemed reason to think that
Lord Lyndhurst's manœuvre would succeed.   The
King concurred in it, and a new administration was
named to mutilate the bill.   But the nation said No!
The King was obliged to agree, if necessary, to create
the requisite Peers to carry "the bill, the whole bill,
and nothing but the bill."   The dread of being so
"swamped" by fresh creations frightened away a great
many of its opponents, and it quietly passed its subsequent stages unchanged.

Lord Tenterden was as good as his word.   After
the Reform Bill received the Royal assent he never
more entered the doors of the House.

If he had survived a few years, he might have
laughed at the disappointment of those who expected
from this measure a new era of pure public virtue and
uninterrupted national prosperity; yet he would have
witnessed the falsification of his own predictions; for,
while individual peers ceased to be members of a

1. 12 Parl. Deb., 3d Series, 398, 454.

formidable oligarchy, the House collectively retained CHAP.
LIV. its place in the constitution, and, I believe, it has since risen in public estimation and in influence.

Lord Tenterden was sincerely convinced that the His health
declines. House and the country were doomed to destruction, and this conviction aggravated the disorders by which his enfeebled frame was now afflicted. In the follow-ing strain, although almost too feeble to support exist-ence, he poured forth his anguish to Sir Egerton Brydges:

" Russell Square, May 20th, 1832.

"My dear Sir Egerton,

"I have made several attempts to write to you, but have found myself unable to do so; nor can I write as I ought, or wish to do. My spirit is so depressed, that when I am not strongly excited by some present object that admits of no delay, I sink into something very nearly approaching to torpidity. My affection for you remains unchanged. God bless you.

"Your most affectionate friend,

"Tenterden."

Again, on the 8th of June, after addressing the same correspondent upon matters of inferior import-ance, he adds—"We differ upon the great measure that has so long agitated the country. I considered the Catholic Bill as the first, and I consider this as the concluding step to overturn all the institutions of the country. In my anticipations of the effect of the first, I have certainly not been mistaken. The present state of Ireland proves this. Would to God I may be mis-taken as to the effect of the Reform Bill. Great alarm was felt yesterday from the Paris news. I hear to-day that the Government prevailed in the conflict. I have no confidence in a temporary triumph over a principle that I believe was never subdued, and can only be restrained by unintermitting coercion."

He rallied a little, and got through the sittings after term pretty comfortably, giving his annual dinner to the King's counsel; but instead of asking each of them to drink wine with him *seriatim* as formerly, he drank wine conjointly, first with all those who sat on his right hand, and then with all those on his left, hospitably admonishing them to drink wine with each other.

His last
circuit.

In July he went the Midland Circuit, as the lightest he could choose, and he was able to sit in Court and finish the business at every assize town, notwithstanding the annoyance of a violent cough and other alarming symptoms. After a short stay at Leamington he returned to his seat at Hendon, and there spent the long vacation; sometimes yielding to despondence, and sometimes trying to amuse himself with making Latin verses, and with classical reading, which used to be his solace.

The long
vacation
before his
death.

Being obliged to come to town for a Council to determine the fate of the prisoners convicted at the Old Bailey, he wrote to Sir Egerton Brydges the following melancholy epistle, which did not reach its destination till the writer was relieved from all his sufferings, and transferred to a better state of existence.

" MY DEAR SIR EGERTON,

" I came to town yesterday to attend His Majesty on the Recorder's report, and have received your letter this morning. I have lately suffered, and am still suffering, very severely from an internal complaint, which they call an irritation of the mucous membrane. It troubled me during all the circuit. I got rid of it for a short time at Leamington, but it soon returned with greater violence, and has for some time deprived me of appetite, and produced great depression of spirits. Sir Henry Halford, however, assures me that a medicine he has ordered me will in time remove the complaint, and my confidence in him induces me to trust it may be so, though after a trial of six days I cannot say that I find any sensible improvement. God bless you.

" Your most affectionate friend,

" TENTERDEN."

However, his mental faculties remained wholly un- His last impaired; and he was determined " to die, like a camel appearance in court. in the wilderness, with his burden on his back." An important Government prosecution, in which I was counsel—*The King* v. *The Mayor of Bristol*—was appointed to be tried at bar immediately before Michaelmas Term. This excited prodigious interest, as it arose out of the Reform-Bill riots at Bristol, in which a considerable part of the city was laid in ashes. The Chief Justice appeared on the Bench with the other Judges, and continued to preside during the first two days of the trial: I recollect one characteristic sally from him, indicating his mortal dislike of long examinations. Mr. Shepherd, the junior counsel for the Crown, having asked how many horses were drawing a messenger's post-chaise sent in quest of the mayor, and being answered "four," Lord Tenterden sarcastically exclaimed in a hollow voice, "and now, Sir, I suppose you will next get out from your witness *what was the color of the post-boys' jackets*." But his bodily health was evidently sinking. When he went home in the evening of the second day of the trial he had no appetite for the dinner prepared for him, and he fancied that fresh oysters would do him good. He ate some; but they disagreed with him, and an access of fever supervening, he was put to bed, from which he never rose. Although His death.

attended by Sir Henry Halford, Dr. Holland,[1] and Sir

1. "George Calvert Holland, (1801–1865). physician, was born at Pitsmoor, Sheffield. Feb. 28, 1801. He had practically no early education, and his father, a respectable artisan, apprenticed him to a trade. When about sixteen years old he suddenly discovered that he had a facility for writing verses. He thereupon studied the poets. and learned Latin, French, and Italian   On the completion of his apprenticeship his friends, under the advice of Dr. Philipps of the Upper Chapel, Sheffield, placed him with a Unitarian minister with a view to his joining the Unitarian ministry.   After a year he determined to enter the medical profession, and went to Edinburgh, where he graduated M.D. in 1827 with high honors, and, joining the Hunterian and Royal Physical societies, became president of both.   He spent a year in Paris, taking the degree of bachelor of letters, and after another year in Edinburgh began practice in Manchester.   Here he made for himself a distinguished position, but a fierce controversy, in which his advocacy of the new discoveries of Gall and Spurzheim involved him with his professional brethren, led to his finally removing to Sheffield.   His career in his native town was from the first a success.   He at once took a prominent and important position in the Literary and Philosophical Society, Mechanics' Library, and Mechanics' Institution, and an active part in promoting the return of liberal members during the first and second elections for Sheffield under the Reform Act of 1832.   His works, 'An Experimental Enquiry into the Laws of Animal Life,' Edinburgh, 1829, 8vo, and 'The Physiology of the Fœtus, Liver, and Spleen,' 1831, added much to his professional reputation, and he was appointed one of the honorary physicians to the Sheffield General Infirmary.   Holland was an enthusiastic student of the new science of mesmerism.   In the struggle for the repeal of the corn laws he turned his back on his old principles and actively defended protection.   Although his new friends rewarded his efforts with a purse containing five hundred guineas, his action cost him in practice and position more than ten times the amount.   Practically giving up his profession, Holland became provisional director of many of the railway projects at the time of the railway mania, and was also a director of the Leeds and West Riding Bank and of the Sheffield and Retford Bank.   Disaster overtook these latter companies, and involved him in utter ruin.   He retired to Worksop, where he wrote, 'Philosophy of Animated Nature,' 1848, which he regarded as his best work.   After an unsuccessful attempt to establish himself in London, he returned again to Sheffield in 1851, and having changed his views on medical science began practice as a homœopathist.   He was elected a member of the Town Council, but lost his seat in 1858, owing to his advocacy of a Local Improvement Act.   In 1862, however, he was made an alderman of the borough, and that position he held until his death at Sheffield on March 7, 1865.   Holland's principal works are, besides those mentioned above: 1. 'Essay on Education,' 1828, 8vo; 2. 'Enquiry into the Principles and Practice of Medicine,' 2 vols..

Benjamin Brodie,[2] his disease baffled all their skill. He

1833 and 1835; 3. 'Corn Law Repealing Fallacies,' etc., 1840, 8vo; 4. 'Millacrat,' 1841, 8vo; 5. 'The Abuses and Evils of Charity, especially of Medical Charitable Institutions'; 6. 'The Vital Statis tics of Sheffield,' 1843; 7. 'The Philosophy of the Moving Powers of the Blood'; 8. Diseases of the Lungs from Mechanical Causes,' 1844; 9. 'The Nature and Cure of Consumption, Indigestion, Scrofula, and Nervous Affections,' 1850; 10. 'Practical Suggestions for the Prevention of Consumption,' 1850; 11. 'Practical Views on Nervous Diseases,' 1850; 12. 'The Constitution of the Animal Cre ation as expressed in Structural Appendages,' 1857; 13. 'The Domestic Practice of Homœopathy,' London, 12mo, 1859. He also edited a new edition of the poetical works of Richard Furness of Dore, with a sketch of his life 1858."—*Nat. Biog. Dict.*

2. "Sir Benjamin Collins Brodie, the elder (1783–1862), Sergeant-Surgeon to the Queen, was born at Winterslow, in Wiltshire, in 1783. He was fourth child of Peter Bellinger Brodie, rector of the parish, who had been educated at Charterhouse and Worcester Col lege, Oxford. His mother was daughter of Mr. Benjamin Collins, a banker at Salisbury. From his father, who was well versed in general literature, and a good Greek and Latin scholar, Brodie received his early education. In 1797, when the country was alarmed by the prospect of a French invasion, Brodie and two brothers raised a company of volunteers. At the age of eighteen he went up to London, to enter upon the medical profession. There he devoted himself at once to the study of anatomy, attending first the lectures of Abernethy, and in 1801 and 1802 those of Wilson at the Hunterian school in Great Windmill Street, working hard in the dissecting-room. He learned pharmacy in the shop of Mr. Clifton of Leicester Square, one of the licentiates of the Apothe caries Company. At this time Brodie formed a friendship with William Lawrence, the celebrated surgeon, which was continued through life, and he was joint secretary with Sir Henry Ellis of an 'Academical Society,' to which many eminent writers belonged. The society had been removed from Oxford to London, and was dissolved early in the present century. In the spring of 1803 Brodie entered at St. George's Hospital as a pupil under Sir Everard Horne, and was appointed house-surgeon in 1805, and afterwards demonstrator to the anatomical school. When his term of office had expired he assisted Horne in his private operations and in his researches on comparative anatomy. He diligently pursued for some years the study of anatomy, demonstrating in the Windmill Street school, and lecturing conjointly with Wilson until the year 1812. He was selected Assistant-Surgeon to St. George's Hospital in 1808, an appointment which he held for fourteen years, and in the next year entered upon private practice, taking a house in Sack ville Street for the purpose. In 1808 he was elected a member of the Society for the Promotion of Medical and Chirurgical Knowl edge, a society limited to twelve members, founded by Dr. John

became delirious and talked very incoherently.   Afterwards he seemed to recover his composure, and, raising

Hunter and Dr. Fordyce in 1793, and dissolved in 1818. At this
period he contributed his first paper—the results of original phy-
siological inquiries—to the 'Philosophical Transactions,' and was
elected a fellow of the Royal Society in 1810. During the winter
of 1810-11 he communicated to the society two papers, one 'On the
Influence of the Brain on the Action of the Heart and the Generation
of Animal Heat'; the other 'On the Effects produced by certain
Vegetable Poisons (Alcohol, Tobacco, Woorara, etc.),' the first of
which formed the Croonian lecture. So favorable was the impression he produced that the Council awarded him the Copley medal
in 1811, when he was twenty-eight years of age. His unremitting
devotion to the work of his profession, without holiday for the
period of ten years, now told seriously upon his health, but change
of air and rest enabled him to resumed his duties. His interest
when he was House-Surgeon having been excited by a case of
spontaneous dislocation of the hip, he was led to study other cases
of disease of the joints, and in 1813 he contributed a paper to the
'Medico-Chirurgical Transaction,' which formed the basis of his
treatise on 'Diseases of the Joints,' published in 1818. This work
went through five editions, and translations of it appeared in other
countries. He again delivered the Croonian lecture at the Royal
Society on the action of the muscles in general and of the heart
in particular, and at this time performed the experiment of passing
a ligature round the choledoch duct, the results of which were
given in Brande's 'Journal.' In a paper on 'Varicose Veins of the
Leg,' published in the seventh volume of the 'Medico-Chirurgical
Transactions,' he described the first subcutaneous operations on
record. He married in 1816 the daughter of Serjeant Sellon, a lawyer of repute, and as practice steadily increased he removed in
1819 to Savile Row. In the same year he was appointed Professor
of Comparative Anatomy and Physiology at the Royal College of
Surgeons, and delivered four courses of lectures. While he held
this office he was summoned to attend George IV., and assisted at
an operation for the removal of a tumor of the scalp from which
the King suffered. He was elected Surgeon to St. George's Hospital in 1822, and his time was now busily employed with his
hospital duties and lectures and an increasing and lucrative practice. In his attendance upon the King during the illness which
terminated fatally he used to be at Windsor at six o'clock in the
morning, staying to converse with the King, with whom Brodie was
a favorite. When William IV. succeeded to the throne, Brodie was
promptly made Sergeant-Surgeon (1832), and two years afterwards a
baronet. His lectures on diseases of the urinary organs were published in 1832, and those illustrative of local nervous affections in
1837. The numerous papers which he wrote from time to time
will be found in his 'Collected Works.' In 1837 he travelled abroad
in France for the first time. In 1854 he published anonymously

his head from his pillow, he was heard to say in a slow CHAP. LIV. and solemn tone, as when he used to conclude his summing-up in cases of great importance, "And now, gentlemen of the jury, you will consider of your verdict." These were his last words: when he had uttered them, his head sunk down, and in a few moments he expired without a groan.

According to directions left in his will, his remains His were, in a very private manner, interred in the vaults funeral. of the Foundling Hospital,[1] of which he had been a

' Psychological Inquiries,' essays in conversational form, intended to illustrate the mutual relations of the physical organization and the mental faculties. In 1862 a second series followed, to which he put his name. He was elected President of the Royal Society in 1858, and this office he resigned in 1861, when he found that failing eyesight interfered with the discharge of the duties. He was President of the Royal College of Surgeons (1844) having been for many years Examiner and Member of the Council, and having introduced important improvements into the system of examinations. He was also President of the Royal Medical and Chirurgical and of other learned societies. The estimation in which he was universally held is shown by his connection with the Institute of France, the Academy of Medicine in Paris, the Royal Academy of Sciences of Stockholm, and the National Institution of Washington; and the University of Oxford conferred upon him the degree of D.C.L. He died at Broome Park, Surrey, in the eightieth year of his age, from a painful disease of the shoulder, Oct. 21, 1862. His wife had died two years previously. As a surgeon Brodie was a successful operator, distinguished for coolness and knowledge, a steady hand, and a quick eye ; but the prevention of disease was in his opinion higher than operative surgery, and his strength was diagnosis. An accurate observer, his memory was very retentive, and he was never at a loss for some previous case which threw light upon the knotty points in a consultation. Unflinching against quackery, he was instrumental in bringing St. John Long to justice, and his precise evidence in the witness-box was effective against the poisoner Palmer. His life was spent in active work, and he devoted it to the arrest of disease." —*Nat. Biog. Dict.*

1. On the east side of Russell Square opens Guildford Street, which leads to the Foundling Hospital, founded in 1739 by the benevolent Thomas Coram, captain of a trading vessel, for " the reception, maintenance and education of exposed and deserted young children." In 1760 the institution ceased to be a " foundling " hospital except in name, but is still applied to the reception of illegitimate children. The girls wear brown dresses with white caps, tuckers and aprons ; the boys have red sashes and cap-bands.—*Hare's Walks in London.*

governor.   At the south-east entrance to the hospital is to be seen his monument, with the following modest inscription, written by himself only two months before his death:

His
epitaph.

> " Prope situs est
> CAROLUS BARO TENTERDEN
> Filius natu minor
> Humillimis parentibus,
> Patre vero prudenti matre piâ ortus
> Per annos viginti in causis versatus,
> Quantum apud Britannos honestus labor
> Favente Deo valeat
> Agnoscas lector!" [1]

Underneath is added, by his pious son—

> " Hæc de se conscripsit
> Vir summus idemque omnium modestissimus.[2]

The impartial biographer cannot say that he was a great man—but he was certainly a great magistrate. To the duties of his judicial office he devoted all his energies, and on the successful performance of them he His charac- rested all his fame.   Authorship he never attempted ter and manners. in his lifetime beyond his law book, which, although it passed through various editions, is already out of fash-ion and thrown aside, like an old almanack, as it was founded on statutes many of which have been repealed, and on decisions many of which have been reversed. A Diary which he kept, from November, 1822, to Feb-ruary, 1825, now lies before me.   The following com-mencement led me to expect much useful information and amusement from it:

"I have often wished that my predecessors had left a Diary, and that I was in possession of it."

But I am grievously disappointed.   It contains

1. " Near by lies Charles, Lord Tenterden, the youngest son of humble parents, born of a wise father and pious mother; for twenty years he was employed in causes ; thus you may know, Reader, how honest labor, with the favor of God, is rewarded among the British péople."

2 " These lines a great and very modest man wrote concerning himself."

very little that is interesting to a succeeding Chief Justice or to any one else. The diarist not only abstains from all notice of public events, but he makes no remark of any value on any professional subject. He never hints at any defects or improvements in the administration of justice in his Court, and never introduces the name of any counsel who practised before him. He confines himself to dry details of the number of causes tried at the sittings, and his expenses on the circuits. One might have expected some satirical allusions to his brother Judges, for whom he had not a very high respect; but nothing is said of any of them that might not have been published at Charing Cross. There is no ground for regret that the Diary was not begun sooner or continued later.[1]

Neither on the Bench nor in society did he ever aim at jocularity or wit, although, by accident or design, he once uttered a pun. A learned gentleman, who had lectured on the law and was too much addicted to oratory, came to argue a special demurrer before him. "My client's opponent," said the figurative advocate, "worked like a mole under ground, *clam et secretè.*" His figures and law Latin only elicited an indignant grunt from the Chief Justice. "It is asserted in Aristotle's Rhetoric "—"I don't want to hear what is asserted in Aristotle's Rhetoric," interposed Lord Tenterden. The advocate shifted his ground and took up, as he thought, a safe position. "It is laid down in

---

1. Beyond the extracts which I have given, I find nothing more curious than the following table of his expenses on the Circuit :

	£	s.	d.
Spring, 1816—Home	243	7	0
Summer, 1816—Oxford	290	9	0
Spring, 1817—Western	323	16	0
Summer, 1817—Norfolk	251	7	0
Spring, 1819—Norfolk	165	15	0
Summer, 1819—Midland	274	9	0
Summer, 1822—Northern	203	3	0
Summer, 1824—Western	374	0	0

the Pandects of Justinian "—"Where are you got now?" "It is a principle of the civil law."—"Oh, sir!" exclaimed the Judge, with a tone and voice which abundantly justified his assertion, "we have nothing to do with the *civil* law in this Court."[1]

The extreme irregularity of the Judges in their conferences, which there has often been occasion to deplore, once forced him into the necessity of coining a word. He said he could not call them *Parliamentum Indoctum*, but that he might well call them *Parliamentum Bablitivum*.

He was courteous in company, but rather stiff and formal in his manners, as if afraid of familiarity and requiring the protection of dignified station—which probably arose from the recollection of his origin and of his boyish days. He would voluntarily refer to these among very intimate friends, but he became exceedingly uneasy when he apprehended any allusion to

Compliment to him by the Lord Mayor of London. them in public. Once, however, he was complimented upon his rise under circumstances so extravagantly ludicrous that he joined in the general shout of laughter which the orator called forth. Sir Peter Laurie,[2] the

1. Townsend, 261. I should rather think, notwithstanding the *Joe Miller* of Garrick catching an orange thrown at him on the stage, and exclaiming, "This is not a *civil* orange!" that the Chief Justice's pun was unintentional, like that of Mr. Justice Blackstone, who says in his Commentaries, with much gravity, that "landmarks on the sea shore are often of *signal* service to navigation."

2. "Sir Peter Laurie (1779?-1861), Lord Mayor of London, born about 1779, was son of John Laurie, a small landowner and agriculturist, of Stitchell, Roxburghshire. He was at first intended for the ministry of the established church of Scotland, but his tastes inclining him to a commercial life, he came to London as a lad to seek his fortune. He obtained a clerkship in the office of John Jack, whose daughter Margaret he afterwards married, and subsequently set up for himself as a saddler, carrying on business at 296 Oxford Street. Becoming a contractor for the Indian army his fortune was rapidly made, and in 1820 he took his sons into partnership; he himself retired from the business in 1827. He was chairman of the Union Bank from its foundation in 1839 until his death. In 1823 he served the office of sheriff, and on April 7, 1824, received the honor of

saddler, when Lord Mayor of London, gave a dinner CHAP. LIV.
at the Mansion House to the Judges, and, in proposing
their health, observed, in impassioned accents, " What
a country is this we live in! In other parts of the world
there is no chance, except for men of high birth and
aristocratic connections; but here genius and industry
are sure to be rewarded. See before you the examples of myself, the Chief Magistrate of the Metropolis
of this great Empire, and the Chief Justice of England
sitting at my right hand—both now in the highest

knighthood. On July 6, 1826, he was chosen alderman for the ward
of Aldersgate. In 1831 he contested the election for the mayoralty
with Sir John Key, who was put forward for re-election. Laurie
was defeated, but served the office in the following year in the ordinary course of seniority. He was master of the Saddlers' Company
in 1833. During his mayoralty and throughout his public life
Laurie devoted himself largely to schemes of social advancement.
He gained the reputation of being a good magistrate, and took an
active part in the proceedings of the court of Common Council,
where he showed himself a disciple of Joseph Hume. In 1825 he
succeeded in throwing open to the public the meetings of the court
of Middlesex magistrates, and in 1835 the meetings of the court of
aldermen were also held in public through his endeavors. He was
president of Bridewell and Bethlehem hospitals, and a magistrate and deputy-lieutenant for the city of Westminster and the
county of Middlesex. His town residence was situated in Park
Square, Regent's Park, where he died of old age and infirmity on
December 3, 1861. He was buried in Highgate Cemetery on the
10th of that month. Laurie had no children, and was left a widower
in 1847. There is a mezzotint portrait of him engraved by James
Scott from a painting by Thomas Philipps, R.A., and published in
1839; and an inferior lithographic print from a drawing by F.
Cruikshank was published by Hullmandel. A portrait by an unknown painter, presented to him by the Company on February 24,
1835, hangs in Saddlers' Hall. Laurie published: 1. 'Maxims
. . . ,' 12mo., London, 1833. 2. 'Substance of the Speech of Sir P.
Laurie on the Question of the Periodical Election of Magistrates in
the Court of Common Council,' March 28, privately printed, 8vo.,
London, 1835. 3. 'Correspondence between C. Cator . . . and Sir
P. L. upon the Minutes of the Court of Common Council,' 8vo.
(1839). 4. 'Speech . . . at the Public Breakfast of the Wesleyan
Missionary Society,' pp. 8, 8vo., London, 1843. 5. 'Killing no
Murder, or the Effects of Separate Confinement . . .' 8vo., London,
1846. 6. 'A Letter on the Disadvantages and Extravagances of the
Separate System of Prison Discipline for County Jails . . .' 8vo.,
London, 1848."—*Nat. Biog. Dict.*

offices in the State, and both sprung from the very dregs of the people!"

His recollections of Canterbury.

Lord Tenterden is placed in a very amiable point of view by MACREADY,[1] the celebrated tragedian, in a lecture which he delivered to a Mechanics' Institute after he had retired from the stage, and which he published with several others, possessing great interest. The lecturer gives an account of a visit paid by him to Canterbury Cathedral, under the auspices of a Verger, who, by reading and observation, had acquired wonderful knowledge of architecture and mediæval antiquities. Having introduced us to his guide, the ex-tragedian thus proceeds: " He directed my attention to everything worthy of notice; pointed out with the detective eye of taste the more recondite excellence of art throughout the building, and with convincing accuracy shed light on the historical traditions associated with it. It was opposite the western front that he stood with me before what seemed the site of a small shed or stall, then unoccupied, and said, ' Upon this spot a little barber's shop used to stand. The last time Lord Tenterden came down here he brought his son Charles with him, and it was my duty, of course, to attend them over the Cathedral. When we came to this side of it he led his son up to this very spot and said to him, ' *Charles, you see this little shop; I have brought you here on purpose to show it to you. In that shop your grandfather used to shave for a penny! That is the*

1. William Charles Macready (*b.* 1793, *d.* 1873), actor, born in London, and educated at Rugby ; made his first appearance at Birmingham in 1810, and was engaged at Covent Garden in 1816. He played Richard III. in 1819, and removed to Drury Lane in 1822, and after a tour in the United States, appeared as Macbeth in 1827. He subsequently visited Paris, and held the management of Covent Garden and Drury Lane. In 1849 he nearly lost his life in a riot promoted by the friends of Forrest at the Astor Opera House, New York; and he made his last appearance at Drury Lane in 1851.— *Cassell's Biog. Dict.*

proudest reflection of my life ! While you live never forget that, my dear Charles.' And this man, the son of a poor barber, was the Lord Chief Justice of England. For the very reason, therefore, that the chances of such great success are rare, we should surely spare no pains in improving the condition of all whom accident may depress or fortune may not befriend."

I have heard some complaint, although I confess I myself never saw any sufficient ground for the complaint, that after Abbott had been several years Chief Justice, he was not only a *martinet* in Court, but that he rigidly enforced the rules of evidence and of procedure when presiding at his own table. The following amusing anecdote, recorded of him in the "Quarterly Review," I suspect is only entitled to the praise of being *ben trovato :* "He had contracted so strict and inveterate an habit of keeping himself and everybody else to the precise matter in hand, that once, during a circuit dinner, having asked a county magistrate if he would take venison, and receiving what he deemed an evasive reply: 'Thank you, my Lord, I am going to take boiled chicken;' his Lordship sharply retorted, 'That, sir, is no answer to my question; I ask you again if you will take venison, and I will trouble you to say *yes* or *no* without further prevarication!'"

At all times he showed an affectionate regard for the place of his early education: "In 1817, the centenary commemoration of the school, he accepted an invitation to Canterbury, witnessed the examination of the scholars, addressed the successful candidates, and, after attending the usual service and sermon at the Cathedral, dined with the masters and members of the institution at the principal hotel of the city. In his speech after dinner he expressed himself with feeling and effect, and declared that to the free school of Canterbury he owed, under the Divine blessing, the first and

best means of his elevation in life. Nor was his gratitude confined to words. With a tasteful retrospect of
the cause of his own success, he founded and endowed
two annual prizes—the one for the best English essay,
the other for the best Latin verse." [1]

Lest I should be misled by partiality or prejudice,
I add, in justice to the memory of Lord Tenterden,
sketches of him by very skilful artists. Thus is he
portrayed by Lord Brougham:

" A man of great legal abilities, and of a reputation,
though high, by no means beyond his merits. On the
contrary, it may be doubted if he ever enjoyed all the
fame that his capacity and his learning entitled him to.
For he had no shining talents ; he never was a leader at
the bar ; his genius for law was by no means of the depth
and originality which distinguished Mr. Holroyd nor
had he the inexhaustible ingenuity of Mr. Littledale,
nor perhaps the singular neatness and elegance of Mr.
Richardson. His style of arguing was clear and cogent,
but far from brilliant ; his opinions were learned and
satisfactory, without being strikingly profound ; his
advice, however, was always safe, although sometimes,
from his habitual and extreme caution, it might be deficient in boldness or vigor. As a leader he very rarely
and only by some extraordinary accident appeared, and
this in a manner so little satisfactory to himself, that
he peremptorily declined it whenever refusal was possible, for he seemed to have no notion of a leader's duty
beyond exposing the pleadings and the law of the case
to the jury, who could not comprehend them with all
his explanation. Although his reputation at the bar
was firmly established for a long course of years, it was
not till he became a Judge, hardly till he became Chief
Justice, that his merits were fully known. It then appeared that he had a singular judicial understanding,

1. 2 Towns., 237.

and even the defects which had kept him in the less
ambitious walks of the profession—his caution, his
aversion to all that was experimental, his want of fancy
—contributed, with his greater qualities, to give him a
very prominent rank indeed among our ablest Judges.
One defect alone he had, which was likely to impede
his progress towards this eminent station; but of that
he was so conscious as to protect himself against it by
constant and effectual precautions. His temper was
naturally bad; it was hasty and it was violent, forming
a marked contrast with the rest of his mind. But it
was singular with what success he fought against this,
and how he mastered the rebellious part of his nature.
Indeed it was a study to observe this battle, or rather
victory, for the conflict was too successful to be appar
ent on many occasions. On the bench it rarely broke
out, but there was observed a truly praiseworthy fea-
ture, singularly becoming, in the demeanor of a Judge.
Whatever struggles with the advocate there might be
carried on during the heat of a cause, and how great
soever might be the asperity shown on either part, all
passed away—all was, even to the vestige of the trace
of it, discharged from his mind, when the peculiar duty
of the Judge came to be performed; and he directed
the jury, in every particular, as if no irritation had ever
passed over his mind in the course of the cause. Although nothing can be more manifest than the injustice
of making the client suffer for the fault or the misfortune of his advocate—his fault, if he misconducted
himself towards the Judge; his misfortune, if he un-
wittingly gave offence—yet, whoever has practised at
Nisi prius, knows well how rare it is to find a Judge of
an unquiet temper, especially one of an irascible disposition, who can go through the trial without suffering
his course to be affected by the personal conflicts which
may have taken place in the progress of the cause. It

was, therefore, an edifying sight to observe Lord Tenterden, whose temper had been visibly affected during
the trial (for on the bench he had not always the entire
command of it, which we have described him as possessing while at the bar), addressing himself to the
points in the cause, with the same perfect calmness and
indifference with which a mathematician pursues the
investigation of an abstract truth, as if there were
neither the parties nor the advocates in existence, and
only bent upon the discovery and the elucidation of
truth."

The following discriminating praise and mild censure are meted out to him by Mr. Justice Talfourd, the
author of " Ion":

—by Mr.
Justice
Talfourd. " The chief judicial virtue of his mind was that of
impartiality ; not mere independence of external influences, but the general absence of tendency in the mind
itself to take a part, or receive a bias. How beneficial
this peculiarity must prove in the judicial investigation
of the ordinary differences of mankind, is obvious; yet
in him it was little else than a remarkable absence of
imagination, passion, and sympathy. In him the disposition to single out some one object from others for
preference—the power and the love of accumulating
associations around it and of taking an abstract interest
in its progress, were wholly wanting. The spirit of
partisanship, almost inseparable from human nature
itself, unconsciously mingling in all our thoughts, and
imparting interest to things else indifferent, is especially
cherished by the habits and excitements of an advocate's profession, and can, therefore, seldom be wholly
prevented from insinuating itself into the feelings of
the most upright and honorable Judges. But Lord
Tenterden, although long at the bar, had rarely exercised those functions of an advocate which quicken the
pulse and agitate the feelings ; he had been contented

with the fame of the neatest, the most accurate, and CHAP.
LIV.
the most logical of pleaders; and no more thought of
trials in which he was engaged as awakening busy
hopes and fears, than of the conveyances he set forth
in his pleas as suggesting pictures of the country to
which they related. The very exceptions to his general impartiality of mind partook of its passionless and
unaspiring character. In political questions, although
charged with a leaning to the side of power, he had no
master prejudices; no sense of grandeur or gradation;
as little true sympathy with a high oppressor as with
his victims. On the great trials of strength between
the Government and the people, he was rarely aroused
from his ordinary calmness; and he never, like his predecessor, sought to erect an independent tyranny by
which he might trample on freedom of his own proper
wrong. He was 'not born so high' in station, or in
thought, as to become the comrade of haughty corruption. If seduced at all by power, it was in its humbler
forms—the immunities of the unpaid magistracy and
the chartered rights of small corporations, which found
in him a congenial protector. If he had a preferable
regard in the world, beyond the circle of his own family
and friends, it was for these petty aristocracies, which
did not repel or chill him. If he was overawed by
rank, he was still more repelled by penury, the idea of
which made him shiver even amidst the warmth of the
Court of King's Bench, in which alone he seemed to
live. His moral like his intellectual sphere was contracted; it did not extend far beyond the decalogue;
it did not conclude *to the country*, but was verified *by the
record*. His knowledge, not indeed of the most atrocious but of the meanest parts of human nature, made
him credulous of fraud; a suggestion of its existence
always impelled his sagacity to search it out; and if
conspiracy was the charge, and an attorney among the

defendants, there were small chances of acquittal.   The
chief peculiarity and excellence of his decisions consist
in the frequent introduction of the word '*reasonable*'
into their terms.   He so applied this word as in many
instances to relax the severity of legal rules, to mediate
happily between opposing maxims, and to give a liberal
facility to the application of the law by Judges and
juries to the varying circumstances of cases, which before had been brought into a single class.   If he would
not break through a rule for the greatest occasion, he
was acute in discovering ways by which the right might
be done without seeming to infringe it ; and his efforts
to make technical distinctions subservient to substantial
justice were often ingenious and happy."

His love of
classical
literature
and talent
for making
Latin
verses.
I reserve, as a pleasing *finale* for this memoir, Lord
Tenterden's ardent and unabated devotion to classical
literature, which confers high distinction upon him, and
is so creditable to our profession,—showing that the
indulgence of such elegant tastes is consistent with a
steady and long continued and successful application to
abstruse juridical studies, and with the exemplary performance of the most laborious duties of an advocate
and of a judge.   Lord Eldon never opened a Greek or
Latin author after leaving college, and Lord Kenyon
could never construe one.   Lord Tenterden in his
busiest time would refresh himself from the disgust of
the *Liber Placitandi*, or the *Registrum Brevium*, by reading a Satire of Juvenal, or a chorus of Euripides.   He
likewise kept up a familiar knowledge of Shakespeare,
Milton, Dryden, and Pope, but he was little acquainted
with the modern school of English poets.   When Sir
James Scarlett on one occasion referred to the poetry
of Southey and Wordsworth as familiar to the jury,
Lord Tenterden observed, that "for himself he was
bred in too severe a school of taste to admire such
effusions."

Although he had long ceased to make verses himself, a few years before his death his passion for this amusement returned, and in the following letter to Sir Egerton Brydges, dated 15th September, 1830, he gave an interesting account of his " hobby."

" I have always felt that it might be said that a Chief Justice and a peer might employ his leisure hours better than 'in writing nonsense verses about flowers. But I must tell you how this fancy of recommencing to hammer Latin metres after a cessation of more than thirty years began. Brougham procured for me from Lord Grenville a copy of some poems printed by him under the title of ' Nugæ,' chiefly his own, one or two, I believe, of Lord Wellesley's, written long ago, and a piece of very good Greek humor by Lord Holland. The motto in the title-page is four or five hendæcasyllabic lines by Fabricius. At the same time John Williams[1] of the Northern Circuit, now the Queen's Solic-

1. "We have in Sir John Williams another example of the union of law and literature, and an additional proof that the deepest scholastic attainments are not incompatible with professional success. Sir John's love of the classics and devotion to the Muses did not prevent him from being a hard-working advocate, a zealous law reformer, or a good practical judge. He was of Welsh extraction, being descended from an ancient family in Merionethshire ; but was born at Bunbury in Cheshire, of which his father was vicar, as well as holding a living in the former county. He was born in January, 1777, and imbibed his classical tastes at the grammar school of Manchester ; from whence proceeding to the University of Cambridge he gained a scholarship at Trinity College at the age of eighteen. In his progress he won many prizes, and graduating as B.A. in 1798 he succeeded in obtaining a fellowship after a strenuous competition. His legal school was the Middle Temple, where he took his degree of barrister in 1804. On the Northern Circuit and at the Manchester and Chester sessions he made his first attempts, and by degrees, for his progress was slow, satisfied the dispensers of business of his skill as an advocate, and of his painstaking zeal for his clients. His merits were so great, and his reputation for accuracy, ingenuity, and boldness became so well established, that in 1820 he was selected to assist Mr. Brougham and Mr. Denman in the defence of Queen Caroline, in the course of which he fully confirmed the character he had obtained. This naturally made him a marked man ; but though it

itor General, who is an admirable scholar, sent me four
or five Greek epigrams of his own. I had a mind to
thank each of them, and found I could do so with great
ease to myself in ten hendæcasyllables. This led me
to compose two trifles in the same metre on two favor-

increased his professional employment, it delayed his acquisition of
professional rank. This, however, may perhaps be accounted for by
his attacks upon Lord Chancellor Eldon in the House of Commons,
of which he had been elected a member in 1823 as the representative
of the city of Lincoln. No sooner had parliament met than Mr. Williams commenced that series of motions upon the delays in Chancery, which ultimately, after some years, led to a commission of inquiry and the introduction of bills for reforming the proceedings in
that court. These motions exhibited undoubtedly too much acerbity,
and seemed to be dictated as much by personal as they certainly
were by political feelings against Lord Eldon. In 1827 he attained
a silk gown; and on February 28, 1834, was advanced to the bench
as a baron of the Exchequer, on the retirement of Mr. Baron Bayley.
In the following term, however, changing places with Mr. Justice
Parke, he took his seat in the Court of King's Bench, having received
the accustomed honor of knighthood. During the whole of this period
he never deserted his classical favorites; contributing several articles on the Greek Orators to the 'Edinburgh Review,' and translat-
ing some of their best orations, one of which, that of Demosthenes'
'For the Independence of Rhodes,' was published in the Appendix
to the authorized edition of the Speeches of Lord Brougham, who
had already shown his estimation of the writer, by dedicating to him
his lordship's 'Dissertation on the Eloquence of the Ancients,' Sir
John was also an adept in the turn of a Greek epigram, and Lord
Tenterden speaks of several that he had written when Queen's solicitor, speaking of him as 'an admirable scholar.' He afterwards
published a collection under the title of 'Nugæ Metricæ.' He remained on the bench for a little less than thirteen years, when he
died on Sept. 14, 1846, at his seat, Livermore Park near Bury St.
Edmunds. At his outset in the judge's office he was ignorant of the
minor details of practice, and many curious anecdotes are told of his
perplexing counsel and attorney by refusing to grant orders of course,
which involved some absurd and since disused fiction of law. He
soon overcame this difficulty and became an excellent judge. With
much eccentricity of manner, and a strong and decided way of expressing his opinions, he was a great favorite, both with his brethren
and the bar, from the cordiality and kindness of his nature. To the
last he would spout Horace and Demosthenes by the hour if he could
obtain an audience; and there was nothing so annoyed him as to
hear counsel perpetrate a false quantity. He married Harriet Catherine, the daughter of Davies Davenport, Esq., of Capesthorne
Hall, Macclesfield, for many years M.P. for Cheshire."— *Foss's
Judges of England.*

ite flowers, and afterwards some others, now I think twelve verses in all, in different Horatian metres, and one, an Ovidian epistle, of which the subject is the Forget-me-Not. One of the earliest is an ode on the conservatory in the Alcaic metre, of which the last stanza contains the true cause and excuse of the whole, and this I will now transcribe :

> ' Sit fabulosis fas mihi cantibus
> Lenire curas ! Sit mihi floribus
> Mulcere me fessum, senemque
> Carpere quos juvenis solebam.[1]

"You see I am now on my hobby, and you must be patient while I take a short ride. Another of the earliest is an ode in the Sapphic metre on the Convallaria Maialis, The Lily of the Valley. I am a great admirer of Linnæus, and my verses contain many allusions to his system, not, however, I trust quite so luscious as Darwin's Loves of the Plants, which, I believe, were soon forgotten. I have not seen the book for many years. I have one little ode written in the present year on a plant called the Linnæa Borealis, which, Sir J. Smith tells us, was a name given to it from its supposed resemblance to the obscurity of the early days of the great botanist. It is not common, and possesses no particular attraction. Smith says it has sometimes been found on the Scottish mountains, and I have a plant sent to me last spring by Dr. Williams. I will send you a copy of this also. You must give me credit for the botanical correctness of the first part; of the rest you can judge, and you may criticise as much as you please. There are three other metres of Horace on which I should like to write something, but what, or when, I know not. It is now high time to quit this subject."

1. " May it be right for me to lighten my cares with songs rich in myths ! May it be right for me to soothe my weariness with flowers, and to enjoy in my old age what I was wont to enjoy in my youth."

By the favor of the present Lord Tenterden, I have before me a copy of all the poems here referred to, and several more which the Chief Justice afterwards composed to cheer his declining days. From these I select a few for the gratification of my readers. It should be known that botany had been taken up by the Chief Justice late in life as a scientific pursuit, and that this gave the new direction to his metrical compositions.

DOMUS CONSERVATORIA.

Haud nos, ut Urbem, Flora, per inclytam
Olim Quirites, Te colimus Deam,
   Fictumve, cœlatumve numen
    Marmoreis domibus locamus ;

Quas impudicis cantibus ebria
Lascivientûm turba jocantium,
   Festis salutatura donis,
    Saltibus et strepitu revisat.

Sed rure ameno Te vitrea excipit
Ædes, remissis pervia solibus,
   Quâ rideas imbres nivales
    Et gelidis hyemem sub Arctis.

Secura jam non hospitio minus
Nostro foveris, sub Jove candidum
   Quam si benigno Tu Tarentum, aut
    Niliacum coleres Syenem.

Cæcis pererrat tramitibus domum
Ardor, quietis læta laboribus
   Servire, jucundoque curas
    Auxilio tenues levare.

Ergo sub auris plurima non suis
Ardentis Austri progenies viget,
   Neve Occidentales Eois
    Addere se socias recusant

Herbæve, floresve, aut patrium dolent
Liquisse cœlum, fervidus abstulit
   Si nauta, mercatorve prudens.
    Vel peregrina petens viator

Misit colendas ; Gentibus exteris
Spectandus hospes ; salvus ab æstubus
   Uliginosis, nubibusque
    Lethiferâ gravidis arenâ.

Non tale monstrum, naribus igneos
Spirans vapores, cessit Jãsoni ;
   Nec tale donum sævientis
    Conjugis innocuam Creontis

Natam perussit : nec vagus Hercules
Tam dira vicit, perdomuit licet
   Hydrasque, Centaurosque, clavo, et
    Semiferum validus Giganta.

Sit fabulosis fas mihi cantibus
Lenire curas ! Sit mihi floribus
   Mulcere me fessum, senemque
    Carpere quos juvenis solebam,

Prid. Cal. Jan. 1828.

GALANTHUS.

Anni primitiæ, Brumæ Phœbique nivalis
   Pallida progenies,
Frigoris atque gelu patiens quæ caulibus albam
   Findis humum teneris,
Seu proprium de lacte Tibi, potiusve cadente
   De nive nomen habes,
Te juvenesque senesque hilares agnoscimus ultro
   Auspiciumque tuum.
Tu monstras abituram hiemem, redituraque vernæ
   Tempora lætitiæ ;
Tu Jovis aspectus mutari, et nigra, serenis
   Cedere fata mones ;
Demittensque caput niveum, floresque pudicos
   Stipite de tereti,
Nil altum moliri homines, sed sorte beatos
   Esse jubes humili ;
Et tua blanditias juvenum nunc virgo suorum
   Accipit, ipsa lubens,
Haud secus ac Zephyros si Sol Aurasque tepentes
   Duceret Oceano.
Scilicet hyberno plantis quæ tempore florent
   Vis genialis inest,
Atque illis miros intus Natura colores
   Sufficit, alma parens,
Æthere sub gelido pecudum licet atque ferarum
   Langueat omne genus,
Et Cytherea tremens, pallàque informis agresti,
   Algeat ipsa Venus,
Maternoque puer vix tendere debilis arcum
   De gremio valeat.

Prid. Cal. Feb. 1829.

CONVALLARIA MAIALIS.

Quo pedes olim valuere, robur,
Lætus et ruentis juvenalis ardor,
Si tuo, dulcis, redeunte curru,
    Maia redirent ;

Quærerem inculti nemorosa ruris,
Impiger densos penetrare valles,
Quà suos gratâ renovent sub umbrâ
    Lilia flores.

Ducat haud fallax odor insolentem,
Et loquax flatu nimis aura grato,
Abditam frustra sobolem recessu
    Prodet avito.

Conditus molli foliorum amictu,
Dum tener ventos timet atque solem
Fortior tandem gracili racemus
    Stipite surgit,

Flosculis nutans oneratus albis ;
Non ebur lucet, Pariumve marmor,
Purius, nec quæ decorat pruina
    Cana cupressos,

Talis et pectus niveumque collum,
Advenâ viso, pudibunda texit
Insulæ virgo, leviterque cymbam â
    Littore trusit ;

Voce sed leni facieque mota,
Hospitem fido prius indicatum
Somniis vati, magicas ad ædes
    Nescia duxit ;

Quæ diu, patris comes exulantis,
Vallium saltus coluit quietos,
Læta si nigros roseo ligaret
    Flore capillos ;

Mox tamen tristi monitu parentis
Territa, absentique timens, puella,
Nobilis supplex, petere ipsa Regem
    Ausit et urbem.

Otii lassum accipitrem canemque
Seque captivum juvenem, querentis,
Et lacus dulces, Elenamque molli
    Voce sonantis,

Palluit cantus ;—adiit trementem
Lene subsidens, generosus hospes,
Simplici plumâ, viridisque veste
    Notus, et ore.

Et su, quem tuâ petis, hìc in arce
Regius jam nunc, ait, est Jacobus ;
Virgini nunquam gravis invocantì,
    Mitte timores ;

Te manent intus pater, atque patre
Charior ; nudis Procerum capillis
Cœtus exspectat, poterisque opertum
    Noscere Regem ;

Et vagi posthàc Equitis pericla
Forsan, et suaves Elenæ loquelas
Et levem vates memori phaselum
    Carmine dicet.

Cal. Maii, 1828.

I have only further to state, that the Chief Justice left not a splendid, but a competent fortune to his family. He is now represented by his eldest son John, the second Lord Tenterden, a most amiable and excellent man. As the title was worthily won, I trust that it may long endure, and that it may be as much respected as if he who first bore it had "come in with the CONQUEROR."

Present representative of the Chief Justice.

INDEX.

393

Lightning Source UK Ltd.
Milton Keynes UK
UKHW021319270219
338009UK00007B/969/P